THE READER'S
COMPANION TO
MEXICO

THE READER'S
COMPANION TO
MEXICO

EDITED BY **ALAN RYAN**

A Harvest Original
Harcourt Brace & Company

SAN DIEGO   NEW YORK   LONDON

Library of Congress Cataloging-in-Publication Data
The reader's companion to Mexico/edited by Alan Ryan.
p.   cm.
"A Harvest original."
ISBN 0-15-676021-5
1. Mexico—Description and travel.   2. Mexico—Social life
and customs.   3. Visitors, Foreign—Mexico—Attitudes.
4. Travelers—Mexico—Attitudes.   I. Ryan, Alan, 1943–
F1215.R3   1993
917.204'835—dc20   92-39391

Designed by Trina Stahl
Printed in the United States of America
First edition
A B C D E

FOR MY SON,
SEAN RYAN,
THIS GIFT FOR THE NEXT ADVENTURE

WE LOVE CARTA BLANCA BEER.
— JOHN STEINBECK

CONTENTS

NORTH OF MEXICO CITY

INTRODUCTION

Not an easy question to answer. Reading time and travel time
are both precious, and the combination even more so. I've spent as
much as three weeks anguishing over what to read on a two-week vacation.

Some travelers make odd but revealing choices.

Joseph Henry Jackson was literary editor of the *San Francisco
Chronicle* in the 1930s. In 1935 he made a motor tour of Mexico.
The early chapters of his book about the trip make it clear that he
went to Mexico suspicious of the place and doubting that he'd like
it. What did he take along to read? Rockwell Kent's new book, *Sala-
mina*. A book about Greenland.

In 1938 Graham Greene traveled for six weeks in Mexico. His
purpose was to investigate the ways in which the government was
oppressing the Roman Catholic church, a state of affairs that Greene
found abhorrent. He knew he wouldn't like Mexico before he even

left home. So, expecting to hate the trip, what did he take along to read? Cobbett's *Rural Rides* and a novel by Trollope. Good places to hide from Mexican reality, both of them.

When I go to Mexico, I don't want to read about life in the countryside of Great Britain. And I would no more take a book on Greenland to Mexico than I would take a book on Mexico to Norway or Nepal. When I go to Mexico, I want to read about Mexico. And the book I've wanted to read about Mexico didn't exist.

I wanted a book that would be like having a trunk filled with letters from a branch of the family that had lived and traveled for many years in Mexico. Some of these imaginary relatives loved the country and made it their own. Some married and set up housekeeping, some went into business, others had terrific adventures. Still others remained skeptical but stayed on and on. Some visited briefly, saw what there was to see, and left. A few disliked the country, complained about everything, and couldn't wait to get away. All of them sent back reports.

Those reports, I imagined, would be filled with commentary on everything Mexican, depending on the writer's own interests: people, places, foods, customs, arts, crafts. There would be eyewitness accounts of historical events. Chance meetings with celebrities. Intensely personal impressions. Carefully documented studies of the culture. Nosy questions and questionable answers. Taken together, they would add up to a kind of multiscreen, time-lapse view of Mexico.

In the capital, for example, the countryside and the cornfields would yield to a broad avenue, the Paseo de la Reforma, where great colonial mansions would rise and then subside to be replaced by modern hotels, embassies, office towers. Buildings and monuments would spring up, tremble in earthquakes, and occasionally fall. And some things would remain comfortingly constant.

In other parts of the country, a road would slowly be cut through the mountains from the capital, and a sleepy Pacific port town, fallen on hard times, would develop into modern Acapulco. Elsewhere, a tiny Maya coastal village, its name unworthy of maps, would be picked by a computer, and modern Cancún would rise like magic from the sand. Ancient Maya and Aztec ruins would be discovered sleeping beneath the jungles of the south and beneath the traffic-clogged streets of Mexico City. Revolutions would shake the country. Volcanoes would shake the land.

If I had a trunk filled with such impressions and reports, I thought, I could gather the best of them into a book, and I could take the book with me to Mexico. I'd be able to read, on the scene, about how this relative faced off against Zapata in Cuernavaca, about that one's view of Acapulco in the thirties, about someone else's visit to Diego Rivera's studio. I could read, while I was there, a description of the hotels where various people stayed in the thirties, forties, fifties, and I could find those hotels myself. I could eat at the same restaurant, say, where one writer had been in the thirties and another in the forties, and I could compare my impressions of the place with theirs. I could walk and stand in some of the very same spots where these people had been, and I could compare my view of Mexico with theirs. I could gain the one thing the unaided traveler always lacks: a tangible sense of the passage of time.

Unfortunately, my family is small and my only relatives live in Akron, Ohio.

So, instead, I have assembled the book I wanted from the large and rich store of travel writing about Mexico.

Mexico has always fascinated foreigners, especially North Americans. As for the United States in particular, while our official involvement with Mexico hasn't always been benevolent, our personal interest has long been intense. Apart from proximity and political and economic reasons, many of the spurs to interest have been cultural, while others have been purely circumstantial.

In 1908 Charles Macomb Flandreau's *Viva Mexico!* painted a picture of that country that whetted the appetite of many travelers. Here, apparently, was a simpler and more romantic world, one that was free of the dreadful and deceitful industrialism that Europe and the United States had inherited from the nineteenth century. And when industrialism exploded in everyone's face in 1929, a country like Mexico seemed all the more appealing. After that, not even a series of revolutions looked very daunting.

In 1909 one of the greatest guidebooks ever written about any place on earth was published. *Terry's Mexico*, by an Englishman named T. Philip Terry, instantly became a bible for the visitor, and all its many later editions were appropriately printed in the same size and shape, and with the same kind of paper and binding traditionally used for the Bible. Thick with detailed folding maps and encyclopedic information, *Terry's Guide to Mexico,* as subsequent editions were called, informed travelers for many decades not only of scenic wonders and local customs but also of a seemingly endless array of startling antiquities.

And—an important point—Mexico was attractively inexpensive.

In the 1920s the sudden renaissance in Mexican art, particularly mural painting, attracted widespread attention, and everyone who cared about such things wanted and needed to know about artists like Orozco, Siqueiros, and especially Rivera. Throughout this period the revolutionary struggle of the Mexican people also caught the imagination of the world.

In the 1930s interest in Mexico intensified. As political strife spread through Italy, Spain, and Germany and a large-scale war seemed increasingly likely to engulf Europe, Mexico and the other countries of Latin America became important as potential allies, Good Neighbors-to-be. And that same turmoil drove the international rich from traditional European playgrounds. They discovered Mexico and, in particular, Acapulco.

In 1931 an American historian named Hubert Herring began his famous Summer University in Mexico City, attracting intellectuals from far and wide. Also, early in the decade, the visits of Diego Rivera and Frida Kahlo to the United States filled both the art pages and the gossip columns of American newspapers. Before they left in 1933, Rivera had also filled the headlines with the scandal over his Rockefeller Center mural. And Mexico further engaged American and British attention in the 1930s by expropriating foreign oil interests.

But in a time of worldwide crisis almost anything could be conveniently forgiven, and in 1940 the Museum of Modern Art in New York presented a huge show of twenty centuries of Mexican art and invited the foremost Mexican conductor and composer, Carlos Chávez, to give a series of concerts.

In the 1940s, with a war on in Europe, Mexico was a particularly good place to visit. And when the war was over, Mexico positively became a party. Acapulco enjoyed a boom, and tourists began discovering the rest of the country.

And it was still inexpensive.

Through the years there were always remarkably good guide-books to Mexico. Besides *Terry,* the American Automobile Association's *Mexico by Motor* made auto trips easy, and there have been good books by Frances Toor and Anita Brenner (both longtime American residents in Mexico), Sydney Clark, MacKinley Helm, Selden Rodman, and Kate Simon.

Mexico has always had a special attraction for creative people and commentators on cultural life. Throughout all these years of growing interest, both as a result of it and as a cause of even more, an amazing number of people have written personal accounts of travel in Mexico. There is a long list of writers, artists, photographers, and others who have either lived there or visited extensively and have recorded their impressions in one medium or another.

Many of the writers are represented in this book. In addition, the list includes such very different figures as Sergei Eisenstein, Edward Weston, Tina Modotti, Laura Gilpin, Henri Cartier-Bresson, Eliot Porter, John Reed, B. Traven, Evelyn Waugh, Hart Crane, Erle Stanley Gardner, Joseph Wood Krutch, George Woodcock, Aldous Huxley, John Dos Passos, Waldo Frank, Carleton Beals, Todd Downing, Tennessee Williams, Norman Mailer, Oliver La Farge, Malcolm Lowry, Leonard Wibberley, Elizabeth Morrow, Anne Morrow Lindbergh, Budd Schulberg, Jack Kerouac, Roberto Matta, Gabriel García Márquez, Oscar Lewis, Carlos Castaneda, Alma Reed, Elizabeth Anderson, and Diana Kennedy.

All the selections in this book are eyewitness accounts. Some are more personal than others—a couple may even tell more about the observer than the observed—but all have the vividness of first-hand reports. They include a wide variety of views, drawn from travel literature, autobiography, and essays, and the writers are as different as, say, D. H. Lawrence and Ilka Chase or Langston Hughes and Elizabeth Borton de Treviño.

The first rule I set myself was not to include Mexicans who have written about their own country. I am a foreigner in Mexico, and I wanted to know about the experiences of other foreigners. We are all outsiders, and we all share the experience of trying to get to know the unknown.

I also set a rule of not going back more than a hundred years or so. I grew up with my grandmother who remembered seeing, as a little girl in Dublin, newspaper headlines about Jack the Ripper's exploits in London. The impressions she formed then still seem very vivid to me now. So a hundred years doesn't seem very remote. On the other hand, you have to draw the line somewhere. And while many of the writers here are literary figures, others are not. I wanted to preserve the experiences—especially in a book on Mexico, about which so much has been written—of some people who simply found the country so interesting that they felt compelled to write about it.

These writers sometimes contradict each other or form very different opinions. Some condemn the bullfights, while others become *aficionados*. Some can't digest the food, or won't even try it, while others prize it as among the world's best. Some dread the traffic, while others are amused by it. Some distrust the Indians, while others study and respect them. Some scorn the crafts, while others are avid collectors. Some worry about the water and the salads and the altitude, while others never spare a moment for such thoughts.

These contradictions, the different ways of human perception, are near the heart of the book. And so are the countless points at which different writers, separated by many years, many miles, and many temperaments, confirm each other's impressions.

I have not attempted to include pieces about every significant place in Mexico. This is not a guidebook. I've limited my choices of locale to some of the most popular destinations, the places that a visitor is likely to have seen or is likely to see or that a reader will most likely want to read about. And I've included some selections that offer multiple views of a place. There are multiple views, for example, of Cuernavaca, Taxco, and Acapulco, of Chichén Itzá and Palenque, and Mexico City is seen at different times and from many different angles.

And not everything here is favorable. Graham Greene, for example, takes great care to detail his reasons for hating Mexico. And while most of the writers are accurate in their reporting and thoughtful in their observations, a few are careless, glib, shallow, or condescending.

And sometimes their Spanish isn't very good, either. While obvious typographical errors in the original publications have been corrected here, the selections are offered as they first appeared. The reader will note some inconsistencies in Spanish spelling (even in proper names), including the use of accents. In some cases, the differences are due to changes in usage over time—in others, to simple ignorance. Don't try to learn Spanish from this book, but do keep in mind that this is the way the writers delivered their views to the public, and this is the way foreign readers learned, little by little over the years, about Mexico.

Of course, much that I would have liked to include has had to be omitted. How nice it would have been, for example, to have here the very different impressions of Baja California formed by Erle Stanley Gardner and Joseph Wood Krutch. Their paths actually crossed once, in Bahía de los Angeles. Gardner was energetically organizing one of his many paramilitary assaults on the unexplored interior of the peninsula when Krutch, along with Roger Tory Peterson, came sailing comfortably into the harbor on some millionaire's yacht.

The label on each selection provides only a rough guide to its contents. And all sorts of tidbits are hidden away here: a young Tennessee Williams knocking timidly at the door; useful help in buying craft items and bargaining in the marketplace; advice on silver; catalogs of exotic fruits; and claims for the invention of both sangría and the margarita.

The introduction to each selection sets it in context and provides information about the author. A few selections contain errors of fact or interpretation, and I've corrected some of these in the introductions. Errors in Spanish remain unchanged. As necessary or appropriate, the introductions also offer some background on the locale or bring the selections up to date with a modern report. I've tried, for example, to locate many of the places referred to and note if they're still there and still in business. Sometimes the introductions refer to other selections in the book or to other travelers who visited the same place. Sometimes they tell stories of their own.

Many of the books from which I've taken selections, and many of those I've relied on for information about Mexico's past, are long out of print and hard to find, even by a very determined collector. I can vouch for it. It's a real pleasure to bring some of them back into the daylight—preferably into the Mexican sunshine—where they belong.

I am, of course, indebted to everyone who ever wrote about Mexico before me. In addition, I owe warm thanks to the people who, over several years and in a wide variety of ways, helped me see this book through: Homero Aridjis, Sarah Arvio, Bob Booth, Diane Buchanan, Reid Collins, Anne Freedgood, Eleanor Garner, Leigh Haber, Dan Janeck, Ellen Levine, Christa Malone, Marie Marino, Octavio Paz, John Radziewicz, Hanna Rosenberg, Sean Ryan, Alan Schwartz, the late Frank Scioscia, Flo Silver, Cork Smith, Dori Weintraub, and Dave Wood. Special thanks go to John Coyne, for always knowing what needs to be said, and to all my pals at the Chariot, for keeping the friendship warm and the coffee hot.

ALAN RYAN
January 1995

MEXICO CITY

F. HOPKINSON SMITH

Paseo de la Reforma, 1888

"A CARRIAGE PASSES, AND A VELVET-EYED
BEAUTY IN SALUTING AN ADMIRER DROPS HER
HANDKERCHIEF."

*In 1888 an American painter named F. Hopkinson Smith traveled
through the major cities of Mexico. Shielded from the sun by a white umbrella, he sketched and painted the quaintest scenes he could find. His
memoir of the trip,* A White Umbrella in Mexico, *a handsome little
book illustrated with some of his drawings, was published in 1889.*

*In his introduction, Smith declares at once that he never intended
to probe very far below the surface. "I have preferred," he writes, "rather
to present what would appeal to the painter and idler. A land of white
sunshine redolent with flowers; a land of gay costumes, crumbling
churches, and old convents; a land of kindly greetings, of extreme courtesy, of open, broad hospitality." He will leave analysis of church and
state and society to others; he is interested in the things that immediately
strike the sensibilities of the visitor in "the most marvellously picturesque
country under the sun."*

*Despite this painterly emphasis on the picturesque, however, Smith
traveled with an open heart as well as open eyes and never neglected the*

people of Mexico. "To study and enjoy this or any other people thoroughly," he writes, "one must live in the streets. A chat with the old woman selling rosaries near the door of the cathedral, half an hour spent with the sacristan after morning mass, and a word now and then with the donkey-boy, the water-carrier, and the padre, will give you a better idea of a town and a closer insight into its inner life than days spent at the governor's palace or the museum."

The wide, tree-lined Paseo de la Reforma—especially the original two-mile stretch from Avenida Juárez to Chapultepec Park—is one of the most famous boulevards in the world. In centuries past, the lake waters here were filled in to make a causeway and carriage path between the city and Chapultepec Castle. The American generals Lee and Grant, who had fought side by side to conquer Chapultepec in 1847, rode along here to take possession of Mexico City itself. In the 1860s Maximilian and Carlota widened the roadway to suitably royal proportions, added the handsome trees, and called it Calzada del Emperador. After the fall and execution of Maximilian in 1867, it was renamed to commemorate the Reform Laws of 1861.

In August 1892 another American visitor formed an opinion of Mexico City as enthusiastic as F. Hopkinson Smith's. Thomas L. Rogers was commissioned by the Mexican Central Railway Company to write a book of travels following the major rail routes, and if his book incidentally glorified the Mexican rail system as well as Mexico itself, so much the better. Mexico? Sí, Señor was published in Boston in 1893. (The title was used again in the 1930s by Wells Fargo for a booklet advertising its Mexican tours.) Under the circumstances, Rogers wrote a very balanced book, which also includes valuable contemporary photographs. Some of these show the Alameda with young trees newly planted along the curb and Avenida Juárez filled with horse-drawn carriages; the Zócalo with a bandstand, a fountain, and a small park in front of the Cathedral; the Sagrario next to it, noticeably less sunken than it is today; and the National Palace before the third story was added. During his visit, Rogers stayed at the eighteenth-century Iturbide Palace, at Madero 17, which was then a hotel.

Rogers was just as impressed by Paseo de la Reforma as F. Hopkinson Smith had been four years earlier. And he added a little social analysis that was beyond Smith. "The Paseo between four and six o'clock on any day in the year, but particularly on Sunday," he wrote, "is another sight which is worth going a long way to see. The boulevard itself is one *of the finest driveways in the world. . . . Two miles in length, one hundred and seventy feet in width, with its glorietas and magnificent trees, . . . the royal avenue is the pleasure drive of the people. Here may be seen a larger number of fine horses and carriages and, in general, more display of wealth than in the park of any city in the world with twice the population of the city of Mexico. When it is remembered that but a small proportion of the population is either able or pretends to be able 'to keep a carriage,' this statement is the more worthy of note. It carries its own lesson, and comment is unnecessary. The Paseo is Vanity Fair on wheels."*

THE ENGLISH DOGCART AND THE FRENCH bonnet have just broken out in the best society of Mexico. The disease doubtless came in with the railroads.

At present the cases are sporadic, and only the young caballero who knows Piccadilly and the gay señorita who has watched the brilliant procession pass under the Arc de Triomphe are affected. But it is nevertheless evident that in the larger cities the contagion is spreading, and that in a few years it will become epidemic.

Nowhere should the calamity of a change in national habits and costumes be more regretted than here. Stroll up the Paseo de la Reforma at sundown,—the Champs Elysées of Mexico,—and watch the endless procession of open carriages filled with beautiful women with filmy mantillas shading their dark eyes, the countless riders mounted on spirited horses, with saddle pommels hung with lasso and lariat; run your eye along the sidewalk thronged with people, and over the mounted soldiers in intermittent groups, policing the brilliant pageant, and tell me if anywhere else in the world you have seen so rich and novel a sight.

A carriage passes, and a velvet-eyed beauty in saluting an admirer drops her handkerchief. In an instant he wheels, dashes forward, and before you can think, he has picked up the dainty perfumed cambric from the dust without leaving his saddle, and all with the ease and grace of a Comanche.

Should a horse become unmanageable and plunge down the overcrowded thoroughfare, there are half a dozen riders within sight who can overtake him before he has run a stone's throw, loop a lasso over his head, and tumble him into the road. Not ranchmen out for an afternoon airing, but kid-gloved dandies in white buckskin and silver, with waxed moustaches, who learned this trick on the haciendas when they were boys, and to whom it is as easy as breathing. It is difficult to imagine any succeeding generation sitting back-a-back to a knee-breeched flunkey, and driving a curtailed cob before a pair of lumbering cart-wheels.

Analyze the features of a Spanish or Mexican beauty. The purple-black hair, long drooping lashes, ivory-white skin, the sinking, half-swooning indolence of her manner. Note how graceful and becoming are the clinging folds of her mantilla, falling to the shoulders and losing itself in the undulating lines of her exquisite figure. Imagine a cockchafer of a bonnet, an abomination of beads, bows, and bangles, surmounting this ideal inamorata. The shock is about as great as if some scoffer tied a seaside hat under the chin of the Venus de Milo.

Verily the illustrated newspaper and the ready-made clothing man have reduced the costume of the civilized and semi-barbarous world to the level of the commonplace! I thank my lucky stars that I still know a few out-of-the-way corners where the castanet and high-heeled shoe, the long, flowing, many-colored tunic, the white sabot and snowy cap, and the sandal and sombrero, are still left to delight me with their picturesqueness, their harmony of color and grace.

All these reflections came to me as I strolled up the Reforma, elbowing my way along, avoiding the current, or crossing it, for the shelter of one of the tree trunks lining the sidewalks, behind which I made five-minute outlines of the salient features of the moving panorama. When I reached the statue of Columbus, the crowd became uncomfortable, especially that part which had formed a "cue," with the head looking over my sketch-book, and so I hailed a cab and drove away towards the castle of Chapultepec. The Paseo ends at this famous spot.

The fortress is built upon a hill that rises some two hundred feet above the valley, and is environed by a noble park and garden, above which tower the famous groves of hoary cypresses. On this commanding eminence once stood the palace of Montezuma, if we may believe the traditions. Indeed, Prescott dilates with enthusiasm upon the details of its splendor, and of its luxuriant adornment, these same cypresses playing an important part in the charming extravaganza with which he delighted our youth. The records say that when the haughty Spaniard knocked at the city's gate and demanded his person, his treasure, and his arms, the vacillating monarch retired to the cool shadows of these then ancient groves, collected together a proper percentage of his wives, and wept. This may be fiction, and that pious old monk, Bernal Diaz, Cortez's scribe, inspired by a lively sense of the value of his own head, and with a loyal desire to save his master's, may alone be responsible for it.

For this I care little. The trees are still here, the very same old gnarled and twisted trunks. The tawny Indian in feathers, the grim cavalier in armor; fine ladies in lace; hidalgos in velvet, all the gay throngs who have enlivened these shady aisles, each bedecked after the manner and custom of their times, are gone. But the old trees still stand.

What the great kings of Tenochtitlán saw as they looked up into their sheltering branches, I see: the ribbed brown bark sparkling with gray green lichen; the sweep of the wrinkled trunk rushing upward into outspreading arms; the clear sky turquoised amid matted foliage; the gray moss waving in the soft air. With these alive and above me, I can imagine the rest, and so I pick out a particularly comfortable old root that curves out from beneath one of the great giants, and sit me down and persuade myself that all the Aztec kings have been wont to rest their bones thereon. From where I lounge, I can see away up among the top branches the castle and buildings of the military school, and at intervals hear the bugle sounding the afternoon's drill. Later I toil up the steep ascent, and from the edge of the stone parapet skirting the bluff, drink in the glory and beauty of perhaps the finest landscape in the world.

There are two views which always rise up in my memory when a grand panoramic vision bursts upon me suddenly. One is from a spot in the Sierra Nevada Mountains, in Granada, called "La Ultima Suspira de Mores." It is where Boabdil stood and wept when he looked for the last time over the beautiful valley of the Vega, — the loveliest garden in Spain, — the red towers and terraces of the Alhambra bathed in the setting sun. The other is this great sweep of plain, and distant mountain range, with all its wealth of palm, orange, and olive; the snow-capped twin peaks dominating the horizon;

the silver line of the distant lakes, and the fair city, the Tenochtitlán of the ancient, the Eldorado of Cortez, sparkling like a jewel in the midst of this vast stretch of green and gold.

Both monarchs wept over their dominions. Boabdil, that the power of his race which for six hundred years had ruled Spain was broken, and that the light of the Crescent had paled forever in the effulgence of the rising Cross. Montezuma, that the fires of his temples had forever gone out, and that henceforward his people were slaves.

Sitting here alone on this stone parapet, watching the fading sunlight and the long creeping shadows and comparing Mexico and Spain of to-day with what we know to be true of the Moors, and what we hope was true of the Aztecs, and being in a reflective frame of mind, it becomes a question with me whether the civilized world ought not to have mingled their tears with both potentates. The delightful historian sums it up in this way:—

"Spain has the unenviable credit of having destroyed two great civilizations."

Full of these reveries, and with the question undecided, I retraced my steps past the boy sentinels, down the long hill, through the gardens and cypresses, and out into the broad road skirting the great aqueduct of Bucareli. There I hailed a cab, and whirled into the city brilliant with lights, and so home to my lodgings overlooking the old convent garden.

KATHERINE ANNE PORTER

The Fiesta of Guadalupe, 1919

"A GROUP OF INDIANS, FANTASTICALLY DRESSED,
EACH CARRYING AN ARCH OF FLOWERS, WERE
STEPPING IT BRISKLY TO THE SMART JANGLE OF
THE BELLS."

Katherine Anne Porter was born in San Antonio, Texas, in 1890 and grew up hearing her father's tales of Mexico, where he had lived in his youth. Through the 1920s and into the thirties, she lived and wrote in Mexico for long periods of time, calling it "my familiar country." She was especially moved by Mexico's artistic renaissance. "It would be difficult to explain in a very few words," she wrote, "how the Mexicans have enriched their national life through the medium of their native arts. It is in everything they do and are."

Several of her stories, including "Flowering Judas" and "Hacienda," are set in Mexico, and the opening scene of her 1962 novel, Ship of Fools, *takes place in Veracruz. With a friend, Porter also translated into English* The Itching Parrot, *a nineteenth-century picaresque novel by the Mexican writer J. J. Fernández de Lizardi.*

The Aztecs once worshiped the earth goddess Tonantzin on the hill now known as Guadalupe. Within a few years of their arrival, the Spaniards put a stop to that by destroying the site. Then, in 1531, an Indian convert named Juan Diego reported seeing an apparition of the Virgin there, and Guadalupe has been a site of Christian pilgrimage ever since. Porter's description of the fiesta was published in 1920.

In the 1930s, when the Mexican government took a hard stance against priests and churches—the situation that brought Graham Greene to Mexico in 1938—and even changed the old Christian names of many locales to new revolutionary ones, Guadalupe became known officially as Villa Madero. The 1935 edition of a reliable guidebook written by Anita Brenner, the author of Idols Behind Altars and a longtime resident in Mexico, reports this: "The date, December 12, once meant vast pilgrimages from all over the country to the shrine, and no true believer was worth a snap who did not go there—partly on his knees—at least once in his life. The best dancers, drummers and chanters congregated here yearly for a week, along with the sickest, the lamest, haltest, blindest, and everybody with something to sell. Nowadays this festival has gone into a decline along with most other religious celebrations and ancient folklore. People blame (or praise) the government, the revolution, the advance of the machine."

But the Virgin of Guadalupe was and is at the heart of Mexican consciousness and identity, a living presence in the mind, and no government decree could change that. In more recent times, the crowds visiting the shrine and attending the fiesta grew so great that the old basilica became inadequate. A new basilica—modern, larger, in the shape of a volcano, and the fifth to be built here in four centuries—was consecrated in 1976.

☀ I FOLLOWED THE CROWD OF TIRED BURDENED pilgrims, bowed under their loads of potteries and food and babies and baskets, their clothes dusty and their faces a little streaked with long-borne fatigue. Indians all over Mexico had gathered at the feet of Mary Guadalupe for this greatest *fiesta* of the year, which celebrates the initiation of Mexico into the mystic company of the Church, with a saint and a miracle all her own, not transplanted from Spain. Juan Diego's long-ago vision of Mary on the bare hillside made her Queen of Mexico where before she had been Empress.

Members of all tribes were there in their distinctive costumes. Women wearing skirts of one piece of cloth wrapped around their sturdy bodies and women wearing gaily embroidered blouses with very short puffed sleeves. Women wearing their gathered skirts of green and red, with blue *rebosos* wrapped tightly around their shoulders. And men in great hats with peaked crowns, wide flat hats with almost no crown. Blankets, and *serapes,* and thonged sandals. And a strange-appearing group whose men all wore a large square of fiber cloth as a cloak, brought under one arm and knotted on the opposite shoulder exactly in the style depicted in the old drawings of Montezuma.

A clutter of babies and dolls and jars and strange-looking people lined the sidewalks, intermingled with booths, red curtained and hung with paper streamers, where sweets and food and drinks were sold and where we found their astonishing crafts—manlike potteries and jars and wooden pails bound with hard wrought clasps of iron, and gentle lacework immaculately white and unbelievably cheap of price.

I picked my way through the crowd looking for the dancers, that curious survival of the ancient Dionysian rites, which in turn were brought over from an unknown time. The dance and blood sacrifice were inextricably tangled in the worship of men, and the sight of men dancing in a religious ecstasy links one's imagination, for the moment, with all the lives that have been.

A woven, moving arch of brilliant-colored paper flowers gleaming over the heads of the crowd drew me near the gate of the cathedral as the great bells high up began to ring—sharply, with shocking clamor, they began to sway and ring, their ancient tongues shouting notes of joy a little out of tune. The arches began to leap and flutter. I managed to draw near enough to see, over the fuzzy poll of sleeping baby on his mother's back. A group of Indians, fantastically dressed, each carrying an arch of flowers, were stepping it briskly to the smart jangle of the bells. They wore tinsel crowns over red bandanas which hung down their necks in Arab fashion. Their costumes were of vari-colored bits of cloth, roughly fashioned into short skirts and blouses. Their muscular brown legs were disfigured with cerise and blue cotton stockings. They danced a short, monotonous step, facing each other, advancing, retreating, holding the arches over their crowns, turning and bowing, in a stolid sarabande. The utter solemnity of their faces made it a moving sight. Under their bandanas, their foreheads were knitted in the effort to keep time and watch the figures of the dance. Not a smile and not a sound save the mad hysteria of the old bells awakened from their sleep, shrieking praise to the queen of Heaven and the Lord of Life.

Then the bells stopped, and a man with a mandolin stood near by, and began a quiet rhythmic tune. The master of ceremonies, wearing around his neck a stuffed rabbit clothed in a pink satin jacket, waved the flagging dancers into line, helped the less agile to catch step, and the dancing went on. A jammed and breathless crowd and pilgrims inside the churchyard peered through the iron fence, while the youths and boys scrambled up, over the heads of the others, and watched from a precarious vantage. They reminded one irresistibly of a menagerie cage lined with young monkeys. They spraddled and sprawled, caught toeholds and fell, gathered themselves up and shinned up the railings again. They were almost as busy as the dancers themselves.

Past stalls of fruits and babies crawling underfoot away from their engrossed mothers, and the vendors of images, scapulars and rosaries, I walked to the church of the well, where is guarded the holy spring of water that gushed from beneath Mary's feet at her last appearance to Juan Diego, December twelve, in the year of grace fifteen and thirty-one.

It is a small darkened place, the well covered over with a handsomely wrought iron grating, through which the magic waters are brought up in a copper pail with a heavy handle. The people gather here and drink reverently, passing the pail from mouth to mouth, praying the while to be delivered of their infirmities and sins.

A girl weeps as she drinks, her chin quivering. A man, sweating and dusty, drinks and drinks and drinks again, with a great sigh of satisfaction, wipes his mouth and crosses himself devoutly.

My pilgrimage leads me back to the great cathedral, intent on seeing the miraculous Tilma of Juan Diego, whereon the queen of Heaven deigned to stamp her lovely image. Great is the power of that faded virgin curving like a new moon in her bright blue cloak, dim and remote and immobile in her frame above the soaring altar columns.

From above, the drone of priests' voices in endless prayers, answered by the shrill treble of boy singers. Under the overwhelming arches and the cold magnificence of the white altar, their faces lighted palely by the glimmer of candles, kneel the Indians. Some of them have walked for days for the privilege of kneeling on these flagged floors and raising their eyes to the Holy Tilma.

There is a rapt stillness, a terrible reasonless faith in their dark faces. They sigh, turn toward the picture of their beloved Lady, printed on the garment of Juan Diego only ten years after Cortes had brought the new God, with fire and sword, into Mexico. Only ten years ago, but it is probable that Juan Diego knew nothing about the fire and sword which have been so often the weapons of the faithful servants of our Lady. Maybe he had learned religion happily, from some old gentle priest, and his thoughts of the Virgin, ineffably mysterious and radiant and kind, must have haunted him by day and by night for a long time; until one day, oh, miracle of miracles, his kindled eyes beheld her, standing, softly robed in blue, her pale hands clasped, a message of devotion on her lips, on a little hill in his own country, the very spot where his childhood had been passed.

Ah well—why not? And I passed on to the steep winding ascent to the chapel of the little hill, once a Teocalli, called the Hill of Tepeyac, and a scene of other faiths and other pilgrimages. I think, as I follow the path, of those early victims of Faith who went up (mighty slowly and mighty heavily, let the old Gods themselves tell you) to give up their beating hearts in order that the sun might rise again on their people. Now there is a great crucifix set up with the transfixed and bleeding heart of one Man nailed upon it—one magnificent Egoist who dreamed that his great heart could redeem from death all the other hearts of earth destined to be born. He has taken the old hill by storm with his mother, Mary Guadalupe, and their shrine brings the Indians climbing up, in silent groups, pursued by the prayers of the blind and the halt and the lame who have gathered to reap a little share of the blessings being rained upon the children of faith. Theirs is a doleful litany: "In the name of our Lady, Pity, a little charity for the poor—for the blind, for the little servants of God, for the humble in heart!" The cries waver to you on the winds as the slope rises, and come in faintly to the small chapel where is the reclining potent image of Guadalupe, second in power only to the Holy Tilma itself.

It is a more recent image, copied from the original picture, but now she is lying down, hands clasped, supported by a company of saints. There is a voluptuous softness in her face and pose—a later virgin, grown accustomed to homage and from the meek maiden receiving the announcement of the Angel Gabriel on her knees, she has progressed to the role of Powerful Intercessor. Her eyes are vague and a little indifferent, and she does not glance at the devout adorer who passionately clasps her knees and bows his head upon them.

A sheet of glass protects her, or she would be literally wiped away by the touches of her devotees. They crowd up to the case, and rub their hands on it, and cross themselves, then rub the afflicted parts of their bodies, hoping for a cure. A man reached up and rubbed the glass, then gently stroked the head of his sick and pallid wife, who could not get near enough to touch for herself. He rubbed his own forehead, knees, then stroked the woman's chest. A mother brought her baby and leaned his little toes against the glass for a long time, the tears rolling down her cheeks.

Twenty brown and work-stained hands are stretched up to touch the magic glass—they obscure the still face of the adored Lady, they blot out with their insistent supplications her remote eyes. They have parted a carved bit of wood and plaster, I see the awful hands of faith, the credulous and worn hands of believers; the humble and beseeching hands of the millions and millions who have only the anodyne of credulity. In my dreams I shall see those groping insatiable hands reaching, reaching, reaching, the eyes turned blinded away from the good earth which should fill them, to the vast and empty sky.

Out upon the downward road again, I stop and look over the dark and brooding land, with its rim of mountains swathed in layer upon layer of filmy blue and gray and purple mists, the low empty valleys blackened with clumps of trees. The flat-topped houses of adobe drift away casting no shadows on the flooding blue, I seem to walk in a heavy, dolorous dream.

It is not Mary Guadalupe nor her son that touches me. It is Juan Diego I remember, and his people I see, kneeling in scattered ranks on the flagged floor of their church, fixing their eyes on mystic, speechless things. It is their ragged hands I see, and their wounded hearts that I feel beating under their work-stained clothes like a great volcano under the earth and I think to myself, hopefully, that men do not live in a deathly dream forever.

WITTER BYNNER

D. H. Lawrence at his first bullfight, 1923

"THE BULL SHOVED AND GORED AND RIPPED;
AND WHILE THE CROWD GAVE A SIGH OF RELIEF,
LAWRENCE GROANED AND SHOOK."

In 1922, at the suggestion of Mabel Dodge Stern, D. H. and Frieda
Lawrence visited the home of the American poet Witter Bynner in Taos,
New Mexico. Lawrence—shrill voiced, always dissatisfied, and con-
stantly complaining—was a difficult but fascinating guest. After some
months in Taos and Santa Fe, Lawrence, as always, grew restless to
be somewhere else and began studying a Spanish grammar and Terry's
Mexico. By January 1923 he was making plans, and in March he and
Frieda left by train for Mexico City, with Bynner and Bynner's lover,
Willard (Spud) Johnson, to join them within a week.

They all stayed at the Hotel Monte Carlo, at Avenida Uruguay 69,
next to the National Library, at the corner of Isabel la Católica. The hotel was once described by Carleton Beals as "a smelly Italian hostelry"
and by a 1935 guidebook as "very modest." It's still there, and it's still
modest in every way.

Lawrence was soon eager to be off elsewhere again, but the group
saw the sights in and around the capital, examined early frescoes by the

young artists Rivera and Orozco, and visited Puebla, Cholula, and Cuernavaca. One episode was typical of Lawrence's behavior. A friend arranged for the group to have lunch with Carleton Beals and the Minister of Education, José Vasconcelos, who at about that time was doing much to launch Mexico's artistic renaissance. But when Vasconcelos had to postpone the lunch by a day, Lawrence lost his temper and refused to meet him.

From May to July of 1923 the Lawrences rented a house on Lake Chapala, with Bynner and Spud staying nearby, and there Lawrence worked on the first draft of The Plumed Serpent. He completed the novel later in Oaxaca, adapting and re-creating many of his experiences and impressions from three visits to Mexico. Witter Bynner appears in it as the character called Owen Rhys.

On Easter Sunday, April 1, 1923, Lawrence, Frieda, Bynner, and Spud went to the bullfights. The Gran Plaza de Toros they visited no longer exists. It stood just off Avenida Oaxaca, between Durango and Colima and between Salamanca and Valladolid, within easy walking distance of what is today the Zona Rosa. Built in 1907, the structure contained, appropriately enough, both a chapel and an infirmary, had a ring diameter of 450 feet, and seated 20,000 spectators—nearly 7,000 more than the largest bullring in Madrid at that time.

Despite his reaction to this bullfight, Lawrence did attend another, six months later in Tepic, and he describes a bullfight—incorrectly—in the first chapter of The Plumed Serpent.

It was, of course, the frequent goring of the horses that most often spoiled the Sunday dinners of tourists. By the 1930s the horses were regularly fitted out with padding of cloth and leather that somewhat protected them from the horns of the bull.

The edition of Terry's Mexico that Lawrence was reading concluded its lengthy section on bullfights with the comment that "in the last analysis, the bull-fight is a curious and picturesque spectacle—one no doubt doomed to disappear soon from Mexico."

Terry, of course, was wrong, because the bullfight, to those who love it, is much more than a picturesque spectacle. In the ring, strict formality (order in the universe, some would say) confronts the wild and savage. And so anything can happen.

A Mexican bullfighter named Luis Procuna was nicknamed El Gitano (The Gypsy) by the crowds because his performances were so unpredictable. On good days, he could work within inches of the horns *and bring the crowd to its feet shouting "Torero!" over and over. On bad days, he could be moved almost to tears of frustration as the crowd shouted that he was a coward for running from the bull and leaping over the barrera. And there is a close-up photo of him in the ring with a look of genuine fear and horror as he faces the bull.*

One famous incident, involving a matador named Alfonso Ramírez, demonstrates the spontaneous passion that bullfighting can inspire. One Sunday in 1946 in Orizaba, Ramírez had such a great afternoon that he was awarded both ears and the tail of the bull he fought so spectacularly. His performance was so exciting, in fact, that at one point the bandleader ordered the band to strike up the national anthem. This, alas, is specifically forbidden by law, and the enthusiastic bandleader was carted off to jail. But not for long. Ramírez's grateful fans soon bailed him out.

Among the Mexican bullfighters Langston Hughes saw during his teenage years in Mexico was the great Rodolfo Gaona, famous as the inventor of a thrilling pass known as the gaonera, in which the capa is held behind the back while the matador faces the charging bull. Hughes thought bullfighting "the most beautiful and dangerous of sports in the world."

The first bullfights in New Spain were held in the sixteenth century in the Zócalo, after the market was cleared out for the occasion. The bullring in Morelia is generally agreed to be the prettiest in the country, but the capital's modern, functional Plaza Mexico, on Insurgentes Sur, which opened in 1946 and seats 50,000 spectators, is the largest in the world. The bullfights start at 4:00 P.M., and they start on time, a tribute to the place they hold in Mexican culture.

LAWRENCE HAD HEARD IN EUROPE HIGH praise of the famous Spanish matadors, Belmonte and Joselito, the latter killed in the ring only three years before; and we were told that the Mexicans, Rodolfo Gaona and Juan Silveti, were performers of comparable skill and prowess. Silveti was to be the star on Sunday.

On Easter morning, having been to churches Friday and to a sacred movie on Saturday, we were wakened by bells of resurrection and in the afternoon attended the bullfight. It was a first experience for all of us, and we approached it curious but apprehensive.

At the entrance to the arena Lawrence, Johnson, and I, like

other males filing through, were frisked for firearms: it had been announced that President Obregón would be present. At the last moment, word spread that he could not attend; but other dignitaries entered the presidential box escorting three or four bright-fluttering women who wore flowered mantillas and high combs.

Since seats cost but half as much in the sun as in the shade, we were sitting in the sun, except that this day, to Lawrence's special pleasure, there was no sun. Our backless bench tier of concrete was within five rows of the ring. Below us, paralleling the wall of the ring, was a circling five-foot wooden fence with here and there a gap and before each gap a small barrier, making safety boxes for performers when hard pressed. The crowd, now thickening and seeming less an assemblage than a single mass monster, was already—with its murmurs, growls, and yells—grinding our nerves a little.

"I begin to feel sick," whispered Lawrence. "Look at their faces. The eyes don't seem hard, or the mouths. It's that cruel dent of relish above the nostril."

Opposite us rose a roar of voices. Somebody's hat had been tossed across the tiers into a group which was scrambling for it. Other hats followed, on our side too. Orange peels began flying. A shoe landed in Lawrence's lap. He sat immobile while someone from behind him seized it and sent it scaling again.

"Shall we leave?" asked Lawrence, his head twitching upward like that of a horse.

Half an orange just missed my bald spot. A second half hit it. Other bare heads were being hit. A kindly Mexican motioned that I should put on my hat. Obeying him, I was spared further pelting. Apparently uncovered heads were permissible targets.

Three bands, one at a time, entered their sections near the President's box and were shouted at for *musica!* When a rousing Mexican march blared out, the vocal din was only accelerated. The crowd had not wanted music so much as a beat for their own noise.

What looked like a folded coat landed in the arena. It seemed a signal. Like water from a broken dam, the mass of men in unreserved seats swelled over the reserved section which in a trice was filled solid. Seatholders who came later were vain claimants.

On the exact moment advertised, a wide gate opened, a square colorful procession strutted with music into the arena toward the

President's box to make bows, with waists and trim buttocks held tautly, shoulders back; two groups of fine-stepping *toreros* with bright cloaks above their embroidered boleros and half-length, skin-tight trousers and salmon-colored stockings; then mounted picadors; then *banderilleros* with silver embroidery; then matadors with gold and with red capes, all these men wearing berets over abbreviated pigtails; and finally, in red harness, two dingy teams of three mules each, ready to drag away carcasses. "The right symbol!" muttered Lawrence. "They're all jackasses." The procession, after circling the ring and receiving a round of plaudits, dispersed.

Then, with no warning, no noise, a huge white bull swam into the arena and stood a moment, his tail waving, his head bewildered, apprehending foes. Lawrence's head rose and sank with the bull's. "The bull is beautiful, Lorenzo," said Frieda. The foes were there, the first of them: two stationary horsemen. When the lowered head made clumsily for a horse, the rider warded it off with a lance. The second rider did likewise. And then into the ring came the toreros, to nag him with scarlet mantles. He saw them one at a time. He snorted. He charged a cloak. It was whisked over his head. He curved quickly and charged again, cleaving the air with his horns under a swing of color. Now and then he would corner a torero who, amid jeers and whistlings, would either dodge into one of the safety boxes or vault the *barrera* into the shielded alley way. All of a sudden the bull too had heaved his pawing bulk over the fence. Attendants scurried to cut off a section of the gangway by closing gates. Commotion subsided. "He beat them," Lawrence said as though to himself. "They should let him go." A fluttered cape teased the bull out again into the ring, where he stood still, waving his tail. His belly lifting, falling with his heavy breath, he looked round and lowed; then once more he leaped the fence, this time breaking it. And once more the blocked exit, once more the flashing taunts, the deft weavings and wavings of five toreros; once more his return to the ring, his half-seeing eye, his wasted strength. "They're dastardly!" Lawrence exclaimed.

He turned to us. He had been shifting in his seat and looking sharply at us now and then as if to see what we thought of it all. We could tell that the teasing of the beast, the deliberate baiting and angering had made him as tense as the animal, with whom he was almost identifying himself. "They keep him starved and in the dark," he snapped, "so that when he comes into the ring he's angry but can't see. He's the only one among them with heart or brain. He despises them, but he knows what they are; he knows that he's done for. The toreador jumped the fence to get away from the bull; the bull jumped the fence to get away from the lot of them. They let the toreador get away. Why don't they let the bull get away?" he exhorted us. "Why don't they respect his intelligence and bow to him instead of to those nincompoops in the box? He's not the brute; they're the brutes. He abhors them and so do I. But he can't get away and I can. Let's get away." He was on his feet. None of us stirred to follow him. He sat down again.

"It sickens me too, Lorenzo," I agreed. "But hadn't we better see at least one round of it through, to know what we're talking about when we say we don't like it? I shan't want to see another bullfight any more than you will."

"Very well," he glared. "But I don't need to see a round through, as you call it. The trouble is that you're as bloodthirsty as the rest of them. You can't resist it. Frieda can't resist it. Spud can't. I could resist it, but I'll give in to you." He sulked back on the bench and looked away from us, away from everything.

But now came a change, a chance for the bull to vent his disgust, if not on a man, then on a decrepit, blindfolded horse. The rider spurred toward him. The picador, with armor under his trousers, urged the shivering mount to expose its belly. The crowd was hushed, expectant, on the edge of its seats. Lawrence was breathing hard and glaring. Suddenly, given a chance not so much by the rider as by the bull, the horse struck with his thin hind legs, fought free and stalked off with an air of doddering valor, only to postpone a next encounter not at the center of the ring where he had had clearance, but close to the barrera, with no room for him to dodge; and though the picador was supposed with his blunt lance to shunt the bull off, the crowd knew better. The bull pawed up earth, slowly bent his head. The lance was futile. The horse reared and floundered. In and up went the horn. While the picador tumbled against the fence and sheepishly found his feet, the bull shoved and gored and ripped; and while the crowd gave a sigh of relief, Lawrence groaned and shook. By the time the toreros had again drawn their prey toward the cloaks and the picador had remounted and forced his steed into motion toward the exit, the horse's bowels were bulging almost to the ground, like vines and gourds. But the bull had not had enough. "Stop it!" cried Lawrence to the bull, jumping out of his seat. But just before the picador reached the gate, horns were lowered again for another snorting plunge, and this time the entire covering of the horse's belly was ripped off. He fell dead, his contents out on the ground, with earth being shoveled over them by attendants. Lawrence had sat down again, dazed and dark with anger and shame. Frieda was watching him. The proud front of the bull—head, neck, chest, leg, hoof—shone crimson in a moment of sun. The crowd was throatily satisfied!

There had been something phallic, Lawrence might have noted, in this fierce penetration, this rape of entrails, this bloody glut. But his nerves exploded. Fortunately people were too intent on the ring to notice him, and only a few of them heard a red-bearded Englishman, risen from his seat, excoriating cowards and madmen. Frieda was as alarmed as Johnson and I, for he was denouncing the crowd in Spanish. But he sickened suddenly, plunged away from us, treading toes, and lurched down the row toward the exit.

"I'll go with him," exclaimed Frieda. "I'd better. There's no knowing. You stay. He'll be worse if you come. You stay. Leave him to me. Ja!" And she squeezed her way out.

"Yes, I think we'd better stay," said Johnson, with a drawn face. And we did stay, though we were as revolted by the performance as are most Europeans and Americans. I supposed the audience had more than once seen outraged foreigners bolt away, and learned to ignore them as barbarians. I dreaded what we were still to watch, felt my insides sift like ashes, was sorely tempted to follow the Lawrences. But we did stay.

Lawrence wrote Knud Merrild: "We saw a terrible bullfight and ran away after ten minutes." But he was wrong: the time had been triple that.

I noticed then that a rain had begun, with large drops. A shower fell quickly. It became a downpour. Many of the onlookers scattered for cover. But most of them, including Johnson and me, remained, huddling from the wet and not feeling it much. In spite of rain and mud, the show continued.

A banderillero advanced toward the bull, with no protective cloak, but holding up in each hand a pink-stemmed barb. He coaxed the brute, wheeled him, yelped at him, hopped in the air, with feet clicking together below him and darts clicking together above him. Lawrence might have admired the birdlike poise. Now on this side, now on that, he waited and watched till the bull gathered its puzzled wits again and charged. In a flash the man had leaped aside and in the same flash had planted the two barbs jiggling at a neat angle on the shoulders. He did it again with green *banderillos*, shorter ones — an alert and precarious performance; and though the deed seemed ignoble to us, we applauded, feeling at the same time relieved that Lawrence was gone and could not see us.

For a moment the animal shook his body and bellowed slightly. Then came the matador, his scarlet cape hung athwart a long sword. Here came a sudden, sure, personal authority. Lawrence would have liked this presence, this sureness, this motion of a bird with wings slow, then swift. This was different. Directly facing the bull, choosing a moment when the horns hung toward him at precisely the right slant, this lordly authority, this death-dealer, thrust the *espada* half to its hilt in the vulnerable spot exposed between lowered shoulder blades. There with the banderillos the sword joined a halo like a section of the nimbus around Our Lady of Guadalupe; I would tell that to Lawrence.

The bull stood stock still, seemed to be wondering how these pains could have reached him. For a last few moments before the end, he faced and followed his enemies, but with weaker and weaker lunges. His knees crumbled. He sank. He was up, but only for a second, then down again, a grisly likeness to a bull at rest in a meadow. His eyes glazed. He acknowledged death. Thereupon, with one swift jab, an attendant dispatched him. In came the mules. Proud and stalwart until now, now flabby and ignominious, the bull's body was dragged out at one gate, and the horse's body and entrails out at another. The drenched crowd was ready for scene two. Now I could feel again the presence of Lawrence's thin, tortured face and Frieda's eyes, watching him. Perhaps we should have left with them.

Rain over, the wet people were gay again. There was more tossing of orange peel and this time soaked wads of newspaper.

By now Johnson and I knew that we were staying to the end. We felt ashamed but hypnotized, cataleptic. Later, we held our breath when Juan Silveti, in the very act of executing the firm, delicate master stroke, slipped and fell and might have been injured but that his huge victim at once drooped and stood quiet, stricken from within by a mortal vent of crimson, triply spilling with his breath from throat and nostrils. In a few moments he was dead from that one stroke, and the matador was gracefully acknowledging gusty applause, striding and bowing past section after section of the amphitheater. If Lawrence had stayed this long, he might have been hissing the hero—and might have been roughly handled.

In the fourth round one of the horses, receiving a horn in the chest, managed to walk all the way out with a steady spurt of blood from above his forelegs, like a jet from a wall fountain. In the fifth round Juan Silveti relinquished to one of his lesser fellows a bull not fierce enough or not foolish enough for heroes.

Then in the sixth and last round the banderilleros inserted their gay darts as neatly as ladies used to adjust hat pins; and Silveti kneeled to let the clumsy beast attack, as ever, the cloak instead of the man. By adroit passes, he attracted two or three charges in the customary time of one, then walked nonchalantly away with his back to the bull, dragging his cape at his heels. Finally he placed a handkerchief on the ground and succeeded in so directing his victim's attack that he could thrust the *espada* without budging from his small white foothold. The game needed these variations, these graces, this ballet precision; Johnson and I reluctantly confessed to each other that the crowd's enjoyment was not altogether blood lust, and wished that the Lawrences might have seen the artistry and considered it as something apart. At least Frieda would have granted it a reluctant but admiring "*ja!*" Experienced Mexican eyes could of course see far better than we the exact gaugings, manipulatings, side-steppings, balancings, and piercings. We vowed, though, as we filed out, that it was our last bullfight.

In the corridor we came upon a middle-aged Polish professor of psychology, whom we had casually met at the Monte Carlo. He was vacationing from some American university, spoke fair Spanish, and was with a Mexican friend, both of them gesticulating with joy over the events of the afternoon. "Magnificent!" he exclaimed. We bowed, without assenting but without disturbing the ecstasy of chatter between the two. "We are going to Silveti's hotel," the Pole called out. "Why not come with us? My friend knows him well." "Thanks," I answered, "but I must join our own friends. They were shocked and left." "Yes, I saw them," he laughed. "They shouldn't be shocked. They are just new to it. But we'll see you later at the hotel, unless

Mr. Johnson will come with us." "Go ahead," I urged. And Spud went.

Lawrence greeted me at the hotel with a hard look of contempt. "So you stayed through all of it. I thought you would. You Americans would run to any street accident to see blood. You are as bad as the dirty Mexicans. You would have held Frieda there in that slaughter-house. You tried to keep her there."

"No, Lorenzo!" she protested.

"But they wanted you to stay. I know. They not only fooled themselves with their nonsense about 'seeing it through,' they wanted to fool you as well, but you were too fine for them."

"He compliments me," smiled Frieda. "How angry he must be with you!"

At supper, after Johnson's return from the bullfighter's hotel, Lawrence expatiated. "What we saw this afternoon," he snorted, "was the grandeur of Rome, soiling its breeches! You like scatological jokes, Bynner. No wonder you liked this dirt."

"He didn't like it," Spud defended me mildly, "any more than I did."

"You both stayed it through," flamed Lawrence. "The way not to enjoy it was not to stay it through."

The Pole was with his friend at a nearby table and, when they had finished eating, came over to ours and asked if they might join us. But before bringing the Mexican, he touched off the fuse. "It was my sixth bullfight," he gloated. "I was shocked at first, like you, Mrs. Lawrence. I saw that Mr. Lawrence had to take you out. But I've learned now. Didn't you see how happy the bulls were?" He beckoned to the Mexican and continued, "I'd like to have you meet my—"

"No," said Lawrence firmly. "I do not wish to meet your friend, or anyone else in this loathsome country. And I have seen, as well, all that I wish to see of you."

"Ja!" nodded Frieda vigorously.

The Pole was silenced. But as most Mexicans react when bull-fights are condemned, the friend was kindled and, more because Lawrence had left the ring than because of this rudeness, he came close and took up the cudgels. "You are English," he challenged in our tongue. "You run after animals, little foxes, tire them out and then let dogs tear them to pieces, while you ride your high horses.

We Mexicans face big animals, stronger than we are, and we are not dogs. We face them as men and kill them with our hands. You English hunt little people too and make dogs of your soldiers to tear little people to pieces."

"I abominate fox hunts," sparred Lawrence, in confusion.

But the Mexican did not spare him. "You have judged all Mexico by one bullfight, but I will not judge all England by one Englishman." He bowed to Frieda, turned on his heel and conducted the Pole with him out of the dining room, out of the hotel.

By now Lawrence was seething, and I expected further outbursts against one or all of us. To my surprise the seething settled; and, with no more mention of Poles or Mexicans, we had a pacific session in their room, during which he opened one of those stores of information with which he frequently surprised us. He had been studying somewhere the history of bullfighting and had taken notes, in fact he produced a page of data and he half read, half remembered for us:

"In the sixteenth century the Vatican took a stand against the filthy business, which was going on here even then. Pope Pius V," he glanced at a note, "banned it. So did Sixtus V. But a great protest followed, led by poets," he gave me a look, "and by the whole faculty at Salamanca. With the next Pope," and here a final use of the paper, "yes, Clement VIII, the Church gave in, just as it had to give in to your Penitentes in New Mexico and to letting your Indians add their pagan rites to the Mass. That was different. I like that. I suppose a Church which murdered heretics shouldn't mind the murder of a few bulls." He dropped the sheet of notes into a wastebasket and smiled indulgently when I picked them out again.

I have been reminded of Lawrence's running away from the bullfight by a passage in Catherine Carswell's *Savage Pilgrimage* telling of his similar flight from a performance in 1920 of Tolstoy's *Living Corpse:* "It made him so unhappy," she says, "that before the performance was half through he found himself unable to endure it longer, even with his face buried in his hands. . . . There was nothing for it but for us to squeeze our way out . . . earning, as we did so, black looks from a long row of earnest Russophile playgoers."

But it was only five months after the Mexico City bullfight, when Lawrence had returned to Mexico with the Danish painter, Kai Götzsche, that the latter wrote Knud Merrild, October 15, 1923, concerning a village near Tepic: "As we came into a small town, a bullfight was to be staged, so we stopped to take that in. . . . Interesting, but how raw it was. We saw four bulls, of which two were killed. . . . The poor animal, he tried to lie down and die. But he was constantly aroused to make hopeless attacks at a red rag. . . . I got provoked and furious just to think of the yellow and dumb performance."

This time Götzsche was the outraged dissenter. Lawrence not only stayed and watched the show but wrote a short story later about a bullfighter and his cruelty to an enamored rich woman. The story was called "None of That" and reported the lady's initial experience at a bullfight: "At first she was very disgusted, and very contemptuous, a little bit frightened, you know, because a Mexican crowd at a bull ring is not very charming." Finally, because of the torero's vicious cruelty to her, the woman poisoned herself and left him half her property.

JOSEPH HENRY JACKSON

Toluca market, 1935

"WE BEGAN OUR BARGAINING. BEFORE WE WERE
DONE WE HAD A CIRCLE OF INDIANS STANDING
SILENTLY BEHIND US, THEIR HEADS SWINGING,
LIKE A CROWD AT A TENNIS MATCH."

Joseph Henry Jackson was literary editor of the San Francisco Chronicle *in the twenties and thirties. He wrote several books about his home
state, concentrating on the Gold Rush period, and edited an excellent an-
thology of writings about California. In the fall of 1935 he and his wife,
Charlotte, drove to Laredo and then started down the new Pan American
Highway to Mexico City. He recorded the journey in* Mexican Inter-
lude, *published the following year.*

*Jackson wrote the book as he traveled and it reflects his own feel-
ings at least as much as it reports what he saw. He starts out suspicious,
protected against harm by only a few words of Spanish and a bundle of
letters of introduction, including ones from "our Governor, our Mayor
and Chief of Police, complete with gold seals and silk ribbon," meant,
one assumes, to ward off the evil intentions of simpleminded and dangerous locals. He fears the salads and the water, marvels constantly at the
relative cheapness of everything but congratulates himself on not tipping
25 centavos when 15 would do, and averts his eyes from Mexican reality*

by reading Rockwell Kent's new book on Greenland, which, we are not surprised to learn, he finds "immeasurably soothing."

But the deeper he gets into Mexico—in distance, time, and intimacy—the more his attitude and his book both change. Confronted everywhere by good manners and good cheer, he becomes noticeably less tense, more tolerant, and willing to let Mexico and the Mexicans simply be themselves. In the following passage, his change of heart is clear in his reasonable method of finding an acceptable restaurant and in his remark on restaurant kitchens.

When Jackson and his wife reached Mexico City, they had a room waiting for them with a friend of a friend, but they didn't know how to find the address. So they followed signs for Shirley Courts through the city, relieved to know that at the end of the route there would be a friendly American who could give them local directions.

Shirley Courts and Automobile Service was located at Calzada Villalongin 153, just north of Paseo de la Reforma and near the Colonia passenger train station. After the street name was changed, its address became Sullivan 166. The site of the train station is now Sullivan Park, which, on Sundays, becomes El Jardín del Arte.

The enterprising proprietor, a Texan named James Shirley, had responded quickly to modern trends in auto travel by promising American motorists the very latest thing, a California-style tourist court. He offered deluxe housekeeping apartments and such amenities as lawns and gardens, artesian water and hot running water, heated rooms and refrigerators, parking spaces and complete auto service, all at moderate prices, in a converted hacienda setting. Tourists from the north must have blessed him when they spotted the first of his many signs, each bearing a bright orange arrow. Those arrows led drivers unerringly from the Pan American Highway (which actually entered the city fairly close by), through the complicated local streets of the outskirts, right into a parking space at his door.

Shirley Courts continued to be a beacon for American tourists as late as 1965, when it offered sixty-seven rooms at $6.40 double and, according to one guidebook, was "well run" and had an "excellent coffee shop." The coffee shop offered Americans country-style breakfasts, chicken à la king, club sandwiches, and, like Sanborn's, a soda fountain. The restaurant business prospered too, and in the sixties Shirley's provided the in-flight food for Pan Am and American Airlines service from Mexico City to the United States. Today there are six Shirley's restaurants in Mexico City, famous for their buffet meals and serving both traditional Mexican and American foods. In keeping with the Shirley tradition, one of the specialties is Yankee pot roast. In its own way, Shirley's has been as central to life in Mexico City as its classier rival, Sanborn's.

In this prewar age, Americans of a certain sort who traveled abroad were in the habit of stopping by at the American consulate to sign the register. This allowed other Americans of the same sort to know that they were in town and where to find them, and vice versa. When the Jacksons went by to sign the register, they discovered that John and Carol Steinbeck were in Mexico City, staying in Frances Toor's apartment while she visited the United States.

Frances Toor was an American who had established herself at the center of Mexico City's cultural life. She edited and published the popular Mexican Folkways, wrote a very useful guidebook, directed an art gallery, encouraged many writers and artists (both Mexican and American), and—like Gertrude Stein in 1920s Paris—was hostess of the capital's liveliest literary and artistic salon.

The Jacksons and the Steinbecks quickly established a friendship and planned their first outing together. The Steinbecks are the unnamed "friends" in the following account of a visit to Toluca market.

BETWEEN MEXICO AND TOLUCA THE ROAD IS good highway all the way and it needs to be; you climb in the first twenty miles from Mexico's 7,200 feet to a high point at Las Cruces of something like 10,000. Of all the scenery after we crossed the border this reminded us most of our own country. Evergreens and oaks cover the hills, and near the summit there are wide stretches of meadow land dotted with lumps and chunks of gray granite that recalled the California Sierra so vividly as to give us one or two sharp twinges of homesickness. The air here is light and heady and the clouds that almost always hang about the high peaks are magnificent; the temptation is to spend half your time stopping to point your camera at the mountains and the sky. We did stop several times, going through the complicated routine of wide-angle and telescope lenses and yellow filters and such, and we got some good pictures for our trouble. All, that is, but one which neither of us can remember taking. It is a very simple picture; indeed its simplicity is perhaps its best feature. It contains only a very large field of corn, and, lurking in the background, a smallish, inoffensive sort of hill. In it there are no clouds, no handsome peaks, nothing at all, in fact, that could possibly be considered a picture. When we saw the print C. said she believed she remembered our making the exposure in order to demonstrate when we got home that a good deal of corn grew in Mexico; but even the exceptional altitude couldn't have made us as light-headed as that. Yet there is the damning evidence; we took it, unless the camera simply snapped its shutter and wound the film of its own accord. A hundred acres of dryish, unimportant-looking corn and nothing else. Perhaps some night our reason for doing it will come to us in a dream, but we are inclined to think that we shall never really know. In the meantime we keep the print as a reminder of the curious aberrations from which the amateur photographer may sometimes suffer.

Twenty urchins sprang for the bridle of the car the moment we stopped in Toluca's main street, across from the market.

The custom in Mexico is to put your car in care of a boy when you leave it, no matter where you are. In the City there are uniformed men who make a business of watching the parking spaces; you pay them ten *centavos* if you are away less than half an hour and say twenty or thereabouts if you are gone longer. It is one of the recognized schemes by which a man may pick up a little change, and after all it is worth the fee, ten *centavos* being a shade under three cents American. But in the smaller towns and villages, any small boy that comes along will do, and plenty of them come along. In Toluca we hired the boy who addressed us as *jefe*. The flattery was brazen, but the other boys had not been able to match it; the best any of the rest could do was *patrón,* and while it is pleasant to be spoken to as "Landlord," after all, the term "Chief," with all its connotations (it is used today in Mexico as the approximate equivalent of our "Big Shot"), is a blandishment difficult to ignore. The rest of the yelling group (they yell, but politely) faded away. We waved off the women who wanted to sell us wooden ashtrays and carved *molinillos,* which are the instruments you twirl between your palms to make Mexican chocolate frothy. One or two beggars spotted us and drifted over to ask for money, but in country towns like Toluca beggars are not hard to dispose of; you simply shake your head, waggle your forefinger from side to side with a rolling wrist motion and look sad. After you have done that seven or eight or maybe ten times they see what you mean and drift off again.

There were a dozen women at the curb with bright woven baskets, but even though they began at ten *pesos* and came down to four before we were across the street we did not buy. There was the whole market to see and it was a feast day besides. If we felt that we had to have baskets we could get them later. It was just as we came to the edge of the market place that we heard for the first time the cry that later became one of the most familiar sounds in Mexico. Right in our ear a tall, serious Mexican, thinly whiskered like a Chinaman, roared "Aylaao*woose!*" When we got our balance again we read the sign on his little pushcart. It said, much more simply, "*Helados*," which means merely ices, sometimes ice-cream cones, sometimes frozen sherbets on a stick. His pushcart was named, too. In accordance with some mysterious and wonderful compensatory law which appears to operate in Mexico, that roaring, bellowing hokey-pokey man had called his ambulating shop "*La Violeta.*"

The confusion of your first market day in Mexico is something you never forget.

Toluca is a country town, but it has an exceptionally large market that draws customers from the little villages for miles around. We entered at the wrong side—the section given up to booths in which were displayed the cheap calicos and rayons, children's patent-leather shoes, combs, brushes, costume jewelry in the Woolworth manner, socks, tennis-shoes, low-priced factory-made toys and such things. Each merchant was singing out his goods and his prices at the top of his voice and having a grand time doing it. "Cheap" is the key-word, shouted "*Barato-barato-BARATO!*" in a triple burst of machine-gun fire that almost bowls you over when you hear it for the first time. Indians from the hills round about fingered the sleazy materials wistfully and wandered on; not many of them have any money to speak of. It was all a good deal like New York's Canal Street in the old days, with booths instead of carts, cheap goods and insistent merchants peddling them. Even cigarettes (an old New York trick) were sold in broken packages; little bundles of five, tied with a bit of string. We saw Indians buying those often; the full package of twenty for about seven cents American comes too high for them.

We made our way through this section of the market, dodging the fantastically rigged cotton awnings stretched from makeshift poles to keep the sun from beating down too strongly, avoiding the neatly piled stacks of merchandise that crowded the sidewalks, stepping carefully to keep from crushing bare toes. Because it was a holiday the market was twice as full of people as usual and ten times as busy, yet no one pushed, no one was irritated, everyone took his time. Everybody that passed in front of us said *"Con permiso!"* and smiled. It's in the city streets that you find your slick-haired, pushing, impolite Mexican, just as it is in American cities that you find the same type. But these were country people, slow and courteous and ready to smile and make allowances for the strange *Norteamericanos* who did things all backwards. We had the familiar "Good-bye!" shouted at us a dozen times at least, but it was not until we were just about to debouch into the part of the market we had been looking for, with its bright *sarape*-booths and counters full of embroidered cloths and headbands and belts, that we were given a really ambitious salute. A large Mexican (he was selling poisonous blue and pink combs, fine-toothed ones that he knew we didn't need) swept off his *sombrero* and in a frenzy of good-humor fairly blasted us into the *sarape*-zone with "Aow de do! Helloh! Sure!"

All Mexico loves a bargainer.

That doesn't apply, perhaps, to the stores whose rents are fixed and which cater to the tourist trade. In the City of Mexico, for instance, such places of business operate on a fixed price basis, take it or leave it, just as stores do in the United States. But a market is different, particularly a country market such as Toluca's. True, the *sarape*-booths are there to catch the roving eye of the tourist, but their proprietors sell to the Indians also, and they are ready for half an hour of bargaining any time.

We had seen the typical Saltillo *sarape* in Monterrey and didn't care for it. In spite of its fine weave and texture there is something about its rainbow stripes and violently combined colors that suggests the factory, even though the blanket may be as hand-made as ever was. But these booths in Toluca had all kinds, and it was no time at all before we had dozens of them spread out for us to admire. It didn't take those merchants two minutes, either, to find out how our tastes lay. After the first two or three, no bright ones were even offered us. They knew exactly what they were doing, those salespeople.

But prices were something else. We had our friends with us, and we had learned from them, on the road coming up, all we could about the technique of buying. For there is a technique. No matter how sharp your saleswoman or salesman may be, you can eventually get a better price if you keep at it, and no matter how much they may want their profit they may still be pleased by a heartfelt "*Qué bonito!*" And those *sarapes* were lovely; we didn't have to force ourselves to say so just for business reasons. The rather loosely woven type that is predominantly Tolucan has a softness and a woolly warmth that struck us, at least, as being infinitely more desirable than the tighter, harder fabrics. Besides, they were the kind the Indians all around us were wearing. We liked the rich browns and blacks and grays and the flexible looseness of the weave, and we began our bargaining. Before we were done we had a circle of Indians standing silently behind us, their heads swinging, like a crowd at a tennis match, first toward us and then over toward the *puesto*-keeper. It was a show; their show; one of the reasons they had come to market. A really good bargainer, an artist at it who has a rich vocabulary and a touch of the actor in him, can easily gather an audience of hundreds to watch him work, and before we left Mexico we saw some magnificent performances staged. But we were rank amateurs with nothing but our persistence and our patience to recommend us and our circle was small. Nevertheless we were encouraged; at least we were getting somewhere, even though the merchant swore we were breaking his heart. And our patience was rewarded. Eventually two blankets for which we had originally been asked twenty-five *pesos* each were engineered down to twenty-seven-fifty for the pair. Our friends had draped themselves in embroidered belts and tablecloths and none of us could carry any more of anything. We made up our minds to eat. The afternoon was still before us, and we could always come back later. We left the booth with smiles all round and polite good wishes. The vendors had made a profit; they thought better of us for bargaining; we had got what we wanted for forty per cent less than we would have paid for the same articles in a City store. Everything was lovely. Besides, as we were leaving, another group of

Americans had come up. As we turned away, the same capable and earnest saleswoman who had asked us twenty-five *pesos* was showing almost the same *sarape* to the new customers who, unhappily for them, had no Spanish at all. With as expressive a wink in our direction as I have ever seen, she was saying, in the amused tone of one who names a ridiculously small amount, "This one? A mere forty *pesos!*" We have wondered ever since if they got her down to thirty.

On ordinary market days there are reasonably clear alleyways through which you can pick your way, but this was *fiesta,* the Day of the Child Dead. Between booths, straying across the paths wherever we turned, were the tiny temporary tables of the women who sold the *muertos,* the sweetbreads and cakes and candies symbolic of the children that have died. The variety of these articles was extraordinary. Mexico has more kinds of bread anyway than any American can hope to keep track of, and now there were also the special candy figures to add to those. Life-sized sugar skulls, tastefully trimmed with blue or red or gilt paper, stared at us from every side, all of them named in sugar scrolls across the forehead. There were more Marías and Panchos than anything else, but the chances were distinctly in favor of finding any Spanish name you fancied. As for pigs, sheep, goats, tigers, burros, horses, cats and dogs in candy, there was no end of them. We photographed two elegantly smug sugar pigs, together with the proprietress of the stall who was trying to capture the fancy of a customer with a fine pink sheep, and squeezed past. The street was straight ahead of us and we were all hungry.

Lunch in Toluca on market day (the Spanish equivalent is *lonch,* so spelled on restaurant windows and everywhere else; something like the linguistic compromise in *biftek* and *futbol*) was rather a problem.

There were, of course, no American restaurants; Toluca does not cater to the tourist because the tourist spends little time there. So we set out in search of a Mexican place that would be reasonably quiet and reasonably clean. We found one before long, using a simple test of quality which consisted in poking our heads in at the doors and counting stray dogs and cats. We took the restaurant with the fewest of either, on the principle that the restaurateur that spent the most energy chasing such animals away had probably the neatest instincts. We went into no kitchens. It is best not to go into Mexican kitchens, at least in places in which you expect to eat. I shouldn't like to say outright that they are dirty, because I have never actually gone round peering into corners. But the effect, to the American eye and nose, is decidedly not appetizing.

In this case the food was very good; after all, we didn't see where it came from. There was a vegetable soup with pieces of goats'-milk cheese floating in it; Mexican rice, very dry and good; chicken (try to escape chicken in Mexico) and a salad which we did not eat because it was of uncooked vegetables. We took beer as always, and finished with a *café chico*, a small coffee, black as your hat and with that concentrated power of the Mexican brew which digests everything that has gone before it by sheer strength and awkwardness. While we were lingering over cigarettes, an Indian woman came in selling *ciruelas*, a kind of wild prune, undried, which is eaten everywhere in Mexico. We did not want any and she did not press us in the manner of the basket vendors with their wares. But she asked quite simply whether, if we had no use for the chicken we had left on our plates, she might have it. There was no mock servility about her, no trace of the typical Mexican beggar who follows you whining for blocks if you are not firm with him. The idea was merely that she could use the food if we did not need it. We said yes, of course; and she wrapped the remains in a twist of paper, thanked us with pleasant dignity and moved on with her flat basket of *ciruelas* to the next eating place. We liked her enough to photograph her a little later when we passed her in front of the embroidery stalls. I still think hers is one of the most interesting faces we saw in Mexico.

When we passed our *sarape*-sellers again we were no longer merely *turistas* but friends. We exchanged greetings, quite as though we had not parted only an hour or so before, and inquired where we might buy the best embroideries. Naturally they knew the answer; in fact they went with us to the keeper of the booth who had, so they explained with flourishes, the very finest embroidery work to be found in all Toluca, or in the City of Mexico either. Later we learned that same concessionaire owned both stalls, but it was a pleasant gesture just the same and everybody felt the better for it. And they were exceptionally fine embroideries, too. The patience with which the Indian women stitch those long strips of cotton cloth (descendants of clerical stoles perhaps?), working the bright patterns over every available fraction of the six feet by four inches, must be the equal of Job's. And when they are done and sold and the market booth has its profit, you have bought them for anywhere from one to five *pesos*—twenty-eight cents to a dollar and forty cents American—depending upon how elaborate the work happens to be and how badly the *puesto*-keeper thinks you want the piece. We had the morning's experience to give us confidence, and our *lonch* to give us strength, and we held out to the last. Especially admirable, we all thought, was the deal C. worked out, by which two of those long belts (asking price five *pesos* each) were ours for two *pesos* apiece, provided we would also buy six handbags that she wanted for presents at home. The catch in it was that those handbags were first priced at one *peso* seventy-five, but in view of our buying the whole lot they were cut to one *peso* each. It still sounds to me as though we were paid a premium for arguing down the price on the belts, but no doubt the merchant knew what she was doing. No doubt at all.

We had bought one large woven basket when we got back to the car, but since there were two couples of us the basket-women felt that was not enough. One in particular was persistent; her basket was something we simply must not leave Toluca without; it was very much prettier and very much rounder and very much better in every way and wouldn't we please just take hold of it and look? We looked, as we had been looking for five minutes, but all we could see was that it was smaller than the first one, not so good in design and done in colors we didn't like. We told her so, but it made no difference; she tried another line of attack. Could we not see for ourselves that the first basket was of quite inferior workmanship and weave? That hadn't occurred to us, and we looked. We also looked for the first time at the woman. She was the same who had sold us the first basket. When we told her so, accusingly, she burst into giggles, and so did the swarm of others in the background who had everything from wilted flowers to pottery jugs to sell. We left Toluca with that laughter in our ears, nor are we yet certain whether it was directed at the basket-woman or ourselves.

LANGSTON HUGHES

Bohemian life, 1934–1935

"I TOOK A TINY GROUND-FLOOR FLAT NEAR THE
LAGUNILLA MARKET ACROSS FROM THE STALLS OF
THE COFFIN MERCHANTS, AND CONTINUED TO
HAVE A WONDERFUL TIME."

*Around the time Langston Hughes was born in 1902, his parents sepa-
rated because "my father wanted to go away to another country, where a
colored man could get ahead and make money quicker, and my mother
did not want to go. My father went to Cuba, and then to Mexico, where
there wasn't any color line, or any Jim Crow." When Hughes was five,
his father sent for him and his mother. At 11:34 P.M. on April 14,
1907, an earthquake shook Mexico from the capital to Acapulco for
four and a half minutes. The Cathedral was seriously cracked, the new
Palacio de Bellas Artes (then under construction) sank a little, scor-
pions crawled out of exposed earth, and hundreds of people were killed.
Hughes's mother took him home immediately, and all he remembered
was his father carrying him in his arms through the Alameda as the
ground trembled beneath them.*

*Then, in 1919, his father showed up in Cleveland and took the
seventeen-year-old Hughes with him to spend the summer in Mexico.
The young man had only one night in Mexico City. This was spent at*

the Grand Hotel (built in the nineteenth century as a department store and today the Gran Hotel Howard Johnson) on the Zócalo, with time only to visit his father's friends, the Patiño sisters, at 16 Calle Santa Teresa, just behind the Cathedral. This area has changed over the years, especially since 1978, when power-company workers stumbled on additional ruins around the buried Aztec Templo Mayor near the northwest corner of the Cathedral. Many colonial buildings were razed in order to expose the ruins.

The summer, which Hughes called "the most miserable I have ever known," was spent in Toluca, where his father lived in a house at 3 Plaza de la Reforma. His father, a man driven to make money and alienated from the United States by racial prejudice, pushed Hughes hard at everything, especially the need to learn business skills, but otherwise gave him little attention.

After that summer and during his final year in high school back in Cleveland, Hughes came to realize that neither of his parents could provide the psychological support and the direction he needed. He made up his mind to return to Mexico after graduation and persuade his father to send him to Columbia University in New York.

That summer of 1920, when he was eighteen and earning money of his own in Toluca, he was able to visit Mexico City on weekends and quickly fell in love with the bullfights. The bullring was the same one from which D. H. Lawrence would flee in horror three years later.

By the time he next visited Mexico, Hughes had traveled extensively and had won a place of his own in the literary world, although he was still living on charity and loans. When word of his father's death reached him, he left for Mexico City in December 1934 to settle the estate.

James N. Hughes had held a low opinion of American blacks, who, he often said to his son, were content to be waiters and Pullman porters. He would have been interested to meet another black American who was living in Mexico at the time. In 1934, the year the elder Hughes died, Harry Franck traveled in Mexico and wrote of meeting "an American negro," a retired Pullman porter, who had built a splendid home for himself and his family facing the blue Pacific from the cliffs above the beach at Acapulco. This man kept a small food stand in the plaza and carefully cultivated the trade of American visitors by serving apple pie and other reminders of home. Franck notes that "he can't build up the business he might, however, because if the authorities should think he is making anything more than a bare living they would take it away from him in taxes." Even so, Franck can quote the man as saying that he "wouldn't go back to the States if you gave 'em to me."

Langston Hughes mentions another black man, Butch Lewis, who had established himself very successfully in the capital at that time. Lewis was the owner of Butch's Manhattan Cafe, a popular American-style lunch counter and restaurant. Writing about it twenty years later in I Wonder As I Wander, *the second volume of his autobiography, Hughes remembered Lewis's restaurant as being on Avenida 5 de Mayo. It was actually one block over, at Avenida Juárez 58. It was a good location in the heart of "American" Mexico City, within a block or two of Sanborn's, the Lady Baltimore, the bar in the Ritz, the American Book Store, the offices of Pan American Airways, and Wells Fargo, where Americans gathered every morning for their motor tours.*

The Patiño sisters, who had helped Hughes's father in his business affairs and looked after him in his illness, were now living a couple of blocks farther north, on Calle de San Ildefonso. They received everything from the estate, which turned out to be small, and even after they insisted that Hughes share in the proceeds, he had only enough money to repay his aunt what she had loaned him for the trip. "So I stayed in Mexico," *he wrote later,* "until I could make enough money from writing to come home."

After this trip, Hughes visited Mexico only once more, and only for a few hours. In 1953, while passing through El Paso, Texas, he crossed the border to see a bullfight in Ciudad Juárez.

☀ FOR ME IT WAS A DELIGHTFUL WINTER. I have an affinity for Latin Americans, and the Spanish language I have always loved. One of the first things I did when I got to Mexico City was to get a tutor, a young woman friend of the Patiños, and began to read *Don Quixote* in the original, a great reading experience that possibly helped me to develop many years later in my own books a character called Simple. I also began to translate into English a number of Mexican short stories and poems by young writers for publication in the United States. I met a number of painters, the sad Orozco, the talkative Siqueiros, and the genteel Montenegro, whose studio was across the street from where I lived.

Every Sunday there were the bullfights. After the regular

season in the big ring, young fighters at Vista Alegre were pitted by unscrupulous promoters against enormous bulls, their bodies tossed, trampled and gored with frequency by animals too swift and tricky for beginners. I watched two boys killed. Every week after such a spectacle, I would swear each Sunday night never to attend another bullfight. But the next Sunday afternoon I'd be there before the gates opened. From the days of my adolescence when I first saw the famous Mexican matador, Rudolfo Gaona, and the great Spaniard, Sanchez Mejías (of Lorca's *Five O'Clock in the Afternoon*), I have been fascinated with bullfights—to my mind the most beautiful and dangerous of sports in the world.

At Lupe Marín's home I met the young Spanish matador, Juan Luis de la Rosa, a handsome lad who was having a rough time with the Mexican public. Armillita and Domingo Ortega were the favorites at the big ring, El Toreo, and Alberto Balderos was a runner-up until he was viciously gored as, after a beautiful pass, he turned to walk away. The bull caught Balderos in the seat of his golden trousers, lifted him high on a single horn, and tossed him halfway across the arena. Juan Luis de la Rosa fought more carefully, and so was more popular at parties than in the ring. One Sunday Lupe Marín gave a big dinner for de la Rosa—the traditional Mexican turkey with *mole,* a sauce that takes days to make. But Juan Luis did not show up. Hostess and guests waited, waited and waited. Finally, Lupe, instead of blessing the succulent bird on the table, with carving knife poised delivered a few choice words concerning bullfighters and their worthless mothers, then we all fell to and demolished the fowl.

By spring I had sold a few stories so, with a young French photographer, Henri Cartier-Bresson and a Mexican poet, Andrés Henestrosa, I took a tiny ground-floor flat near the Lagunilla Market across from the stalls of the coffin merchants, and continued to have a wonderful time. The darling old-school Patiño sisters had not approved of the artists, writers, models and bullfighters who sometimes came by their house looking for me. As young ladies, my father's friends had worshiped President Porfirio Díaz. They hated the leaders of the Mexican revolution, as well as all its art and artists. The mere name, Diego Rivera, caused them to turn pale and cross themselves for protection. When the three sisters learned that I had been to Diego's studio at San Angel, they were horrified. And one day when his former wife, Lupe Marín, came by to call for me with some other friends, they looked at Lupe without smiling and spoke only with formal politeness to this exotic Mexican whose lips were a bright red and who dressed in so colorful and careless a way. To make matters worse, however, Lupe was entranced by the three Patiño sisters, who she thought were like quaint figurines under glass, lovely leftovers of distant days beyond even Díaz. So Lupe came back to their house especially to see them and to admire the precious lace mantillas they wore about their shoulders in the chilly stone rooms where candles before the madonnas provided the only warmth.

The Patiños liked Miguel Covarrubias and Cartier-Bresson a little, but the others of my friends not at all. It was mostly for this reason that in the spring I sometimes stayed with the three sisters, but more often in the flat near the market where no one was embarrassed by bohemian company.

With a photographer and a poet as roommates, and none of us with any money to speak of, I recall no period in my life when I've had more fun with less cash. From our poor neighbors we learned how to cut down on electricity. Instead of allowing lights to burn on the meter, the neighbors taught us how to attach our wires to a long, heavy, copper wire with a hook at one end. At night, through our grilled window, with the aid of a broom handle, this attachment could be looped over the power line that ran across the courtyard. Thus one had lights for nothing. None of the other tenants got electrocuted. We didn't either.

Henri Cartier-Bresson had come to Mexico from Paris on a sight-seeing trip and had liked it so much that he did not want to return home when the francs his father gave him for his vacation ran out. His father wrote that Henri might stay in Mexico then and starve if he chose! He did not send him any more money. But Cartier, in love with a camera, still managed to take pictures. And in March he had a joint exhibition of his photographs with Manuel Alvarez Bravo at the Palacio de Bellas Artes. This was Cartier-Bresson's first major showing of his photographs. Some of the pictures that hung in this show were taken in our Lagunilla courtyard, and in the streets surrounding the market. When the show came down, Cartier generously gave Andrés and me several of the prints.

Andrés Henestrosa was a little Indian—a white Indian from Oaxaca—a poet and transcriber of folk tales, who was busy beginning to make the first dictionary of his own Indian language. He later completed this at Columbia University, and then went on to become a politician and a congressman in his native Mexico. Andrés was courting a beautiful and much-photographed Indian girl, dark brown in complexion, whom he later married. And Cartier was in love with another Indian beauty from Tehuantepec who went barefooted. My favorite girl was a tortilla maker's daughter named Aurora. All three of us in the Lagunilla flat were interested in the folk dances, songs and night life of the Mexican capital. When our daytime work was done, if there were no parties to which we were invited, we would often seek out the little bars and clubs where the *mariachis* played their guitars and wailed their *corridos* and *huapangos*. Once I went with Cartier to the hot springs on a picture-taking trip. Aside from that, other than one excursion to Guadalajara to see the Rivera frescoes, one to Taxco, and another to my old home of Toluca, I remained in the capital.

The artist, Miguel Covarrubias and his wife, Rose Rolando, I had known in New York in the days when Harlem was in vogue. For my first book, *The Weary Blues,* Miguel had done the jacket, and he had tried several times to do a caricature of me, but finally said I wasn't caricaturable. He and his wife had a charming house outside Mexico City where more and more Miguel was turning toward serious painting and serious writing, documenting the history, folk life and Indian art of his country. It was Covarrubias who introduced me to Diego Rivera, that mountain of a man, darker than I am in complexion. When I told Diego he looked more like an American Negro than a Mexican Indian, Rivera said, "One of my grandmothers was a Negro."

Then he and Covarrubias told me about the African strains to be found in Mexican blood, particularly in the Vera Cruz section of the coast where many of the people are dark indeed. Certainly, Diego Rivera had large and quite Negroid features and a deep bronze complexion. But fortunately in Mexico color did not matter as it does in the United States. My father had gone to Mexico when I was a baby, to escape the color line in Oklahoma, where he had been refused permission, because of race, to take the law examination for the bar. He practiced in Mexico City instead, and came back only once in thirty years to his native land. When my father wanted a vacation, he went to Europe instead. He hated Jim Crow, and thought I must be crazy to live in the United States. But then my father, although himself a Negro, was not fond of Negroes. He felt that they were too passive in the face of prejudice. In Mexico City I missed Negroes in large numbers. There were some there, long-time residents as my father had been, but most of them had so merged into the Mexican community that they were hard to find. However, one old friend of my father's, a successful colored business man named Butch Lewis, owned the largest and most popular (next to Sanborn's) American-style restaurant in Mexico City. Mr. Lewis finally dug up a few other Negroes for me, when I convinced him that I really wanted to find some. That winter, too, I met the boxer, Henry Armstrong, when he came down to fight Casanova. And José Antonio Fernández de Castro, my journalist friend from Havana, had become a diplomat in Mexico, so he introduced me to the Cuban Negro drummers about town, since both of us could listen to bongos for hours.

But José Antonio, when he found out I was in Mexico, immediately began broadcasting to the Mexican press what an (in his view) "important" writer I was, and he himself wrote a long piece about my poetry, which was published. The result was for me a number of newspaper interviews, sessions with photographers and artists, and translators asking me how to translate the syncopated rhythms and Harlem slang of my poems into Mexican idioms and Spanish meters. Javier Villarrutia, José Mancisidor, and Heliodoro Valle, among others, wrote articles about my work. The big newspaper, *El Nacional,* published a page of my poems with my photograph in its Sunday supplement. Requests for me to speak at literary soirees began to come in. And for a while it looked as if I were going to be lionized—which I never liked very much. I get embarrassed. So in the late spring I began to think about going back to California to find peace for writing again.

I never lived in Greenwich Village in New York, so its bohemian life—in the old days when it was bohemian—was outside my orbit. Although once I lived for a year in Montmartre in Paris, I lived there as a worker, not an artist. So the nearest I've ever come to *la vie de bohème* was my winter in Mexico when my friends were almost all writers and artists like Juan de la Cabada, María Izquierdo, Luis Cardoza y Aragon, Manuel Bravo, Rufino Tamayo and

Francesca and Nellie Campobello. Most of my friends were almost always broke, or very nearly so. But then we didn't care. Henri declared his father in Paris—who rumor said was a wealthy industrialist—could keep his money. He, Henri, would get along. Andrés said he'd never had much money anyway, so *no le hace*. As for me, I'd often lived hand-to-mouth. But when I got really hungry, the gracious Patiños always set a good noonday table, and every evening had an enormous *jarro* of steaming chocolate and sugared rolls for supper. Sometimes José Antonio would invite me to dine in a good restaurant where foreign diplomats ate. Or Butch Lewis, my father's old friend, would see me passing the windows of his café on Calle 5 de Mayo and beckon me to come in and have some chicken. Or Andrés might sell an article on Tehuantepec and all three of us would go to Las Casuelas—a restaurant with an open kitchen where you could look in the pots and see the food cooking. On Sundays after the bullfights, Lupe Marín might have a feast.

Once I went with Lupe to collect her alimony from Diego Rivera. We had been that day to luncheon with Miguel and Rose Covarrubias in suburban Tizapán. On the way back into town, Lupe said, "Let's go by San Angel and see Diego. He's behind on my payments. Maybe I can catch him."

But she did not find him. There was no one at his studio, a box of modern French architecture built high in the air on stilts of steel with the pipes of the plumbing exposed beneath. There was a similar companion studio a few yards away which Lupe said Rivera had built for Frida Kahlo, herself a fine artist. Some twenty feet up in the air connecting the two buildings, there was a little bridge.

"That," said Lupe, "is the catwalk. How it supports Diego's weight at night, I'll never know. Where is that big hunk of Mexican mud, anyhow?"

Both Lupe and Diego were famous for the names they called each other. The ample and voluptuous Lupe had been not only his wife, but for years his favorite model. Now, parted, they were fighting friends, or friendly fighters, according to their moods on meeting. Their alimony meetings were always dramatic, their friends said, and usually of sufficiently public a nature to furnish the capital's cocktail parties with a fresh supply of quotes and anecdotes every month. Lupe's language was often most vivid, but it does not stand up well in print. Many writers have tried to write about her, and she herself wrote one or two *Lives,* but none as alive as herself, by a long shot.

Anyway, having heard that she and her former husband some-times indulged in head-on collisions, the day I went to San Angel with her and she called up to the open windows of Diego's studio, "Come out, you rock-hearted heathen idol!" and there was no an-swer, I thought maybe a picture might come flying down on our heads. (Gossip gave them credit for fantastic fights.) But nothing happened. Only silence, and the rustling of the eucalyptus leaves in the tall trees. Disappointed, Lupe gazed at the studio above her head, and spat at the pipes of the plumbing beneath it.

"I guess I'll have to climb those *malditas* steps," she said.

Up the stairs she went and flung open the door, which was not locked although there was nobody home.

"Look at this crap in here," said Lupe.

Large paintings and small paintings, sketches half finished and unfinished were all around—a fortune in Riveras—and nobody home.

"I can't stand the sight of these pictures," said Lupe. "None of them are of me. Let's go sit in the yard. He'll come. He scents me. Something always tells Diego when I'm around, so he'll come."

Sure enough, we had hardly been sitting in the eucalyptus shade ten minutes when down the road came a little car and out stepped a huge man, Diego Rivera. He greeted us jovially, but asked us to do him the favor of remaining in the yard "Because," he said, "look! Buyers!"

Trailing his car came a long luxurious motor with a well-dressed American couple of obvious means in the back. A chauffeur let them out. Diego had guided them in from the city to take a look at his paintings. They disappeared into the studio.

"They'll pay a year's fortune for something he painted in half an hour," said Lupe. "But I'm not going to wait while he entertains tourists. I'll be back, don't worry about that. Adios, pumpkin-belly!" she called.

Without further ceremony we drove off into town. I did not hear how or when she collected her month's alimony. But there was a story current that once when Diego thought he had no money, he simply gave Lupe a blank check which he signed and said, "Maybe there's a little something in the bank, Peso-eater, go get it."

That very morning it seems, according to the tale, without his knowledge, one of Diego's foreign dealers posted to his account a quite large sum of several thousand dollars. Lupe drew it all. Anecdotes about Diego and Lupe were as common in Mexico City then as were tall tales about Robinson and Una Jeffers at Carmel, or stories of the amazing doings of Mabel Dodge Luhan and Tony at Taos. Rivera and his ex-wife were favorite conversation pieces in the capital. But not with the Patiño sisters! My father's old friends would have none of them.

My last few weeks in Mexico I spent at the Patiño home, because I knew they would feel hurt if I didn't. I went to vespers with them every night in the old church just across the street, lighted by tall candles and smelling of incense. Sometimes I even got up early in the morning to attend mass. And I still cherish the lovely old rosaries they gave me. These sisters were very sweet, kindhearted women. But sometimes I thought their kindness was a little misspent. I was then all in favor of working to change the *basic* economics of the world, while they were engaged in little charities widely dispersed to help various indigents a *little*. From their small income they gave, in proportion, generously—five pesos here, ten there, two to this brotherhood, three to that sisterhood, one peso to one organization, a peso and a half to another—and regularly each week to the church. Then from their home they had their own little private dispensation every seventh day to the poor of the neighborhood.

This weekly ritual seemed touching, but very futile to me. There were literally thousands of poor people in the neighborhood, since the Patiños lived in the heart of Mexico City, not far from the Zócalo. In our block alone there were perhaps two or three hundred shoeless or nearly shoeless folks. Personal charity for a handful, I felt, was hardly a drop in the bucket for so great a need. But these elderly women had been doing this for years, so I said nothing to discourage them. Every Monday, early in the morning they would busy themselves, these three sisters, packaging in separate cones of newspapers little cups of beans, a tiny scoop of sugar, perhaps two or three onions, a bunch of grapes or an orange, and a small slice of laundry soap. Several dozen such little packets of each thing they would make. Then from eleven to twelve, just before midday dinner, the poor of the neighborhood would come to receive their gifts. To each who asked, a set of these tiny packets would be given at the door, with a "Bless you, Marianita! . . . Bless you, Luz!" as each filed past with open hands. But the food each got was not enough for even one good meal. And the tiny piece of soap would hardly wash anyone's hands and face more than a day.

But there was among the deserving poor in the neighborhood one woman who must have felt as I did—concerning this small donation—because she always stayed to dinner. After she got her tiny packages, she would squat on the floor just inside the dining-room door, and no one could move her until the three sisters sat down to eat their noonday meal and she was served on the floor, too. Her name was Carolina (pronounced Car-o-*lean*-a) and she was a leper—a very old, sick and repulsive-looking leper. Her hands were calcified and spotty with horrible gnarled fingers. Her face was peeling and her eyes were rheumy. Her distorted lips drooled. But she could talk very fast and quite continuously, and would do so until fed. She was hardly decorative to have around during dinner.

"God give me the grace to bear Carolina," Lola, the youngest of the Patiño sisters, would sigh.

"Isn't she one of God's creatures? Isn't she one of God's creatures?" Fela, the eldest, would mutter rapidly with upturned eyes. "She belongs to God."

"That's right," Carolina would say. "I'm in God."

Cuca, the middle sister, who had a sly sense of humor, would murmur softly—so I could hear, but not her more serious sisters or *la pobre* Carolina, "Oh, would to God that He'd take care of you at the hour of *our* dinner!" I would bow my head to hide the laughter in my eyes. Carolina had a sense of humor, too, and knew well what she was doing—that she wryly amused Cuca and me while she irritated the more fastidious younger sister and the pious elder one. Sometimes the unrotted side of Carolina's mouth would flash Cuca and me a quick smile. Then her face would become woeful again as she lamented her plight, her poverty and her hunger, as she turned her pus-filled eyes on Lola and Fela. Carolina knew well that none of us would sit there in the name of God and eat a hot full-course meal and not give her some of it, too. Yet she wailed like a beggar as a preliminary to each course.

The problem was that the Patiños always had a really big dinner with several courses, a soup, a meat, two or three vegetables, tortillas, salad, the final customary plate of Mexican red beans, a dessert and coffee. Carolina had only one spoon and one eating utensil in her possession, a kind of large clay cup the size of a bowl, which she tied to her belt. She, being a leper, could not be served from any of the Patiño dishes. So all of her food had to go into this one cup—first soup, then a mixture of meat and vegetables, then salad and beans, then dessert. Carolina wanted some of everything—and chattered until she got it. Finally at the end, into the greasy and unwashed cup was poured her coffee. The servant would touch nothing belonging to Carolina for fear of contamination. No one could blame her—for this decaying leper was a sight to behold. Sometimes I would deliberately not be at home for Monday's dinner, just to miss looking at Carolina. But whenever I did see her, I always gave her a few pesos, and she gave me a smile from the good side of her mouth, plus a blessing. Once I went to help her up from the floor when she seemed weak, but the two serious sisters both cried aloud, "Don't touch her! For the love of God, don't touch her!"

They explained after Carolina left that touching a leper might give one leprosy. Cuca looked at me slyly and whispered under her breath, "You might get it quicker from just looking at her. Imagine Christians saying, 'For the *love of God,* don't touch her!' " Then, mocking her older sister, she intoned aloud, " 'Isn't she one of God's creatures, Fela? Isn't she one of God's creatures?' "

I once said to the Patiños that I thought it would be better, instead of giving once a week to so many people so many *little* bags of beans, if *all* those beans were put into one *big* bag and given to Carolina; she could live the whole week—then at least one person—and the most needy one—would be fed adequately. But they didn't see it that way. They prayed a lot for everyone, and gave a little to everyone, too.

MACKINLEY HELM

With Diego Rivera at San Angel, 1930s

"I WAS TAKING COFFEE WITH HIM AFTER LUNCH
ONE DAY, ON A BALCONY OVERLOOKING THE
STUDIO, WHEN A LARGE, EXPENSIVE-LOOKING
AMERICAN WOMAN SWEPT IN."

MacKinley Helm, an American who lived for some time in Mexico in the thirties and forties, was an early and important advocate of the new Mexican painters. He amassed a very important collection of pictures, and his Modern Mexican Painters, *published in 1941, did much to explain and popularize Mexican art in the United States. In later years Helm remained a friend of Mexico.* A Matter of Love, *a book of short stories about life in a small Mexican town, based on his own experiences, was published in 1946. (Retitled* A Month of Sundays, *it was published in England in 1949.)* Journeying Through Mexico, *a travel guide, appeared in 1948. And a verse drama about eighteenth-century California, called* Fray Junípero Serra, the Great Walker, *was published in 1956.*

In the following excerpt, Helm is wrong about Frida Kahlo's age at the time she married Rivera, but he can't be blamed for it. Kahlo was born in 1907 but, moved by patriotism, she liked to tell people she was born in 1910, with the Revolution.

Rivera's home in San Angel (Villa Obregón) was designed for him by Juan O'Gorman. It contained his studio, a private apartment, and a matching and attached apartment for Kahlo. Langston Hughes came here one afternoon in the spring of 1935 with Lupe Marín. The San Angel house was for years one of Mexico City's most glittering salons. Painters and writers flocked here, strangers and friends, including everyone from Leon Trotsky to Nelson Rockefeller, as well as an endless stream of buyers who carried away hundreds, maybe thousands, of his pictures. The inexpensive watercolors that he produced quickly, effortlessly, and beautifully for this steady market have been selling at recent Sotheby's and Christie's auctions in the $30,000-to-$40,000 range.

Selden Rodman tells a story, which he had "from an eyewitness," that reveals clearly the different personalities of Rivera and fellow muralist José Clemente Orozco. In 1934 both artists were working simultaneously on murals in the Palacio de Bellas Artes, Orozco on his Catharsis, Rivera on his Man at the Crossroads. (This was his re-creation of the mural on which work had been stopped, amid loud controversy, and which was then destroyed, at Rockefeller Center in New York the previous year.) "One day as they were working on their scaffolds, back to back, a dozen students drifted in and called up to Diego that they had sketches to show him. He lumbered down, ordered drinks for all of them, called their sketches 'very promising,' even bought one. Then they turned to Orozco. 'Maestro . . .' Annoyed at being interrupted in what to him was a very private struggle, Orozco glanced down at the students and their sketches and said, 'Art, gentlemen, is like parachute jumping. Sometimes the parachute never opens. In art, this is almost always the case. You are parachute jumpers. Your parachutes have not opened.' And back to work he went." These murals are at opposite ends of the third floor, before one enters the theater. There are also murals here by Siqueiros and Tamayo.

After the death of Frida Kahlo, Diego Rivera married Emma Hurtado. He died on November 15, 1957, at the age of seventy. His house and studio, at Palmas and Altavista, across the street from the San Angel Inn, were opened to the public as El Museo Estudio Diego Rivera in 1986.

THE FIRST TIME I VISITED DIEGO RIVERA IN his pink and blue studio in San Angel, a suburb of Mexico City, there was handed in, from the afternoon post, a printer's dummy of Bertram D. Wolfe's biography of the painter. Rivera was pleased with the format. It was evident that the book was going to be impressive, with its gilded blue cover and profusion of reproductions. Of the text, Rivera gave me the impression that he had scanty foreknowledge. He explained that he had given the biographer access to a disorderly collection of letters and documents, and he expected a book which would do him credit in English-speaking countries. From what he had been able vaguely to gather of the contents at that time he had concluded, he said, that the publishers had given it the wrong title.

"They have called it *Diego Rivera, His Life and Times*," he told me. "From what I know that Wolfe is going to say, they should have called it *Diego Rivera, His Wifes and Times*."

When the book eventually came out Rivera professed to be furious. He says he supposed that only political letters would be used in the book, although it seems clear that he permitted his biographer to see his papers indiscriminately. He was therefore annoyed when he discovered that some private letters had been put to what he felt was scandalous use. Perhaps his displeasure was augmented by the rage of Guadalupe Marín, who, when she learned that some of her intimate correspondence had been published, threatened suit against the publishers in the American courts. Frida Kahlo, a more recent wife, not to be outdone by her predecessor's indignation, actually went to New York in defense of her reputation.

Rivera was especially vexed because, as he thought, the book challenged his integrity as a painter. He objected to Wolfe's judgment that his Cubistic pictures were imitative of French Cubism, and irrelevant to the painter's own experience. That criticism made Rivera really angry and provoked him into finding and advertising errors from the beginning to the end of the book; and led him, so he says, to the renunciation of another of his many fateful friendships.

Rivera was born on the Feast of the Immaculate Conception, December 8, 1886, in Guanajuato, the birthplace of Mexican Independence, — a small, clean, colonial city lying out in the hot, dry sun on the hills of the richest mining country the world has ever known. Rivera's father was a schoolteacher. His paternal grandmother was a

Mexican girl of Portuguese and Jewish descent; the grandfather, a Spanish-born Mason and freethinker, was a soldier in the Juárez revolution against Maximilian. Diego's mother, who was of mixed Spanish and Indian blood, was fond of reminding her family that her mother, who was clearly part Indian, had descended from a line of Spanish nobles. Baptized with nearly a dozen of their aristocratic names, Rivera has signed his pictures with only three of them, Diego for his father, María for his patroness (while his father lived, and then usually only by way of the initial letter), and his patronymic. Since his father's death he has signed his pictures merely "Diego Rivera."

From his childhood Rivera remembers an elderly cousin, Rodríguez Campaces, a silversmith who died one night over his worktable; and the exquisite silverwork that was done in Guanajuato in those days, figurines and filigree. His mature feeling for the local pottery, famous for the purity of its lines, is rooted in early familiarity with the provincial arts. He is today a sympathetic and tireless collector of objects of popular Mexican art.

At the age of ten Diego entered the Academy of San Carlos as a pupil of Velasco and Rebull, under whose direction he particularly enjoyed drawing and painting from plaster models. He is innocently pleased to show to this day a grisaille of a Greek philosopher which he painted when he was fifteen. As a matter of fact, it has many of the illusory qualities of the friezes which accompany Rivera's frescoes in the Cortés Palace in Cuernavaca, and the archaic grisailles in the Ministry of Education in Mexico, works to which the painter himself frequently calls attention.

In 1907 Rivera set out for Spain with the promise of a pension from the governor of Vera Cruz, money in his pocket from the sale of pictures to friends of Dr. Atl, and Dr. Atl's letter to Eduardo Chicharro, whose pupil Diego became in Madrid. Of the work of this period there are examples in the collection of Salo Hale and don Jesús Luján of Mexico City. One of them is a carefully painted street scene from Vizcaya. Both subject and style are in the Spanish romantic vein, neither affording any suggestion of the painter's identity. There is Rivera color in a painting of the cathedral of Avila and in a portrait of a dancer of Madrid, but otherwise these are school pieces, craftsmanlike imitations of painters he used to admire. Probably no one but Picasso in modern times is as erudite as Rivera in the technical aspects of the art of painting. He painted in scores of styles before he developed his unmistakably personal formulas on Mexican walls.

For some months he wandered about in the northern European capitals, looking at pictures, painting, meeting people. Amongst his new friends was Angeline Beloff, the gentle little creature who lived with him and took care of him in Paris, and followed him, years later, to Mexico, where she was hurt to discover that he had forgotten how she looked. In Paris he knew all the artists, *Fauves* and Cubists, Picasso, Derain, Braque, Gris, Modigliani; and besides the painters there were sculptors and poets, novelists and critics. He liked everybody and everybody liked him. His Mexican friends, of whom there were many in Paris at the time, remember seeing his huge bulk wrapped in all weathers in a flowing cape, and recall fantastic accounts of visions which startled him at night and followed him by day along the streets of Paris.

From 1913 to 1917 Rivera painted in the Cubistic style. The professing Cubists never quite accepted him as an honest and sincere convert because he was not prepared to go the whole way with them. In most of his Cubistic pictures there are distinctly representational elements,—as, indeed, there are in many of Picasso's. Bertram Wolfe, who reproduces fifteen works of this period, explains that Rivera "reconstituted" his figures "before he had completed, so to speak, the chopping up." The purists of the Paris school, who preferred to make new patterns out of broken-down elements, were inclined to think that Diego was a little too conservative to be accepted as a fellow-traveler.

Still, in all the crowded years of his painting, Rivera has never produced richer and more harmonious color patterns than in his Cubistic works. The *Man with a Cigarette* from the collection of Salo Hale (Plate 22 in Wolfe), executed in a wide range of soft colors in which violets and blues predominate, is one of Rivera's most beautiful paintings.

It was during his Cubistic period that Rivera was introduced into the company of a group of Russian painters, in discussion with whom he formulated theories which he was later to expound in his Mexican murals. Indulging the revolutionary passion for manifestoes, the Russians in Paris drew up a collective resolution somewhat after this fashion: "We must give art to the masses. As industry must be made to provide goods for everybody in a socialist society, so must art be made to give itself to the workers."

Rivera speculated about this resolution. In the back of his mind he was amused by the thought of stupid Russian peasants gaping at the Cubistic canvases which the young revolutionary painters proposed to take home to them, but he phrased his ultimate dissent in tactful Marxist terminology. He suggested to the comrade-artists that they were involved in a confusion of categories, a phrase which made them instantly respectful. The enjoyment of art, he intimated, is a product of the simultaneous activity of the nervous apparatus and the mind, both of which faculties, physical and psychical, are conditioned by experience. He went on to explain that without training in looking at objects of art a man not only will not enjoy them but is likely to receive positive harm; just as a man who is not accustomed to certain food, say to Chinese or Mexican cooking, will not only find no pleasure in it but is likely to get indigestion.

Rivera was convinced that if ordinary people are to be expected to look at art with enjoyment, the artist must provide them with forms which not only employ the techniques of modern art and reflect its qualities, but are also of sufficiently simple design and engaging content to be interesting and comprehensible at first glance. This principle of spectator-aesthetics ought, I should think, to be valid for all places at all times.

The Marxist theoreticians did not object to Rivera's criticism but they asked for examples of the kind of art he meant. Rivera explained that modern forms such as he had in mind did not yet exist, but he said, he has told me, that he was thinking of mural painting because it could be produced on large spaces in public buildings. It would be easy to look at and there would be plenty of people to see. He refused an invitation to go to Russia on the spot and paint cubistically there, whilst enlarging his thesis, and made ready to return to Mexico. At home, judging from what he had heard from Siqueiros, he was sure he could find walls on which to illustrate his doctrines.

Rivera began his Mexican mural demonstrations by painting in encaustic, an example of which technique, his *Flower Festival,* is in the permanent collection of the Museum of Modern Art in New York. He scratched his designs for the *Creation of Man* deep in the wet cement so that the outlines, at least, would be imperishable, and laboriously applied the melted wax color. When he discovered that it was going to take months to do a small area in that medium, he joined in the general experimentation in the more rapid technique of fresco. Like others, he discovered that the government changed its mind and its personnel swiftly in those days, and the painter who wanted to cover an appreciable amount of space had to work fast.

Shortly after his return to Mexico, Diego met Xavier Guerrero, whom he promptly employed to assist him in the *Anfiteatro Bolívar*. Guerrero came from the northern mines, where he had worked with European muralists on the decoration of mine-owners' houses. He knew the technique of painting on gesso applied to wet stucco, a process in which the painted surface is immediately rubbed with a hot iron. Because the color dries rapidly this process lacks flexibility; it is suitable only for pure decoration, such as geometrical figuring and stylized floriation. Still, when Guerrero went up to the capital he knew something about wet-wall painting, and that was more than anybody else in Mexico City knew at the time. Before Rivera's return he added somewhat to his knowledge by making a small fresco in the Ministry of Education. It appears that Rivera eventually removed Guerrero's panel to make room for a work of his own, but while the two painters were still on good terms they conducted experiments together and evolved a formula which they first used in the newly built Ministry.

So much of what has been written about fresco methods in Mexico has been either confusing or wrong that I asked Guerrero to tell me in some detail about the way in which he prepared walls for Rivera to paint. First, he explained, he spread over the whole area to be painted a one-inch layer of full-bodied plaster of slaked lime and clean mineral sand. The lime had been burned for at least two months to insure solubility: the filtered lime which is manufactured today having been not yet available in Mexico in 1922. The sand, transported from mines because Guerrero found it more free from fungus than river sand, received in Mexico City a cyanide wash of Guerrero's own devising, a further guarantee of purity. Guerrero has been justified by his works. Many Mexican frescoes have been spoiled by the outgrowth of fungus on improperly prepared walls, but Rivera's have remained relatively clear of this defect.

The first layer of plaster was permitted to dry for a month or more, until it became resistant to humidity. Plaster applied to porous brick dries quickly, but old Mexican walls were commonly compounded of brick, stone, adobe and rubble, a mixture of masonry which requires more caution in handling than mural painters are obliged to take with standardized American building materials.

When the first layer of plaster was thoroughly dry it was brushed with distilled water. Then to the limited surface which Rivera could, on a given day, be expected to paint, the assistant applied a second layer of plaster, of less than a centimeter to two centimeters in thickness, depending upon the smoothness of the first layer. The mixture of sand and lime contained less body than that prepared for the first layer, the sand having been more finely screened. Over this layer of plaster, just before it dried, Guerrero finally applied a paste of pure lime with a trowel. He had discovered that the lime paste enhanced the brilliance of the colors.

When Rivera made his first frescoes he drew his designs directly on the surface of the wall at this moment of preparation. It was important to move rapidly because both drawing and painting had to be accomplished while the thin plaster coating was still moist. The colors do not actually *penetrate* the plaster, as is sometimes loosely said; rather, they *become* the surface of the plaster when, in the process of drying, the lime is carbonized and at length recovers its original properties as calcium carbonate, or limestone.

It was, of course, enormously difficult to draw the designs and then paint them before the plastered surface dried out. Rivera ultimately added a further, now an invariable, step in the process. He drew the designs upon the first coat of plaster and transferred them thence to transparent paper, from which an assistant could quickly return them to the wall by stencil, when the final surface was ready for the colors. His basic palette was eventually composed as follows: vine blue made from calcined grape-seeds, ultramarine, cobalt blue, emerald green, raw and burnt sienas, almagre morado (red oxide of iron), Pozzuoli (Italian red earth), dark ochre and yellow ochre.

If scientifically correct processes had been used consistently, the frescoes in the Ministry of Education would have been, technically, more successful than they proved to be, but something untoward happened which both Rivera and Guerrero are now shy of discussing. It appears that Guerrero one day suddenly announced that the Aztec painters had used nopal liquor, the juice of a common type of cactus, as a body-making color vehicle. Perhaps this information was communicated to him in a vision: it could not have been established in a laboratory. But it was a romantic idea calculated to appeal to Rivera, and nopal juice went into his mixtures of color and distilled water. The organic substance of nopal could not be chemically combined with the mineral substances of the plaster, it simply dried out on the surface; hence some of the early frescoes were disfigured by water blisters which formed under scales of nopal. Rivera has never been able to repair more than a small part of the damage.

Guerrero has described to me Rivera's first approach to his job in the Ministry of Education. The *maestro* nervously examined the area prepared for the day's assignment and somewhat uncertainly set to work reproducing his sketches. By the time he was ready to paint he was shaking with excitement. Within a quarter of an hour he had decided that the painting was bad. Before he had worked half an hour he was convinced that the informal technique would never please him. He snatched up a hammer, assaulted the wall and powdered the surface he had painted. But the next day he was calmer. He said he could not see that there was much difference, after all, between water-color and fresco painting, when you got down to it, and since he had always been a magnificent water-colorist he was presently working with the rapidity and rhythm of a born technician.

The building which houses the Ministry of Education in Mexico City is an immense structure in the neoclassical style of the eighteenth-century Jesuit monastery which it displaced. It is divided into two courtyards or patios of unequal size and rises to three stories, each of which is encircled by a corridor or cloister. José Vasconcelos, who let the contracts for the murals, originally commissioned Rivera to paint the three floors of the smaller patio, including the great staircase, and assigned to Charlot, de la Cueva, Guerrero and others the decoration of the large patio.

It appears that Rivera did not have, in the beginning, any generally conceived design for his part of the ambitious work. Fresh from visits to Yucatán and the Tehuantepec peninsula, he painted first some purely decorative panels representing the statuesque and Amazonian women of the South. These picturesque ladies proved to have no more connection with the social problems of Mexico in revolution than the portraits of buxom Lupe Marín and the cadaverous poetess Nahui Olín in the *Anfiteatro*. Considerably embarrassed, Diego thereupon began to cultivate a pictorial interest in social conditions, and shortly went to work upon a succession of panels of people at work: weaving, dyeing, harvesting; refining sugar, molding pottery; heaving and sweating in blacksmith shops and foundries.

The Tehuantepec women were painted in bright, clear colors, many of which proved to be impermanent. In the industrial designs Rivera began to use dull earth-browns and grays, colors which now appear, especially in the panel of the dyers, a little dirty. As the design developed, he introduced richer tones, adding to his palette brighter purples, deeper yellows, reds built up into flame.

Finally the first floor of the first patio was finished. Rivera looked upon it and saw that it was good and called it the Court of Labor.

Three particularly interesting characteristics of Rivera's mural style can be observed in the Court of Labor: the progression from flat to modeled painting, the development of the Rivera Mexican type, and the emergence of the propaganda motif. Beginning by drawing his figures relatively flat against backgrounds with few planes, in a manner obviously suggestive of Gauguin, Rivera proceeded to introduce modeling in the full round; although, except in the nudes, he rarely, even in the later murals, modeled in detail.

Again, beginning with individualizing figures, he went on to develop the typical small, flat-nosed, round-shouldered brown man who became the world's symbol of the Mexican Indian: a little fellow with a globular head attached to a neckless, egg-shaped torso poured into a white shirt.

The first notes of social indignation occur in panels which show the searching of miners as they stream up from the mines, and the weighing of grain by an ungenerous overseer. Sometimes the moral is pointed out in a text, as in the quotation, "They defame and despise us because we are common people." Against these scenes of oppression are set engaging aspects of the work of the benevolent revolutionary party, such as the unselfish labors of the rural teachers, those ascetic modern missionaries to the illiterate peasantry.

When Rivera had finished the walls of the ground floor of his patio it was discovered that half-a-dozen painters had covered only a few square meters of the larger courtyard. Early in 1924, therefore, he received contracts to take charge of the decoration of the entire building and proceeded to the ground-floor corridor of the large patio, the Court of Festivals. Here he began to let go with color. Some of the panels are rich with ochre and flamboyantly decorated with bright floral backgrounds. On one hand a colorful ribbon dance; on the other a row of effigies of Judas Iscariot, awaiting consumption in the streets in a sputter of fireworks, on Holy Saturday. Using some of the choicest paper Judases in his own collection as models—several of them were on exhibition in the Museum of Modern Art in 1940—Rivera provided them, in these murals, with the faces of unpopular citizens: a priest, a general and a financier.

Four frankly popularizing panels represent parades on the First of May, Labor Day in Mexico. The pictorial fascination of this theme persisted with Rivera for a long time. In Moscow in 1928 he made forty-five May-Day water-color sketches which Mrs. John D Rockefeller, Jr., has presented to the Museum of Modern Art. In the Mexican version the parading workmen carry banners printed with trite exhortations: "Workers and Peasants of the World, Unite," and "Peace, Land, Liberty and Schools for the Oppressed Masses." Several portraits are worked into the text. There is one of Guadalupe Marín, who had modeled for Woman in the early encaustic, and had now come from her home in Guadalajara to live with the painter. It was she who inspired probably his greatest work, the murals at Chapingo. Other portraits are those of Jean Charlot, who contributed to the Court of Festivals two panels in something approaching the monumental style; Máximo Pacheco, a poverty-stricken Indian muralist who at that time assisted Rivera at the rate of three pesos a day; and Paul O'Higgins, another Rivera helper who has become a sound painter on his own account. Besides these, there is a generous assortment of self-portraits.

At the entrance to the staircase which makes its way up through the gloomy interior of the Ministry a marine allegory peopled with luminous nudes initiates a series of prospects illustrating the geographical ascent from Vera Cruz to Mexico City. Up in the highlands, where clothing is customary and a moralizing purpose appears, an *hacendado* takes his ease while the workers toil. Toward the top of the *escalera* the design becomes complicated, the propaganda explicit, the subject matter symbolic. Most of the revolutionary iconography is present: a peasant (presumably an economic martyr) is buried, lightning strikes clerical and military oppressors of the people, the land is divided, the ignorant receive instruction, the sick are healed; and at the exit to the third-floor corridor, to the left, a self-portrait crowns the work.

A final series of frescoes, painted in 1927 and 1928 in the third-floor corridor of the large patio of the Ministry of Education, illustrates two revolutionary *corridos,* the verses of which appear on overhanging festoons. The ballads recite a kind of popular commentary on the Constitution of 1917 and, like that hopeful document at the end of its first decade, describe the aims of the Revolution rather than its accomplishment. Rivera illustrates them with thousands of the little egg-shaped people who await the liberation the Revolution promised them: *paysanos* in straw *sombreros* (which economically obscure their faces), tight-fitting shirts and seamless trousers. Their clothing adheres snugly to plump bodies, a little like old-fashioned balbriggan underwear bleached to chalky white. The real Mexican, who is bony, muscular and lithe, perhaps even a little angular because of his ascetic diet, looks in wonder at Rivera's version of his figure.

Contrasted with the peasant figures are caricatures taken from what Diego would have called the capitalist society, the Rockefellers, the Morgans and the Fords, mopping up champagne—little did Rivera understand the puritanical inhibitions of really rich Americans—at a table decorated with streams of ticker tape; and mocking portraits of contemporary Mexicans who had engaged the muralist's ill will, like Vasconcelos, whom Rivera had known from boyhood and never liked and now ridiculed upon a white elephant.

Rivera's caricatures are not grim and violent, like Orozco's; they are grossly, hilariously funny. Diego told me one time that the Rockefellers had decently professed amusement over his portraits of themselves and even took photographs of them. This event occurred, I believe, several years before Rivera raided Radio City.

The color patterns throughout the Ministry seemed to me to be somewhat impaired by occasional compromises between close and remote effects. Immediately in front of the murals it is impossible to get proper perspective, the corridors are too narrow, while from across the patio important elements of design are lost. Orozco had a much simpler problem in the Preparatory School where his frescoes are separately framed by cloister arches. They look whole and finished when seen from the patio, although actually the transitions between them are abrupt and sometimes ugly. Rivera's frescoes, to their great disadvantage, are separated by doorways which lead to interior offices and bear no balanced relationship to the cloister arches. Some of them are confronted by solid columns which entirely hide them from a spectator standing in the patio. To offset this disability, from the standpoint of design, Rivera has drawn carefully disposed diagonal lines to intercept the prevailing verticals of the Court of Labor and the prevailing horizontals of the Court of Festivals. The diagonals have the effect of lending movement to the interrupted sequences when seen in panorama from the open court.

Before he had finished his work in the Ministry of Education, Rivera additionally undertook the decoration of a large chamber, a onetime chapel, in the National School of Agriculture at Chapingo, about forty minutes by motor from Mexico City. If this is not his most significant work— he himself puts the Detroit murals in first place—it is certainly the most beautiful. It has the feeling of a thoroughly modern Sistine Chapel, in which lip service to revolutionary doctrine is substituted for skin-deep Christian piety as a background for sheer plastic virtuosity.

Lupe Marín, the principal model for this work, appears first as a classical recumbent nude set in a lunette over an arch in the entrance to the chapel. Her black hair falls sweepingly over her eyes, her left arm follows the limpid lines of her body, the left hand gracefully at rest upon the thigh. In her right hand she holds a cactus plant, a device which Rivera often uses as a phallic symbol. Here Lupe is the freshly created Earth, an unawakened virgin. At the opposite end of the chapel a pregnant Lupe represents the Earth Mother, fecund and liberated. Finally, she appears as Earth enslaved, half reclining in a typical Michelangelesque slave posture, imprisoned (Rivera-wise) by the priest, the soldier and the capitalist.

These splendid female nudes, together with eight vignetted male figures in the ceiling, fill the space with haunting beauty not to be felt elsewhere in Rivera's monumental work. A few panels of social themes expounded in duller color and flatter modeling, although they spoil the ideal unity of the design, scarcely divert the eye from the strong accents of the major panels with their rich color and rounded forms.

For seven fat years Rivera fed the Mexican populace with

murals. Whether the people liked them or not, most of them were at least digestible food. The Chapingo designs may have been a little too rich for their taste, but Chapingo stands by itself, both artistically and geographically. The frescoes in Mexico City are as easy to look at as an illustrated primer. Meanwhile the same years had been lean in Russia, where Cubism had proved to be not in the least nourishing for the masses. In 1927 Rivera, who had been in and out of the Party, was therefore invited to go to Moscow to illustrate his theories of Communist painting. This he did with great satisfaction, producing before the Communist Academy a pocketful of photographic illustrations of the thesis he had compounded in Paris.

Altogether he had a great success. The Academy elected him to membership in the October Group, the students of the School of Plastic Arts in Moscow appointed him to an honorary professorship, and the auto mechanics' union commanded him to stay in the USSR to decorate buildings which had not yet been built. Before the year was out, however, Rivera's friends in Russia found themselves in disfavor, after some characteristic domestic political crisis, and he was persuaded to go home to assist a Communist candidate to become President of Mexico. In 1929 he was expelled from the Party at a trial which was as incoherent as it was pretentious. Although he was later reinstated, for a time, Rivera never forgave his colleagues for humiliating him. His turning to toryism was a part of his revenge.

Rivera's next important commission came from the late American Ambassador to Mexico, Dwight W. Morrow, who engaged him to paint the walls of the loggia of the Cortés Palace in Cuernavaca, a pleasant provincial capital some fifty miles south of Mexico City. Here he produced his most colorful, objective and unified frescoes, dramatizing the history of the State of Morelos from the Conquest to the Revolution. In well-known panels of which the rhythms and rose and blue colors are enchanting, Spanish cavalrymen invade the little Aztec city. Cortés, elegantly attired, superintends the construction of his Cuernavaca palace, this very palace where the murals are. A languid *hacendado,* like the gentleman in the Ministry staircase, lies in his hammock and sips a cool drink while his agents draw blood from the backs of peons at work in the cane fields. The Church despoils and oppresses in the persons of gross and greedy monks, composed in the stereotyped Rivera form, and consoles in the tender portrait of the Franciscan Father Motolinía. It will be seen that Rivera was not wasteful of symbols.

In August, 1929, when he married Frida Kahlo, it appears that Rivera was legally married for the first time in his life. There had never been any pretense of marriage to Angeline Beloff, and whatever the ceremony was of which Lupe Marín is said to have boasted to her friends, it was sufficiently informal to allow her to take another husband without the public formality of divorcing Rivera.

Frida Kahlo, hastening the blossom before the leaves, had announced at the age of thirteen that she desired to have a child by Diego Rivera. When she was seventeen she was modeling for him, having usurped, at least in his studio, the place of Lupe Marín. At nineteen she married him. A year later she was still sure enough of him to allow her sister Cristina to model for a panel in the modernistic Public Health building, and when these frescoes were finished— they are too hygienic to invite aesthetic emotions—she went with him to California where Rivera had been commissioned to paint, of all places, in the San Francisco Stock Exchange.

Having covered acres of walls with frescoes, Rivera has been concentrating, the last few years, on work in his studio, enjoying as privately and quietly as he can, what with daily tourist invasions, the pleasures of drawing and easel painting. Now he professes to be interested in painting small surfaces, in the refinement of forms. He is absorbed in translating from fresco to oil painting the technique of securing the maximum of expression with minimum means; but above all, at least for the moment, he relishes the profounder qualities, the more varied textures and the more leisurely use of oil and tempera, as compared to fresco painting.

There is no official catalogue of Rivera's work, but he has produced altogether probably one thousand paintings and drawings,— not counting the notebook sketches, of which some Italian drawings sold by Angeline Beloff to the Gallery of Mexican Art in Mexico City are the choicest. Of this great number of works about half of the paintings and many of the drawings are in European galleries and private collections. Several important pieces painted during the last three or four years have gone to a mysterious collection in Italy, of which the rumored owner is Mussolini, whom in the old days Rivera scarcely professed to admire. Most of the remaining pieces are in the United States, although Rivera has reserved for himself a sheaf of his finest water colors and scores of Chinese ink drawings. Probably the greatest American collection of Riveras in North America is that of Mr. Albert M. Bender of San Francisco.

Amongst his most recent works are two nude portrait studies and about thirty posture drawings of Maudelle, an American negro dancer. One of the oil paintings was lent by the painter for the "Twenty Centuries of Mexican Art" exhibition at the Museum of Modern Art and was reproduced in color in the catalogue. A few luminous and tender nudes have been done from a new model, a pretty little Mexican girl who, between his divorce from Frida and his remarriage, presided over Diego's dinner table. Besides these, there have been two or three not very convincing experiments in Surrealism. These suffer from the artist's greater interest in the several forms than in composition as a whole. Because the cheap peso has attracted throngs of tourists to Mexico, there still come from his brush, alas, dozens of identical little Indian children in blue dresses.

It seems less remarkable, when you see Rivera at home in his studio, that he should produce occasional stereotyped pieces than that he is able to paint at all. In tourist season his establishment is crowded with sightseers who waste his time wantonly, and he is kind and patient to them all. I was taking coffee with him after lunch one day, on a balcony overlooking the studio, when a large, expensive-looking American woman swept in, followed by a group of chirruping dependents. She bagged two autographs and a photograph before she consented to look at some small pictures. Diego showed her a series of water colors taken from the new model, who was helping him display the pictures for the lady.

"Oh," said she, "I don't care for these squaws. Can't you show me something with a cute little village?"

I asked Diego how he could stand that sort of thing, why he let such people come in. He loftily said he thought it was an obligation to make his ancient works of art available to the public; and it is true that he has archaeological treasures which great museums covet. But more probably that extraordinary man, who likes praise and admiration no less than any of us, loves the excitement of working and talking in the market place which his studio seasonally becomes. He admits the rude with the gentle, the dull with the apt, lest he miss something which even for an instant might engage his inexhaustible resources of mind and heart, or at the least, contribute to the publicity. If in his politics he is often a pretender, and in his rages a man of violence, in his ordinary daily relationships he has a great capacity for genial friendship, and sincerities far deeper than his showmanship.

PAUL BOWLES

Diversions and excursions, 1937–1940

"THE WOMEN WERE THE MOST BEAUTIFUL IN ALL
MEXICO, AND THEY BATHED NAKED IN THE RIVER
EVERY MORNING."

Paul Bowles, with the friendship and support of Aaron Copland and Virgil Thomson, was earning a growing reputation as a composer when he made the first of his four trips to Mexico in 1937. Bowles was twenty-six that year. One night in February, in the lobby of the Plaza Hotel in New York, friends introduced him to Jane Auer. It was Jane's twentieth birthday. By the beginning of April, along with their friends Kristians and Marie-Claire Tonny, they were off to Mexico together.

Jane turned out to be a poor traveler and was not cheered by the bus ride down the Pan American Highway, parts of which were still under construction. When they finally reached the capital, Jane disappeared. Three days later the friends located her in the Hotel Guardiola.

The Hotel Guardiola, at Avenida Madero 5, next to the Church of San Francisco and across the street from Sanborn's, was one of the oldest in Mexico City but had been modernized early in the thirties. Its Lady Baltimore tearoom was cheap and popular with Americans and, since 1920, had made its own famous chocolates. It was over lunch at the

*Lady Baltimore, late in 1929, that William Spratling and Diego Rivera
discussed the artist's commission from U.S. Ambassador Dwight Morrow
to paint murals in the Cortés Palace in Cuernavaca. Spratling had arranged the commission and now suggested that Rivera charge by the
square meter. After lunch they hired a car and went down to Cuernavaca
to measure the walls. The proposed charge came to $12,000, and the dis-
believing Rivera promised Spratling a fee of $2,000 if Morrow would
pay. Morrow agreed, and Spratling used the fee to buy his house in
Taxco.*

*The restaurant Bowles tells Jane about, Las Cazuelas, was at Co-
lombia 69A, near Calle del Carmen, four blocks north of the Cathedral.
A 1935 guidebook described it thus: "Picturesque, Mexican proletarian-
Bohemian. Caution." In that year, just two years before Bowles's visit,
Langston Hughes ate here with his roommates, Andrés Henestrosa and
Henri Cartier-Bresson, whenever they had money. Walking there from
the Zócalo, Bowles might have passed within sight of where Hughes's
friends, the Patiño sisters, lived on San Ildefonso. Still at the same
address, in an eighteenth-century mansion in a run-down but historic
neighborhood, Las Cazuelas remains popular with both local people and
visitors for its inexpensive and authentic Mexican food. Diners can still
look into the open kitchen and the huge pots, just as Langston Hughes
did in 1935. Families have replaced the bohemians, and the "caution" is
now out of date.*

*Bowles was always interested in folk music— in later years he per-
sonally recorded a large and important collection of traditional music in
Morocco—and one of the first things he did in Mexico was to seek out
music. It had a considerable effect on his own work. This was, writes
biographer Christopher Sawyer-Lauçanno, "a fertile period for Bowles.
Caught up in the local music scene, he quickly began to write several
compositions directly inspired by the various folk melodies and rhythms
he was hearing on the streets and in the bars." Two of his most beautiful
piano pieces, "Huapango No. 1" and "El Sol (Huapango No. 2)," come
from this experience.*

BEYOND MONTERREY THEY WERE STILL LAY-
ing the highway, which often became barely passable. The
buses were even more primitive than those of North Africa. Tonny,

Marie-Claire, and I were delighted with the hairpin curves, the sheer drops, and the unfamiliar, savage landscape, but Jane had lived a relatively sheltered life in New York and Switzerland and found it all terrifying. For two days going through the mountains she crouched, frightened and sick, on the floor at the back of the bus, unmindful of Tonny's scornful remarks. *"Ecoute, ma petite, tu aurais mieux fait de rester chez ta mère,"* he would tell her, or: *"On a marre de toi et ta frousse,"* or: *"Tu nous emmerdes avec tes histoires de gosse de riches."* The night we arrived in Mexico City Jane jumped out of the bus, seized on some porters, and announced: *"Moi je file pour le Ritz."* I tried to stop her, but Tonny and Marie-Claire thought we should let her go. We three ended up in a cheap hotel on the Calle 16 de Septiembre. The next day we went around to the Ritz and failed to find Jane's name in the register. We discovered her three days later at the Hotel Guardiola in bed, recovering from a flash fever that had struck her the night of her arrival. She said firmly that as soon as she could walk, she was going to the airport and get on a plane for the United States. We chaffed her, gave her enthusiastic accounts of the bullfight we had seen and of the music at Tenampa and the food at Las Cazuelas, and before leaving promised to come by at lunchtime the following day to see if she might be well enough to go out to eat with us. When we called by for her, they told us at the desk that she had taken the plane for San Antonio.

"Tant mieux," said Tonny with bitter satisfaction. He was on edge because he had not managed to get anywhere with her during the trip. I knew he was not going to be able to, because from New York to Monterrey she and I had sat together and engaged in many hours of conversation. She had her own ideas on the subject: she was a virgin and intended to remain in that category until she married.

"If you hadn't been so mean to her she'd have stayed," said Marie-Claire, who was upset by the sudden departure.

"I said so much the better she's gone, didn't I?" he demanded. It was clear that Jane had been a sore point between them for some time.

"Tu es dégoûtant." That was Marie-Claire's way of putting an end to a conversation.

Aaron had given me a note to Silvestre Revueltas, saying I would like both him and his music. I went down beyond the Zócalo to the conservatory where he taught. By coincidence I arrived there during the course of a concert at which he was conducting his *Homenaje a García Lorca*. I was immediately struck by the luminous texture of the orchestral sound. It was music of impeccable style. After the performance I presented my note to him, and was once again impressed, this time more deeply, by the quality of the man himself. He had a truly noble face, one side of it slashed across by a terrible knife scar, with an expression of impossible purity. It was a purity, alas, maintained at the cost of life itself. Revueltas was an incurable dipsomaniac; he spent six months of each year in the gutter. By the time I met him he had arrived almost at the end of the line. He died the following year. The conditions under which he lived, in a distant slum quarter, scarcely left him an alternative to death. Never had I seen such poverty in Europe or North Africa. There were no walls, properly speaking, between one apartment and another. Partitions went up eight feet or so and stopped. The hubbub of voices, radios, dogs, and babies was infernal. It seemed particularly cruel that a composer should have to live in such a place.

It was Revueltas who took me to the *Grupo de los Cuatro*: Ayala, Moncayo, Contreras, and Galindo, all composers in their twenties. They were fun to be with, and all of us together went around the capital for several weeks, having a great time. Then they proposed a concert of my music, to be presented by *El Grupo de los Cuatro*. The programs were printed, and the small *sala* at the Palacio de Bellas Artes rented for the night, but each time rehearsals were called, only a few of the musicians appeared, so that no rehearsals ever took place. Nor, needless to add, did the concert.

Shortly before leaving New York, I had gone to see Miguel Covarrubias, the Mexican painter whose caricatures in *Vanity Fair* had impressed me fifteen years earlier when I was a boy. Covarrubias said he had gone with Diego Rivera to southern Oaxaca, to the Isthmus of Tehuantepec. His descriptions of the place made me resolve to see it myself. The women were the most beautiful in all Mexico, and they bathed naked in the river every morning. There was an oasis, he said, which would remind me of North Africa; he considered it the most exotic and fascinating region in the Western Hemisphere. Whenever we mentioned Tehuantepec to the Mexicans, we found that they agreed with Covarrubias, although none of them had visited the place. It seemed essential that we go to see for ourselves.

The journey to Tehuantepec was arduous, but never boring. First we took the train down to Veracruz; there we waited to get the semiweekly train which ran between Veracruz and the Guatemalan border. We had intended to spend one night at a place called Jesús Carranza. When we arrived there in the evening, we got off the train and walked to the hotel, a desperate-looking construction run by a group of Chinese. Having eaten nothing but fruit since the day before, we set our luggage down in the dining room and ordered large bowls of hot soup. It was very tasty, with pieces of ginger root among the solid morsels floating in the stock. The kerosene lamp shed just enough light to enable us, once we had emptied the bowls of their liquid, to distinguish the corpses of the slugs which lay at the bottom. This was not really surprising, inasmuch as *gusanos de maguey* are considered edible items in Mexico. However, it was sufficient to banish our appetites and startle us into action. We got up from the table and asked to see the rooms upstairs. A balcony ran around the outside of the second story, its railing a single strand of barbed wire. Apparently the rooms were given an annual cleaning. Under each bed lay a great pile of garbage, pushed there so it would not show at first sight. Quickly we went downstairs and paid for our soup, took our valises, and began to run toward the station. We need not have hurried; the train did not move for another hour and a half. We settled into a different third-class coach, ate some avocados, along with pineapples and bananas, bought a bottle of *habanero,* a Mexican rum that cost a peso and a half, and applied ourselves to being comfortable and happy as we rattled along all night through the jungle.

Tehuantepec was unforgettable. Everything Covarrubias had said was accurate (save that he had not told us there were always female guards at the early morning bathing in the river who threw stones at any man or boy approaching within a thousand feet), yet his description had not prepared me for the particular atmosphere of the place. I had imagined it as a more-or-less African landscape dotted with Spanish-looking towns. But the countryside did not remind me of North Africa, nor did the villages, in spite of their Andalusian grilles, ever make me think of Spain. There were indeed oases (the *labores*) of coconut palms towering above the mangos, zapotes, and bananas. A highly spiced hot wind blew incessantly across the country, which was not really desert, but an impassable wilderness of bare thorny trees and cacti. To me it was a more forbidding prospect than the Sahara: the vegetation also looked mineral, but the forms it had taken were far more suggestive of hostility than any rock formation ever could be.

We ate our meals at a stall in the market, where the cook would swing the hens by their heads to break their necks. The women in the market had all the money there was in town and did all the work save picking the fruit and caring for the children. Often we looked into a patio and saw a man sitting by a hammock gently rocking it, and in the hammock a baby.

Just before leaving New York I had bought a used accordion for $125. The instrument was inlaid with rhinestones and paste rubies and emeralds—a fancy object with the lush sound characteristic of Italian made accordions. Evenings when we walked to the park, I would carry it with me; it had a swift success with the townsmen. Very shortly I was Don Pablito. As we went along in the moonlight fifteen or twenty Zapotecans would accompany us.

May Day was about to arrive. We offered them our help in preparing for the parade. I bought all the red cotton bunting in town to make into banners. The slogans they wanted were POR UNA SOCIEDAD SIN CLASES and SALUDAMOS A LOS MARTIRES DE CHICAGO (the latter referring to the Haymarket Riots of the 1890's, of which I had never heard until I got to Tehuantepec). I rented a house, and ten of us spent several days there cutting, sewing, and painting banners. I added my own MUERA TROTSKY to be included in the parade, as well as one which read EL COMUNISMO ES LA RELIGION DEL SIGLO VEINTE. It seemed to me to concertize a tendency already extant in the region—that of putting photographs of Marx and Lenin in the votive niches along with *Jesucristo* and *Santa María*. I remarked several times on the custom and got a simple explanation: Marx and Lenin were for the men, the others for the women. During the last few days of April the churches were full of women on ladders, building altarpieces and arches of fruit, flowers, and palm branches. In each church there was to be a festival with dancing and fireworks. When the day came, the parade included about 80 percent of the inhabitants. We marched for miles along dusty roads from village to village. A few old people holding babies waved from the doorways. Practically no one watched the parade in the outlying villages, so it headed back to the main market, where the few *burgueses* were, so that fists could be raised, not in salute but in defiance, at particular individuals watching from their shops or houses.

After May Day a delegation of country people came to the Hotel La Perla. The group consisted of nine men, all of them mute but respectful as only Mexican peasants can play it—all, that is, but the spokesman, who with his hat in his two hands, murmured that everyone was saying we had been sent from the capital to teach and that we could teach them about Communism, and of course everybody wanted to learn how to do Communism, and were we going to open a school for them?

This seemed to me very bad. Tonny laughed and thought it *marrant;* Marie-Claire was overcome with pity for the little men. I was appalled at seeing myself thrown into a false category which implied assuming responsibility. I shrugged and smiled sadly; I could not do anything like that, for it was necessary to have permission to teach, which I did not have. "Then why did they send you?" the spokesman asked.

"We were not sent from the capital," I told him, and he appeared to accept the statement. Nevertheless, he was determined to go away with something. "Tell me just one thing," he said. "*Qué es el comunismo?*"

Since I could not answer the question in a way satisfactory either to him or to me, I brought out some books and pamphlets in Spanish, including one called *El ABC del Comunismo,* but he was not interested. Then I realized that none of them could read and that he was the only one who spoke Spanish. He explained to them in Zapotec what I had said; they shook hands with us and filed out into the street.

We were only a day and a half by train from the Guatemalan border, and we thought that before turning north again, we should look inside. The proximity proved illusory, for when we got to the frontier at Suchiate I was turned back by the Guatemalan authorities for having written the word *ninguna* opposite *Religión* on the application form. Since they were suspicious of me, they said I must get letters from six businessmen of Tapachula. We returned to that godforsaken town where we had just spent a night, all three of us in an ugly mood, passed two days vainly trying to get even one such document, and, finding it impossible (since the pillars of society there were almost all Germans and not at all inclined to be either helpful or friendly), consulted the local headquarters of the Mexican trade unions. The third day they sent a man with us all the way to Suchiate, where we waited and were presented during off hours to an official who not only filled out a new application form for me, but got the Guatemalan authorities to stamp it and engaged a punt to ferry us across the Río Suchiate to Ayutla on the Guatemalan side. Thus we had a rapid three-week glimpse of the decorative little republic before returning to Mexico City.

This time we wanted to live in the country. Tonny had done no work since leaving Paris and felt a productive period coming on. We took pension with an American family who had been living for years in Malinche's palace (built for the Aztec lady by her lover Hernán Cortés, conqueror of Mexico). It was a huge old building with plenty of rooms, and it lay about halfway between Tlalnepantla and Atzcapotzalco. When summer came, I had a wire from Lincoln Kirstein saying that *Yankee Clipper* was to be presented in Philadelphia, and I must get to New York as quickly as I could. This was a dubious triumph: I wanted to hear the Philadelphia Orchestra play my music, and so of course I must go, but the peculiar rustic charm of the life in the place where we were living and the melancholy magnificence of the vast landscape roundabout had already captured me. I had looked forward to a long summer of hearing the roosters crow at Malinche's palace, and now I would not have it.

Paul and Jane Bowles—they were married in 1938—returned to Mexico early in July 1940 and stayed until September.

In Taxco, Jane spent a great deal of time in the cafés but continued working on the novel she had started in New York. It was in Taxco that she met Helvetia Perkins, with whom she would have a long affair. Perkins, it appears, was in Mexico to work on a novel of her own.

During this period of his life, Bowles, no matter where he was, was always eager to be someplace else, a condition that persisted until he settled permanently in Tangier in the late 1940s. In 1941 he and Jane returned to Mexico and stayed for a little more than a year. Jane spent most of the time in Taxco, working on Two Serious Ladies, which she finally completed in 1942. Bowles, as always, traveled.

In 1944 Bowles spent a month in Mexico by himself, staying in Manzanillo but visiting Uruapan to see the volcano, Paricutín.

THE MEXICAN ELECTIONS WERE COMING UP. WITH the fate of Spain at the hands of General Franco still fresh in everyone's mind, liberals feared that General Almazán, an avowed Fascist, might possibly win. Civil war would then be inevitable, the border would as a matter of course be shut, and my chances of getting to Mexico City would be reduced to zero. The more I read about the situation, the harder I worked to finish the score for *Roots in the Soil* and get across the Río Bravo into Ciudad Juárez before the trouble began. The Department of Agriculture people thought I should visit the Jemez Mountains where several tens of thousands of pure Spanish peasants still lived. It was beautiful high, rugged country; sometimes I could have thought myself in some poor remote hamlet of the Sierra Nevada in Andalusia. Under any other circumstances I should have been fascinated by this ethnic enclave. The government people offered to fly me up and down the Rio Grande Valley, so I could get "the feel of it," but as I never liked flying enough to do it unless it was necessary, I declined, and they took me on some tours by automobile.

Just before I completed the score, Saroyan's libretto arrived. It was called *Opera, Opera!*, and it was not a libretto any more than Gertrude Stein's text for *Four Saints in Three Acts* was a libretto; it needed a Maurice Grosser to provide one for it. I was at a loss how to proceed, but I took it along with me when we left for Mexico, in order to study it.

We spent a week in Zacatecas. Now that we were across the border I was in no hurry to get anywhere. Still, we had promised Peggy and Louis Reille to be in Mexico City by mid-July, and so we continued on our way over the lilting roadbed of the Mexican Railways. We got to the capital in time for the trouble, and were in the Alameda on election morning, hiding behind the stone benches like everyone else, as the cars and trucks roared past, spraying bullets indiscriminately. The shooting went on all day, and there were the sounds of heavy explosions from time to time. Avila Camacho won the day, luckily for everyone. We forgot about General Almazán's Fascist threat and began to look for a place to live. Remembering Malinche's palace, I wanted to find something similar and even more remote, if possible.

I found it at Jajalpa, an old hacienda 10,000 feet up, on the road to Toluca. It was a huge place with many rooms around a great courtyard. The mountaintops were on all sides, and the volcano of Toluca was there in all its detail, across a wide valley. I used to sit in an abandoned upstairs room and look at it. The vastness of the landscape had a paralyzing effect on me, and I remembered Thomas Mann's observation that being in the presence of a great natural spectacle impedes the desire to create.

Jajalpa was so isolated that it was impossible to keep a staff of servants functioning. Someone was always leaving, and we often went into the capital to see if an agency could get us an immediate replacement whom we could take back with us in a taxi. It was a melancholy place; the fact that it was so beautiful made the melancholy more insidious, more corrosive. The maidservants insisted that evil spirits wandered around at night in the rooms. They would come from their quarters long after we had gone to bed, knock rapidly on the door, and whisper: "Señor! Señora! Hay pasos, pues." This was how they announced the fact that they were going to spend the night in our room with us, in the corner on the floor. If there were footsteps, then etiquette demanded that we allow them to sleep with us. This did not happen every night, nor was it all the servants, but it happened regularly with certain of them. Each master bedroom was provided with a loaded rifle, standing by the head of the bed. We thought of the old firearms purely as part of the somewhat comic decoration, but the servants took them with complete seriousness.

I went down to party headquarters in the capital and offered my services. They wanted to know where I lived. When I told them, they decided to run Sunday bus excursions to Jajalpa for tourists who wanted to visit a real, old-fashioned hacienda. This happened on only two Sundays. The sightseers were largely American, although there were a few Europeans among them. They looked at the livestock (we had eighty-five cows and hundreds of sheep) and the chapel and the immense courtyard, and wished they were back in Mexico City. But they had to have lunch first, for they had paid the agency for that before starting out. Jane was stoical about the situation. It gave the Mexican party a little extra money, more, certainly, than we could have given them.

Slowly I became aware of a constant feeling of repletion and incipient nausea. I found it impossible to eat; the thought of food made me shudder. I realized that the altitude was interfering with my digestion and decided to get out quickly. I went down to the capital. Lou and Peggy Reille were there with Esteban Francés, the Spanish painter, and were about to drive down to Acapulco. I went with them; they had rented Bill Spratling's beach house there, a fine long house on top of the cliffs, shaped like a bent dumbbell whose rod was a huge terrace connecting the two parts of living quarters. Spending the whole day in the sea for a fortnight helped me a great deal; my appetite returned with a vengeance. A wire from Jane announced that she and Bob were arriving and asked me to find a house immediately. Lou was an old Mexican hand who later married Dolores del Rio; he found a house with a patio 150 feet long, shaded by avocado and lemon trees. There was a wide covered *corredor* between the rooms and the garden, strung with hammocks.

Jane and Bob arrived with two dwarfish, popeyed Indians they had found in Toluca, a youth and a girl, who under the guidance of an older local woman in the kitchen would constitute our staff. They told a strange tale about the owner of the hacienda, the grand lady we had visited at her ostentatious house in the city when we had signed the lease. She had prepared a typed list several pages long of objects which she said were missing from the hacienda. It included furniture, farm tools, and pigeons, among other things. They could do nothing but stare at the list. Bob singled out one item, a *zarape* valued at an unheard-of figure—enough to buy twenty *zarapes*—and called her attention to the price she was asking for its replacement. It was not the *zarape* that was valuable, she explained; it was the bullet hole in it that made it valuable. Her brother had been wearing it the day he was shot and killed. They got the bill down by $100 before they paid. I was indignant, but since I had left Jane to do the boring work of getting things out of the hacienda, I could say nothing.

The two Indians soon began to weep as they worked. They wanted their mothers, they explained, as though it were natural for people eighteen or twenty years old to need maternal protection. They could not sleep at night because their mothers were so far away. We tried to get them to bathe in the sea at Los Hornos, but they would not even walk onto the sand. At the end of their month they had to be put onto the bus and sent back home. They did not understand Acapulco at all.

The house lent itself to the collecting of birds and animals. One merely let them loose in the jungle of the garden, and they enjoyed themselves. This was not true of the two coatimundis; they insisted upon being with people. One of them would sleep only on Jane's head, wrapped in her hair. If she slept late, so did the coatimundi. I learned not to try to remove it; its resistance was expressed in two phases, the first of which consisted of covering its eyes tightly with its two paws and chattering rapidly, and the second of suddenly sinking its terrible little teeth into my hand.

One morning when we were getting ready to leave for a day at the beach, someone arrived at the door and asked to see me. It was a round-faced, sunburned young man in a big floppy sombrero and a striped sailor sweater, who said his name was Tennessee Williams, that he was a playwright, and that Lawrence Langner of the Theatre Guild had told him to look me up. I asked him to come in and installed him in a hammock, explaining that we had to hurry to the beach with friends. I brought him books and magazines and rum and Coke, and told him to ask the servants for sandwiches if he got hungry. Then we left. Seven hours later we got back to the house and found our visitor lying contentedly in his hammock reading. We saw him again each day until he left.

Presently Jane drove up to Taxco for a weekend with some Americans. She stayed on a few extra days, and then sent me a telegram saying that she had taken a house there. I was annoyed, because Taxco was the one town in Mexico where I did not want to live. I had spent a week there with Tonny and Marie-Claire three years earlier, and the carefully nurtured bohemian atmosphere depressed me. The place had been adopted by foreigners, and as a result, it attracted too many visitors.

We moved up to Taxco; it was more comfortable, and Jane

seemed much happier, but after Acapulco I found the still mountain air oppressive. I was sorry, although not desperately so, to be suddenly called back to New York by the Theatre Guild. Helen Hayes and Maurice Evans were signed to play Viola and Malvolio in *Twelfth Night*. The production needed a score.

GERTRUDE DIAMANT

The other side of Paseo de la Reforma, 1941

"I KNEW IN ONE GLANCE THAT I HAD FOUND
MY HOME."

*Early in the 1940s, while ethnologist Gertrude Diamant was working on
a study of the Otomí Indians, she took a furnished apartment in Mexico
City and hired—at the child's insistence—a ten-year-old named Ofelia
as her maid. Diamant's life was never the same again.*

*Ofelia proved to be more than a vivid personality. Rural people,
like their counterparts throughout Latin America, were beginning to
move to cities in large numbers, seeking a better life among the perceived
virtues of the urban world. But the urban world was not ready to receive
them. The problem was especially difficult in Mexico because the country's people—and their cultures and languages—are so varied. And Mexico City, which of course attracted most people, was expanding at a rapid
rate, faster, in fact, than its means permitted. Ofelia and her family became the focal point for Diamant's examination of this phase in the city's
development.*

The Days of Ofelia *was published in 1942 and quickly became
one of the most popular books about Latin America in a period when*

countless books on the region were being written. Apart from its value as a study of Mexican society, it offers a tale of a charming young heroine, sentimentally but lightly told. Today its appeal is even greater, as it vividly records private life in Mexico City half a century ago.

The street known as Río Atoyac, where Diamant rented her apartment, is in the section called Cuauhtémoc. Only a few blocks long, stretching from the Diana fountain at the eastern edge of Chapultepec Park to Río Mississippi, it runs parallel to Paseo de la Reforma and one block north. Thanks to Diamant's descriptions, modern visitors can picture this section—then near the edge of the city—when it still had cornfields. Today the region is transformed. On Reforma, only a five-minute walk from Río Atoyac, and where Ofelia must have passed every day on her way to the market, she might have been dazzled in the 1960s by the colored fountains of the new and luxurious María Isabel Hotel. That hotel is now the high-rise María Isabel Sheraton, with 850 rooms. Next to it is the U.S. embassy, and just across Reforma are the fashionable shops and restaurants of the Zona Rosa.

Of course, Ofelia might still be walking these same streets and marveling at how they've changed in her lifetime. She would be about sixty-four years old in 1995.

THE STREET BEHAVED JUST LIKE A RIVER. IT rambled through empty lots and circled a field of corn, and then it disappeared. There was a high white wall where it disappeared, but not a sign or a person to tell me where the street had gone. Presently a boy on a bicycle came by, and seeing me standing in perplexity, he waved and called: "Follow the wall." I followed it, and there was the street again.

I was looking for Atoyac number 82, where the morning paper said there was a furnished apartment—cheap, comfortable, decent, ideal for an American. And I was in that part of Mexico City where all the streets bear the names of rivers. Already I had crossed the Tiber, the Rhine, and the River Po, old favorites familiar from high-school days. But what of the River Atoyac? Nobody knew where it was, and nobody seemed to have heard of it. The sun was high and the sidewalk burned my feet, and I wandered on, hoping that the street would not disappear again. For I was carrying the two big valises which I had brought with me to Mexico, and which now contained all that I owned in the world.

It was a way of burning my bridges behind me. I was tired of living in boarding-houses (those beautiful old colonial mansions of the guide-books) with their damp dark rooms, slippery floors and dreadful furniture. I had vowed never to enter another old colonial mansion, but to leave them all to their decaying splendors and to the Spartan Mexicans. And if there was no place in the city with an easy-chair and a comfortable bed and dry and sunny, then I would go back to the States. But I did not want to go back, either. There are three hundred thousand Otomí Indians in Mexico, and I had tested a mere one hundred. I must test another two hundred at least to prove—but no, it is not scientific to know in advance what one is going to prove.

I put my valises down, flexed my arms and looked around. There were houses now, but not a sign to tell me if I had come to the River Atoyac. To know where you are in Mexico City, you must look at the corner houses; and with luck you will see a tiny plaque which bears the name of the street. But usually it isn't there at all, and the Mexicans have a sweet reasonableness when they cannot enlighten you. "Pues . . . you see, señorita, the signs are missing which should bear the names of the streets. So I cannot tell you, señorita, forgive me." It was Sunday and the stores were closed and the street deserted. I left my valises standing and walked until I came to where a man was sitting on the curb. He looked up from under a wide sombrero. "No, señorita," he said, "really I cannot tell you. I have little time here." "Time!" I thought scornfully. "What time do you need to tell me the name of a street?" And then I remembered my still meager Spanish. It is an idiom meaning that one has only just come to a place. "But if you ask the señor at the little stand over there," he went on, "possibly he can tell you. He has much time here." So I crossed to the little stand.

"Atoyac!" mused the man of much time. "Atoyac!" He smiled engagingly. "Forgive me, señorita, but I am unable to say. I do not concentrate on the names of the streets. However, if you should wish for the Street of the River of the Plata"—he pointed with an exquisite grace—"it is over there, señorita, just two blocks over there." "Thank you," I said, "I do not wish for the Street of the River of the Plata." And I went back and gathered my valises and wandered on.

There were empty lots again and many blocks where the houses were still being built. Soon I would come to the city limits. I could see fields of corn and beyond them the mountains, splendidly luminous in the afternoon light. But at the last corner before the fields began I came to a house that miraculously bore the number 82. Five little girls sat on the doorstep.

"Is there a furnished apartment here?"

They chorused raggedly, pointing. "Arriba . . . upstairs." And I saw that they all had the same shade of brown-green eyes. Then they rose in a body and we all went up.

I could not tell in that mass of brown arms and legs and serious faces that escorted me upstairs which one was Ofelia. But at the top of the stairs one child detached herself, took a bunch of keys from under her apron, and turning, waved her hand at the others with a royal gesture, as who should say: "Away, O profane ones! Efface yourselves."

The other little girls turned as one man and slunk down the stairs again, submissive as lambs. Then she of the keys opened the door. "I have such trouble with them, señora," she said, sighing. "They are very presuming children. I alone am supposed to show the apartment, but they always come up with me. If you should wish to see it again, please ask for Ofelia. Ofelia Escoto at your service."

But I knew in one glance that I had found my home. It must have been the casement windows that decided me, and the way the rooms made a corner so that I could spy on myself, a nice diversion for one who lives alone. And there were two "closts," rare in any Mexican apartment, and I would not have to go to the market to buy those hideous guarda-ropas, which come from the time of the Count of Monte Cristo. Ofelia must have noticed my pleased expression, for she ran to the window. "Ramona, Lupita, Cristina, Elodia," she called. "Run and call father. The señorita will speak to him."

There was a chorus of sí's and the sound of a stampede, and I gathered that the herd had been waiting obediently under the window for just such a signal. Presently Ofelia's father came, followed by all the children, who now entered fearlessly as under a higher authority. Señor Escoto had very blue eyes. It was the first thing you noticed about him, and the thing you would always remember about him. It was a deep blue, untamed and challenging, and when he looked at me sideways and smiled with the very white teeth that Mexicans have, I found myself thinking, inevitably, "Handsome devil." Only his smile was soft and lazy, and I liked him because it contradicted the fierce blaze of his eyes. It was very easy to arrange things with him, because all he did was to smile and say softly, "Yes, that can be arranged." Meanwhile the children stood by with their hands behind their backs, and I thought how there must have been a Scotch ancestor, perhaps far back, who had given them their name of Escoto. But the Scotch blue had skipped the children, or at least it had compromised with the Indian black to give them those bronze, brown-green eyes.

Ofelia was the last of the children to go, and Señor Escoto waved her away with the same imperious gesture she had used on her little sisters. "Señora, you must forgive me for Ofelia," he said earnestly. "Do not let her bother you. She is a very presuming child."

Then they were gone. Only the door opened again, and Ofelia put her head in. "Señora," she whispered sibilantly, "when you wish for a maid, remember me. Ofelia Escoto, at your service." She closed the door lingeringly and I turned back to the apartment. But the windows drew me, flooded with a blue so clear that I had to go and look down on the lot below, to make sure I was not floating through space. The Escoto children were playing there, and from somewhere came the music of a harmonica and the sound of metal clinking, over and over again. At the far end of the lot men were playing a game, tossing a little piece of metal into a cupped stone. It was late, yet the day still lingered, the long golden Mexican day which seems as though it could never die. In the morning it lifts the spirit, but in the late afternoon, when the air is saturated with golden light and unmoving as if it had stopped breathing, one feels a great sadness— the weight of time, a premonition of eternity. That sadness I felt now, looking out on the lingering day while it grew dark in the apartment where I was not yet at home, and very much alone. And because I did not want to feel that sadness I quickly unpacked the valises and spread the intelligence tests on the desk. And very soon I was checking and adding and dividing, figuring I.Q.'s for the Otomí Indians.

IN MEXICO YOU MUST HAVE A MAID IF YOU WISH to be considered a person of consequence. Someone who does the washing on the roof, while she sings at the top of her voice and the sun makes splendid ebony of her hair, and who bargains with the butcher and who fetches your tortillas, and goes to market for you. I had no maid and so I did the marketing myself, going out every morning with a basket and a bag swinging from my arm. It was the wrong thing to do. In the corner grocery Manolo and his wife, leaning elbows on the counter, gave me good morning as I passed; but their eyes followed me disapprovingly, and I am sure they thought: of these Americans any queerness may be expected.

But how could I explain to them my great delight in going to market, or tell them that it was circus and holiday, theater and fair and folklore to me? The market of the Merced is on the other side of town, a long bus ride from Atoyac 82. But I preferred it because it is such a large market, a city in itself where one can wander and get lost. And it has infinite variety—green glass from Monterrey, and baskets from Toluca, and sombreros from every state in Mexico; and sandals hanging from the stalls like meats being cured, and leathers and cloths from Tlaxcala, besides every fruit that grows in Mexico, and every herb for medicine or witchcraft.

You cross the Great Plaza and go east, in the direction where the volcanoes show on a clear day; and even before you come to the market there are covered stalls, and the cries begin. "Buy, marchante, choose! What were you looking for, what did you desire?" A marchante, I take it, is one who marches around presumably looking for a bargain. "What do you need, marchante, what will you carry home? A bargain, a bargain, take advantage!" It is an endless litany, soft and cajoling. "Buy, my little blonde one, buy, my pretty one! I bring oranges from Córdoba, let's see if they please you."

Then comes the market proper—the difficult walking between the stalls, the dusty air and the slippery dirt, the smell of tortillas frying in bubbling fat, and the smell of leather and grass mats still green; and the din of strolling musicians and the whine of beggars, and the cries of the cargadores bent double under huge bags of produce, blindly charging through the crowd. "Make way! Make way!"

The church where the prostitutes come to pray to their patron saint is near the market, where the stalls end in a slum more terrible than any in Mexico City. But before you come to the church there is a chapel, where the women come to spend a moment out of the sun, and to say some prayer that they have in mind. It has a terrifyingly realistic Christ who sits leaning forward, the beads of blood bright on his waxen cheek, and one pale hand uplifted in the twilight air. I remember the chapel because I took refuge there on the Day of the Dead. I had made the mistake of going out bareheaded on a clear day and very soon I felt dizzy; for the Mexican sun is no pleasant benediction like our northern sun, but a fierce stroke of consuming light. Still, I did not want to turn back. The gleaming gay skulls, sugary-white and with splendid gold trimmings, lured me on, and I walked farther and farther into the market, bewitched by the cries of the women. "Skulls, skulls—two for five." I thought of buying a skull and having my picture taken, holding it in the crook of my arm like some medieval alchemist. Nobody would have thought it strange, on that day, if I had wandered through the city carrying a skull. For the whole city is given over to death, and there is feasting in the cemeteries and everywhere there are dancing skeletons, and pastries and candy take the shape of skeletons as naturally as our gingerbread takes the shape of Santa Claus. You cannot even open the paper without seeing skulls. All the famous men from the president down are pictured with fleshless grins, and someone writes very nasty epitaphs for them. It is a day for morbid joys and gruesome delights, for death casts its jigging ribaldry over everything.

But not a day for walking in the sun. I was beginning to feel sick from the smell of burning copal, the incense of the ancient Aztecs, with which they perfumed the stench of their human sacrifices. And the skulls no longer stayed in the stalls, but began to rise and float around me like balloons, and I felt myself rising too, and all of us jigging like motes in a sunbeam to the cry of "Two for five, two for five." Somewhere, I thought, there must be shade, where I can find reality again and escape from these white skull-bones. But there was no shade, only the merciless sun, chalk-white on the awnings over the stalls, sugar-white on the skulls that floated around me.

I saw brown hands molding cool ices of a poisonous febrile pink, and brown hands extended strange fruits to me with seductive cries. "Buy, my pretty one. Buy, my little blonde one." But they were the ices and fruits of death, sweet and poisonous, and I floated past them and smilingly rejected them with a wave of my hand. At which the skulls that floated with me also smiled; for while they were thus cheated of me for a time, at least I continued to suffer a fiery thirst, and that pleased them. I remember in particular one skull with the name Guadalupe beautifully inscribed on her white forehead in red icing. I had seen her first in a stall with some other female skulls— Ramona, Esmeralda, and Eusebia; and she seemed to have joined my floating escort and taken the lead, a merry wench if a bit unfleshly.

It must have been high noon, for there was no shade anywhere, and I longed for a church, a dim Christian interior to absolve me from the sun. There, I knew, the skulls must disappear, for clearly they were demons of the fierce Mexican sun and in the dark they could not exist. By now I had come to the slum, and beggars stretched their stumps of arms toward me, and the lazars, the blind and the maimed streamed past me, phantasma stepped out of some medieval painting. The buildings too were fantastic. They leaned gently awry, sinking into the earth. *Mexico is built on a filled-in lake, and old buildings with poor foundations sink slowly into the swampy ground.* It was a nice cool note to remember from the guide-books, and I hoped it was so. For if not, I was quite mad. But I remembered also what one of the Spanish conquerors had written: that the stench of human sacrifices in the Aztec temples was so great that his nostrils could not abide it. Surely that blood-thirst of the ancient Aztecs had not died out, but still claimed its living victims. I was convinced of it and already imagined the headlines: GRINGA DIES OF SUNSTROKE IN THE MERCED MARKET. And then I came to the chapel and went in, and leaned against the cold marble wall, while the air whirled around me and whirled the waxen Christ, with his pale hand lifted in reproof. The women there had put their market bags aside to kneel and pray, but they looked at me slyly while their lips moved. They were all decently shawled in long black rebozos. And as I went out one of them said to me, gently rebukeful: "Yes, one must cover the head."

Whenever I went to market Ofelia watched me. The Escotos lived in a hut on the lot next to the house, and I had to pass it to take the bus. One day she waylaid me.

"Señora, you are going to market," she said, respectfully accusing. "I too wish to go."

Since in dealing with children precedent is everything, I at once said no very firmly, and then thought of all the reasons for it. I was in a hurry, the market was far away, there would be heavy things to carry.

"I will help you carry them," she said.

"No, there's a little boy in the market who helps me."

"Ah, señora," she sighed. "Those rascals. They are shameless ones. They carry little and charge much. I will carry your things without payment. And as for the fare . . ." She showed me a ticket she had found, good for one ride on the bus. "I have that too."

"It is not the fare," I said.

Her eyes filled with tears. "But I long so to go."

"What for?"

"To buy something that pleases me."

"And what pleases you?"

"I don't know, señora. How can I tell? I would have to go to the market to find out."

"Then why don't you go?"

"There is no one to take me."

"And your mother never goes?"

"Never, señora. There is no occasion for it, because she lacks the money to buy things."

"And your aunt, the young and pretty one?"

"She too lacks the money. Besides, she says the market is very dirty."

"Yes, it is very dirty."

"But so many things! Ay, señora, what a mountain of things!" And she looked off into the distance, as if she could see the market and all its wonderful variety.

I had to give myself for vanquished, as the Spanish says. "Come," I said, and took her hand.

We did not return from the market until dark, for so many things pleased Ofelia that she could not make up her mind. We had explored all the stalls before the choice narrowed—a pair of blood-red earrings, or the blue cotton drawers, both for thirty centavos. She bought the earrings with money she had earned carrying tortillas for the Señora D'Arce in the house. "But I am not her maid," she reassured me, "and so should you need me, señora . . ."

After that I never went to market alone. I would wave my bag when I stepped out of the house, and Ofelia came flying like a bird to the signal, and took the bag from me and off we went together. She insisted on carrying it even when it was full, swinging it up to her shoulder. And when we came home the spoils had to be disgorged at once, and we would congratulate ourselves on the cheapness of this or that, or deplore the high cost of something else. And there were always new fruits to savor, which Ofelia chose for me. She watched, very distraught, while I tried them, as if the future of the whole species depended on my verdict. But I liked everything except the mangos, which have a musky rich after-taste not for my simple palate.

Very soon Ofelia began to hint that it would be a fine thing if I would let her go marketing alone. "A fine thing for you, señora," she said. "Then you could sit at your desk all day without interruption."

"But your mother would never let you go so far alone," I told her, distractedly trying to concentrate on the intelligence tests.

"Pues, it is far," she admitted, "but then if I were really your maid . . ."

"Child! You are too young to be a maid."

"Oh no, I am ten. And my sister Aurora, who bears very few years more than I, already has employment. If you would only speak to my mother . . ."

She leaned on the desk and looked with her head on one side at the drawings made by the Otomís. Problem: it is raining, draw the object which you use to protect yourself from the rain. Only it doesn't rain in the Valley of the Mesquite where the Otomís live, and the problem is how to get water, water to drink and water for the soil.

Ofelia nudged me gently. "Señora, if you would only speak to my mother . . ."

I had seen her mother often, but never spoken to her. She was tall, much taller than Señor Escoto, and in her long black skirt and black rebozo sheathing head and shoulders she looked like some figure from mythology. Whenever she met Señor Escoto on the street one could imagine that Fate herself had accosted him for the final reckoning. And usually he took a few coins from his pocket and reluctantly gave them to her. But one night Mrs. Escoto knocked at my door. In Mexico when you open the door to a neighbor, you must at once bid him come in, come in, whether you know him or not. Never let him stand on the threshold, for the Mexicans consider it a dangerous and unhallowed place. So I bade Mrs. Escoto come in, and she apologized profusely for coming in, and it made a fine chorus all the way to the living-room.

"You must forgive me, señora, for disturbing you," she began, "but it's about this Ofelia here. She is a very presuming child. I have such trouble with her." Ofelia had come in too, and stood with her hands behind her back, watching me intently from under her long lashes. "She says you have taken her for your maid and that I am to buy her an apron."

"Why, no, we only go to market together."

"There, you see?" Mrs. Escoto turned wrathfully on Ofelia. "The señora does not confirm your story. It is another one of your lies. Just imagine, we have not enough to eat in the house and I was to go out and buy her an apron! Go!"—she waved Ofelia away. "Go, presuming one! You are not wanted here."

Ofelia went out slowly, looking back at me with a beseeching urgency in her eyes, and I found myself saying, "But now that I remember—yes, we did talk of her being my maid. But not about the apron, of course. I will buy that for her myself."

"Go!" Mrs. Escoto waved again, fiercely unsatisfied until Ofelia had quite disappeared. And then, to cover a change of mood, she rearranged her rebozo and smiled at me. "Ay, señora, the trouble I have with these children. One never knows what to believe. And they are growing up so wild, so wild here in the city. We are not of the city, señora. We are of Jalisco, from the pueblo of Atotonilco near Guadalajara. And we came here of necessity, so that we might live and have a shelter over us. Such a shelter as it is! In our pueblo it would have served for the beasts." She sighed and looked around. "But here you are in glory, with such a wealth of things. In our little house in Atotonilco we too had a table and chairs and a bed, all that which makes the felicity of life. Ay, señora, what pleasure it is to have many things, many things as you have here."

"Yet more than I need. Being alone . . ."

"And look you, now we have two daughters to go out and work as servants. The sadness of it. Two daughters to be serving-maids. Aurora, who is thirteen, she already has employment, and Ofelia. Ofelia is ten. And what I wanted to ask you—what I came to find out—señora, could you give her a little salary, just a tiny little salary?"

In Mexico the diminutive is so common, for flattery, for wheedling or for sheer adornment, that one never knows whether to take it seriously or not. So I felt called upon to explain. "It will have to be a tiny little salary in all truth. I could not give the child more than ten pesos a month."

A purr of satisfaction escaped Mrs. Escoto before she shook her head. "Yes, that is little, to be sure. But then Ofelia is young, and as yet of little use."

"And she will eat with me."

Mrs. Escoto smiled deprecatingly. She had strong white teeth, but her gums were covered with red sores. "Ah, no, señora, I was not thinking of that. There is always something to eat in our house. Not much, but a mouthful can always be found."

"She will eat with me," I insisted. And, as if the little salary had expanded visibly, Mrs. Escoto instructed me sternly: "And set her to work on her knees. Do not spare her, not for a moment. For she must learn, she must learn her trade, which is that of a serving-maid. Because look you, señora, we are not young—I and her father. I have a little one, Lolita—perhaps you have seen her? She can hardly walk yet, but for all that we are not young, we are well advanced in years. It is only that one goes on having children until the thing finishes itself. And if, God forbid, they should one day be left orphans . . ." She rose after a while, fatefully tall, and adjusted her rebozo and smiled at me. She had a gaunt prettiness, but it was ravaged by time and illness, and I thought there was something very sad about her. "And forgive me, señora, that I came to disturb you. But the child bothered me so . . ."

While we were preparing the supper that night, I asked Ofelia: "What do you eat in your home?"

"Pues—" She hesitated only because the answer seemed so obvious to her. "Pues," she said, "we eat tortillas."

"Yes, but what do you have for breakfast?"

"Tortillas."

"And for lunch?"

"Tortillas."

"And for supper—"

"We do not eat supper, only Daniel and my father, because they are men. But Daniel is not here now and so it is only my father. He eats the tortillas which are left over."

"And are there many left over?"

"It depends. You see, my mother gives me a peso in the morning and I buy two pounds of dough, and with it my mother and my aunts make the tortillas. Two pounds is not much, señora, and they finish quickly."

"Yes, I see."

"And then we are twelve, counting my little grandmother and my two aunts. There's my Aunt Delfina, her husband has left her, and my other aunt who is very ill."

"But do you never have anything else?"

"Pues, sí! We have black beans from time to time, and eggs when my Aunt Delfina goes to her village, which is Saint Pedro of the Pines, to fetch them. And meat on Sundays. But it's never very good meat. Just imagine, señora, we pay the butcher thirty centavos for a piece of meat, and it's pure nerves. My father says it's a shame. And we have coffee, too, but my father says it is bad for one. Is it so, señora?"

"Oh yes, coffee is bad."

"My aunt, the older one, cannot sleep when she drinks coffee. But then she is very sick, and the pains keep her awake too."

I asked what the sickness was, and Ofelia shrugged and said, "Quién sabe? . . . who knows?" Spoken like a Mexican, who never says "I don't know," with its ring of personal responsibility. But he says "who knows," and he says it with a great weariness, as if the thing in question were utterly unknowable, or as if it would be asking too much of him to find out.

SO OFELIA BECAME MY MAID. DEAR OFELIA! HOW ardently you craved the martyr's crown, and begged to be set sweeping and scouring and scrubbing on your knees. And how busy I was, keeping you busy, lest you suffer a moment's idleness and so fall from grace. I wanted to dismiss you a hundred times in those early days, but I couldn't. Because it would have been an expulsion from paradise for you, because your new maidhood was seventh heaven and a crown of glory to you.

And how patiently in those early days you listened to my wisdom, the well-fed wisdom of my race, of which I delivered myself while we sat eating the raw carrot—telling you of the wonderful vitamin and other magical entities. You listened patiently but without belief; and yet you grew bright-eyed and rosy-cheeked, and different from your little sisters who were waxen and pale as the very tortillas of their diet. "We shall turn into horses," I observed once, as we sat munching our raw carrots. "Or into burros," you said, and then you turned serious. "Yes, señora, there are people who remain burros all their lives. Those who have never been baptized in the Holy Church. All their lives they never have the wisdom of human beings." You were old, Ofelia, with the ancient wisdom of the Church; and old with the ageless dignity of the rebozo that framed your face. And only when you looked longingly at the ugly little celluloid dolls in the market did I remember your scarce ten years. Mornings, when I drew the curtains aside and looked down on the lot, I saw you standing at the door of the hut and braiding your hair. Already you had been to church. You had risen at five, weary and dirty from unrestful slumber on a straw mat, and unwashed but decently sheathed in your rebozo, you had walked many blocks to hear a Mass in the great golden church on the Reforma.

And now, your peace made with God, you were preparing for the secular duties of the day. You braided your hair without a mirror. It was long chestnut hair, which the Mexicans call blond, as they call any hair blond which is not of an Indian blackness. No doubt the Scotch ancestor who gave you your name also gave you your chestnut hair. But your skin was for Mexico—dark dark. When, obeying my orders, you scrubbed your face, you looked at yourself in the mirror and said despairingly, "But I am dark dark, just the same, señora." And you hated your dark skin, because everyone knows that true beauty is white as the driven snow. And after you had braided your hair you went into the hut and came out wearing your black rebozo—the coarse cotton one, for the silk one was only for church—and with a basket on your arm and a peso in your hand, the single peso that must buy the day's food, you went to market for the pound of dough and for my paper. You did not understand why I must have another paper every day. "Haven't you yesterday's?" you asked. And then I explained that the news is created fresh every day; and after that, with lofty understanding, you asked each morning as you gave me the paper: "And what is the news today?"

"Well, Mexico is going to elect a president." Or, "The war in Europe continues." You did not know that Mexico had a president, or that there was a place called Europe. These were faraway things of no importance. But on the other hand, all the saints were near, and you knew the days of each and how one must honor them; and you knew what is mortal sin and what is forgivable. And you knew how to bargain in the market-place, and how to pound chile and make tortillas—things adequate for your world.

And you knew also how to behave in difficult circumstances. For I believe it is a difficult circumstance to sit down at table with one of a strange race, to eat strange foods. That first time we sat down at table together—you did not touch the food and I wondered why you sat so quietly without eating. And then you said, with great dignity and with that Mexican way of half-statement: "I, señora, as I do not eat at table . . ."

"But eat any way you like," I said. And you fell to, tearing the meat with your hands. But you did that also with reserve and a certain dignity.

And you knew the gracious courtesy, the wonderful politeness of your people. "Well, señora, I am going," you said when the day's work was over. But you lingered. "With your permission, señora."

"Well, señora, until tomorrow," and now you were at the door, where you waited a decent moment. "Well, señora, until we meet again. May it go well with you." And then the door closed softly, and your "Adiós, señora," floated back to me. And thus, at the end of each day you left me, for leave-taking is a delicate matter, and one must never go abruptly.

Dear Ofelia! You kept me so busy that my Otomís languished without their I.Q.'s. And I had to work far into the night, and I was tired with the altitude and dozed over the papers. And so I would put them away with nothing done, and go to bed, and sleep was only a small moment before the sun sprang up from the mountains, and I heard the women making tortillas—the steady slap-slap as they tossed the dough between their palms.

It is the sound of Mexico, as the blue of the sky is its color. And the cold of the mountain night is still in the air when it begins. I would rise and draw the curtains, and see the sun low and clear on the level white buildings. From the huts came a haze of smoke and the morning noises—chopping of wood, water splashing, and the pigs squealing; and Ofelia's little sister singing shrilly over and over, "To heaven, to heaven let me go, to receive the blessed crown, the blessed crown." And through it all the insistent slap-slap of tortilla-making, a rhythmic sound like part of a ceremonial, and one seems to hear far off the accompanying beat of feet in some primitive dance.

I could see the women working in the smoky huts where the night still lingered, their hands twinkling in the obscure light, their faces bronze and shadowy as if emerging from a dark canvas. Outside the men were washing, dousing their heads in the dirty water in the barrels; and then, drying their faces, they went into the huts to eat. They squatted on the dirt floor, and took many tortillas at a time, and folded them and downed them with black coffee. All the men of the huts worked on the houses that were being built on the block; and after breakfast they strolled over to the foreman's shack, a leisurely stroll with hands in pocket and much jesting. "Ay, how lonely I was last night!" It was the sung-out complaint of one of them—no doubt a bachelor; and every morning the men laughed at it, standing in front of the foreman's shack, and singing back retorts that increased the laughter. For singing is the word for Mexican speech. It is most noticeable in the working people, when they call to each other, talk loudly or jest. Then something happens to their speech— a lilt at the end of each phrase, a musical cadence always the same, with the last note fading away sweetly resonant. I used to think there was an opera company under my windows, for it was not speech that I heard, but a recitative always straining to break into song.

The roll-call was always a long and elaborate business, and I am sure that the first step in bringing the Mexicans up to our northern standards of efficiency must be to shorten their names. "Señor Ildefonso Sánchez Morales." "Señor José Herrera Rodríguez." The foreman intoned each name with long-drawn sonority, and each man answered, "Presente, maestro." Then the men who had come from other parts of the city went into the shack and hung up the woven bags in which they carried tortillas. But the foreman more often than not stands frowning at his list. "Juan! Juan!" he calls into the shack. "Are you drunk again?" Everyone looks toward the shack and Juan comes out, and he is drunk again. And grinning happily and waving his arms as if he were flying. No doubt he had been in the cantina a few blocks away, which bears the name: I Feel Like an Aviator.

Ofelia calls the men who work on the buildings "los peones," the peons. This used to be the term for the serfs on the large estates before the Revolution. But now, either with land of his own or the right to acquire it, the rural laborer of Mexico is called a campesino—a peasant or farmer. Yet the word peon still persists, both for the rural laborer and the hired hand of the city. Nearly all the men who work on the buildings come from the provinces. They are not men of the city, not skilled builders. They have only recently been on the land, and the planting of a field of corn is more familiar to them than the processes of brick and mortar and the plumbline. Perhaps that is why the hammering on the buildings sounds much busier than it really is; for the men work at their own rhythm, very relaxed and slow about whatever they are doing. And if a peddler passes they all stop work, looking on while one of their number drives a bargain, at great length and with sallies of wit.

There are always peddlers coming to the street. There is the old man who trots along under a perilous tower of painted straw chairs. He has to trot very fast to keep them from falling. And the Indians come with flowers from Xochimilco, and with berries and herbs. And a man and a woman come driving a small herd of goats before them. They are very young goats, uncertain on their legs, and they stop stupidly before no obstacle at all. Then the man and the woman scold them in an Indian language which is probably Aztec. They are both very small, and ragged and barefoot, yet somehow proud and indomitable in their rags. The man's hair is a matted black mass under his sombrero, but the woman's two braids lie like carved wood against the high cheekbones. And there is a woman who comes selling live chickens, their dangling heads showing more life than the baby she carries on her back, half suffocated in her rebozo. And there is a man who comes flailing a flock of turkeys, that invade the street like mummers with their cries and strut and color. And work must stop and everyone must watch while one of the peons buys something, for a good bargain is a public concern. And why should there be haste to make a building that will be only two stories high? Of course, building a skyscraper is different.

But the women really worked. They washed clothes every day, though the only water they had was carried from the buildings in old gasoline cans. I used to watch, and marvel at the way they treasured every drop of water, at their intricate system of wringings and rinsings that turned the clothes out as spotless as if a whole ocean had cleansed them. Mexican women always wash clothes horizontally on a stone, working their arms back and forth, instead of up and down. Perhaps it comes from the practice of washing clothes on a river bank, or because they have grown so used to moving their arms that way from grinding corn on the metate. But in any case it is certainly contrary to gravity, and very hard work. And it would be a good thing if the feminists who agitate for communal mills to grind the corn would also ask the Government for hundreds and hundreds of wash-boards. Then, when the clothes had been hung on the fences to dry, the women aired the sarapes and the straw sleeping mats. And then all the earthenware pots were scoured with great wads of coarse hay, rinsed and turned upside down to dry. In the sun their burned bottoms gleamed like ebony.

Ofelia and I worked also—the morning warfare against the flea. For it is ironical that in the high Valley of Mexico, where the mountain forms bespeak cosmic geologic upheavals, the greatest menace to man is the tiny flea. Let every resident of Mexico City put pesos for "fleet" on his budget. Fleet (the American Flit) is the name that Mexicans have adopted for any insecticide. You may buy a Mexican brand of fleet, but my grocer did not advise it. "Yes, señorita," he said, "I recommend the American fleet, even though it be dearer. The American product truly kills. The Mexican merely stuns the animal." And he gave a fine imitation of a stunned flea. Ofelia loved spraying fleet. The smell of it enchanted her, and she would go around inhaling it as though it were perfume.

Ofelia could not tell time, but she went by the sound of the hammering. When it ceased altogether, she would announce: "Las dos, señora. Two o'clock"—very proudly, as though she had looked at the clock. Then the peons invaded Manolo's store, calling loudly for beer and soda pop—the busiest hour for Manolo, who never took a siesta. The men who did not live on the lot ate in the scant shade of the buildings; but the others ate in the huts—tortillas not so fresh as in the morning, and perhaps a paste of black beans fried in lard. I would hear Mrs. Escoto calling Ofelia's little sisters for this, their last meal of the day. At night there would be no supper call to take them from their playing. Yet they would play in the darkening air with tireless energy, and with no knowledge that they were hungry. Only they were thin and bony, and waxen as the image of the Virgin that stood on a packing-case in the hut.

Ofelia called them her little pigs. "Pues, I am not hungry any more," she would say, laying down the knife and fork which she now used with some facility. We would agree that it was a sad waste of food to throw away what was left on her plate, and, since she had been talking about her tierra and the ranch where they used to live, she would suggest casually: "I could feed it to my little pigs." Which continued the talk and allowed her to carry off the food without embarrassment. "Tierra" literally means earth, and thus the Mexican designates the region from which he comes, the place of his birth and childhood. Ofelia loved to talk about her tierra, like all good Mexicans, though she never seemed sure whether they had owned their ranch or whether it had been part of a great estate. But she said there were abundant fruits there, wood to be given away, oranges ripening faster than they could be picked, and eggs at two centavos in near-by Atotonilco. Yet they left their tierra and came to the city.

"But why?" I asked.

"Well, my father came first."

"Yes, but why did he leave the ranch?"

She considered. "Pues . . . you see, señora," and her words gathered aggrieved momentum, for she remembered now exactly how it had been. "They paid him only fifty centavos there on the hacienda where he worked. Imagine that! Only fifty centavos for so much work every day, and for the family that we are, too. It was unjust, wasn't it?"

"Certainly it was unjust. But still you were better off there than here, weren't you? You had everything to eat, and a real house, and beds to sleep on . . ."

"Yes, señora, but we went barefoot all the time, and my father was angry that they paid him only fifty centavos."

"And now?" I asked, looking down at her torn shoes.

She sighed. "Now there is no money for shoes, either. Still, it is better that we came. My father earns more, oh, much more. It's only that we are so many—so many of us."

She feels so sure that it was better, yet I cannot quite understand. Perhaps they did not own the land after all, and the abundance was none of theirs, but only a charity from a kind hacendado. Or perhaps they did own the land, only that it gave them a surfeit of fruits where there was no one to buy, and what good is abundance if one cannot see a silver peso from one year's end to the next? Or perhaps it was simply as she said: "My father got angry that they paid him only fifty centavos." A man may well get angry at that and feel himself worth more, and leave everything he has to prove it.

"Still," I reasoned, "why didn't your father, when he found work here, send money back to the ranch? Why did all of you come to the city?"

"My father wrote us one day to come, and we came," she said, with the air of one who gives more than adequate reason. And then with even more conviction, "Nor did we wish him to be alone here in the city."

I had to let it go at that, though I was still troubled; for it seemed to me that they had made only an illusory change. They were still barefoot and poor as they had been before, and now they were starving too.

"And doesn't your father ever think of going back?"

"Well, no"—she considered. "My mother talks of it often, but without much purpose. And the city is better, señora. Just imagine, in Atotonilco the streets are so narrow that an automobile could not pass through them, that is, if ever one came."

"Just imagine."

"And besides, my brother Daniel is coming now. He stayed behind so as not to forsake his sweetheart. But now they are going to get married and they are coming here for the nuptials. And Daniel will work and we will have more money."

And more mouths to feed, I said to myself, thinking how little simple mathematics counted with them. "And will Daniel and his sweetheart sleep in the hut?"

"Pues, sí. My father wishes it."

"And won't you be rather crowded?"

She did not think so. "What does it matter," she sighed, "while we sleep?"

SYBILLE BEDFORD

Living on the Alameda, ca. 1950

"IN THE SPACES OF THE PLAZA MAYOR, WALKING
OVER THE GRAVE OF A PYRAMID, ONE IS
ASSAILED BY INFINITY, SEIZED AT THE THROAT
BY AN AWFUL SENSE OF THE PAST."

The English writer Sybille Bedford traveled with a friend in Mexico in
1950. The Sudden View, *her account of the trip, was published in
1953 but attracted little attention at the time.* Retitled A Visit to Don
Otavio *and published in England and the United States in 1960, after
the appearance of Bedford's novel* A Legacy, *it was hailed as a modern
classic of travel literature.*

*Bedford is caustic, funny, frustrated, and patient by turns, and her
companion, called simply "E.," is a good foil for her opinions. Despite
grumblings—her descriptions, for example, of tortillas and of Sanborn's—Bedford is game for anything. Imagine Barbara Pym in a really
feisty mood.*

*Bedford doesn't name the hotel where she stayed in Mexico City,
but it was the Hotel de Cortés, at Avenida Hidalgo 85, facing the northwest corner of the Alameda park. The Cortés was described by various
contemporary guidebooks as a "modernized colonial convent," offering
"modern comforts in a handsome 17th [century] mansion, with rooms*

around a beautiful patio." A 1949 guidebook calls it "a colonial palace intelligently modernized to meet the requirements of modern travel. Its romantic appeal is great," and, the guide adds, one should not be deterred by its location "on the edge of an extensive red light district."

No wonder Bedford was told that she was on the "wrong" side of the Alameda. The "right" side of the Alameda was clearly opposite, on Avenida Juárez, where the spectacular Hotel del Prado had opened at number 70 in 1948 and was immediately hailed as the greatest hotel in all of Latin America. It had six hundred rooms, sixty-five suites, a four-story lobby with a handmade Mexican carpet that looked and felt like grass, a shopping arcade, a sundeck with a real lawn, a heated swimming pool, a three-hundred-car garage, and a rooftop belvedere with a view of the volcanoes. The lobby murals were by Covarrubias, those in the cocktail lounge by Montenegro, and those in the breakfast room by Ledesma, while the dining room became a center of heated controversy because of Rivera's A Dream of a Sunday Afternoon in the Alameda Park, which in later years was moved to the lobby. Like New York's Waldorf-Astoria, the del Prado was the traditional host to visiting heads of state and everyone else of note, from the Duke and Duchess of Windsor to Emperor Haile Selassie.

At 7:18 in the morning of September 19, 1985, an earthquake of magnitude 8.1 shook Mexico City violently for more than three minutes. The Alameda region was struck particularly hard. Rivera's famous mural escaped damage and is now on display in the nearby Museo de la Alameda. The Hotel del Prado was destroyed.

So was the grand and huge old Hotel Regis—"where the American Rotarians go," Graham Greene had complained in 1938—that had stood across the street on Juárez, at the southwest corner of the park, since 1910.

The small Hotel de Cortés survived the earthquake, just as it had survived demolition in the 1970s when Paseo de la Reforma was extended northeastward from its original termination point at Avenida Juárez. The new extension cut through many local streets but angled past the Cortés. Built in the eighteenth century as the Hospedería de Santo Tomás de Villanueva, it sheltered traveling missionaries. Under private management, it opened as a hotel in 1943 and through the years has hosted, besides Syhille Bedford, such guests as Georgia O'Keeffe, dancer José Limon, and San Francisco columnist Stanton Delaplane. Today it's still proud, still beautiful, still a bargain, still has a fountain and tables *in the courtyard, and its corner suites still have a view of the Alameda. The eighteenth-century hostel for traveling friars is now, like the Ritz and the Majestic, part of the Best Western chain.*

THE FIRST IMPACT OF MEXICO CITY IS PHYS- ical, immensely physical. Sun, Altitude, Movement, Smells, Noise. And it is inescapable. There is no taking refuge in one more insulating shell, no use sitting in the hotel bedroom fumbling with guide books: it is here, one is in it. A dazzling live sun beats in through a window; geranium scented white-washed cool comes from the patio; ear-drums are fluttering, dizziness fills the head as one is bending over a suitcase, one *is* eight thousand feet above the sea and the air one breathes is charged with lightness. So dazed, tempted, buoyed, one wanders out and like the stranger at the party who was handed a very large glass of champagne at the door, one floats along the streets in uncertain bliss, swept into rapids of doing, hooting, selling. Everything is agitated, crowded, spilling over; the pavements are narrow and covered with fruit. As one picks one's way over mangoes and avocado pears, one is tumbled into the gutter by a water carrier, avoids a Buick saloon and a basin of live charcoal, skips up again scaring a tethered chicken, shies from an exposed deformity and bumps into a Red Indian gentleman in a tight black suit. Now a parrot shrieks at one from an upper window, lottery tickets flutter in one's face, one's foot is trodden on by a goat and one's skirt clutched at by a baby with the face of an idol. A person long confined to the consistent North may well imagine himself returned to one of the large Mediterranean ports, Naples perhaps: there are the people at once lounging and pressing, there is that oozing into the streets of business and domesticity; the show of motor traffic zigzagged by walking beasts; the lumps of country life, peasants and donkey carts, jars and straw, pushing their way along the pavements; there are the over-flowing trams, the size and blaze of the Vermouth advertisements, the inky office clothes, the rich open food shops strung with great hams and cheeses, and the shoddy store with the mean bedroom suite; the ragged children, the carved fronts of palaces and the seven gimcrack skyscrapers. Nothing is lacking: monster cafés, Carpet Turks, the plate-glass window of the aeroplane agency, funeral wreaths for sale at every corner and that unconvincing air of urban modernity. One looks, one snuffs, one breathes—familiar, haunting, long-missed, memories and present merge, and for a happy quarter of an hour one is plunged into the loved element of lost travels. Then Something Else creeps in. Something Else was always here. These were not the looks, not the gestures. Where is the openness of Italy, that ready bosom? This summer does not have the Southern warmth, that round hug as from a fellow creature. Here, a vertical sun aims at one's head like a dagger—how well the Aztecs read its nature—while the layers of the air remain inviolate like mountain streams, cool, fine, flowing, as though refreshed by some bubbling spring. Europe is six thousand miles across the seas and this glacier city in a tropical latitude has never, never been touched by the Mediterranean. In a minor, a comfortable, loop-holed, mitigated way, one faces what Cortez faced in the absolute five hundred years ago: the unknown.

Well, what does one do? Where does one begin, where does one turn to first? Here we are in the capital of this immense country and we know nothing of either. We don't know anybody. We hardly know the language. We have an idea of what there is to see, but we do not know where anything is from where, nor how to get there. We do not have much money to spend, and we have much too much luggage. Winter clothes and clothes for the tropics, town clothes and country clothes and the bottom of our bags are falling out with books. We have a few letters of introduction. They are not promising. From vague friends to their vague friends, Europeans with uncertain addresses who are supposed to have gone to Mexico before the war. Guillermo had pressed a letter into my hand at the station; a German name covered most of the envelope. "Great friends," he had said, "they have had such trouble with their papers." E. had been told to put her name down at the American Embassy. Nobody seemed to know any Mexicans. No one had written to people running a mine or a sugar place; or heard of some local sage, a Norman Douglas of the Latin Americas, who knew everything, the people and the stories, plants and old brawls, how to keep the bores at bay and where to get good wine.

God be praised we have a roof over our heads and it is not the roof of the Pensión Hernandez. The spirit that made us fall in with

Guillermo's suggestion has waned, already there is a South-wind change. A man on the train told us about a small hotel, Mexican run, in front of a park. To this we drove from the station, and found a Colonial palace with a weather-beaten pink façade. Of course there were rooms. We have a whole suiteful of them. Bedrooms and sitting-room and dressing-room, and a kind of pantry with a sink, a bathroom and a trunk closet and a cupboard with a sky-light. Everything clean as clean and chock-full of imitation Spanish furniture, straight-backed tapestry chairs, twisty iron lamps with weak bulbs. There is a balcony on to the square and a terrace on to the patio. The patio has a pleasant Moorish shape; it is white-washed, full of flowers, with a fountain in the middle and goldfish in the fountain, and all of it for thirty shillings a day.

The first step obviously is luncheon. Time, too, we were off the streets. That sun! E.'s face is a most peculiar colour. One had been warned to take it easy. One had been warned not to drink the water, to keep one's head covered, to have typhoid injections, beware of chile, stay in after dark, never to touch ice, eat lettuce, butter, shellfish, goat cheese, cream, uncooked fruit. . . . We turned into a restaurant. I had a small deposit of past tourist Spanish to draw on; it did not flow, but it was equal to ordering the *comida corrida*, the table d'hôte luncheon. Every table is occupied with what in an Anglo-Saxon country would be a party but here seems just the family. Complexions are either café-au-lait, nourished chestnut, glowing copper, or milky mauve and dirty yellow. Everybody looks either quite exquisite or too monstrous to be true, without any transitional age between flowering ephebe and oozing hippopotamus. The male ephebes are dressed in extreme, skin-tight versions of California sports clothes, shiny, gabardiny, belted slack-suits in ice-cream colours, pistachio and rich chocolate; their elders are compressed in the darkest, dingiest kind of ready-made business outfits, and ladies of all proportions draped in lengths of sleazy material in the more decorative solid colours, blood orange, emerald, chrome yellow, azure. There is a wait of twenty-five minutes, then a succession of courses is deposited before us in a breathless rush. We dip our spoons into the soup, a delicious cream of vegetable that would have done honour to a private house in the French Provinces before the war of 1870, when two small platefuls of rice symmetrically embellished with peas and pimento appear at our elbows.

"*Y aquí la sopa seca.*" The dry soup.

We are still trying to enjoy the wet one, when the eggs are there: two flat, round, brown omelets.

Nothing is whisked away before it is finished, only more and more courses are put in front of us in two waxing semi-circles of cooling dishes. Two spiny fishes covered in tomato sauce. Two platefuls of beef stew with spices. Two bowlfuls of vegetable marrow swimming in fresh cream. Two thin beef-steaks like the soles of children's shoes. Two platters of lettuce and radishes in an artistic pattern. Two platefuls of bird bones, lean drumstick and pointed wing smeared with some brown substance. Two platefuls of mashed black beans; two saucers with fruit stewed in treacle. A basket of rolls, all slightly sweet; and a stack of *tortillas,* limp, cold, pallid pancakes made of maize and mortar. We eat heartily of everything. Everything tastes good, nearly everything is good. Only the chicken has given its best to a long and strenuous life and the stock pot, and the stewed fruit is too sticky for anyone above the age of six. The eggs, the stew, the vegetables, the salad, rice and beans are very good indeed. Nothing remotely equals the quality of the soup. We are drinking a bottled beer, called Carta Blanca, and find it excellent. At an early stage of the meal we had been asked whether we desired chocolate or coffee at the end of it, and accordingly a large cupful was placed at once at the end of the line with another basket of frankly sugared rolls. This *pan dulce* and the coffee are included in the lunch. The bill for the two of us, beer and all, comes to nine pesos, that is something under ten shillings.

It is four o'clock and the sun has not budged from its central position in the sky. We do not fool with hats and shade, but return to the hotel by cab. I close the shutters, lie down, and when I wake I do not know where I am nor where I was just now. I hardly know who I am. These pieces of escaped knowledge seem immediately paramount; hardly awake I struggle to fill the blanks as though it were for air. When identity is cleared, I cannot put a finger on my time, this is When? At last the place, too, clicks into place. It must have taken half a minute, a minute, to catch up with my supposed reality. It seemed much longer. One sleeps like this perhaps two or three times in a life and one never forgets these moments of coming to. That intense pang of regret. For what? The boundless promise of that unfilled space before memory rushed in? Or for the so hermetically forgotten region before waking, for the where-we-were in that sleep which we cannot know but which left such a taste of happiness? This time reaction is reversed, opportunity lies before not behind, adjustment is a joy. I am at the edge of Mexico—I rush to the window. It must have been raining. It has. This is the rainy season, and it does every afternoon from May till October. The square looks washed, water glistens on leaves and the sky is still wildly dramatic like an El Greco landscape. Half the male citizenry is unbuttoning their American mackintoshes and shaking the water out of the brims of their sombreros; the other half is huddling in soaked white cotton pyjamas, their chins and shoulders wrapped in those thin, gaudy horse blankets known as *sarapes* in the arts and crafts. It is no longer hot, only mild like a spring evening. Two hours ago we were in August, now it is April.

I take a look at a plan and set out. I cross the Alameda, a rather glum squareful of vegetation cherished as a park. It was started, like so much else in Mexico, in honour of some anniversary of Independence, and its plant life seems to be all rubber trees. I come out into Avenida Juárez ablare with juke-box, movie theatre, haberdashery and soft drink parlour. Our street, Avenida Hidalgo, was handsome if run down—a length of slummy *palacios* with oddments of Aztec masonry encrusted in their sixteenth-century façades, and no shops but a line of flower stalls selling funeral *pièces montées,* huge wreaths and crosses worked with beads, filigree and mother-of pearl skulls. The wrong side of the Alameda, we are later told. The right side looks like the Strand.

I walk on and am stunned by the sight of as amazing a structure as I could ever hope to see. It is the National Theatre and was obviously built by Díaz and in the early nineteen-hundreds. I had best leave the description of this masterpiece of eclecticism to *Terry:*

> "*El Teatro Nacional, an imposing composite structure of shimmering marble, precious woods, bronze, stained glass and minor enrichments, stands on the E. end of the Alameda. . . . It . . . cost upwards of 35 million pesos. The original plans, the work of the Italian Adamo Boari (who designed the nearby Central Post Office), called for a National Theatre superior to any on the continent. . . . The Palacio presents a strikingly harmonious blend of various architectural styles. . . . When about half-completed the enormously*

heavy structure began slowly to sink into the spongy subsoil. It has sunk nearly five feet below the original level."

This sounds an optimistic note. But no, the Teatro Nacional is no iceberg, there are still some three hundred feet to sink.

When I reach the centre it is quite suddenly night. On Avenida Francesco Madero—a murdered President—the shops are bright with neons. Wells Fargo, where I had hoped to collect some letters, keep American hours and are closed. Everything else is open and bustling. After the three-hour lunch, the siesta and the rains, a new lease of business begins at about eight. The food shops are as good as they look. Great sacks of coffee in the bean, York hams and Parma hams, gorgonzolas, olive oil.

"May I buy all the ham I want?" I feel compelled to ask.

"How many hams, Señora?"

I have no intention of leaving this entrancing shop. It is as clean as it is lavish, and they are so polite. . . . One might be at Fortnum's. Only this is more expansive: that warm smell of roasting coffee and fresh bread. And the wines! Rows and rows of claret, pretty names and sonorous names of *Deuxième Crus,* Château Gruaud-Larose-Sarget, Château Pichon-Longueville, Château Ducru-Beaucaillou, alas all are expensive. A tray of small hot pasties is brought in, *mille feuilles* bubbling with butter.

"*¿Qué hay en el interior?"*

"Anchovy, cheese, chicken."

I have some done up to take back to E. There is French brandy, Scotch whisky, Campari Bitter, none of them really ruinous, but none of them cheap. Decidedly, the local produce. I get a quart of Bacardi rum, the best, darkest kind. Five pesos. A peso is almost exactly a shilling. And a bottle of Mexican brandy. The name of this unknown quantity is appropriate, *Cinco Equis,* Five X's. It costs nine pesos and has three stars. We shall see.

As I leave the shop, a small child relieves me of my parcels. She does it with dignity, hinting that it is not so much her wish to earn a tip, as that it is not suitable for me to go about the streets with bottles done up in brown paper and half a dozen meat pasties dangling from my fingers by a string. I do not like being fetched and carried for by persons older or smaller than myself, but realise that here I must submit to so comfortable a custom. There are more shops like the first, and thanks to my companion I am now free to enjoy them all. I buy a bottle of tequila (two pesos a quart and every pint guaranteed to give D.T.s), succumb to Campari, but resist Spanish Pernod. After these additions I have a suite. But it is always the first child who receives the parcels from my hands and distributes them among the other tots. We have some stilted conversation. A young man is sitting on the pavement outside a branch of His Master's Voice with six avocado pears for sale. He shifts them before him in a pattern and as they are moved about in the dusk the avocados look like trained mice. I buy his stock. He has nothing to wrap it up in, so my head-child commandeers three passing babies with two empty hands each. The notion of having acquired half a dozen avocado pears for threepence makes me slightly light-headed. I do not buy the two puppies from the man who came rushing out of a church, but I buy a pineapple, a heap of papayas, a straw hat, some plums, some sweets for the porters (squeamishness about plain money to children), some hot chestnuts and some flowers: two armloads of tuberoses, and they too cost next to nothing. As we trail back through the business streets, *Bolívar* and *Cinco del Mayo,* and the pitch black *Alameda,* I feel like the Pied Piper. In the lobby, the children accept their fruit drops and pennies with self-possession. They thank me and express wishes for my well-being in this world and the next, *que Dios la proteja, que la vaya bien,* hand their parcels to a rather older hotel child and depart like well-bred guests at an Edwardian dinner-party without haste or lingering.

I had the impression that the desk clerk was obscurely distressed by my purchases. Sure enough, ten minutes later we are visited by the housekeeper. She looks Spanish, one of those neat, middle-aged, efficient Latin women who are so much better at their linen cupboards than one can ever hope to be at anything. She does not come to the point. Does Mexico please us?

Oh, indeed.

"Yes, it is pretty." We were not displeased by the rains?

We reassure her.

The hotel is also to our taste?

We try to say how pleased we are.

Yet those flowers. We did not like their flowers?

The vases were already filled with lilac and narcissus. Mexican hotels, that is Mexican-run hotels in Mexico, put flowers in their guest rooms with the towels and the bottle of drinking water. Fresh flowers every day, all year round. I try to explain that we had not been aware of this charming practice. We are not believed. The housekeeper leaves in a confusion of mutual apologies. Then the boy comes in from behind the door and bears away the lilac and narcissi. Next day, a great sheaf of tuberoses appears in my bedroom, and all during our stay there are fresh tuberoses every morning. I love them, and I am delighted.

☀

THERE ARE THREE CLIMATIC ZONES IN MEXICO, one hot, one cold, one temperate. The *Tierras Calientes, Fría* and *Templada.* The Hot Zone is very hot, the Cold not as cold as it sounds; the Temperate is celestial perfection.

It is also the most inhabited portion of the Republic—the best part of the *Mesa Central* lies in *Tierra Templada.* Yet this plateau is not a temperate place at all: the mildness is luxuriant and dynamic, the temperance the product of the clash between two intemperances. It is a tropical region anomalously cool, combining the geographical extremes of Switzerland and Central Africa, high as Mont-Blanc, equatorial as the Sahara. At sea-level, the Mexican latitudes would be desert and jungle; in the north, the Mexican heights would be Alpine wastes. Joined, these excesses of parallel and altitude created a perennial Simla better than Simla. As a matter of recorded fact, the annual mean temperatures of the *Tierra Templada* vary between 66° and 73° Fahrenheit. The average rainfall is some 80 inches a year and concentrated within four months, June to October. In terms of human experience this means: it is always warm; it is never hot; it is never cold. It only rains in season and when it does it pours at fixed and regular hours, and afterwards the air again is dry and light, leaves and fields shine, there is no damp, no mud, no dripping, only a great new freshness.

Grey days are unknown. Except for a few minutes of dramatic preparation for the actual burst, the sky is always clear. There is little difference in the weather between July and February; it may get rather warm in the late spring and there are chilly evenings when the wind is blowing from the Coast, yet a person with a change of clothes suitable for an exceptionally fine English June, a blanket and a hut made of waterproof leaves and bamboo canes would be comfortable day and night from one end of the year to the other. Ownership of a mud cottage and some pine cones for a fire around Christmas would assure a sybaritic existence. This opens, and shuts, economic vistas. A promoter from Germany, Gruening tells us in his wonderfully detailed *History of Mexico,* arrived some time in the nineteenth century full of business projects, and departed so disgusted that he wrote a long and angry volume on the natives' cursed lack of wants, their *verdammte Beduerfnigslosigkeit.* He should see them now, poor man, sipping their Coca-Colas.

The second zone is at sea-level and frankly tropical. Hundreds of miles of jungle, beach and silted port on the Pacific. The Gulf, with Veracruz, the oil trade, coffee *fincas* and a certain commercial bustle. The deep South: Chiapas, Tabasco, Campeche—swamps and forests, the Graham Greene country of *The Lawless Roads;* Yucatán and the pre-Columbian ruins. The third zone is not a region but a number of separate points of especial altitude. It is a matter of exposure, on the whole every place above seven thousand feet is considered to be *Terra Fría.*

Thus Mexico City belongs to the cold land. It is, however, a rule unto itself. It has four distinct climates, one for the night—which is bitter—and three for every day. In the morning we are on the coast of New England. It is autumn. A golden late September; the air is brisk but informed with warmth, luminous with sun. The kind of morning when one cannot bear to be in bed, when numbed insects stir to a new lease and one picks up one's teacup and walks out into the garden. Here the unexpected gift comes every day. Breakfast is laid in the patio: there is fruit, the absurd goldfish are swishing in the fountain and everything smells of geranium; warmth lies gently across one's shoulders; E. has ceased to talk politics, the housekeeper stops to chat, the boy comes running with hot rolls and butter. . . . It is good to be alive.

At eleven, the climate becomes continental. It is the height of summer on the top of a mountain. The sun is burning, brilliant, not to be fooled with; the *fond de l'air* cool and flowing like fine water. One feels tremendously exhilarated, charged with energy. This is the time of day when I like to pick my way through the streets, walk slowly across the Cathedral Square under the shade of the brim of my hat. This full noon lasts for several hours. Then comes the cloudburst and through the early evening, rain falls with the sound of rain falling in the hot countries all over the world, in Egypt, in Burma. . . . Later, it is a spring evening in a large city: mild, tenuous, nostalgic, laid out to be long. It is not long. Darkness descends with a sudden extinguishing sweep like the cover on the canary's cage. Energy ebbs, the heart contracts with fear. This is no time to be out in the streets, this is the hour of return, of the house, the hearth, the familiar ritual. *Alors, il s'est retiré dans son intérieur.*

The hotel room is desolate, the lamp dim. There is nothing then but the panicked dash for the clean, well-lighted places.

There are none. The current is wretched all over the city. The story goes that the last President's brother is still selling power across the border. There are no cafés, no pubs, only bars for men and huge pastry-shops. You do not dine before ten, unless you are willing to eat waffles in a pharmacy got up like a mosque at Sanborn's astonishing emporium; the cinemas waste no money on illumination; there is going to be a concert on Friday week. . . . Some of the hotel bars are open to women. They are full of tourists and Mexicans emphatically without wives. Besides, this is not a good country to drink in: in daytime one does not want it at all, and at night one wants it too much.

We decide to have dinner at X's, a French restaurant that enjoys a reputation in the hemisphere. We push through the doors. One night in the early nineteen-thirties, a friend was good enough to take me to a restaurant in London which in its day had been a very famous restaurant indeed. The list of its patrons was literary and glamorous, the wine and cooking admirable; it had a speakeasy cachet. Our elders and betters had talked and drunk there through the nights of the First War when they were young and notorious; they had dined there in the 'twenties when they were well-known and middle-aged. It had had the honours of at least five contemporary novels. Let us call it Spisa's. I had never been there, and I believe it was my twentieth birthday, or the eve of my twentieth birthday. When we got to Spisa's the shutters were down, the dining-room was dark and the owner dying. I mean literally dying. Mr. S. was on his death-bed and the priest had just been. My friend was a face from the better days, so they were much touched to see her at this hour. She was also a Catholic. They took her in to Mr. S.'s where she stayed in prayer for some time. I was put into a parlour where an Austrian waiter and an Italian waiter were saying their rosaries.

I had no rosary, but the Italian waiter went and found me one. Later they would not let us go but insisted that we have our dinner. They sent out for some chops and lager from the pub in Charlotte Street and made us eat it in the dining-room. There was just one lamp lit above our table, otherwise it was quite dark. As we ate people came to us and whispered to my friend in Italian. I could see she had been weeping. Presently we walked home and later became quite unreasonably gay.

As E. and I pushed through X's swing doors, there was just one lamp lit above one table. The waiters stood huddled in gloom. I sank, into self-pity. I know it is futile to indulge in my regret that I came too late upon this earth to enjoy the pleasures of the table at Edwardian house parties, but to think what I missed in my own time— I have never been to the Chapon Fin at Bordeaux, I was too late for Voisin's at Paris, too late for Spisa's, and now too late for X of Mexico City. Then I pulled myself together: a fellow creature was dying; I still had no rosary but I was ready to pay such respects as I could.

A second lamp was lit with small effect above a second table, chairs were pushed back and one of those French menus, large as a poster, was laid before us decorously like a floral tribute. Service as usual? But no, the place was too preposterous: the lush, the darkness, the gloom; no funeral parlour in the U.S.A. could stay in business for a week with such an atmosphere. We had yet to learn that this was merely the regular nightly aspect of public eating-places all over the Republic.

I must try a Mexican wine. I order a bottle of something called Santo Tomás. When poured out, it looks quite black. I sniff before tasting, so the shock when it comes is not as devastating as it might have been. I yell into the darkness to have the bottle removed.

The head waiter shuffles up gracefully. "Anything wrong, Señora?"

"Taste it."

He does. His face stays serene. Sheer self-control.

"There is something very wrong with this bottle. Taste it again."

"? ? ? *es regular.*"

Regular? Cheap ink dosed with prune juice and industrial alcohol, as harsh on the tongue as a carrot-grater? Regular! What a country, what palates, what digestions. They refuse to change the Santo

Tomás for another bottle of Mexican wine—rather disobliging of them I thought then—but insist that we take an imported wine instead. I choose a Spanish claret, one of the Marqués de Riscal's honest *riojas*. It is good, but it costs ten shillings a bottle, which is too much to pay for one's glass or two at dinner in a wine country. Perhaps, it begins to dawn on me, Mexico is not a wine country. It was by nature and in God knows what fashion before the Conquest; then the Spanish dug up the vines, the idea being to import wine from Spain and charge duty. For the same reason they cut down the olive trees and forbade the culture of silk-worms. Oil, silk and wine were to New Spain what rum and tea were to Massachusetts and Maryland. After Independence, everybody was too busy murdering each other to plant vineyards and olive groves, and what is being produced now is only a new incentive to murder. Santo Tomás comes from some infernal valley in Baja California where the climate is so unsalubrious that the very grapes breed acid antidotes inside their skins. And what the Indios do not do to those grapes . . . Santo Tomás is the best wine in the Republic. For one thing it contains only a limited amount of syrup, and the vats are always rinsed after being scrubbed with turkey excrement. I learned to swallow my Santo Tomás, with a liberal admixture of water, like a man.

The service at X's is as regular as the lighting and the wine. To sit in the penumbra with nothing but death and Santo Tomás to occupy one's mind is unnerving. My cries rend the shadows for something to eat.

"Where is that *Terrine* we ordered? It must be ready."

"It is ready. But the Prawns-and-Rice are not."

"But we are having the *Terrine* first."

"Yes, the *Terrine* comes first, but the Prawns are not ready."

"We are not going to eat them at the same time. Please bring us the *Terrine* now."

"Señora: we must wait for the Prawns. Then you will eat the *Terrine* first."

"I mean first now, not first then."

"Yes, Señora, first. First in a little while."

"Will you please bring the Terrine *at once."*

"At your taste, Señora. I shall run to tell the chef to hurry up the Prawns."

We wait. Then the *Terrine* is brought over from the sideboard in the Stygian corner where it had been reposing, and here on its heels are the Prawns, sizzling. So much is clear now, everything is allowed to take its time but once your dinner is on its breathless way, there must be no pause. The custom must have ruined tempers and digestions. It is unfathomable, and it is bedrock.

WE HAVE BEEN TO THE PENSIÓN HERNANDEZ.

We were walking along Isabel la Católica, a smart street in the business quarter, when we had to do the equivalent of taking cover, we flattened ourselves against a wall to avoid being crushed by a train of mules carrying boulders; the mules were flattening themselves against us to avoid being barged into by a motor hearse that was avoiding a tram. The tram, tramlike, pursued its way; we fell backwards through a door into a patio. Above our heads, like the finger of providence, was a plate saying *HERNANDEZ Casa de Huéspedes.*

One is sometimes less intrigued by the future than by what the past might have held. "Let us go in," I said; "there may be letters."

The pensión was on the third floor. An old Indian, barefoot and very clean, conveyed without uttering a single word that he was entirely at a loss as to who we were and what we had come for. He edged us into a sombre parlour. In the exact centre of this apartment stood a large, brand-new sewing-machine. It was covered, like a concert grand, with a tapestried runner representing several phases of the life of Geneviva of Brabant in port-wine colours. On the runner was a vase with a neatly rounded bouquet made of artificial flowers and barbed wire. The remainder of the parlour was stocked like a cross between the votive chapel at Lourdes and a cupboard of Queen Victoria's presents. Everything was spotless. We spent a long time looking at water stoops, statues of the Virgin clothed in doll's dresses, bronze stags and leaning towers, and absolutely nothing happened. Then we opened the door. The Indian had gone. We began to walk downstairs. Something compelled us to look up. An exquisite apparition wrapped in a foulard dressing-gown, looking as though it had been kept pinned in the glass case for rather a number of years, was leaning over the banisters.

We started. It spoke.

"You are the friends of Guillermo's," it stated in Central European English.

We edged two steps down.

A second apparition from a butterfly collection appeared behind the first. "I was shaving."

"I adore New York," said the first.

"I thought it was bailiffs," said the second.

"Guillermo wrote to look you up," said the first.

We put a foot on the landing.

"Do you know Bubi von der Witzleben?" said the second.

"They should go to Taxco," said the first.

We had turned the landing. There was the door. We bolted.

The mules had passed. There was only an old man milking a goat into an empty tin of Campbell's Cream of Tomato, and a taxi. We took the taxi.

Concert at the Teatro Nacional. Virtuosi from the U.S.A. The National Orchestra. Brief Bach. Brahms. A contemporary suite, not brief at all, thumping with fiesta motives, failing to do for Mexico what Ravel does for Spain. The public is cosmopolitan provincial, like an afternoon audience at the Casino in Nice. At midnight, more stanzas of the national anthem are played than is usual elsewhere at such occasions. Then we disperse from the stuffy foyer into a remote and silent night, bitter as a night in the desert. On the pavement hundreds of Indios are curled in sleep.

The city has many open squares in which markets are continuously held and the general buying and selling proceeds. . . . There are barber-shops where you may have your hair washed and cut. There are other shops where you may obtain food and drink. There are street porters such as there are in Spain to carry packages. There is a great quantity of wood, charcoal braziers made of clay, mats of all sorts, some for beds and others more finely woven for seats, still others for furnishing halls and private apartments. All kinds of vegetables may be found there, in particular onions, leeks, garlic, cresses, water-cress, borage, sorrel, artichokes, and golden thistles. There are many different sorts of fruit, including cherries and plums. They sell honey obtained from bees. . . . All kinds of cotton threads in various colours may be bought in skeins. . . . A great deal of china-ware is sold, including earthenware jars of all sizes for holding liquids, pitchers, pots, tiles and an infinite variety of earthenware all made of very special clay and almost all decorated and painted in some way. Maize is sold both as grain and in the form of bread. . . . Pasties are made from game and fish pies may be seen on sale and there are large quantities of fresh and salt fish both in their natural states and cooked ready for eating. Eggs from fowls, geese, and all others may be had, and likewise omelets ready made.

The last paragraph was written in 1520. It is part of a letter by Cortez to the Emperor Charles V on the Aztec capital as he found it on his first entry as a guest of Montezuma's. The description still serves.

When I join E., I find her at a table with a stranger and some bacardies.

"S., S.," she cried across the room, "this kind lady from Ponkah City wishes to know whether she should visit the Pyramid of the Moon?"

We end up all three eating the rather rustic luncheon—rice and pork, chickpeas and goat, and such portions—the Ritz serves for seven pesos in a tight, gilded back parlour.

Ribera's frescoes in Cortez' Palace are hard, flat and huge. The figures are flat, static and huge; the colours flat and drab. They are as narrative as the illustrations to the rhyme sheet, but without innocence. They have a dead serious over-emphasis that results not in power but in boredom. The subject is a pageant of Mexican history culminating in the Apotheosis of the Revolution, a kind of Dialectical Last Judgment, one of the many remarkable features of which is the five times life-size figure of the wife of Carlos Marx standing almost haloed among the elect with the tool-bearing worker and the sheaf-laden peasant, while the Señora Doña María-Carmen Romero Rubio Díaz hovers on the other side in murky shadow with bankers and the members of the upper clergy.

"Can you make me a pair of these sandals?"
"No, Señora."
"I mean, can you make me a pair of these sandals?"
"No, Señora."
"But you do make sandals?"
"Yes, Señora."
"Then why can't you make me a pair?"

"I made sandals yesterday."

"That's no reason."

"It is, Señora. I have got all I need."

"All you need? You're not going to retire on yesterday's sandals?"

"Who knows, Señora? I have all I need now."

The note of fear again.

The rains were late to-day and I was caught by them and darkness, alone and far from the shop-lit streets of the centre. One was aware of the presence of silent people sitting in doorways. Nothing happened, but I was seized by such a sense of desolation that several times I broke into a run. Once I thought that I had lost my way. I made the hotel and E. in the state of a person reaching shelter from a panic. It was half past eight in the evening.

Homage to D. H. L.

"We have had a letter from Anthony," said E. "It is his vacation. He's going to join us."

"How nice."

"He's coming out to Mexico City by air."

"We must wait for him."

"Of course, we must."

"Of course."

It appears that we have been called upon by Rosenkranz and Guildenstern.

"Do make some sense out of the porter," said E.

The porter said there were two gentlemen and these were their names.

We find their cards in our rooms upstairs.

> *Freiherr Karl-Heinz-Horst von Rautenburg zu Landeck*
> *Baron Guenther von der Wildenau-Schlichtleben*

"Golly," said I. "Pensión Hernandez."

"The long louche arm of Guillermo," said E.

"What do they want?"

"We shall see," said E.

———

Already a week in Mexico City. One entire day we were gated by the housekeeper. Not exactly polling day, but some kind of recount of a previous election we gathered, perhaps incorrectly, from the papers.

"Yes, yes, an *eleccioncita,* a tiny election. It is of no matter," said the housekeeper.

But why should we not go out? Was it not safe?

"Yes, safe. Very safe. Safe as safe. Only a little shooting. Quite safe. *But it is better to stay in.*"

On the day the massive front door of the hotel stayed barred and bolted. The hotel has no restaurant, nevertheless from dawn to dusk our detention was enlivened by a succession of trays—sandwich trays and cold meat trays, fruit and cake trays, tea trays, trays with covered dishes and chafing dishes, trays piled with tiered triple boilers balancing casseroles, until one could no longer tell snack from meal. We were never charged for these treats. We did not hear any shooting. Next morning the housekeeper told us that there had been a few dead, one hundred? two hundred? just a small election.

Other days pass in a rhythm of going out and exhausted return to the cool, flower-scented peace of the patio. Outside everything is just a bit too near, too loud, too much. One is always pressed upon, there is always something to dodge—the beggars, the insane traffic, the sun, pineapples cascading off a stall.

The Baedeker round is quickly done.

Palace and Cathedral are vast Spanish Colonial edifices conceived in ambition and the high if interested purposes of the Counter-Reformation, and built with rather more than the usual deal of delay through low funds, change of policy and volcanic tremor. The Paseo de la Reforma, Maximilian and Carlota's Champs-Elysées, casts a dank Victorian pall, dispiritedly *dépaysé* with its unbending line of tropical trees mercilessly clipped à la française. The Gallery has its Rubens (a religious subject), its Murillo, "what," I am quoting *Terry,* "is believed by many to be a genuine Titian," cracked and darkened portraits of Spanish gentlemen with heads like Spanish Gentlemen painted by El Greco, many battle-pieces and room upon roomful of Schools. The Museum has the Aztec Calendar Stone, an assortment of sacrificial stones of all sizes and a large collection of imp-faced deities, but Pre-Columbian sculpture can be seen bigger and better in Oaxaca and at the British Museum.

Yes, the show-pieces on the itinerary are numbered and on the whole disappointing. But how much there is to see. Everywhere. No need, no point, to plan and rush, only to stand, to stroll and stare; to connect. Not great beauty, not the perfect proportions, the slow-grown, well-grown balance (you will never be further from Greece), not the long-tended masterpiece of thought and form, the tight French gem, but the haphazard, the absurd, the over-blown, the savage, the gruesome. The fantastic detail and the frightening vista; the exotically elegant; the vast, the far, the legendarily ancient.

Everywhere. In the thoroughfare where the baby mule is born; by the fountain in the cool courtyard of the Spanish merchant's house where the Churrigueresque façade is gently weather-worn like a half-wiped slate; in the Street of the False Door of Saint-Andrew where two lovely, epicene young workmen are weaving a custom-made cage of soft twigs for a waiting parrot; in the lobby of the Ritz where of a Sunday morning Creole business-men sit, heavily powdered, missals on their laps, discussing fat deals.

The Church of the Assumption of María Santísima, the Cathedral of Mexico City, the Archiepiscopal See of the Distrito Federal, the Holy Metropolitan Church of Mexico, the Patriarchal Basilica of the Americas, *l'Iglesia Mayor,* the First Christian Church on American Soil, is dense from sunrise to nightfall with a religious rabble, the vagrant camp-followers of holy shrines, prostrate, agape, chanting, swaying, scraping on their knees, hugging images with oriental intensity—mindless, far-gone, possessed, separate and at one, unarrestable, frightening to the pitch of panic.

The City is full of bookshops, large recent establishments stocked with cheap, well-turned-out paper editions of *David Copperfield, Le Père Goriot, The Mill on the Floss, Point Counter Point.* The showcases are stuffed with the translated editions of Stephan Zweig, Emily Brontë and Professor Sigmund Freud. Who buys them? One quarter of the people cannot read. Another quarter can only read laboriously. Every grown-up, who can, is supposed by law to teach his letters to one illiterate grown-up a year. The question is often what letters. The current language is Spanish, but there are still two million Mexicans who speak only one of sixty different pre-Columbian tribal dialects. In the State of Sonora, they do not even use Arabic or Roman numerals, but a system they invented on their own.

I bought a Manual of Conversation. In the section headed *Useful Words and Phrases,* I find on page one:

"Are you interested in death, Count?"

"Yes, very much, your Excellency."

One of the happiest places in this town is a room of early nineteenth-century Creole genre paintings in the Chapultepec Museum. These graceful pictures of hummingbird, butterfly and country life (unusual subjects of inspiration in Latin America) are quite unlike anything one has ever seen, luxuriant but domestic, naïve and worldly, fresh, faintly absurd, wholly delicious. Young women in striped silk on a verandah mocked by a lemur, a muslin dress shimmering through magnolia trees, fruit like flowers and flowers like birds, give intimations of a better world. One can hear the leaf fans rustling through the afternoon, soft sucking of bare feet on patio tiles, ice clinking in punch glasses. . . .

But here, too, the other note is sounded. There is a picture of a small boy led by a governess through a most peculiar garden of sugar cane and coffee bush, followed by a curly lap dog and an Indian boy carrying his doll, a neatly dressed and bonneted baby skeleton.

There are three active volcanoes in the valley, all within easy lava-throw of the City. Popocatépetl, Iztaccihuatl, Xinantecatl — monsters in name and size, fragile in appearance; Japanese contoured shapes of pastel blue and porcelain snow, and three thin formal curls of smoke afloat in a limpid sky. There is also an unobtrusive mound, a tiny volcano now quiescent, Peñon, which according to the geolo gists will one day destroy the City.

In the spaces of the Plaza Mayor, walking over the grave of a pyramid, one is assailed by infinity, seized at the throat by an awful sense of the past stretching and stretching backwards through tunnels of time. . . . Can this be Here, can one be in it? One is in a legend, one is walking in Troy.

THE TOURIST ROUTE

ROSA E. KING

The Revolution comes to Cuernavaca, 1910

"THE ONLY WAY I KNEW TO STOP THE
DEPREDATION WAS TO GO TO SEE ZAPATA
THE CHIEF, AND INSIST ON MY RIGHTS AS AN
ENGLISHWOMAN."

*A young Englishwoman named Rosa King first went to Cuernavaca in
1905 with her husband. Two years later she returned as a widow, "a
woman alone, with my way to make, and two young children waiting in
Mexico City, depending on me." Never having worked before, and with
little money and only one servant, she opened a tearoom in a street just
off the zócalo. Cuernavaca even then had large British and American colonies, and tourists visited regularly, staying at the town's two "modern"
hotels, the Bella Vista and the Morelos opposite. These were the years of
the Díaz dictatorship, a period of placidity and prosperity . . . for all
those who were already rich and powerful. Rosa King and her tea shop
were well situated in every way, and she prospered.*

*She soon discovered that tourists would buy crafts from her at twice
what she paid in the market (without even haggling over prices with the
artisans), and her business grew still more. By 1910 she was able to buy
the Hotel Bella Vista, a handsome sixteenth-century structure with gardens and fountains, where she herself had first stayed in Cuernavaca.*

She refurbished and redecorated it, enhancing the provincial graciousness of the old hacienda, and the formal opening, on Saturday evening, June 9, 1910, was the social event of the Cuernavaca season. Everyone who was anyone stayed at or visited the Bella Vista, and that summer was a whirl of excitement amid the concerts and dances she organized.

With an election coming up, in which Francisco I. Madero would oppose Díaz, Mexico was preparing to celebrate the one-hundredth anniversary of its independence. On the Centenary, September 16, the parades, the fireworks, and the gala balls in Mexico City were splendid indeed. But it was the end of the party. Decades of dictatorship and oppression finally had to be paid for. Within months of the celebrations, blood had been shed, Díaz was running for his life, Madero was leading a ragged army on Mexico City, and a Guerrero Indian named Emiliano Zapata was stirring up the peones in the hills around Cuernavaca.

Both Rosa King and the Bella Vista survived all the years of revolution. Anita Brenner's 1935 guide calls the Bella Vista "one of the nicer oldish Mexican hotels," and MacKinley Helm's 1948 guide praises the "spacious Hotel Bella Vista, whose cocktail terrace faces the municipal bandstand and surrounding garden." The hotel, with fifty rooms, was still in operation as late as 1965. In later years, after she sold it, Rosa King stayed on as a resident, receiving visits from hundreds of old friends and newcomers alike.

She told the story of her years in Cuernavaca in Tempest over Mexico, published in 1935. I own a copy of this book that she signed for visitors in 1948. In a rather tremulous hand, she inscribed it, "From Lovely Cuernavaca."

☀ "QUICKLY CLOSE EVERYTHING, SEÑORA KING! The fierce Zapata is coming, killing and destroying everything in his path!"

It was one of the leading men of the town who stood panting in my *portal.* "The rebels met our garrison at Cuautla, and cut it to pieces. Only a handful of troops are left to tell the tale; you will see them limping in."

Wounded, on foot, tied up in old rags they came—the remnant of Cuernavaca's invincible garrison. Most of the men would never have made the thirty miles from Cuautla if it had not been for the help of their women, who had pushed them and dragged them along. The doors of the townsfolk were closed to them. With the fierce Zapata coming, the people no longer knew the Federals and the belligerent *soldaderas* who cared for them. In the end we foreign women, who had nothing to fear from either side, sent out coffee and bandages. An American named Robinson, a mining engineer, went out to the crest of a hill at the entrance to the town to await the approach of Zapata, and to assure him and his ally Asúnsolo, both of whom were known to him personally, that no further resistance would be made.

I was more interested than alarmed myself, but it occurred to me that the American lady who was running my tearoom for me was alone with two pretty daughters, and might be frightened. I sent word for her and her daughters to come over to the Bella Vista, and together we stood at the window to watch the Revolution enter Cuernavaca.

No Cæsar ever rode more triumphantly into a Roman city than did the chief, Zapata, with Asúnsolo at his side, and after them their troops—a wild-looking body of men, undisciplined, half-clothed, mounted on half-starved, broken-down horses. Grotesque and obsolete weapons, long hidden away or recently seized in the pawnshops, were clasped in their hands, thrust through their belts, or slung across the queer old saddles of shapes never seen before. But they rode in as heroes and conquerors, and the pretty Indian girls met them with armfuls of bougainvillea and thrust the flaming flowers in their hats and belts.

There was about them the splendor of devotion to a cause, a look of all the homespun patriots who, from time immemorial, have left the plough in the furrow when there was need to fight. I thrilled with the remembrance that Don Miguel Hidalgo y Costilla, the father of Mexican independence, had led an army equipped with weapons as crude as bars of iron, shovels, and pitchforks.

All afternoon the wild-looking bands rode in. At six o'clock we heard shots and screams and feared that fighting had begun among them. Instead we found that the shots were fired in jubilation: the prison doors in the old palace had been opened and all the prisoners set free; political prisoners, murderers—all free! I shall never forget those men and women as they ran like hunted animals past my house seeking cover. In the old days they would have been shot as they ran, and they still believed they must be targets.

The generals had closed all places of drink, so far as they could, knowing that their men would be unmanageable if permitted to become intoxicated. A pathetic band of eight or ten pieces played that night in the Zócalo to excited throngs—strange music on unheard-of instruments, sometimes wailing, sometimes riotous with a tumultuous sweetness, and again harsh and discordant. They played the wailing of four centuries of wrong that had been done them, and the awakening of justice. It was music to those savage men and to those who loved the cause for which they fought; but as I listened I shivered a little, and I was glad that I was an Englishwoman and this was not my Revolution.

Two days later I was forced into contact with the Revolutionists to protect the little factory I had established at San Anton. Much to my indignation, I heard that the men were sacking it.

The only way I knew to stop the depredation was to go to see Zapata the chief, and insist on my rights as an Englishwoman. I told my manager, Willie Nevin, what I meant to do, and added, "You must come with me as interpreter."

Willie Nevin was aghast, and at first refused to accompany me; but I insisted. I know now that it was only ignorance that gave me courage.

When we reached the military headquarters, the troops pointed their rifles directly at me, and at trembling Willie behind me, and while many of the guns were antiquated there were plenty, taken from the Federals at Cuautla, that looked as if they would shoot—and straight. I knew so little Spanish that I could only make them understand I wished to enter by parting their rifles right and left with my hands and saying firmly *"Jefe,"* which I knew meant "Chief." They allowed me to enter, but stared at a woman who dared to face them in this manner. Perhaps it was their very amazement that made them let me pass to Zapata's quarters. But my efforts to see him were in vain; the beloved general was sleeping, and could not be disturbed.

By this time the succession of guns and savage looks I had been meeting was having its effect on me, and my knees were trembling. I knew, however, that I must hold my own or my prestige was gone, and without that I could do nothing in Cuernavaca. On I marched, with Willie still behind me, to find the next chief, General Asúnsolo. We climbed upstairs in the old barracks to the room a young Indian pointed out with his rifle. To my surprise the room was perfectly clean, the bed spotless, order and neatness on every hand—something I knew to be unusual with an army on campaign. The man who received me addressed me courteously—in English. It was General Asúnsolo himself.

From the time I met General Asúnsolo I had no more fear. Asúnsolo was different from the grim, determined Indians about him, more like the men to whom I was accustomed. He was, oddly enough, a young man of aristocratic family, educated in the United States of America, and full of life and the love of American "ragtime" "jazz," they call it now. He had joined the Revolution for the adventure, I think, and because he thought it likely to succeed.

His mere presence in the Revolutionary army was reassuring to me. When I told him my trouble he said courteously, "The raids on your factory shall end at once, Señora King," and he kept his promise. Nor did his kindness end there, for I could not have wished better care than was taken of me and my property during the six weeks he was in Cuernavaca with his troops.

One little incident occurred about this time which, if I had taken it more seriously, might have suggested to me that the peace and order we were enjoying depended on a very delicate balance between explosive elements.

I was sitting on the verandah one evening after dinner with the two pretty American girls, the daughters of the American lady who had taken over the tearoom for me. We were watching the antics of the invaders, who were amusing themselves in the plaza. To our surprise, one of the Indians suddenly came over and sat down next to the elder of the two girls. He was a young fellow, hung with pistols, and with very little clothing on under the three or four cartridge belts that covered his body.

The girl was too frightened to say anything. My indignation was tremendous. I went over to the boy and told him to move at once, thinking my size, as I am quite tall, would quell him. To my great wonder he simply turned around and said, "Oh, no, madam, these are different times. The *peon* is now the master." The girl translated for me.

My English blood was boiling. It was all I could do to refrain from knocking him off the chair. Instead, however, I went to some Mexicans who were sitting near by and asked their help. One of them, a young doctor, promptly took the Indian by the neck and threw him out of his seat. The boy, on the floor, pulled a pistol.

Luckily for us, at this moment two or three other soldiers, who had seen the trouble from the plaza across the street, seized their companion-in-arms and held him fast. I do not know which of us the boy meant to shoot, and I do not think he much cared, but it probably would have been me because of my interference.

When the soldiers had been told what happened they carried off the boy as a prisoner to General Asúnsolo, the man I had made my friend. The general sent word at once to ask if I would like to have an example made of him; if so, he would have him shot that night or in the morning. This message alarmed me more than the boy had. I sent word please not to do anything quite so desperate, just keep him locked up for two or three days. I had not been living among and observing these people without learning a little about them, and I realized that what the boy had done had been occasioned simply by his elation over the glory of his troops. Their victories had gone to his head. After he was released he came to me to apologize, and was soon made happy by the present of a little money. From that time on until Asúnsolo's troops left town, he acted as the personal guard for all of us at my house; and very good he was to us.

On the twelfth of June Mr. Madero, the presidential candidate who had led the movement to overthrow the dictatorship, came to Cuernavaca to confer with General Zapata, who had been fighting in his behalf. Zapata arranged a "review" in his honor, and we all turned out to see the show. We were not disappointed.

Surely, all the strength of the Zapatistas was kept for action, for they wasted none on uniforms or martial drill. Poor fellows, in their huge straw hats and white cotton *calzones,* with cotton socks in purple, pink, or green pulled outside and over the trouser legs. They were equipped with rifles of all sorts, and one poor little cannon. But even the cannon looked proud of being a follower of the brave leader, Emiliano Zapata. Among the troops were women soldiers, some of them officers. One, wearing a bright pink ribbon around her waist with a nice big bow tied in back, was especially conspicuous. She was riding a pony and looked very bright and pretty.

Treacherous little ribbon! It gave the game away, for it was soon seen by that vivid bit of color that the troops were merely marching around a few squares and appearing and reappearing before Don Francisco Madero. The pathetic attempt to please Madero by seeming stronger in numbers than they were was funny, but it was sad, too. Behind that sham was indomitable spirit. Mr. Madero's face, far from expressing any consciousness of the amazing reappearance of the same "battalions" in such quick succession, was perfectly impassive. He knew that passing before him was the embryonic power that would win the Revolution.

Shortly afterward the election took place which made Madero legally president, and he came a second time to Cuernavaca. It was rumored that Zapata would now be appointed governor of Morelos, and I for one was quite content with this prospect. Rough and untaught as his followers were, they had treated us with true kindness and consideration during their occupation of the town, and I had come to have confidence in their natural qualities. Since my friend Don Pablo Escandon had long ago resigned the governorship and left the country, the post was being temporarily filled by Mr. Carreón, the banker. One morning just before this second visit of Madero's, Mr. Carreón and a delegation of men appeared at my door to ask me to go to the railway station to meet the president elect, Don Francisco, and his wife when they arrived. I was surprised and rather pleased, and consented on condition that one or two of the American ladies in Cuernavaca go with me.

When the day came, the governor's carriage was sent for us, drawn by two most spirited horses. Now horses are one of the Mexican passions, and at this time they had a particular fascination for the Revolutionaries, because always before their possession had been limited to the ruling classes. For fear this fine pair would be seized by the Zapatistas, they had been kept upstairs in hiding, in a bedroom, for five or six weeks, and were so full of life they could hardly be driven. We passed through streets lined with Zapata's soldiers, and accustomed as I had become to these Indians, my heart rather failed me at the sight of them all together, with their heavy armament and their look of wild men of the woods.

When we reached the station the horses became very restive. General Emiliano Zapata, riding a beautiful horse, with his brother Eufemio beside him on another fine animal, gave the order for me to move.

I told him rather frankly that I would not move, as I had been requested by the governor of the state to await the arrival of Mr. and Mrs. Madero. He did not insist, but sat silent with his long sensitive fingers quiet on the reins; a graceful figure of a man, with a kind of natural elegance. He was swarthy, as the men of Cuautla are apt to be, with beautiful white teeth beneath the heavy black moustache, and he wore the *charro* suit of the ranchman, always neat even when made up, as his was, in coarse materials.

As I look back now on that scene—the calm assurance with which I stood firm upon a point of etiquette, and the simple manner in which the commanding general accepted my objections—it seems to mark an epoch in the Revolution. In later years I should probably have been shot for countermanding the orders of any chieftain. I do not believe that Zapata understood any more than I did, at this time, the full splendor of what he was doing, or that the day would come when, in the social emancipation of Mexico, he would stand third in rank after Hidalgo and Juárez.

The little black engine finally puffed its load of celebrities and soldiers into the station. As Mr. and Mrs. Madero stepped from their coach, there was a fusillade of shots from the soldiers on the train and an answering volley from the Zapatistas who lined the street. Both volleys were friendly salutes, but the horses who had drawn us in such stately fashion to the station apparently thought otherwise. Less considerate of our dignity than the general, they reared, bucked, and finally dashed for home and safety—the driver struggling with the reins and an Englishwoman and two Americans struggling to catch their breath.

Shortly after, President Madero and Zapata met again at Cuautla, and on this occasion the president gave our general the famous *abrazo*, perhaps as a seal of what we had already heard, that he had promised to make Zapata governor of the state as evidence of his appreciation of all Zapata had done for the Madero cause. An *abrazo* is an embrace between two men who are considered true friends. The confidence between the leaders which this act implied promised peace for Cuernavaca, and when I heard the news, I said to myself, "The Revolution is over." I was equally pleased with the success of the Revolutionary movement and with the quick, rather orderly fashion in which the turnover had been accomplished.

But I spoke too soon. If the promise was made to Zapata, it was not kept; for the coveted office of governor was given to General Ambrosio Figueroa.

From this time on our troubles began in the State of Morelos. The Zapatistas swooped down on trains whenever and wherever they could. They galloped over the rich fields, destroying crops and millions of dollars' worth of machinery imported from England and the United States; and woe to the *administradores* of the *haciendas* when they tried to resist the onslaught.

I was vexed rather than alarmed by the turn affairs had taken. We were safe in Cuernavaca, as Zapata had moved out of the town some time before his break with Madero, and the new governor, Figueroa, and his troops were well established among us. Yet we were inconvenienced by the raids in the outlying country. Traveling became unsafe and few people ventured far from home. My hotel business, which had already declined because of unsettled conditions, suffered still more. At the same time, I simply did not believe what the newspapers said, that the Zapatistas, who had lived among us so peaceably for weeks, had turned overnight into villainous desperadoes. Beneath their quite terrifying exteriors, the Zapatistas had seemed to me more like harmless and valiant children than anything else, and this sudden burst of destructiveness seemed to me a childish reaction to the slight they had suffered.

I know now that there was something more behind their defiance.

Victim of the *hacendados*, Emiliano Zapata had been constantly exasperated by the landowners, who reigned with all the despotism of feudal lords over the *peones* and working classes of the rural population. His personal experiences had inspired in him an ideal— "Land and Liberty" for the downtrodden Indian—which was perfectly clear to him, and which his followers comprehended to an extent that preserved their faith in their leader through all the strife that followed. The new governor, Figueroa, was himself an *hacendado,* the owner of great tracts of land in the State of Guerrero; and Zapata doubtless felt that such a man would not help the people of Morelos to realize their dream.

Personally, I liked our shy, serious young governor and believed him sincere. I think that he, like Madero, was a man of wealth who recognized his obligation to improve the lot of the masses. Looking back, it is easy to see that President Madero made a crucial blunder in passing by Zapata, and that this was the first of the rifts in the Revolutionary Party which later brought ruin on Madero and on the rest of us. But at this time Zapata was an almost unknown Indian, whose genius for leadership had not yet blazed forth to its full extent, and it is not surprising that the president should have believed Figueroa better suited for authority. We all regretted that the new governor's first official job was the unpleasant one of putting down the men of the state.

For the rest, life in Cuernavaca took on a new interest.

The townspeople sympathized covertly with the Zapatistas, but were too sensible to say so openly. Though the disorders in our vicinity were very bad for my own business, since the hotel depended on transients, the town had never been so prosperous before as it was with six thousand Federal soldiers spending their pay. The newspapers talked constantly about the bravery of these troops and how the ragged rebels fled when they met them. The trouble was that the ragged rebels ran only as far as the nearest shelter, from behind which they sniped the Federals; and a good deal of fun was made of the professional soldiers behind their backs because they could never quite stamp out this guerrilla warfare. Figueroa was eventually recalled because he could not catch Zapata, and a succession of military commanders followed him.

We were very gay. The commanding general and his staff always stayed at the Bella Vista, and when the officers were not out fighting, they were dancing or drinking or gambling, and our quiet country town had never seen the like of it. I often wished for the old peaceful times and quieter civilian guests, but it was diverting to watch the antics of these reckless young blades.

They thought it great luck to be on campaign again, after it had seemed almost sure that the Revolution was over and there was nothing ahead of them but a long, dull stretch of peace-time service. They played harebrained jokes on each other, and quarreled endlessly about the superiority of their favorite horses. They were all inordinately vain of their horsemanship, which was superb, and how they would make a horse prance when a pretty girl was looking! More alarming were the disputes they had about their marksmanship, for these were apt to end in a hasty, impromptu shooting match, when the bullets might take off the neck of the bottle set up at so many paces, and then again might miss it altogether.

They were always respectful and deferential to me, and took to calling me *"mamacita"* (little mother). This flattered and pleased me, in spite of the fact that I was not old enough to be their mother; for Mexican boys are devoted sons, and I knew they were paying me their highest compliment. I let them pour out their troubles to me, and tried to help them when I could.

Looking back, it always makes me happy to remember that even at this time my favorite among them was Captain Federico Chacón, who later turned out to be the best friend I had, and to whom I owe my life many times over. Federico Chacón was an upstanding, swashbuckling fellow from the north, who looked just like an American and was always being taken for one, which half disgusted and half pleased him. I was always scolding him about his bad habits— for he had them all!—but I think he liked this, for no one had ever troubled before to tell him why things should be done or not done from the standpoint of ethics. At any rate, he would listen very attentively. When I tried to explain to him that too much indulgence in some kinds of enjoyment was to enjoy life only in a small way, and that there was much more in life to live for, he said he would try to be more serious. But this was so hard for him, and he was such a fine, generous person with it all, that I really felt better when he slipped now and again into his old ways, after which he would return to apologize and ask for forgiveness.

I recall one day when I was sitting in my *portal* with a sedate, elderly British couple, who were feeling very adventurous because they had made the trip to Cuernavaca in spite of the raids of the Zapatistas in our district. Across the way, in the *portal* of the Hotel Morelos, Chacón sat drinking with a group of other men. Suddenly, as we sat idly watching them, a fight began. Over went a gentleman I recognized as a judge of the town. Chacón's driving shoulders thrust about in the midst of the tangle; a moment more and he had bowled over all five of them. He came striding out of the arcade, shaking himself like a big dog—head up, the way he always walked. "By Jove, I can't help liking that man," said the mild-mannered gentleman at my side. "Do you think he'd come over and talk to us?"

I beckoned to Federico and he sat down with us and chatted over a *copita*—a small glass of cognac. Nothing that was said by him or anyone else made any particular impression on me. The noteworthy thing about that conversation was the blank stare with which Federico greeted me the next morning when I recalled it. He had been so drunk all the time that he had no recollection whatever of the fight or what had followed.

Lively as Cuernavaca was with the *militares* in possession, it was hardly the setting I should have chosen for my young daughter. Both my daughter and son were now in boarding schools. My son went to school in Canada, and as the Revolution later destroyed our railroad communication with the countries to the north of us, it was a long while before he was able to return, and he does not enter this story at all. My daughter's school was in Tennessee, and when she came home for vacation I had kept her with me, because it was my wish to take her to England shortly and place her in the school that I had gone to.

It never occurred to me that I should not soon be able to take a holiday. I had implicit confidence that at any moment the ragged handful of Zapatistas with their blundering methods, as the newspapers described them, would be finally overcome by the brave Federals. But I did begin to chafe at the way the fighting dragged on, delaying our departure. My daughter was hardly more than a child, by English or American standards, but a very pretty one—*la guerrita* (the little fair one), the officers called her; and I did not want her head turned.

For this reason, I was glad when they told me that Mexico City had determined to end the struggle. One of the best generals in the republic had been ordered to Cuernavaca and Zapata's fate was sealed.

One afternoon I heard a spirited firing of rifles, and saw from my window that the soldiers already stationed at Cuernavaca and the troops of the incoming general were firing at one another. This was a habit they had, and there was no reason behind it, I was sure, except that there was always more or less jealousy among contending troops, even though fighting in the same cause, and always bitter rivalry between their chiefs. The firing continued and, looking out from a place of safety, I saw a man conspicuously apart, sitting on a very fine horse. He sat as though made of iron, without a motion of his body, his face without a smile, almost without expression, as careless of the bullets flying around him as though they were feathers.

I said to my manager, "Who is that man on the beautiful horse, who sits there in a shower of bullets with no more fear than if they were raindrops?"

"That," said Willie respectfully, "is General Victoriano Huerta. There's nothing he's afraid of."

Later, when they had desisted from their little pastime of fighting and killing each other—for General Huerta soon mastered the troops already with us, as he had good fresh horses and better rifles to help him—he was brought to my house and introduced to me. I knew so little about the politics of the day that I did not realize General Huerta was one of the most prominent men in the country, but it was plain to me that I had met a man of strong and decisive character.

General Huerta remained at the Bella Vista and it amused me to see the stiffening of the military morale when this dynamic leader took command. He allowed no laxness in his troops, but they adored him because he always led them to victory. He himself drank heavily, and nearly every evening had to be led off to bed; but he was always up in the morning bright and early, looking as though he were not even acquainted with the odor of drink.

I often saw him at breakfast and he would try to talk to me, telling me as much as he could of the state of affairs whilst we were peacefully eating *ciruelas*—the plums for which Cuernavaca is noted. The general and I were very fond of these plums and ate them every morning. Looking back, it seems a curious thing to me that this trivial taste that we shared should have played a part in the web of intrigue in which I later became entangled.

My Spanish was still so poor that I could not understand much that the general said, but I did make out that he always told me that he was going to capture Zapata.

The day the army was to set off on the crucial expedition, which required complete concentration of attention on the delicate manœuvrings that were planned, an American turned up who attempted to invite himself along. He said he had come from the American Embassy in Mexico City, which was true, but I hardly think his government can have known what he was up to.

General Huerta was not at all taken with the stranger, a foreigner, who came among us, it seemed, only from motives of inquisitiveness, to gratify a personal curiosity about how Mexicans conducted their military campaigns. But the American—shall we call him Mr. Smith?—was too self-complacent to perceive that behind the general's courtesy there was an astuteness that had penetrated the impertinence of his request. He was quite insensitive to the general's polite rebuff and graceful invitation to take himself off, and insisted on joining Huerta and his officers to find out where they were going.

General Huerta came over to me and said, "Oh, Señora King, I am sure Mr. Smith would like to hear of your experiences in Mexico. I know you will entertain him for me. Mr. Smith, will you sit here with Mrs. King? Be kind enough to take this chair."

I naturally wished to help General Huerta. I knew the nervous tension he must be under because of the character of his errand, and could understand how this intrusion was annoying him.

Mr. Smith, however, did not seem to find me very interesting. He was more intent on finding out what he was after than on talking to me. In a few minutes he got up and went back to the general.

General Huerta turned to him with the air of one who has just seen the light. "Ah, *señor*," he said, "you probably wish to ride out with us; do you not?"

Mr. Smith signified that that was his wish, and thought he had won his point and was going to be permitted to accompany the general and his officers on their campaign. General Huerta then turned to one of the officers and gave a rapid order for a horse to be brought. I did not understand what he said, but my manager, who could speak Spanish like a native, understood and said to me, "I am afraid they are going to play some trick on this man." I did not think it mattered much, as by his persistent intrusion where he was not welcome he had invited punishment.

A fine-looking horse was brought, with a handsome saddle. Mr. Smith went delightedly forward to mount, thinking surely he was to share the honors of the day. I then saw a spectacle such as I had never seen in my life. I do not understand how the man escaped alive. The horse bucked, jumping up and down, fore and aft, kicked, snorted, pawed the ground like a mad bull, stood on his hind feet pawing the air, stood on his tail and then on his head, leaped back and forth, flung himself right and left—made every frantic movement known to a horse mad from some unknown emotion. At last our man slid off, and indeed it was a mystery that he stayed on as long as he did.

Not a line of General Huerta's sphinx-like face changed. Without a smile he said, "My dear sir, I fear there is something wrong. I will have the horse unsaddled that we may see."

The saddle was removed in the presence of us all. Under the blanket were found three big thorns with which the horse was well pricked as soon as the man was in the saddle!

General Huerta's face was something never to be forgotten. A silent smile came over it—a thoughtful smile—even an innocent smile. But he only turned to me and said, "*Señora*, I do not think the gentleman will ride with us to-day."

It was all I could do to keep my laughter back, but it had to be done, for no one dared to make a sound or even to smile while the now abashed Mr. Smith went to his room, packed a valise, and left for Mexico City at the first opportunity. When will the foreigner learn that a Mexican's politeness can be as final as an American's curt "Get out!"

Whether or not this annoying incident had taken the edge off the general's keenness to start on the expedition, I do not know; but he took a drink and another drink. The troops were kept standing all that day in the pouring rain. When night came on, I could stand it no longer and sent out great pots of coffee to warm the poor fellows. Finally, at daybreak, General Huerta got over his intoxication and was able to mount his horse. The troops moved off—artillery, infantry, and cavalry—to comb the mountains in search of Zapata.

I had got up to see them go, and as General Huerta said goodbye he assured me that he would be back in two or three days with the prisoner on exhibition.

He did return in a few days, but not with the prisoner as he had expected. I found out that he had actually succeeded in surrounding Zapata and his forces and was on the verge of closing in when a sharp order had come to him from President Madero to return at once with his troops to Mexico City. Huerta was very, very angry and like an Indian swore revenge on Madero. He felt he had been made a fool of. We all trod cautiously in the face of his wrath and hoped that it would blow over. I marveled at the incredible innocence of Mr. Madero, who seemed to think he could play fast and loose with men like this. He had made a foe of Zapata by just such an about-face, and now, to save Zapata, he had perhaps made a foe of the more formidable Huerta. But it never occurred to me that the relations of these two men would affect me personally.

General Huerta was his usual bland self when he left for Mexico City. "Never fear, Señora King," he said as he shook hands, "that the music will stop in the Zócalo because I am taking away my fine band that you like so much. I have given orders, and you shall have music every night as before." And indeed, whether this was the reason or not, from that time on, even when things were worst, a band played every night in the plaza.

We hoped that Huerta's serenity was a good omen, but I can see now that it was more likely the calm of resolution; and I myself believe that the seed had then taken root in him which later bore bloody fruit.

The evidence of a weak hand and a vacillating will in the capital did not help our situation in Cuernavaca. The morale of the soldiers was impaired by the suspicion that the government was not squarely behind them in their campaign. Some of them deserted and went over to the Zapatistas. The Zapatistas raided with new boldness and confidence, closer to the town. Our newspapers continued to print the usual reassuring accounts, but I could not help noticing that less was coming into the markets; which meant that surrounding villages were being cut off.

A charcoal seller who was a Zapatista, and perhaps a spy, said to me one day, "*Señora,* they always say we are running away and being killed, but they do not tell how many we catch and kill when we are hiding in places where we can shoot on them." This was translated to me in a significant tone by Willie Nevin, my manager, his eyes frightfully crossed as they would become when he was upset.

Although the Federal officers who lived at my hotel continued to be courteous and affable to me, I could see that the campaign was being pushed harder. None of the succession of generals who followed Huerta seemed able to cope with the wily Zapata and his constantly growing bands of untrained Indians. The rebels knew all the mountains and *barrancas* and shot from ambush. The skilled tactics of the Federals were useless against this kind of guerrilla warfare, and the ease with which the rebels picked off their comrades seemed to madden the Federal soldiers. They burned the crops that sustained the rebels and the houses or huts that sheltered them, and shot in their turn at anyone wearing the white *calzones* of the *peon*. Zapata's men not only fought; they had, in between, to work to provide for their families, cultivating their patches of corn and beans. My friend Federico Chacón told me how many of these men were surrounded by Federals while thus working unprotected in the fields. They were made prisoners and driven to the nearest towns, where they were forced to dig their own graves before they were shot—if one can call "graves" the holes into which their bodies were thrown.

Long afterward, in Cuautla, a mason who was working for me told me how the Federals, in the name of the Revolutionary government, had come unexpectedly upon the little piece of ground his father owned, and had shot his father dead before his eyes and his mother's, and then set fire to their poor hut, all to steal the corn they had planted. He and his mother fled, hiding in the fields and woods, anywhere for safety, until they could find Emiliano Zapata, the protector and avenger. The boy was only fifteen at the time, but his father lay dead and his home was in ruins. The Zapatistas gave him a gun. "With my gun in hand and hatred in my heart, I killed and destroyed wherever I could," he told me.

One day I had occasion to go up to Mexico City with my daughter Vera. We were going on the military train, since regular trains were often attacked in the mountains. As I stood looking at the soldiers who filled the first car and bristled on the roofs and running boards of all the cars, and on the cow-catcher, I wondered whether the sight of such an escort aroused in me a feeling of security or of greater trepidation. Just then a young colonel I knew came up and proudly invited me to see some prisoners he had captured.

Never shall I forget the sight of those poor wretches standing tied together, not one uttering a word; looking like the farmers they were, caught unprotected in their *milpas*.

"The only way we can quiet down Morelos," explained the colonel, "is to ship out these Zapatistas. If we break up families doing it—well, our families have lost their husbands and fathers, too. I tell you, *señora,* when these warlike rebels find themselves a thousand miles from home with nothing to eat and no place to go, among people who speak a different dialect, they will not be so brave!"

"Oh," I said, trembling with indignation, "how can you be so cruel? How can you teach them to respect the government if you are not better than they?"

The soldiers were hustling the poor wretches into a cattle box car, pushing them in till there was not even standing room. They boarded up the doors and nailed them shut. Vera turned away and would not look, but I had seen in the car an Indian who had worked for me for four or five years, faithfully, and I began to protest very bitterly.

"They will smother, Colonel Lugo, before they reach their destination!" I cried, with a kind of presentiment—for four or five in that car were later found dead, among them Pepe, my servant.

The colonel shrugged and turned away. "Orders," he said briefly.

Down the way I saw the commander, General Robles, inspecting the guard on the train. He lived at my house, and a few days before, on my birthday, he had commanded the military band to play in the dawn, beneath my windows, the softly swelling "Mañanitas"—the birthday serenade.

I rushed up to him. "Oh, General Robles," I said, tears streaming down my face, "you don't know what they're doing. Make them let those poor people go."

To my horror, he smiled. "Now, now, *señora,*" he chided indulgently, patting my arm, "you must not take it so hard. You are only a woman and you do not understand these things. Why, I am trying to clean up your beautiful Morelos for you. What a nice place it will be once we get rid of the *Morelenses!* If they resist me, I shall hang them like earrings to the trees."

And being what they are, the people of Morelos did resist his will to wrench them from their beloved soil. The women cooled and reloaded the guns and scoured the country for food for the fighting men, and old people and young children endured the hardships of their lot without complaint. The Zapatistas were not an army; they were a people in arms.

Those of the rebels he caught, General Robles strung up on the trees, where their companions could see them, and the passengers on the trains that passed that way. My daughter and I often saw the sickening sight of bodies swinging in the air. At that high altitude they did not decompose, but dried up into mummies, grotesque *things* with the toes hanging straight down in death and hair and beard still growing. We thought at first we could not live among such sights; but, as I look back, I realize that the worst part of all was that in time we grew hardened to them and they no longer bothered us.

The savage persecution by the Federals, who seemed to have lost all sight of the fact that they too were supposed to be Revolutionaries, champions of freedom and justice for all, turned the Zapatistas into fighting demons. Our newspapers lashed on the Federals with tales of atrocities committed by the rebels. I think this was largely propaganda, but if there was some truth in the tales, the acts were retaliation for the cruelty of the Federals, who should have known better, and if I had been one of those ignorant, hounded people, I think I should have acted as they did.

The rebel forces continued to grow, swelled by deserters from the government ranks, and Zapata raided to the very edge of the town. We were safe in the Bella Vista only because it was located in the very heart of the town. Willie Nevin's mother had long been begging him to leave Cuernavaca, and he now decided to accede to her wish I was left without a manager, which in itself was not so serious, as goodness knows I had little enough business in the hotel. I had shut down the tearoom altogether, the *militares* preferring stronger drinks than tea, and the pottery factory had been abandoned Nevertheless, there had been a certain comfort in knowing that a man of my own people was close at hand.

It was then that I began to appreciate the man that Chacon was. Hitherto I had regarded him more or less as a scapegrace one couldn't help liking. Now Federico constituted himself the protector of Vera and myself because, he said, I reminded him of his own mother; and I began to understand as never before that beneath his incorrigible gayety there was a steady loyalty and devotion that was not common. Nothing that would reassure us was too much trouble for him, but he carried off his little acts of kindness with a brusque nonchalance that was in itself a tonic.

One night when my drawing-room was full of people, we heard the sound of heavy firing alarmingly close, on the edge of the town.

Chacón received orders to start out with his men at once, and the other officers likewise prepared to join their troops. Before he left, Federico came to me hurriedly and said, "Mother"—he always called me "Mother" in English, not Spanish like the others—"Mother, play the piano and keep the women quiet; and remember, if we are driven back, wait for me, and I will take you and Vera to safety."

I sat down at the piano and played then, but I could see that my audience was only half listening. Their ears were strained to catch the crack of rifle fire that sounded when my swelling chords sank to *pianissimo*. Nearly all the men had gone to fight, and what I saw before me was a group of women, forlorn and frightened-looking. One superb brunette, however, stood at the window and looked down the street, dramatically fingering the crucifix she wore about her neck. "Doña Luz is going to be tragic!" I thought. "She will upset the few who still are calm, and throw the others into a panic." I knew I had to think quickly.

"Heavens, ladies," I rallied them, "how dismal you look! Your men have only gone to fight; one would think they were courting other girls! Come, let us try to be gay by ourselves, or they will find out how much we miss them. . . . Señora García, Señorita Mendoza"—I was dragooning the timidest—"come sing for us! Doña Luz, we need your rich contralto."

As the sound of shooting grew louder, I demanded more spirit of my chorus. The songs I played grew "louder and funnier," as the Americans say. Finally I swung into the joyous "Jarabe Tapatío," and the rollicking strains of the national dance brought all of them out on the floor in an impromptu, helter-skelter *baile* (dance).

All the while I was thinking that if Federico lived, he would come back for Vera and me and take us to safety, no matter how difficult that might be. But thanks to God's goodness, it was the enemy that was driven back after three hours of hard fighting.

Another day, when there was fighting on the outskirts of the town, the Zapatistas galloped past my windows shouting their blood-curdling cry "*Mueran los gachupines!*" (Death to the Spaniards)—a class to them, as much as a nationality, whom they held responsible for their suffering.

Chacón was out with his troops and I did not know where to turn. I called a servant, Julio, who looked braver than the rest, and placed him close to my daughter and me with a pistol in his hand.

I told him to fire if the enemy came, while Vera and I ran out the back way.

To our great relief, however, the Zapatistas did not return. When Federico came home I told him how frightened I had been, but what presence of mind I had shown. I brought out the pistol I had found for Julio to use in our defense. Federico pretended to be much impressed and stretched out his hand for the pistol, which he had seen before. His laughter was good to hear when he showed me that it was empty.

But after that, I kept the pistol loaded.

WILLIAM SPRATLING
Taxco, 1930s

"MANY OF THE BEST-RUN SILVER SHOPS IN TAXCO
HAVE BEEN SET UP BY SILVERSMITHS WHO HAVE
BEEN ENCOURAGED BY DETACHED AMERICAN
WOMEN."

*Americans began coming to Taxco in the 1920s, as soon as the road
from Mexico City reached that far. Because of the atmosphere and beauty
of the place, many of them stayed, and the town has had a large resident
foreign colony ever since. So large, in fact, that there's an old Mexican
joke about turning down an invitation to Taxco because, the speaker
says, he doesn't speak English.*

*Many of the foreign colony are, or claim to be, writers and artists,
though they have traditionally seemed to do most of their creative thinking over drinks at Paco's or Berta's cafés on the plaza. Comments to this
effect began early in the modern history of Taxco. In 1934 Aldous Huxley wrote, "Taxco is a sort of Mexican Saint-Paul largely inhabited by
artists and by those camp-followers of the arts whose main contribution
to the cause of Intellectual Beauty consists in being partially or completely drunk for several hours each day." Later in the thirties, Rodney
Gallop observed them and thought "it remains uncertain whether they are
painters who have gone there to drink or drinkers who have gone there to*

paint." In the forties, Paul Bowles said he disliked Taxco because there were so many foreigners there—residents, tourists, and "wealthier New York and Connecticut people who stop on their way to Acapulco in their cars." The saving grace, however, Bowles wrote in a letter to Virgil Thomson, was that "unless you seek them out, all these people, you never see them." (Obviously Bowles did see them.) And in the early fifties Sybille Bedford commented that "the foreigners who live at Taxco take villas and stay a very long time. Some may once have thought of writing a book; a few do paint."

The one thing that seems certain is that everybody goes to Taxco, including the writers who write about the writers—to make no mention of writers who write about the writers who write about the writers. In any case, it seems fair to say that it all started with William Spratling.

Spratling was born in 1900 in New York State but grew up in the South and studied architecture at Alabama Polytechnic Institute, now Auburn University. Although he was teaching classes there while still an undergraduate, he left without a degree. Even so, he next went to Tulane to teach architecture. While he lived in New Orleans his circle included William Faulkner (with whom he collaborated on a book), Sherwood Anderson, Roark Bradford, Hamilton Basso, and many other literary figures. His friendships with Oliver La Farge and Frans Blom led to an interest in Mexico, and he spent the summers of 1926 through 1928 there.

Spratling was talented and gregarious, a born hustler, a fixer, a bit of a charlatan, and a tireless self-promoter. He met everybody who mattered, everybody who had money and power. On the strength of his Mexican connections, a New York publisher commissioned him to write a book to be called Little Mexico, and that was reason enough for him to head south again in 1929. Spratling was on his way.

For a young man like him, Mexico was a land of opportunity. He quickly made local friends, moved in the best expatriate and artistic circles, and supported himself by writing articles about the booming renaissance in Mexican art and music. "I became known among the Mexican intelligentsia," he wrote, "as a sort of door-opener for their public-to-be." His friends quickly came to include the new U.S. ambassador, Morgan banker Dwight Morrow, whose daughter Anne was soon to marry Charles Lindbergh. And it was Spratling who suggested that Morrow have Diego Rivera paint murals in the Cortés Palace in Cuernavaca as a gift to the Mexican people. The Morrows had a luxurious house in

Cuernavaca, called Casa Mañana, and when Elizabeth Morrow wrote a book about it, Spratling illustrated it with pencil drawings.

In 1930 Spratling moved to Taxco and soon turned his great energies to developing the art of silversmithing there. The experiment worked, and Taxco has been famous ever since for its silver. Equally famous and prized today are Spratling's own silver designs, based on pre-Columbian motifs. He also managed to finish Little Mexico, which was published in 1932. It is—as Spratling himself clearly believed—one of the best books ever written about that country.

In the letter from Lesley Byrd Simpson that Spratling quotes at length, Simpson refers to a bookstore on Avenida Madero in Mexico City. This was—and still is—the American Book Store, at Madero 25. On the same street as both Sanborn's and the Lady Baltimore and near Butch Lewis's Manhattan Café, it was a central meeting place for the capital's large American colony. Until World War II it even stocked the convenient English-language Tauchnitz and Albatross Editions from Germany.

There was nothing humble about William Spratling, and he was quick to claim credit whenever it was due. One day, as he tells it, after a long ride on horseback, he took John Dos Passos into Berta's Cantina on the plaza in Taxco. "I had Berta prepare him a tall lemonade"—actually a Mexican limonada, made with lime juice—"with a hefty slug of tequila in it." The drink, soon known as a "Berta," became popular, and its fame quickly spread to the capital. "Perhaps in order to lose sight of its humble origin," Spratling writes, the drink eventually became known as a margarita. This time he was willing to share the credit, although not with the humble Berta. "Dos Passos and I," he declares, "can claim credit for its invention."

Another of Spratling's inventions drew on his skill as an architect. He hadn't been in Taxco very long before Wells Fargo, which operated far-flung tours from Mexico City, decided to capitalize on the new road and build a hotel in Taxco. The company commissioned Spratling to design it. The Hotel Rancho Telva re-created a hacienda setting and was named for Marion Telva, a star of the Metropolitan Opera and the wife of Wells Fargo's president. A 1939 advertisement simply listed some names from Rancho Telva's guestbook; they include George Bernard Shaw, Lady Bismarck, Mrs. William Howard Taft, Chief Justice and Mrs. Harlan F. Stone, Vincent Astor, Fannie Hurst, Mrs. C. S.

Heinz, Mr. and Mrs. King Vidor, and such Mexican celebrities as Dolores Del Rio and Miguel Covarrubias. Located on the hillside above the plaza, Rancho Telva has now been combined with the old Victoria to form the present-day Hotel Rancho Taxco-Victoria.

Antonio Castillo, whom Spratling mentions as a young apprentice, went on to direct a famous silver company of his own. Elizabeth Anderson, whom he also mentions, was the widow of Sherwood Anderson. With Spratling's help, she settled in Taxco and opened a clothing boutique, designing her own fashions on Mexican themes. That was also the key to success for another popular designer who began in Taxco in the thirties. In addition to her own creations, Bernice I. Goodspeed's shop, at Arco 9, sold high-quality craft items and books she had written and published, which recounted the local legends she collected.

The following selection, about Spratling's early years in Taxco, is from File on Spratling, an autobiography published in 1967. Like the man himself, it is bluff, boastful, name-dropping, clever, pretentious, and fascinating. On August 7 of the year it was published, William Spratling was killed in an auto accident on the Acapulco road about nine miles south of Taxco.

Today Taxco has a street named after him, and his house is the Museo Guillermo Spratling. Berta is gone, but Berta's Cantina and Paco's Bar are still on the plaza facing Santa Prisca. So are the writers and painters, who, one day real soon now, are going to write or paint something.

BUYING THE HOUSE IN TAXCO HAD BEEN A SO-lution for the writing of *Little Mexico;* being the first house I had ever owned, I rapidly fell in love with it. For the sixteen years I lived there, it never ceased to give me a deep and very personal satisfaction.

One of the first things I did was to make a map of the house as it was, locating and identifying every tree, bush and herb in the garden. The abruptness of the terrain in Taxco is probably what is mainly responsible for its charm. It is practically a vertical site—the variety of combinations, as rooms are adjusted to the separate levels, plus the fact that most of the domestic architecture is humble and on a small scale, with red tile roofs, distinguish this village from the more palatial architecture of San Miguel de Allende or of Guanajuato. Its very poverty has thus contributed to its character.

Taxco has always been famous for the ingenuity and cleverness of its masons. Probably a good twenty per cent of the male population could be called upon to do competent masonry. As I began certain reforms in the house, using local masons for a window this month, or a new roof next month, construction was easy and extremely inexpensive. I felt that building done little by little always has more flavor, more significance.

Situated a stone's throw upward from the plaza, say a hundred yards in front and nearly a hundred yards higher than the square, this house was a sort of island bounded by streets on three sides and a precipitous *barranca* at the back. On the north side, a seventeenth-century stone wall dropped to the narrow street some thirty feet below, while on the other side of the house the street had its level some two yards above my floor level. Even the garden surrounding two sides of the house was on two different levels, each one a mystery in light and shade with winding mosaic-paved paths among the *misteros,* ginger plants, begonias, lemons and oranges, a few roses, *piñones,* figs and, dominating the house at the back, a massive Indian laurel overhanging the garden wall and the *barranca* below. From the front gateway, the Calle de las Delicias dropped abruptly downward toward the square.

There were a few problems at first. The roof leaked, the cook claimed there were ghosts in the bedroom and made me dig up the floor where we did find some bones. The only bathing facilities consisted of a masonry reservoir in the middle of the back patio, but even this was rather pleasant in the shade there, with a basin in hand to pour water over one's body. I remember the gardener was shocked when he found the pink curves of Susan Smith one day in the process of bathing.

In the rough house plan is shown the *"escusado,"* which was then a two holer. At this particular point in the construction, years later, I had acquired the *barranca* and over that rocky declivity added a small apartment for Elizabeth Anderson. But that was not until 1938. The original owners, as is usual with the humble people of the interior of Mexico, believed that the fewer the windows the safer the house. Many windows had to be added and to have an extra bedroom the only way was to add it on top. Eventually a little tower was built at the entrance, a square *mirador*, from which the spires of the cathedral were visible at close hand. It was almost as though you could reach out and touch the top of the laurels there in the Plaza Borda in front of the church. I learned later that all those beautiful laurels in the center of Taxco had been planted from cuttings from my own Indian laurel only thirty years previously.

The neighbors were all helpful, and Rafael Domínguez insisted on painting my furniture for me and the saddle-maker who lived back of the house sold me some old furniture for a song, and I was able to persuade a little girl, named Amparo, to come and cook for me for three pesos a week, which the neighbors thought was too much. Susan Smith was there with me for a while and helped me move in in 1929.

Stuart and Marion Chase came through on their way to Acapulco. Stuart and I had much in common, including the writing of a book. Stuart had told me that Macmillan had asked him to do a book on Mexico, but that he had told them that he could not do this unless he were allowed at least two years in Mexico, and I agreed with his point of view.

It just happened that, a week later, on their way back up from Acapulco, they came to stay in the house again, and that same day, I got Don Antonio Pineda, the judge, to come up to the house and get them married. There was a little fiesta, and Pancho Oton painted a retablo of the scene which the Chases still cherish.

That night I told Stuart that we would put Marion and Susan in the one bedroom and that he and I would have pallets on the floor of the living room. When dawn came the next morning I looked across the length of the floor under the table to where Stuart Chase was lying, hands under head, gazing upward at the ceiling. I said, "I bet you didn't sleep." Stuart said, "That's right, I didn't sleep a wink, but I want you to know, Bill, that I now have the book for Macmillan all laid out in my mind, and I think I'll go to Mexico City today and lock myself in a hotel room for a few days until I have the whole thing knocked out." Which he did. The book was called *Mexico: A Study of Two Americas*. The first printing was 60,000 copies and, being one of the first important books on modern Mexico, it was received with vast interest in the U.S. My copy is inscribed, "To Bill Spratling—without whom this book could not have been written."

He should have referred to a sleepless night in my house and the discomfort of a brick floor.

Many people came and went, as for example, Dos Passos, Lesley Simpson, and many great Mexicans, including Diego Rivera, Carlos Chávez and Moisés Saénz. I built a little house for Saénz, then Secretary of Education, also a house for Hubert Herring. I bought horses on the lower coast of Guerrero where I had gone on a trek with Siqueiros, and the horses were an excuse to travel into the interior, the length and breadth of Guerrero.

My publishers, Cape and Smith, had expected the manuscript for *Little Mexico* to be completed in three or four months. But by that time I had written only two chapters and, needless to say, they were completely superficial and did not click. It took me three and a half years to write the book. And when it was finally cleanly typed and ready to be mailed to the publishers, I again sat down with it that night and chopped out one hundred and thirty-two pages of text, my feeling being that to do a concise portrait, another thousand words or a thousand lines in the drawing would not make it more vivid or acute.

The book finally appeared in 1932 and received generous reviews. I remember John Chamberlain writing two columns in the *New York Times,* claiming that here was one of the three classics on Mexico. Stuart Chase had a page about it in the *Herald Tribune* and there were many other very flattering reviews. Tragically, however, the firm of Jonathan Cape and Harrison Smith was dissolved just as the book appeared, and it was not offered for sale to bookstores. It was sold down the river as a "remainder."

About that time I had two house guests, Clare Spencer, the wife of Harrison Smith, and Katie Seabrook, Bill Seabrook's wife. Natalie Scott's house, across the *barranca,* had been rented by a fine young man who was recovering from a divorce, a friend of mine, named John Evans, Mabel Dodge Luhan's son. John was not feeling social, but finally agreed to join me at dinner with these, to me then unknown, ladies. The next morning Katie and I had breakfast alone; it seems that Clare and John had left for Acapulco. Today I still have a lurking suspicion that Clare's marriage to John affected Hal Smith's decision about his list of authors, keeping Faulkner and letting Spratling go.

To bring the history of *Little Mexico* up-to-date, it was thirty-two years later when Little, Brown republished, paper and hardback, under the new title, *A Small Mexican World*, with considerable success. Lesley Simpson then wrote me:

Dear Bill . . . in the summer of 1931, when I'd not even heard of Bill Spratling, a friend at the American Embassy invited me to spend a weekend in the Morrow house in Cuernavaca. I was completely charmed by its warmth and grace, and heard that a young architect named William Spratling had restored it. (Actually, you had made the illustrations for a book about it, but no matter.) I decided that I should have to know him.

The opportunity soon came. Brownie Aguirre took me to Taxco and put me up in the house you had built for Moisés Saénz. There I inevitably met Natalie Scott, the grande dame of Taxco, with whom I fell in love, as did everyone who knew her. Natalie, who had a passion for taking care of lost gringos, had me up to her funny little house perched on the edge of a barranca. While we were having tea and habanero (a gruesome combination), we were interrupted by a barking of dogs and a clumping of boots, and a character in blue jeans, followed by his dogs, strode across the verandah. He greeted Natalie briefly, dismissed me with a glance, and walked off. I must have looked puzzled, for Natalie said: "Oh, don't mind him. It's only Bill. He thinks you're a tourist. I'll fix it up." Which she did that afternoon at Doña Berta's Bar, where, over several glasses of Doña Berta's best, I made the great breakthrough. Shoals of refugees, fleeing the Great Depression, were coming to Mexico, the New Land of Promise, advertised by Stuart Chase, in his Mexico: A Study of the Two Americas, as a country that had solved the problem of living with itself. Painters, writers, and scholars swarmed in to breathe the invigorating air. They gathered round the towering figure of Diego Rivera, and soaked up his startling mixture of Karl Marx and nonsense, along with his vastly stimulating ideas about what could be done with an art deriving from the rich heritage of aboriginal Mexico. They collected in bars and studios and talked endlessly. It was an intoxicating and delightful interview, described many years later by Carleton Beals, in A House in Mexico. Hart Crane was nursing a hopeless plan to write an epic poem on the Conquest, and drowning his frustrations in tequila, while Peggy Baird and Mary Doherty

*undertook the equally hopeless task of domesticating him. Paca Toor,
an old Mexican hand, was publishing her Mexican Folkways, and
at the same time holding a kind of salon at the top of a crazy apartment building on Abraham González, resembling the Leaning Tower
of Pisa, which one ascended by an elevator like an inclined plane
railway. The floors slanted correspondingly, and one rather expected
the rickety structure to collapse when Diego's immense bulk slid to
the lower end of the room. At Paca's place, and Emily Edwards'
studio, one met a whole constellation of celebrities: Carlos Mérida,
Jean Charlot, Miguel Covarrubias, David Siqueiros, Rufino Tamayo, María Izquierdo, René d'Harnoncourt, and Juan O'Gorman.
I don't remember seeing you there, for you rarely came to the city in
those days, being fully occupied with your dream of reviving the ancient art of the silversmiths in Taxco. Tamayo and Angel Salas were
easily persuaded to play and sing the shocking ballads of the Revolution, which had to compete with the roar of conversation. Our dear
Marian (Simpson) joined us at the middle of that year and gathered
impressions that have lasted until this day and enriched her own
painting.*

*We were all writing, or intending to write; painting, or intending
to paint. Hart Crane, after his year of agony, completed his last great
poem, "The Broken Tower," and died.*

*Then one day in the spring of 1932, while I was strolling down
Madero, you clutched me by the arm and steered me into a bookshop.
"This caballero," you said to the clerk, "wants to buy a copy of*
Little Mexico!" *Which I did, whereupon we repaired to Bach's Bar
to celebrate. And then came the heartbreaking word: Cape and
Smith, the publishers, had dissolved their partnership, and* Little
Mexico *was left an orphan. I forget where we sought comfort, but I
think it was at Doña Berta's in Taxco.*

*This was sad, for I now loved the book, and the Mexico it pic-
tured: the lovely, cruel, simple (perhaps not so simple) life of remote
villages lost in the mountains of the south. The story of your voyage
down the Balsas, admirably illustrated with your sensitive and vigorous drawings, is unforgettable.*

. . . And now that Little Mexico *has been born again I am now
able to reread one of my most treasured volumes, which occupies an
honored place between Charles Flandrau's* Viva Mexico! *and* Fanny

Calderón's Life in Mexico . . . *what a vivid portrait it is of our* patria chica, *and what a host of memories it brings tumbling into my mind!*

Lesley Simpson, the author of that great history of Mexico, *Many Mexicos,* and I have ever since those early days shared an enthusiasm and a nostalgia and a closeness to Mexico and things Mexican.

In 1931, the new highway which connected the capital, Taxco and Acapulco was finished. It was not paved but, for the first time in history, one could travel to Acapulco in less than three or four days. From Taxco, Acapulco could then be reached on the new road in about ten hours. Today tourists complain that it takes three hours to reach Acapulco.

In 1931, then, I took the Morrows, the Ambassador and his wife, and Elizabeth and Allen Dawson to Taxco and Acapulco. In Taxco the Morrows had a "suite" at the only boardinghouse, and the cost, as I remember, was ten pesos a day, including food, for the whole group. There were no tourists then. At breakfast, Mr. Morrow, whose brain worked interminably and constructively all day long, remarked to me, "What a pity, Bill, that of all the thousands of tons of silver sent back from Taxco to the old world over the centuries, that none of this ever stayed here nor was utilized to create an industry or economy for Taxco." This was the germ of a thought which caused me to bring, a little later, some goldsmiths up from Iguala, and to set up what I then thought of as a single experiment, the making of silver articles in Taxco.

The experiment was, of course, a "natural." Thirty-five years have since passed and that single experiment has borne fruit. Taxco has now become known as the Florence of America and has an economy of its own based primarily on the handcrafting of silver.

This new economy, by 1940, produced a prosperity such as Taxco had not enjoyed since the days of Borda. With the prosperity came, every year, an increasing flow of tourists who had money to spend, many of them of course, consciously or subconsciously, looking for romance. I believe most people will agree today, many of the best-run silver shops in Taxco have been set up by silversmiths who have been encouraged by detached American women. In 1940 the main gathering place was Berta's Cantina where, treating that epoch with intimacy, Kim Schee wrote his *Cantina*.

☀

TAXCO IN 1931 WAS A QUIET LITTLE VILLAGE, everyone was poor, the few mines open were "high grading," that is, working out only their richest veins, since silver was at an all-time low and could be bought for fifteen pesos a kilo. Mining, of course, had for four hundred years been Taxco's basic industry, since 1528, in fact, when Alvarado, a lieutenant of Cortés, came to get silver for Spain. Silver now sells for over five hundred pesos a kilo. There is no lack of ore in the Taxco region, though most of it is rather low in yield, probably giving less than three kilos per ton of ore worked.

When Mr. Morrow suggested to me the desirability of creating an industry in Taxco, the local people could not imagine why anyone should want to buy silver. Besides, who would want a silver belt buckle if a gold-plated brass one cost less.

In Iguala, just below Taxco, gold had always been worked, and the "silversmiths" there considered it a little beneath their dignity to employ their "art" on the white metal. However, I persuaded two boys who were good goldsmiths to come up to Taxco from Iguala. I rented a vast hulk of an old building called La Aduana (the Customs House), a three-story semi-ruin with no windows or doors or stairways, though the floors were intact. The rent was twelve pesos a month. There we began making some silver buckles and some very simple half-orange earclips which could be sold for two pesos a pair. That summer the first seminar, a group of editors and civic leaders, was brought down by Hubert Herring and they were in Taxco for two or three weeks. We began to sell silver, sometimes up to a hundred pesos a day. That seemed like good business, and the shop expanded and I was able to add a group of tinsmiths, some carpenters and an iron man.

It should be noted here that only ten years later came the day when, with sales at 8,000 pesos a day, the shop was losing money.

One night, about nine o'clock, some Indians from Coatepec, where they make sarapes, knocked on my door to offer me some weavings. They were good mountain people, who, for generations, had done nothing but card and spin wool and weave it in a traditional simple type of sarape. The forms were geometric and the colors were the natural tones of wool, from black to brown and white. I had had them making a couple of sarapes for me.

There they were at my door. It was a rainy night and I asked them in and offered them beer. After a while I was suggesting that perhaps some day they would like to set up their looms in Taxco and work in my shop. This was merely a tentative idea of mine, and I had forgotten about it when one morning, there they were, three whole families with six mules on which they had loaded their three looms. Happily there was plenty of space in La Aduana and I even arranged cooking and sleeping quarters for them there.

This had news value for the people of Taxco since they had never seen weaving done there. Some friends in Mexico City wanted a supply of articles in tin, and since tin has always had a long tradition in Mexico as "the poor man's silver," and since some of the old pieces were extremely lovely, I persuaded Don Isidro Jejía, the local tinsmith, to bring his helpers over to the old building, and we began work on this order for tin. The possibilities of tin are almost unlimited and it has now become fashionable for modern interiors. Also it is intensely Mexican.

Since I needed some furniture for my house, I proceeded to take on some local carpenters to make some cabinets, chairs and tables. There were friends from Mexico City who ordered this simple, provincial furniture with enthusiasm.

The shop there in La Aduana, later called Las Delicias, had already become a four-ring circus.

At this point I should make a confession· my idea in setting up a silver shop had been simply planned as an interesting experiment, with the thought that, certainly within six months, things would run themselves, and I would be free to stay home and write something. After all, I was supposed to be a writer, since *Little Mexico* had just appeared.

Las Delicias began to attract attention to Taxco and to give people an excuse to go there. I was even invited to talk at one of the seminars. It was a good group of some twenty-five people, and Mr. Trotsky was there. The house had been furnished with chairs by Spratling. When my talk was over, there were a few questions. I remember one little old lady who said, "Mr. Spratling—these people here, what is their life expectancy?" I was at a loss for what to say, not being versed in the language of sociologists, and I asked her to explain herself. She replied, "You know . . . what about the old people? What happens when they get old?" I answered, "They die." Another asked me, "Now what about those people in your shops? Can they read and write?" I replied, "I don't think you should let it get about, but it's just like it is in New York; some do and some don't."

Las Delicias prospered from the very beginning. Everything was very free and easy and nobody watched the clock. Government taxes were not complicated, but as soon as the Presidente Municipal found we were actually making sales, the municipal taxes were arbitrarily doubled.

At about this time, the presidential candidate General Cárdenas was making his campaign and was scheduled to appear in Taxco. The mayor came to the shop and told me that he needed a great silver key to present to the candidate. We worked on it night and day since time was short. The key was a monstrous thing, weighing a couple of kilos. When I took it to him, the mayor was very pleased indeed. But he added, "We will pay you for this next year."

"No," I said, "all you have to do is to give me my tax receipts for a couple of years. Otherwise, you don't get the key." Since this did not call for a cash outlay, it was a deal. Things are different today.

My architectural background made it a natural to take up where other people had left off and achieve a certain amount of improvement in the silver, the tin, the furniture and the weavings, since an architect is primarily concerned with materials and their possibilities, particularly in design. One has to be aware of the possibilities of a given material and of combinations that are proper or perhaps improper. Silver, for example, needs surface and body, plus a good convincing weight. Gold, on the other hand, by its very rarity has been traditionally worked delicately and preciously.

I've always had the conviction that certain materials have the right to be worked in a given community because they are native to that area and that the work of the designer is to utilize these materials and to dignify them. I see no point in importing to Mexico synthetic stones from Germany nor in trying to improve here on something that was better done by the Chinese. Danish silver is properly made in Denmark; Zuñi bracelets are properly made by the Zuñis; Belgian lace is properly made in Belgium.

Beginning from scratch with the problem of styling my articles and being fearful of treading on the toes of Mexican traditionalists, I had gone back to the pre-Columbian clay seals for motifs. Though this was an improper application, that is, taking a clay design and executing it in an entirely different material, people liked the things and they sold.

Actually Mexico had had no continuing thread of tradition in silver except for certain Colonial articles such as basins, candlesticks, and, particularly, churchware. Such styles taken from the past, however, could not properly be applied to the needs of a modern apartment nor for modern commerce. At the time that Las Delicias began, almost the only silver being done in Mexico were the little fish earrings from Pátzcuaro and the necklaces of cast silver from Yalalag in Oaxaca. And, of course, silver was used for application to saddles.

A style does not develop by itself overnight. It must be confessed though that design content has come a long way in Mexican silversmithing since those days in 1931.

About 1931, with Las Delicias expanding, I decided to make an attempt to smelt ore in Taxco the way they used to do it centuries ago. This was, of course, an anachronism but I went ahead, renting an old abandoned smelter just over the hill from my house. Ore was bought from out-of-work miners who were accustomed to handstrip the old mines back in the hills. Many of these people were good friends of mine and, of course, they largely persuaded me that the ancient smelting process was practical. After all, the furnace was there and the tile roof was still intact. These people would supply me the ore on an assay basis. There was one hitch. The few samples we assayed had been placed in the top of the bags and naturally showed a silver content. We stockpiled these sacks until there was enough to make the first run.

My carpenters built a bellows, the kind you fan a fire with, which was ten feet long and six feet wide. It took three entire cowhides to make the sides, then the thing was rigged and placed and counterweighted and, with a rope passed through a pulley to a beam overhead, we were ready to begin.

Teams of men were then employed to haul on this cord, there

were four to a team and the work had to continue twenty-four hours a day for about three weeks. That is about the time it took to build up the temperature necessary to smelt the ore.

This round-the-clock performance provided a highly dramatic spectacle. Friends would come down from Mexico City and we would walk over the hill at night under the stars on footpaths across the rough *barrancas*, watching the fiery glow as we approached this ancient living mural.

One evening García Cabral, Manuel Orta and René d'Harnoncourt were with me. The scene was like something out of Dante's *Inferno*, and I still remember the effect on these city dwellers, watching from the outer rim of darkness where the sweat trickled down the bronze backs and flanks of the four men pulling rhythmically on the bellows. The surrounding faces of the spectators reflected the glare of the furnace, roaring blue and red out of the top.

At the end of three weeks, we were ready to pull the plug on the lower part. The ashes in the pit were carefully scooped out and patted to form a depression. Then the plug was yanked, and precious white metal trickled out and formed a little white puddle. While the pool of metal was still incandescent, it was necessary to perform the very delicate operation of ladling off the metal on top—the lead— leaving only the lower, heavier layer of silver. After a while, this cooled and hardened into an irregular slab.

It was a good show while it lasted, but that little slab of silver, so laboriously produced from all that ore, weighed about six-and-a-half kilos. In short, slightly over one hundred pesos' worth. We had achieved the miracle of producing silver in a silver country at a production cost of about fifteen times what it was worth on the world market. Furthermore, I had casually signed a rent contract for the furnace without noting there was a two-year clause in it.

In Mexico, silversmithing has always been considered a folk art, since it has traditionally been produced for domestic or personal use. I am convinced that folk art is basically possible only when you have a group of people who are happily unburdened with instruction, people who are free to focus and feel the need to produce with their hands in order to make a living. Their imagination is thus poured in an untrammeled way into their products, whether it is silver or the weaving of simple cotton textiles, hand-blown glass or ceramics.

Over the years I have arrived at the conclusion that Mexico is one of the few countries remaining in the world where the people have a sufficient simplicity of outlook, or one-mindedness, which makes the production of handcrafted goods here possible. I am sure that in the U.S., the America of cities and mass production, we will never again see things done in a normal way by people willing to work with their hands to make a living; because in America people no longer respect those who work with their hands. So this leaves Mexico in an almost unique position and comparable only to a very limited number of spots on the earth's surface. The Mexican artisan has always been accustomed to solving his own problems.

Silversmithing is learned best at firsthand. Thus, as only man can produce man, you need silversmiths to produce silversmiths. I have never held classes for my silversmiths nor attempted to instruct them in technique—only in design and efficiency. In this sense, a good artisan can be produced in circumstances which provoke his ingenuity and which feed his daily development. This is like the production of certain gems, where a slight fragment of emerald, placed in certain temperatures with the exact pressure necessary and surrounded by the proper materials, will grow into a full-grown emerald of fine quality.

Emeralds are not produced in Taxco but silversmiths are, of all sizes and temperaments. This has been made possible by the apprentice system which I began in the shop in Taxco in 1931. The system is more or less general throughout Mexico and certainly in the hundreds of shops which exist in Taxco today and at my own shop at Taxco-el-Viejo.

We still put on youngsters—boys who are anxious to learn and who also need to take money home. At the end of the week, the *maestro* will remark whether the boy shows any aptitude or, if he is not interested, he is let go and room is made for another who may show more definite capabilities. The system is very realistic and it works.

In the early days at Taxco, there was only one silversmith, Don Moloton Gomez, about eighty years old and nearly blind, who produced an occasional spoon for a housewife, or silver ornaments for somebody's saddle. In Iguala there were plenty of goldsmiths, and they were called *plateros* though they worked exclusively in gold. Their work, mostly filigree, was sold and is still sold there today, laid out on pink tissue paper on the sidewalks.

For the first three years my Las Delicias, then, was the only silver shop in Taxco. By 1940 many boys had left Las Delicias with my blessing and sometimes help and had set up their own little shops. In 1940 my shop alone was employing over three hundred artisans and we were actually behind on production. Today there are over three hundred big and little workshops in Taxco. These, of course, include the *charreadores,* the small silversmiths, who work at night in their own houses up and over the hills. These supply many of the shops which simply buy and sell, and the poor *charreador,* who neither pays taxes nor keeps books, is frequently forced to sell for less than his actual cost. Their production, usually of very low-grade silver and bad quality of execution, definitely lowers the prestige of Taxco silver. Worthwhile silver requires that it be identified with the name and reputation of its maker. If Balenciaga's designs were reproduced in sweatshops they would probably suffer the same loss of prestige.

My life in Taxco as a silversmith was all detail, sometimes fourteen hours a day of it. Once you lose control of the detail, a silversmith's business begins to unravel. There was a time when labor strikes were the vogue in Mexico, and when the metropolitan newspapers would point out with a certain pride that there had been two thousand or three thousand strikes during a thirty-day period. The labor law, practically unilateral and totally favoring the worker, provoked problems which might occur overnight. A group of workers who had been contented on one day, the next day in the hands of an agitator might turn against the company and present a list of demands which were astronomical in their magnitude.

Thus a strike was declared in my shop in Taxco without any apparent previous discontent on the part of the workers. It simply happened overnight, and I was suddenly faced with a very discouraging situation. I said to the workers, "Since there is no way for me to meet your demands, nor sufficient money, nor credit, I will now leave this small company to its own devices and will be in my house until some solution is found—that is, if the company is to continue to work."

That night, studying the paycards of the workers, my secretary and I sorted them out into groups on the table in my house. We discovered that of the one hundred and forty-four workers, only seventy-two were active strikers. We then proceeded to identify a given striker with one or two of the nonstrikers who happened to be his buddies. The buddies, whom we will call the Whites, were, within a space of a very few days, able to convince many of the strikers, the Reds, that the strike was unfounded and unjust. In this manner, the number of strikers was reduced to only thirty-seven.

As the weeks rolled by, the situation became more bitter, some of the Whites had the idea that they could acquire guns and, by force, overcome the Reds. I ruled that out. About this time a friend of mine, a very able lawyer who had been secretary of the National University and whose brother was on the Supreme Court, came along and laid out plans in a very neat fashion. By this time the number of strikers had been reduced to seventeen diehards. The plan consisted of simply paying these off, giving them all the indemnification conceded by law. Those of the seventeen who were unwilling to accept indemnification, we reported to labor courts as having been offered complete indemnification and that these payments had been deposited in their favor in a local bank. This, of course, left them without a work contract.

One must remember that the Reds were all friends of mine, of this I am convinced. They had merely been badly led. A young apprentice named Antonio Castillo, a boy with much skill and who had considerable influence with his companions, had come up to my house one evening during the first few evenings of the strike to tell me that even though he had taken active part in the thing, he had become sadly aware that the strike was completely uncalled for. I told Antonio that, though I was grateful for his sincerity and frankness, the only way I could accept him back would be that he, in the meeting which was to take place with the strikers the following day, would be willing to speak out in front of everybody and tell why he was leaving the ranks of the strikers. This was indeed a notable occasion, and I think Antonio provoked the admiration of both camps; certainly I myself will forever remember his facing the group as an act of courage and integrity, qualities which have added world prestige to Castillo Silver.

The strike over, within two days the shop was again running smoothly and contentedly: no reprisals and no hard feelings.

Another problem which is peculiar to all craft workers and designers had to do with plagiarism. At one time the average life of a design of mine was no longer than one month, by which time replicas were available in various shops in Taxco, and automatically ceased to interest the buyer since they had been vulgarized and were no longer exclusive. Even my hallmark had been appropriated by one boy. This I had taken from a brand I had used on my horses and consisted of a joined WS. The imitator's name was Serafín Moctezuma, and all he had to do was to use the mark upside down.

He and others had been systematically reproducing Spratling designs, and one day I yielded to the urgings of my store manager and, since the designs had been "registered," proceeded to sue those copyists. There was a lawyer who took the case on a contingent basis, who some two years later appeared in Taxco to tell me that sentence had been passed in a federal court. I paid his fee.

Three years later, during which time there had been no rumor of even an order for an arrest, and when the boys down the street had gotten under way with their own designs and we were all enjoying a normal friendship, the captain of the federal guard in Taxco was changed and the new captain discovered in his office the order for the arrests. He promptly put this into effect, and that same day, these friends of mine were jailed on a federal order.

What followed was a little bit like comic opera; these boys had their friends out with pistols to gun me down. I left Taxco shortly thereafter to make a personal visit to the federal judge who had signed the verdict. I was able to "convince" him that there was a tiny flaw in my perfect case, thereby providing him with an excuse to rescind the order.

Viva la paz.

When the attack on Pearl Harbor occurred, I happened to be in Acapulco. I was back in Taxco the following morning in time to attend a meeting of the silversmiths. They were about to petition the government to be allowed to shut down their workshops. They felt that the war meant an end to the industry and curtains to their prosperity. I told them that I still had some money in the bank, that my shop would keep on working until that ran out. At that point, in a matter of two weeks, the incredible happened. Buyers from many of the finest stores in America came to Mexico, desperately looking for salable gadgets, in other words, luxury goods. Europe was suddenly cut off from them. Until the war occurred, sales of Taxco silver had been mostly retail, and exportation of wholesale orders had been practically nonexistent. Actually the war brought profound changes for all the industries in Mexico. The vision of Mr. Roosevelt and Nelson Rockefeller, his coordinator, was highly beneficial. I had the opportunity of talking with Nelson about problems here and called his attention to the fact that import duties on silver, which did not compete with anything done in the U.S., were at that time one hundred and twenty per cent.

Rockefeller, at my suggestion, managed to get that lowered to one-half. Later the duties were lowered to approximately twenty-five per cent. It should be noted that it was always the policy of Mr. Roosevelt and also of Mr. Rockefeller to prefer a strong Mexico instead of a weak Mexico.

But along with this lowering of the barriers by the U.S., few people now recall one of the most disastrous things which ever happened to the silver industry which was still in its infancy here. The Mexican government, through their Treasury Department, was, by the end of the war, applying three separate export taxes on hand-crafted silver, thus taxing the sweat of the Mexican artisan's own brow.

One day I visited Ramón Beteta, a friend of mine, then Secretary of the Treasury. Beteta smiled and said, "Why, Bill, you silversmiths are now making a lot of money. The government has a right to a share of that income." I said, "Ramón, did you ever see a rich silversmith in your life? I never have." Silversmiths don't seem to get rich. This occurs only when they develop into senseless corporations.

Unfortunately, at the end of the war this incredible export market for all the finest accounts in America which had been practically laid as a gift in the lap of Mexico ceased to exist. The exporters withdrew their trade and went straight back to Europe for their luxury goods. The head buyer of Saks Fifth Avenue remarked, "If the Mexican government does this to us now, what will they do to us next month?"

Mexico missed the train and the Taxco silver industry hit bottom. Five million dollars spent for publicity could never recover the loss of that wonderful market. The export taxes were withdrawn some three months after the war was over, but the damage had been done. In the years succeeding that epoch, silversmithing in Taxco has managed to stay afloat and even to make a slight comeback the hard way. The hard way means keeping the tourist happy with some pretty inferior material.

On the other hand, the very hardships through which the industry has passed have had a certain purifying effect. Competition, which has forced those who never had real criteria to begin with to produce pieces of lesser quality, has had an opposite effect on that minority of the more creative artisans, who now tend to study and refine their design efforts toward a fresher and more vigorous expression in silver. In other words, faced by the overabundance of lesser conceptions, the truly well-conceived and executed pieces become more outstanding by simple comparison.

The element of design is, of course, the most precious element and, as previously noted, a designer's style is not something that may be developed overnight. It is no accident. A style is molded by a sensitive person's own convictions, or tendencies, which he has expressed and experimented with over a period of months, or even of many years. Thus, and sometimes suddenly, an underlying feeling or style commences to make itself apparent in all that the man does, and a piece may be recognized as "by so-and-so." This is a difficult thing to define.

I myself have always gone in for greater simplicity, surface in silver and definition of a refined line. As Greta Pack, in her *Mexican Jewelry,* which was published by the University of Texas Press, stipulates, "designing is not an occupation in itself, but is the result of meeting and solving an occupational problem." I would add to this that designs on paper may be very handsome to look at, but once carried out, may or may not click. From the beginning, my designs have not been intended as "occupations in themselves," are often done on scraps of paper, or backs of envelopes from the trash box.

A ring, when completed in silver, may give an entirely different sensation than it did on paper; it may have to be redesigned over and over and executed six or seven times before it is ready to offer to the public for sale. It pleased me very much to note that Miss Pack states, "Spratling designs are unmistakable."

There are certain materials with which silver is apt to combine very traditionally and very beautifully. There are others which make the metal appear cold and insensitive. A fine Ural amethyst, deep purple, absolutely perfect, mounted in silver, is apt to be taken for synthetic. The extreme cost of the stone would not be in keeping with the economic nature of silver. On the other hand, here from the silver mines of Taxco, and from just south of here in the Balsas region, is obtained an orchid-colored amethyst with flaws which give the stone much character, which is inexpensive, and which combines magnificently with silver. However, in spite of this, people come in who insist that a fine Ural amethyst, worth a couple of thousand dollars, be set in a silver ring worth perhaps fifty pesos.

During the Italian Renaissance, they had very little gold, so they used silver, gold-plated, with which to mount great emeralds, pearls, and other stones which require a richer background. Few people realize this, and in an effort to give a color to silver by gilding it (should we receive an emerald here to be set), we find that very few people realize there is a vast and ancient tradition for gold-plated silver.

Silver embedded in fine woods also has a long tradition. When the Puerto Rican government asked me to make a study on the possibilities of manufacturing silver there, I arrived at the conclusion that Puerto Rico could get a much higher price and offer a much finer product by using silver only to adorn their precious hardwoods. The seed did not sprout; in fact, the idea was not welcomed.

The combination of gold, mounted in silver, exquisitely worked, is also a very felicitous combination, to my way of thinking.

When we come to the point of the finishing of silver, I think it is obvious that for the sculptural piece, in which there is the three-dimensional quality to be admired and become visual, a dull finish is preferable for the simple reason that the highly polished surface picks up reflections all around it, both dark and light, and in a photograph that article appears fragmented. There is a psychological reason, however, which explains why a dull-finished earring does not sell and a shiny one does. Subconsciously, a woman wears jewelry to attract the eye of the male, the shiny finish catches the eye more quickly than the dull one.

Silver with obsidian gives a fine, sharp contrast. Tortoiseshell also combines well with silver. It freshens it, and it has a long tradition. The things done in Central America, and the south of Mexico during Colonial times, were frequently of tortoiseshell with silver arabesque patterns.

I remember years ago that René d'Harnoncourt, who did such a glorious job on revitalizing silver for the Southwest Indians, remarked to me that he had arrived at the conclusion that the definition of a superior *maestro* was "one who could recognize a superior instrument, or tool, and utilize it." A great many people have the black-and-white idea that where machinery comes in, good crafts-manship goes out. René and I agreed that if this were true, we should eliminate rolling mills, and without rolled, flat silver, no sil-versmith could begin to work. Hammers and polishers also would have to be eliminated.

This takes me back to the early thirties, and though I blush to admit it, my old-time silversmiths, coming in from the interior, used the leaf of a local plant to cut down the rough silver surface—instead of what we now have available, various grades of emery paper. The name of this plant, *tlalchichinole,* has now been forgotten by most of the silversmiths here in Taxco. But it was used very effectively. The back of the small, dried leaf had a toothed surface like a file. At that time, the next step in the finishing, of say a piece of jewelry, was the polishing; and for this purpose, the boy would roll up his sleeve, spread a little powdered pumice over the length of his inner arm and proceed to polish the silver vigorously against his own flesh. Silver-smiths of the present generation would laugh out loud if they saw this being done today. Now each one has his own little polishing wheel and cloth disk, and the polishing process is a matter of mo-ments while the boy gossips with his neighbor at the next wheel.

And while all this has been taking place in the silver industry, what has happened to Taxco, as an entity, as a village? The furniture I so modestly made in Las Delicias years ago is now one of Taxco's major products and some of it is very handsome indeed. There are ceramics in Taxco and engraved iron work. Elizabeth Anderson, now an octogenarian, who came to live in my house so many years ago, had an interest in the fine old embroideries, a tradition for needle-work inherent in all Mexican women, and by styling clothing on native garb, she gave rise to a new industry for Taxco. Her creations have frequently been shown in *Vogue* magazine and in fashion shows in New York, San Francisco and Mexico City. Tachi Castillo, also a world-famous fashion designer, is working in Taxco.

And Taxco has its own festival. About 1932, I gave a little cele-bration, a banquet, to mark the beginning of Las Delicias. Each year, thereafter, the day was celebrated by my workers with greater and greater enthusiasm. About 1934 or 1935, it occurred to people in Taxco that this was a date worthy of being commemorated officially. The legislature of the state of Guerrero decreed "The Day of the

Silver of Taxco" an official state holiday, and the Silver Fiesta was born.

Year after year the celebration grew bigger and more ostentatious and by 1940, this celebration could almost have competed with the Film Festival in Cannes. Invited guests came from New York, Acapulco, Argentina and Italy. Dolores Del Rio came; Cantinflas appeared and was acclaimed "favorite son of Taxco." People wept with joy at seeing him, and the great Silver Ball that night was memorable except for a slight note of advertising that had crept in, a sign which said Pepsi-Cola just back of the Queen of Silver's throne.

Only recently has the whole celebration of this very traditional fiesta, which is Taxco's own, been placed in the hands of a non-profit civic foundation, which means that the former celebration for the beginnings of the silver industry in Taxco has become sacrosanct and, as the people of Taxco so earnestly desire, will continue with more and more glorious celebrations.

During one of the celebrations of the *Fiesta de la Plata,* I remember I was delegated to invite some movie stars. Among the most beloved of these in Mexico are Dolores Del Rio and Cantinflas, both of whom have been idolized for many, many years.

The morning I went to invite Mario Moreno, better known all over the world as Cantinflas, his house was not as grand as it is today. Even then, however, Mario was extremely well-to-do, flew his own plane—something we had in common beside and beyond the fact that both of us had been named "favorite sons of Taxco." Jorgo Piño Sandoval, Mexico's Walter Winchell, was also along. The breakfast service was excellent, we had fresh tuna, *chilaquiles* and, of course, *frijoles refritos.* The conversation was lively and I remember Jorgo accused Mario of marrying his wife for her money, because when both of them had been working in a sideshow, she was making eight pesos and Mario was only making six pesos a night.

During the meal, the houseboy came to the table to announce to Cantinflas that there was a committee of Indians waiting out in the garden to speak to him. Deciding it would be best to get this over with, we all trooped out to the front gallery, where the head man of the village, sombrero in hand, began his little speech. He said, "Don Mario, we know you are a great benefactor and that you love your people. We in our village have our little church, but we have a grave problem. Don Mario, our church has no clock in it. We have come to beg you to give us one."

Mario, with just a little bit of double-talk, wound up saying, "just how many fathers of families are there in your village?"

The old man counted slowly on his fingers and finally concluded that there were eleven. Mario then turned to his houseboy and said, "Go tell the Señora to give my friends here enough money for eleven wristwatches."

RODNEY GALLOP

Cuernavaca, Taxco, Acapulco, ca. 1937

"IT REMAINS UNCERTAIN WHETHER THEY ARE
PAINTERS WHO HAVE GONE THERE TO DRINK OR
DRINKERS WHO HAVE GONE THERE TO PAINT."

*Rodney Gallop was born in Folkestone, England, in 1901 and was edu-
cated at Harrow and Cambridge. He entered the diplomatic service in
1924 and was posted successively to Belgrade, Athens, Lisbon, Mexico
City, and Copenhagen. During World War II he served in the Foreign
Office, but his distinguished career was cut short by his death, from
Hodgkin's disease, in 1948.*

*All his life he was interested in folklore and musicology, an interest
enhanced by his diplomatic travels. He wrote a book on the Basques, another on traditional dance, and one on Portuguese folkways, but the book
for which he will always be remembered is* Mexican Mosaic, *published
in London in 1939. This was the same year Graham Greene's* The Lawless Roads (Another Mexico) *appeared in England, and inevitably the
two books were compared. Greene's obviously misanthropic reaction could
not have looked very appealing next to Gallop's warm, well-intentioned,
and well-informed report. Greene himself reviewed* Mexican Mosaic *in*

169

the Spectator *and, misanthropic still, called Gallop "a rare personal-ity—a man who was happy in Mexico."*

Greene held fast to his opinions. In 1967, nearly thirty years later, John C. Lincoln's One Man's Mexico *echoed the same paranoid and negative response of Lawrence's* The Plumed Serpent *and Greene's own book. Greene declared it "the best book on Mexico written this century."*

During his posting to Mexico City, Gallop did his best to avoid the usual diplomatic social schedule and, instead, used as much time as he could to explore the country, mostly on day trips and weekends from the capital. His main interest was in Indian traditions and customs, especially those away from the beaten track that might be endangered by ever-encroaching "civilization." His book vividly describes such traditions as the Flying Game, the Texcoco Passion Play, the Yaqui Deer Dance, and the pagan earth cults of the Otomí Indians.

For the present volume, I've chosen a different kind of chapter from the book. Gallop's account of the route from Mexico City to Acapulco is like no other. He describes the scenery, of course: the twisting mountain roads, the high passes and valleys, the dizzying views, and the glimpses of Popocatépetl in the distance. With a passion for detail, a painter's eye for color, and a connoisseur's knowledge of craft work, he vividly catalogs everything he sees. Here are isolated villages, fiestas and markets, fruits and flowers, serapes and pottery, all of them blazing in brilliant colors untouched by time. Gallop's single failing—more puzzling and sad than serious—is his inability to appreciate Mexican food. But this is clearly the report of a man who knew the country intimately, respected it and cared about it, and, to the extent that he could, tried to preserve it.

☀ IN THE 290 MILES OF ITS LENGTH THE HIGH-way from Mexico City to the Pacific at Acapulco crosses seven mountain ranges. The first, naturally enough, is that which encircles the Valley of Mexico. The road runs out through the gardens of Churubusco and Tlalpam, skirting the Pedregal, and climbs swiftly beneath the shadow of Mt. Ajusco to a broad, undulating upland of pines, tufa rock and dry, tufted zacate grass. Like the Puebla and Toluca roads, it attains a height of 10,000 feet.

These lonely mountain tops long enjoyed an unenviable reputa-tion for brigandage, practised less by outlaw bands than by local Indians who resumed their appearance of peaceful peasants as soon as the soldiers appeared on the scene. Sometimes, too, the soldiers took to brigandage on their own account. Tyler, who travelled to Cuernavaca eighty years ago, describes his feelings on passing a spot "from which forty men had rushed out and plundered the Diligence just ten days before." His worst fears appeared to have been realized when he caught sight of "some twenty wild-looking fellows in all sorts of strange garments with the bright sunshine gleaming on the barrels of their muskets." They turned out to be only the guard, however, "and such a guard! Their thick matted black hair hung about over their low foreheads and wild brown faces. Some had shoes, some had none, and some had sandals. They had straw hats, glazed hats, no hats, leather jackets and trousers, cotton shirts and drawers, or drawers without any shirt at all; and . . . what looked worst of all . . . some had ragged old uniforms on, like deserters from the army, and there are no worse robbers than they." To-day things have changed, and in order that the casinos, bathing-pools and pleasure-gardens of Cuernavaca may be safe for democracy, the road is patrolled by spruce little Indian soldiers in neat khaki uniforms.

Just before the village of Tres Marías the road begins to drop, slowly at first, then rapidly, and not far beyond the village, the traveller is vouchsafed his first breath-taking glimpse of the wide valley of Morelos.

I have seen that view many times in every variation of season and weather, but I shall always remember it one day early in the wet season. As so often happens at that time of year, a pall of cloud lay on the mountains, and it had been drizzling at the top of the pass. Suddenly, as the car swept downwards in wide curves, the curtain of cloud lifted to reveal the bowl of Morelos far below, bathed in brilliant sunshine, pin clear to the far *sierras* away in Guerrero and Oaxaca. Cutting out the high light from the sky, the cloud curtain gave the land a jewelled brilliance, blue and green and gold, which no words could hope to convey.

In about fifteen miles the road drops over four thousand feet to Cuernavaca, twisting and turning along a wooded hillside yellow in winter with Alpine mimosa and with the cistus-like blossoms of the *tronadora,* an infusion of which is said to kill a man or make him mad six months later, when he can no longer recall whose was the hand which administered the potion.

Of Cuernavaca, the ancient Cuauhnahuac of which the Spaniards could make nothing better than their equivalent of "cow-horn,"
I do not find it easy to write. It is attractive, too attractive for a place
so easily accessible from Mexico City, and it has become the Mecca
of week-enders, devotees of a cult which spells death to the *genius
loci*. Outspread at the foot of the mountains on a broad valley-floor
gently tilted towards the south, it enjoys the perfect climate of Mexican *tierra templada*. In consequence, the golden sixteenth century cathedral, Cortés' Palace, the Borda gardens, the old colonial houses
embowered in purple and crimson bougainvillea and misty blue jacaranda trees, have been swamped by what the Mexicans call *tijuaniza-
ción*. Tijuana is a place just across the border from the United States
in Lower California, which has been developed as a Mexican resort
for Californians to the point that the word has become synonymous
with that somewhat meretricious and self-conscious cultivation of the
picturesque which accompanies the development of tourist traffic all
over the world. Cuernavaca's villas are good Santa Monica, but what
place has Santa Monica in Morelos?

I may sound ungrateful to the place which has yielded me many
hours of rest and recuperation from the strain of life at 7,500 feet.
But that is not so. In fact, what I have most enjoyed at Cuernavaca
have been the week-end houses and gardens of my friends, their
deck-chairs, swimming-pools, detective novels and iced drinks. Para-
doxically, I have gone to Cuernavaca not to find Mexico but, on the
rare occasions when I have so wished, to escape from it, to lotus-eat
in luxury and to contemplate the palms, the blue mountains, the
flaming sunsets, with the aloofness of a theatre-goer confronted by a
drama in which he has no part.

From Cuernavaca, the main road slopes down towards a brown
range of mountains, wrinkled with age and erosion. Now winding
down the side of an undivined canyon, now running free across wide,
empty stretches, it drops steadily but so imperceptibly that it is with
surprise that the traveller learns at Puente de Ixtla, three quarters
of an hour further on, that he is only 3,000 feet above the sea, in
tierra caliente.

Bordered by blue hills, the slanting plain of Morelos assumes in
winter the colour of stubble after harvest, broken only by occasional
touches of emerald where a precious thread of water runs along the
bottom of a cactus bordered ravine. The first rains of summer

blacken the volcanic soil, and bring the vivid young green sprouting through, with white clad figures scattered over the face of the land to hold the composition together. The villages are invisible, their presence betrayed only by the orchards of mango, guava, zapote and mamey in which they are hidden. These villages vary extraordinarily in atmosphere as though the few miles which separate each from the next formed an inviolable frontier. Some, like Xochitepec, breathe an atmosphere of dejection and decay. A ruined sugar refinery suggests that for generations its people worked under the broiling sun in the sugar-cane fields, slaving for the hard taskmasters depicted by Diego Rivera in the frescoes bequeathed by Ambassador Morrow to the Palace of Cortés in Cuernavaca. No less ruined are many of the houses of the little *pueblo,* wrecked by the revolution which redeemed it. The "Hill of the Flowers" from which it took its name bears every appearance of having been an artificial pyramid, but on the day I scrambled up, it boasted no flowers but the scrawny *zopilote* buzzards, scavenging in the municipal rubbish dump which crowns the eminence. Down in the *plaza* a *pulquería* bears the name of *La Ilusión del Sueño.* Is even sleep only an illusion here, to be painfully attained through intoxication? A tragic place, whose sorrows are reflected in the faces of its people.

Only a few miles away stands Xoxocotla, an arcadian paradise where Aztec is still spoken and the people lead unchanged the tranquil lives of their forefathers. I have watched them building their houses, white figures against the deep blue of the Morelos sky. Trimmed branches form the uprights and the roof-tree, on either side of which a criss-cross fabric of canes supports the thatching of *zacate* grass. In a corner of each courtyard stand one or two *cuexcomates,* granaries. These are great bowls of dried mud stiffened with a little straw, swelling out from a narrow base to a height of six feet and about the same in diameter, sheltered by a steep conical roof of thatch. At one side beneath the eave is an opening into which as into a letter box are dropped the maize cobs, white or rose-pink when they have dried in the sun on the beaten earth.

The people of Xoxocotla have the blend of quiet dignity and open friendliness which characterizes the village Indians as opposed to those of the *haciendas* and those of the mountains. The people of Tetelcingo lying barely a mile off the highway to Cuautla are unaccountably shyer and more retiring. With their unkempt hair, and skirts and cloaks of blue homespun, the women have misled many into taking them for Otomís instead of *mexicanos* speaking the Tlahuica dialect of Aztec. The schoolmaster knew their language and was using it to teach the little boys the Spanish names of animals. The schoolmistress did not, and was finding it uphill work to induce the tiny children to join in her games and dances.

Driving along the roads of Morelos, you may be fairly sure that anyone you pass on foot has many a weary mile to trudge before reaching his destination. The men walk immense distances in search of work. Nature in Mexico is merciless, and the local drivers, perhaps understandably, are not generous with free lifts. So at least I should judge from the many Indians who would not accept an *aventón* of thirty or forty miles in the hot sun until it had been made clear beyond any doubt that there was no question of payment.

The conversation of these "foot-sloggers" was always entertaining, and their curiosity insatiable. Their questions revealed only the haziest notions of the outside world. The United States always meant something to them, but England generally meant the United States. Then we had to explain that our country was nearly three weeks by sea from Vera Cruz, a statement which was generally greeted with a long-drawn *Caray!* of astonishment. There was room to sleep in the ship, they assumed, never having seen anything much larger than a duck-punt, but what did we do about food? Was there room for cows and chickens? And anyhow, what happened when the boat met a shark? It all reminded me, albeit in a kindlier, more courteous form, of that Don Melchior de Velasco of Chiapa who "in the best, most serious and judicious manner and part of his don-like conference," asked Thomas Gage "whether the sun and moon in England were of the same colour as in Chiapa, and whether Englishmen went barefoot like the Indians and sacrificed one another as formerly did the heathens of that country; and whether all England could afford such a dainty as a dish of frijoles; and whether the women in England went as long with child as did the Spanish women; and lastly whether the Spanish nation were not a far gallanter nation than the English."

The main road turns west at Puente de Ixtla and follows the river up towards its source near Cacahuamilpa, running along the foot of hills which have the bare, primeval look of a relief model for geological students. The river is crossed, and with it the border between Morelos and Guerrero, at the village of Huajintla embowered in yellow *tronadora* and fiery *flamboyant*. A steep climb up the second of the seven ranges, regaining all the height lost since Cuernavaca and a little more besides, brings the traveller to Taxco, one of the loveliest towns in the whole country, but unfortunately in danger of becoming one of the best known and most visited.

The road approaches Taxco along the side of a lofty mountain, thickly wooded. Sheer, naked precipices peer here and there through the trees, with the consciously romantic exaggeration of an early nineteenth century engraving. Round a bend there suddenly appears the pink and white cascade of Taxco's houses looking as though they had been swept down the slope by some cloudburst in the mountains and were struggling to save themselves from slipping into the abyss.

The town takes its full name of Taxco de Alarcón from a Spanish writer who is believed on rather insecure evidence to have been born there. This was not Pedro Antonio Alarcón, the genial nineteenth century author of *The Three Cornered Hat*, but the Golden Age dramatist, Juán Ruíz de Alarcón, author of the neatly turned comedy *La Verdad Sospechosa*, and of the vigorous *El Tejedor de Segovia*. Except in name, however, it is not to Alarcón that Taxco is dedicated but to the great Borda, to whom it owes all that it is and almost all that it has.

Like Taxco itself, Borda owed his fame and fortune to the silver mines discovered on the spot in 1534 by Spaniards in search of iron and tin. The site had not previously been inhabited, and the name was transferred to it from the old Aztec city which has dwindled into an Indian village, known to-day as Taxco Viejo, some eight miles further down towards Iguala. It is derived from *tlachco* the Aztec ball-game, a representation of which served as Old Taxco's hieroglyphic.

The mines had their ups and downs. Gage, passing in 1626, does not mention them but describes Taxco as "a town of some five hundred inhabitants which enjoyeth great commerce with the country about by reason of the great store of cotton wool which is there." It was not until the eighteenth century that the mines yielded their riches, principally to José de la Borda. *El Fenix de los Mineros Ricos* (The Phoenix of Rich Miners), as he came to be called, was born at Jaca in Aragon, in 1699, possibly of French Béarnais parentage, and joined his elder brother Francisco at Taxco in 1716. Here, in 1720, he married one Teresa Verduguillo Aragonés by whom he had two children named Ana María and Manuel. He had had no technical training in mining, but his energy and business ability enabled him to strike one *bonanza* after another, not only in Taxco itself but at the famous Real del Monte in Hidalgo and further north in Zacatecas. He amassed three huge fortunes and lost them all, less through extravagance than through generosity, both to the church and to those around him. "I owe three hundred thousand pesos," he is alleged once to have declared, "but to me they are no more than a *real* and a half." To him the people of Taxco owed not only new roofs for their houses, provisions in time of famine and the water-supply brought by an aqueduct which still spans the main road, but also their splendid parish church, still to-day the pride and glory of the little town. For this munificent gift, Borda was publicly thanked in a Papal Bull by Pope Benedict XIV, and from it came the saying attributed (probably apocryphally) to the man himself: "God gives to Borda, and Borda gives to God." The Phoenix was so far in advance of his time that he abolished in his undertakings the iniquitous system of the *tienda de raya,* not yet fully obsolete in Latin America to-day. By this system, the workman was tied to his plantation or mine by the debts he ran up at a store run by the management at extortionate prices. However hard he worked, he could never rid himself of his burden of debt, which in some cases was passed on to his children.

Borda's fortune reached its apogee half way through the eighteenth century. Yet in 1772, he was compelled to obtain the authority of the Archbishop of Mexico to sell to the Cathedral of *Mexico de Yndias* for 110,000 pesos, a number of jewels and sacred vessels which he had bestowed on Taxco church, but of which he had prudently retained the legal ownership. Chief of these was a golden monstrance, part of which has found its way to Notre Dame in Paris. In 1778, he died at Cuernavaca, in relative poverty.

Against his great qualities must, for the sake of truth, be set some slight faults. He was, it seems, obstinate, passionate and at times violent. With his biographer, Jiménez y Frías, we may try to gloss over these by the discreet remark that "if he sometimes argued with heat it was not to impose his own convictions, but rather that the truth might prevail, and if he was greatly addicted to his own ideas he was so from conviction and not from contrariness."

Two portraits have survived of this great figure. One hangs in the Sala Capitular of Taxco parish church. In this he is seen in the prime of life, dressed in a French coat of the middle of the eighteenth century, with embroidered sleeves and jabot, a powdered wig with a black bow, and white stockings. The features are bold and imperious, the eyes dark and flashing beneath heavy eyebrows. He has the high cheek-bones, tight-lipped mouth and thin, hooked nose, straightening at the tip, of the Basque, and these, coupled with his name, make it probable that Basque blood ran in his veins. A later portrait in the National Museum shows him in profile, dressed in sober black, with a sword at his side and taking snuff. He looks older and more drawn, but the hawk-like gaze is, if anything, intensified.

The great parish church which "Borda gave to God" and to Taxco stands in the centre of the town athwart a ridge running down from the steep and wooded Mount Huisteco. Dedicated to San Sebastian and to Santa Prisca, an obscure Roman martyr, it is one of the jewels of Mexican churrigueresque architecture. It was designed by Diego Durán, and completed in the seven years from 1751 to 1758. Many of the materials were brought from abroad, the tiles for instance from Spanish Talavera as well as from Mexican Puebla, but the exquisite rose-coloured stone which gives the building its principal charm came from no further away than Mount Huisteco. In the light of dawn, Santa Prisca's church has a delicate shell-pink translucence. Under the high noontide sun, it takes on the sheen of burnished copper which the late afternoon warms to ruddy gold.

It was only in 1922 that a motor-car reached Taxco for the first time, and the motor-road followed some years later, bringing with it a more or less residential cosmopolitan colony, of some of whose members it remains uncertain whether they are painters who have gone there to drink or drinkers who have gone there to paint. Yet Taxco has preserved its spiritual integrity. It remains to-day what it has always been, a congeries of white walls and red roofs clambering up the hillside and slithering down the ravines; of arcaded loggias, balconies of open, mauresque tile-work and wrought iron grilles over narrow windows; of hidden patios and gardens betrayed only by purple bougainvillea, scarlet hibiscus, pink *rosa mantana* and the tattered pennants of banana leaves.

Besides Santa Prisca, Taxco counts several churches and chapels: the solid convent of San Bernardino de Sena; the chapels of

Ojeda and Guadalupe perched like falcons' eyries above the town; and, on the ridge below Santa Prisca, the chapel of Nuestro Señor de la Santa Vera Cruz, Our Lord of the Holy True Cross, whose miraculous image attracts crowds of Indians to his *fiesta* on the fourth Friday in Lent.

We were there in 1937. In the tiny *atrio* stood a *castillo,* a tall pole hung at intervals with hoop-shaped frames strung with crackers and fireworks linked by a thin train of powder. When this was lit the fire slowly travelled up the pole, setting each hoop dizzily spinning and flinging off little rockets in the shapes of men and animals. The top ring consisted of six or eight dolls which danced round in a grotesque, agonized rigadoon as the crackers scorched their papier mâché legs. White against the deep blue sky they were like a cruel burlesque of the *juego de los voladores.* I wondered whether there was not some atavistic, sadistic memory of the *auto da fé* in the crowd's laughter at their tortured, writhing antics.

At the foot of the pole the Dance of the Moors and Christians was being performed.

We had hoped, however, that this *fiesta* would bring out Guerrero's speciality, the *Danza de los Tecuanes* or Tiger Dance. Unfortunately, this did not appear, and for my account of it I am obliged to rely on a performance by dancers from Chilpancingo which I saw in Mexico City.

Although it has lost any choreographic virtuosity which it may once have had, the Tiger Dance, like the Yaqui Deer Dance, is a survival of hunting magic, and its theme is the pursuit and death of a tiger, or rather of its Mexican equivalent, a jaguar. The *tecuan* was played by a dancer in a spotted and striped overall and a big tiger mask, its features frozen into something between a snarl, a gape and a grin. The other dancers took the parts of hunters and their servants. The hunters were magnificent figures in broad sombreros, grotesque black or red masks and clothes of sack-cloth, with whips in their hands. They and the tiger skipped backwards and forwards in various dance figures. Then one of the hunters was caught and mauled by the tiger, and a Doctor was produced who cured him in the best tradition of our English mumming-plays. Finally the tiger was killed and, after a brief moment recumbent on the floor, recovered "to fight another day."

That *fiesta* night at Taxco, another speciality of Guerrero appeared, the *Torito,* obviously a near relative of the Spanish St. John's night *toro de fuego.* He was a man carrying on his head a small figure of a bull, like his namesake in the Vaqueros' Dance. From it rose a flimsy frame of bamboo, strung like the *castillo* with squibs, crackers and catherine wheels. To the music of a brass band, he ran about among the crowd with a queer loping step, scattering the small boys and, like a fighting bull from San Mateo or La Laguna, charging the improvised cloaks with which *aficionados* sought to play him. Then light was set to his train and the bull-man was transformed into a flaming monster, crackling and spitting fire. Before his onrush the screaming crowds broke and fled, only to return the moment his back was turned. Coloured flares fell from his frame and flooded him with light in the surrounding darkness or from behind threw him into sinister silhouette. The scene had the fantastic, nightmare quality of a Goya.

To me the most fascinating spot in all Taxco is the little *plaza* before the great west front of Santa Prisca. The other three sides are filled with white houses, the highest of them Borda's, three stories lower on this side than on the other. In the middle, round the municipal bandstand, runs a tiny garden with evergreen American laurels clustering so thick above their bare trunks that the intertwined branches form a canopy casting a green shade on even the hottest day. By day or by night the *plaza* has the heightened colour of a stage setting, dark green of laurels against the rose-pink stone of the church You want to relapse into your stall and wait for the actors to come on and play their parts. There is an atmosphere of suspense. Something, you feel, must happen soon. Then you realize that the actors are there before you. All who walk across the stage, *mestizo,* Indian or even American tourist, become somehow endowed with a new emotional significance. For a moment they have become fragments of a pattern. Then they are gone and the kaleidoscope is shaken up anew.

Here for centuries there used to be held each Sunday the most picturesquely set market in Mexico. From the untouched hinterland of Taxco the Indians came in the night before, spread their wares out on *petate* mats and sheltered them with white awnings which, alternating under the sun or the moon with pools of shadow, made the square look from above like a chessboard. Up the steep narrow lanes the market used to overflow, past the baroque drinking-fountain and down towards la Vera Cruz. Now to make way for tourists and their traffic the *tianguis* has been tidied away, relegated to a cement platform built up in a *barranca* below Santa Prisca. I shall always treasure its memory as one which composed and condensed into a veritable work of art the elements of Indian markets all over the country.

A description of a Mexican market is apt to degenerate into a wearisome catalogue, yet some account must be given of that institution which plays so vital a part in the lives of the inhabitants. Long before the Conquest the *tianguis* was an essential feature of life, and Bernal Díaz has left a vivid description of the great variety of wares exposed for sale in the great market of Tlaltelolco. "Each kind of merchandise was kept by itself," he begins, "and had its fixed place marked out. Let us begin with the dealers in gold, silver and precious stones, feathers, mantles and embroidered goods, slaves, pieces of cloth and cotton. In another part, there were skins of tigers and lions, of otters and jackals, deer and other animals and badgers and mountain cats, some tanned and others untanned, and other classes of merchandise. . . ." So he goes on with a list of wares many of which it would be difficult to find in a modern market. The arrangement is the same, however, and the variety as great, in any rural market to which the Indians flock to-day. Grudging neither time nor effort, they come unbelievable distances to sell their few surplus products, bartering them for others or expending the proceeds on the factory goods of which they stand so greatly in need.

Maize, seed and beans are exposed for sale on *petates* in heaps of varying colour and texture. Fruit, vegetables and chiles are neatly arranged in little pyramids of five. To the amateur of gastronomic tourism they offer wide scope for experiment, seldom entirely satisfactory in my own case, I must confess, for exotic fruits are often a sad disappointment. Juicy pineapples from *tierra caliente* and golden, melting mangoes earn unqualified approval. Equally unqualified is my dislike of astringent persimmon and of the rugous-skinned mamey. Passion fruit, despite its name, is a sad deception with a mouthful of brittle seeds to a trickle of gelatinous, gooseberry-flavoured juice. Between the two extremes lies the whole gamut of *zapote negro*, its dark flesh delicious when mashed up with a little orange juice; the purplish *camote* or sweet potato; the *papaya* or paw-paw, rich in pepsins; the knobbly *chirimoya* or custard-apple; the *jicama* root, in consistency like a flavourless apple yet quenching to the thirst; and the tasteless *tuna,* fruit of the prickly pear. Scarcely to be counted as a fruit, but as fresh to the taste as its purplish-green enamel skin is a delight to the eye, is the *aguacate* or alligator pear.

So much for the fresh, natural foods. Cooked ones sizzling at innumerable booths are as savoury in smell as they are perilous in appearance. Viscerous meats, *tamales* and *tacos* filled with unknown ingredients must take unending toll of digestions weakened by hot chiles.

Pulque flows from inflated pigskin or wooden tub. At the soft-drink stall, mineral waters have not entirely displaced the fruit essences of a more innocent age. In their tall glass containers, they are as vividly coloured as Rosamund's Purple Jar. Orange, lemon, tamarind, crimson *jamaica,* opaque white *orchata* made of barley, and *chia,* dyed arsenic-green by the little black seeds which float in it. No less lurid are the sweets, *jamoncillo* of brown sugar and coconut from Juquila, *chongos* of violent pink cream from Oaxaca, and a hundred others, enticing to the children, alarming to their parents.

At Taxco and throughout Morelos and Guerrero, colour is supplied less by the women than by the men. Here, the soul-destroying blue dungarees which are making such inroads into the native costume on the high plateau have scarcely penetrated to displace the clean white shirt and loose trousers whose twisted cut at the waist makes them appear to stay up of their own volition. In this part of the *tierra templada* there is a great vogue for shirts of coloured satin in every possible hue: crushed strawberry, sky-blue, yellow, pea-green, tangerine, eau-de-nil, old rose, cyclamen and wine. The white *cotones* reflect, the straw *sombreros* refract, a diffused light on the brown faces giving them a golden glow like light shining through alabaster. Often the men gather round some itinerant minstrel with a guitar, singing to a thin, threadbare little tune *corridos,* ballads about the heroes of the Revolution or the latest crime in the capital. He does not pass round the hat but relies for his earnings on the sale of broadsheets with the words of the songs. It is these men who have carried the same popular ditties into every corner of the vast Republic, making Mexican folksong national rather than regional.

Threatened though it is by factory production and by a rising standard of living, the handicraft tradition is still very much alive in Mexico. Arty-crafty shops abound in Mexico City and in the larger tourist centres, but on the whole they cater for the undiscriminating visitor to the point that among Mexicans the term "Mexican curios" has acquired almost a derogatory sense. Nevertheless they drive a lively trade in pictures in inlaid wood or straw, bird pictures made of real feathers which are no more than a hollow memory of the lost art of the Aztecs and Tarascans, lacquered gourds from Olinalá, black, purple or green on a ground of orange-red, embroidered *faja* belts from Milpa Alta, life-sized men in *petate* wicker from Lerma, Oaxaca sarapes in the wrong colours and the wrong designs and a host of other objects, to-day mostly made for the tourist. There is practically nothing you cannot buy, from a *charro* suit to a cake of soap, with the Aztec calendar stone emblazoned upon it.

In the rural markets, on the other hand, handicrafts may be seen fulfilling their proper function, faithful to the true canons of Indian taste. Textiles, pottery and basket-work offer a fascinating range to the collector who will be satisfied only with the authentic and is prepared to take his time and to travel far in search of it.

Sarapes, for instance, must not be judged from the crudely coloured specimens, fit only to adorn the piano of a suburban parlour, into which the wonderful eighteenth century weaving of Saltillo has degenerated. Those of Oaxaca, or to be precise of Teotitlan del Valle, are traditionally correct in sober grey, black and white, and aesthetically pleasing when they preserve the Zapotec designs of deer and tiger with flowers growing from their backs. The plain of Toluca weaves attractive stepped patterns in brown and cream, the natural colours of the wool. These are probably pre-Cortesian as are the diamonds and zig-zags of San Miguel Chiconcuac near Texcoco. San Francisco Xonacatlan has misguidedly taken to weaving, at infinite trouble, *charros* and *chinas,* eagles and serpents in place of the graceful floral designs in blue, red or maroon on a white ground which, with luck, you may buy off the back of one of its inhabitants.

Earthenware, with certain exceptions, is rather disappointing when compared, for instance, with peasant Portugal or for that matter with pre-Cortesian Mexico. Decoration is apt to be restricted to a brown glaze with a few rather haphazard stripes of black. Form, too, is undistinguished, though unglazed water jars, tall in the Mesquital Valley, rounded at Yalalag, are often effective in their simple curves.

Two villages near Oaxaca have each a well-defined tradition of its own. San Bartolo Coyotepec produces a so-called black ware the colour of which is in reality something between gun-metal and pewter. Azumba specializes in a rich green glaze. Both are seen to better advantage in little toys than in utilitarian objects. Coyotepec makes jars in the shape of monkeys and vampires, bells in which the head and torso of an archaic-looking female figure form the handle and her flared out skirt the bell. At Easter time, Azumba produces jars in the shape of angels or animals with glazed heads and roughly corrugated bodies in the interstices of which seeds are placed. Watered through the porous walls of the jar, the seed puts forth a hirsute growth of cress-like shoots appropriate to the season of renewal.

At Taxco, or better still at Iguala, you can buy jars of all sizes in a ware made in the hot country of Guerrero at San Miguel Huapan and other villages. The ground is pale, almost colourless, unglazed and painted freehand in reddish brown. Loops of clay serve as handles and as feet. The designs, stylized floral patterns, birds or animals, strongly recall the geometrical ornament of the Aegean civilization and even include the spreading tentacles of the octopus so closely associated with Minoan Crete.

There is something about Taxco which suggests an island town running down to a sea-shore which is not there. These ridges and ravines, one feels, should lead to storm-beaten promontories and sheltered coves with boats drawn up on the sand, nets spread out to dry and the strong tang of the ocean. Instead there is a deep abyss overhung only by the few houses which have, as it were, rolled over the edge of the Acapulco road. Beyond are bare, lonely hills, cut by a trail which winds over the horizon into the unknown. This marine feeling is to some extent explained when one climbs up along the hillside to the west of the town, and the vast panorama of Guerrero's *tierra caliente* is gradually unfolded. This is indeed a sea, though not of water but of vapours rising from a tangle of age-wrinkled hills and wide valleys stretching away to the heaving, broken horizon of the Sierra Madre.

I have seen this view many times, pin-clear in the rain-washed light of the wet season or reduced to its essential outlines by the heat-haze of the dry, yet I can never grow weary of it, not so much for what it is as for its implications, the spur which it sets to the imagination. This, I never tire of telling myself, is *tierra caliente,* what William Spratling calls "the country's physical uncon- scious . . . vast and fecund, forbidding and promising, practically unexplored and difficult of access." These are the bad lands with their fevers and their strange, disfiguring, tropical diseases. Through them winds the great Río de las Balsas, symbol of unknown Mexico. As I look out upon them from the healthy mountain air and the civilized security of Taxco, I feel as though I am gazing out over the "dangerous and combustious seas" from the safety of a cliff-fortress, or looking down on a riotous street-crowd from the sanctuary of a lofty balcony.

As you walk or ride up the trail behind the town the view grows ever vaster. The near landscape has something of a Japanese quality, with steep rocks among the trees. These are dumpy little cedars or the curious *cucharillo* which I have seen nowhere else, with big vel- vety leaves, rather broader than horse chestnut, which, reversing the ordinary process of nature, are scarlet when they unfold at the tip of the branch and then, shedding their rust-coloured pollen, turn to a vivid green. The Mixteca country climbs up beyond the iron-grey hills. Away to the left, Popocatépetl soars into the sky, its lower slopes lost in the mist, the streaked cone floating in the air, sundered from earth, borne aloft by white-winged clouds. To the left, a side trail leads deep down into a lonely valley, where tropical under- growth has swamped the bleached bones of an *hacienda,* San Fran- cisco Cuadra, picked bare by revolutionary wars as a carcase by *zopilote* buzzards, more heart-breakingly desolate in the brilliant sun- shine and rank vegetation than ever it could be under our cold north- ern skies.

From Taxco, the main road drops down to Iguala in wide circles, dropping 4,000 feet in twenty miles. Here one is in *tierra ca- liente* with a vengeance, steaming hot at all seasons of the year. The road skirts the little town where, on a sultry day in 1821, Morelos made his famous Plan of Independence and designed the Mexican flag. A curious legend has it that, happening to eat a water-melon, he chose its colours, green, red and white, but another explanation is that white stands for purity and religion, green for independence and red for understanding with the Spaniards. So deeply embowered in trees is the little town, that from the highway scarcely a house is to be seen.

Not for many miles does one climb again into cooler air. Dropping even lower, the Río de las Balsas is crossed by a fine bridge at Mescala, full of turbid water as I saw it one September day and flowing with a quiet and sinister purposefulness, out of the unknown and into the unknown, between steep hills which soon hid it from view.

This must be one of the low points of the road. Thereafter, one follows up the bed of a shallow river between wooded hills which gradually close in to become the dreaded Cañon del Zopilote or Buzzard's Gulch, a place of such stifling, oppressive heat that it is easy to believe that none but the croaking carrion-bird finds a home there. To obtain the full effect of the canyon you should be going the other way, dropping from the cool heights of Zumpango ever deeper into this inferno, so that you expect round every corner to come upon Charon and his dark river.

Zumpango and, a little higher, Chilpancingo furnish one of those brusque transitions of climate which are the hall-mark of Mexico. After the first a crest is passed and one finds oneself in a shallow green valley reminiscent, of all things, of Wales. A long ridge cuts the western sky. The road borders on a broad expanse of pasture through which trickles a stream with grassy banks, and Chilpancingo, when it is reached, has an atmosphere of small-town characterlessness which might belong to almost any country.

It is beyond Chilpancingo that the road, narrow and tortuous, attains its full majesty. The four remaining mountain-passes crowded into the last ninety miles can, at a pinch, be distinguished and told off on the fingers, but the impression is rather of a continuous tangle of mountain. The thin ribbon of road, never visible for more than a hundred yards or so ahead, threads its way through the Sierra Madre Occidental, the Pacific *cordillera* which runs almost unbroken from the Canadian Rockies to the great Andean volcanoes. Following a route traced out in colonial times (when the treasure of the *nao de China,* the China galleon, had to be conveyed from Acapulco to Mexico City), the road twists and turns, rises and falls with bewildering rapidity. In retrospect one sees it not with the continuity of a cinema film, but as a series of brilliant, kaleidoscopic snapshots; a group of palm-huts by a stream among the flame-like acacia blooms of the

"Pride of Barbados"; the firs and cloud-enfolded distances of Agua del Obispo; the broad waters of the Río Papagayo and the peripatias of the road first down and then up its tumbling, cascading tributaries; a high waterfall dropping out of a feathery hillside; a glimpse of glistening, brown bodies in the tawny waters of Xaltianguis; and that last steep rise of all, from the crest of which, "in a wild surmise," the Pacific is first seen and the blue horseshoe of Acapulco Bay lies at last at the dusty feet of the traveller.

Acapulco is exactly what you expect of the small tropical harbour. The houses of wood or palm thatch lead down to an untidy, ill-defined water-front. In one-storied shipping offices, perspiring clerks work in their shirt-sleeves, at a temperature which seldom falls below 80 or rises above 90 degrees Fahrenheit. Zopilotes, so noble in flight, so repulsive at rest, roost in rows on the cocoanut palms, and the astonished northerner discovers that cocoanuts growing on the trees are more like clusters of great green cow-bells than the round, hairy skulls at which he has so often shied at village fairs. Overhead, in dignified, streamlined beauty, passes the shadow of a frigate-bird, and off-shore, another lesson in natural history to the Londoner, the pelican, which he deemed such a monster of clumsiness behind the railings of St. James' Park, fishes with swift dexterity.

Of the many sandy bathing-beaches, the most popular are the sheltered Caleta and the Playa de los Hornos beyond the sixteenth century fort, where the Pacific combers come rolling in, their violence tempered by the long arm of land which half closes the bay. More beautiful but infinitely more dangerous is the great expanse of Pié de la Cuesta, on the open sea to the north-west, an unbroken line of white, seething surf as far as the eye can see. The road to Pié de la Cuesta winds corniche-fashion along a mountain-side with glimpses of little rocky coves suggesting a tropical Devonshire. Where it drops down to the sea there is a small fishing hamlet of palm-huts inhabited by Indians and *lobos* (wolves) or Indian-negro half-breeds. At the far end of the beach is another village where naked men, their skins tanned to a rich mahogany, harpoon great fish in the surf with two-pronged fish-spears.

The intervening ten miles form a long, narrow spit of land, never more than a quarter of a mile wide, separating the sea from a wide freshwater lagoon, the Laguna de Coyuca, fringed with impenetrable vegetation, a paradise for naturalists and sportsmen. At early dawn, the mud-coloured caimans may be seen before they hide away from the intense light of the sun. Bird-life of all kinds abounds. Graceful egrets, delicate little stilts and sandpipers, duck of all kinds, fishing pelicans, flocks of green parrakeets and, as once I saw, a great black and gold kingfisher pursue their avocations almost heedless of the intruding stranger.

Behind it all, like a painted backcloth, hang the sultry mountains of the tropics, overgrown with low feathery thorn-trees nameless to all but the naturalist. They are empty of human habitation, of cultivation even, indistinguishable from one another and preserving a sullen, brooding anonymity strangely disconcerting to those accustomed to our individualized northern hills.

STANTON DELAPLANE
AND ROBERT DE ROOS

Cuernavaca, Taxco, Acapulco, 1950s

"SILVER POURS OUT OF TAXCO. DOLLARS POUR IN.
WITH THE DOLLARS THE QUAINT AND UNSPOILED
NATIVES BOUGHT THE LOUDEST JUKEBOXES I
HAVE EVER HEARD."

*In the 1950s Stanton Delaplane's newspaper column, "Postcards from
Delaplane," was a popular feature of the* San Francisco Chronicle, *the*
Louisville Courier-Journal, *the* Houston Post, *the* Honolulu Star-
Bulletin, *and many other papers around the country. Delaplane offered
lighthearted but loving accounts of his worldwide journeys, combined
with well-informed travel advice, both pertinent and impertinent.*

*Drawing on those columns, he joined forces with magazine writer
Robert de Roos for the 1960* Delaplane in Mexico. *After visiting
Puerto Vallarta ("It is a good climate for lizards"), staying in the same
Morelia hotel cottage occupied by Ava Gardner while she was filming*
The Sun Also Rises *("Did Miss Ava crawl under this same bed to re-
trieve the bedside flashlight?"), and coping with Mexico City taxi drivers
("I enjoyed the battle as the bullfighter enjoys the arena. It was full of
tricks and cape work"), he set off on Mexico's most popular tourist route.*

THE BEST ROAD IN MEXICO IS THE NEW TOLL road—four lanes of shiny concrete—between Mexico and Cuernavaca. Cuernavaca where the gentry like to spend the weekend and always have. Gentry like the Emperor Maximilian and his Carlota and Doris Duke. A lot of Americans on the lam have found Cuernavaca a pleasant place to avoid the income tax cops. And, of course, the toll road leads not only to Cuernavaca but also to Taxco and Acapulco and some other spots which will be mentioned. In due course.

Diego Rivera spent his time well in Cuernavaca, splashing some very spectacular paint on the walls of the Cortez Palace, now the state capitol. The Rivera murals showing how the Spaniards snuck across the ravine on vines to sack the city. They came like monkeys, they say in Cuernavaca.

There is a whole breed of dogs which play the Cárdenas delicatessen, a pleasant place to eat on a sunny day. They all have the same shaggy, sad-eyed look. They sit and eye the tourists eating on the sidewalk across from the Cortez Palace.

The tourists are softhearted. They say:

"Oh, the poor starved dog. What a country, where they starve the dogs." They throw him a cracker.

Now these dogs are not starving at all. They are simply fitted to survive because they look like they are starving. They are living in a fashionable tourist town and they are hog-fat inside.

The dogs go over and sniff the cracker. But they do not eat it. They are waiting for the leftovers of the Serrano ham. Or else they want the cracker buttered.

This makes the tourists furious. Because a dog has no right to look like he is starving and then be so ungrateful about charity.

FREEWHEELING

Every Mexican tour agency advises you to see Taxco, the mountain silver town. There is a standard tour—Cuernavaca for lunch, Taxco overnight, Acapulco and return. Five days for $57.

"Suppose I wish only to ride to Acapulco?"

"But it is a tour," said the tourist man unhappily. "Where will you sleep?"

"With friends. Or under the stars."

The tourist man looked worried and looked to the Mexican skies for inspiration. He said it would cost $50 to ride to Acapulco.

I said such a price was fantástico. He said stubbornly it was a tour. Why didn't I go on a nice tour and not make problems?

When you run into this problem in Mexico, take what they call a turismo. All over Mexico they run fast eight-passenger limousines. They are comfortable and cheap. I went over to Los Galgos—Greyhound Lines of Mexico.

"How much for one way to Taxco, cousin?"

The Galgos man punched me out a ticket for exactly $1 American.

Lay off the tours. Go Galgos.

The big Dodge limousine was filled. Three in the back, three in the middle. Two up with the driver.

The driver gave me a front seat where I could see the hairpin twists in the road and measure how close we came to wandering burros.

The road runs high over the mountains where the old stagecoach ran to Cuernavaca. You can see part of the cobbled road. Maximilian and Carlota rode it in gilded Imperial carriages.

There is a new superhighway to Cuernavaca now. But Galgos takes the colorful old road. The driver slid along it in a neat style with a Number 3 pool ball welded to the wheel for easier handling.

Like most Mexican drivers, he cut the engine and slipped it into neutral on the downgrade. To save gas.

He had each turn taped. The curves marked purely right angle, he slowed to 60. (It shows 100 on a speedometer marked in kilometers. It takes constant mental translation to keep your heart flutter down.)

You climb out of the Valley of Mexico at 7,500 feet and rise to about 13,000.

From there it is all downhill to Acapulco at sea level. The driver shut off the key and slipped it into neutral. The speedometer rose gradually to 120. He slid around a burro and took a bending curve along a canyon.

"Freewheeling," he said happily. "Nervous?"

"I have a defect of the heart."

"Tequila," said the driver. "Tequila cures the heart."

I said this ancient cure had been rediscovered by modern medicine. And a fancy New York chain bottles a rare cognac for prescription only.

"This is good brandy?"

"Like gold."

"How unfortunate we do not have a bottle," he said. "It gets boring going downhill."

The speedometer was climbing to 140—about 84 miles per hour. I wished we had a bottle, too. But I was not a bit bored.

The road intercepted the old cobbled road on the edge of Cuernavaca. The driver started the engine and roared into gear. Regretfully. And after coasting an hour or so more on the other side, we swerved around several dogs and climbed the cobbled street of Taxco. All for $1. And not a boring moment.

HI-YO, SILVER!

"Taxco," said the Mexican guide, "is quaint, sleepy and unspoiled. It has 15,000 inhabitants. Fifteen hundred silversmiths. Is it not quaint?"

"Like a three-dollar bill," I agreed. "Likewise sleepy."

If 1,500 Taxqueños beat silver, the rest all beat drums. At 5:30 each morning they beat drums under my quaint windows.

"Who beats the drums?" I asked the sleepy waiter sleepily at coffee.

"The soldiers, señor."

"But why so early?"

"Soldiers must rise early. They are constantly in preparation."

Well, after two days of drum-beating, I rose in curiosity and despair. It occurred to me that drums might be the new secret weapon. Drum your enemies into insensibility.

The drumming had gone on for half an hour. The drums would start under the quaint window. They would fade away as the drummers marched up the street. I would just be getting back to sleep again when—BOOM! BOOM! Rattledy-boom! Back they came.

I got up and looked out the window. It was still dark. Six small boys were marching up and down with drums. They had a leader. Also a bugler. At intervals the bugler let out a few disheartened toots.

At 6:30 they dispersed and I went back to sleep.

At 6:45—WHOOOOOOOOOOOEEEEEEEEOOOOOOO.

The siren at the lead and zinc mines announced the change of shifts.

At 7 o'clock—BONG! BONG! BONG! The church bells in the beautiful pink towers of Santa Prisca. The church built two centuries ago on top of the fabulous silver mine that poured a fortune into the pockets of Borda.

"God gives to Borda and Borda gives to God."

At 7 of a sleepless morning I sort of wished the Almighty had been a little less generous with Mr. Borda.

I got up and went down to coffee. No wonder Taxco is sleepy.

Taxco lies on hills. A hillside town of cobbled streets winding among ancient adobes.

It is considered so quaint and sleepy and unspoiled that Mexico has made it a national monument. This means you cannot build skyscrapers or luxury hotels or serve hot dogs in the plaza.

Many years ago Mr. Bill Spratling came here and saw that it was truly quaint, sleepy and unspoiled. He gathered up the locals and taught them to work silver. Today Taxco beats a ton of silver a month into earrings, bracelets, cups, coffeepots, pins and baby spoons. They ship it all over Mexico.

Some of it is the finest silverwork in the world. Some of it is pure junk.

This put Taxco on the map, as you might say. The town lies halfway between Mexico City and Acapulco, the Miami Beach of Mexico.

Silver pours out of Taxco. Dollars pour in. With the dollars the quaint and unspoiled natives bought the loudest jukeboxes I have ever heard. They bought drums and bugles and hammered at them harder than they did at silver.

I have wanted to talk to Mr. Spratling sometime. I wanted to ask him how he felt about it these days. But founding father Spratling has moved out of sleepy Taxco. He lives on a quiet, quaint ranch about 20 miles away. I imagine on a still morning you can hear the drums of sleepy Taxco.

THE OLD PERCENTAGE

The tourist season is in full swing in Taxco.

The tourist ladies walk uphill in their spike heels and come skittering down precariously. Loaded and ballasted with silver.

This is *the* silver town. Halfway between the tourist Mecca of the Reforma in Mexico City and the elegant beaches of Acapulco.

"It sort of gives you a chance to stop off and see how the natives really live," a tourist lady confided in me the other night at Los Arcos.

The natives live colorfully as befits natives living in a national monument. They run burros up and down the streets. And have been light-metered so much they can take a look at the sky and tell you the camera setting. In English.

I find the major source of alarm in Taxco these days is pretty much like you might find at a luncheon of the Better Business Bureau.

"Some of the silver shops have formed an ethical organization," said an American resident. "But," he said sadly, "they cannot fight the guide racket."

It seems the Mexico City guides—the all-powerful boys who guide the spiked heels up and down the cobbles—cut in for 20 to 25 per cent on all sales.

"You must keep one price or you will drive the tourists away," said the ethical Americans of Taxco.

This seemed like a good idea. Mexico goes strong for booster organizations. Outside almost every town is a listing of when the Lions Club or the Rotary holds meetings.

They formed a sort of Better Business Bureau. Colorfully native but better.

But in every Eden there is a nest of serpents. There were a number of natives who did not want to remain colorful. They wanted to get rich.

They saw quite plainly that the guides were hustling the customers where the pay-off was 25 per cent. They remained colorfully enough in the Better Business Bureau. But they paid a percentage, too.

"It has not been a great success," said the American.

It is a difficult thing to keep a businesslike town quaint and colorful. When you can do so much better by raising the prices 25 per cent. And give it to the guide.

The plaza at Taxco is like a stage setting. A beautiful plaza under the Indian laurels with the pink cantera stone of Santa Prisca Church gleaming in the sunlight.

The plaza is crowded with colorful serape sellers. And colorful basket sellers. And every shop on the four sides gleams with bright silver.

The boy with the baskets made his pitch for me on the bench under the laurels.

"Cuanto?" I said.

"Twenty-five pesos," he said in English. "Look," he said, "you can't get these kind of baskets in Toluca. You put two or three pounds in a Toluca basket, they break."

"I'll give you fifteen."

"Twenty-two. That's my best price. Look, mister, these are the best baskets in Mexico. They are bound all the way around. Not like those cheap Toluca baskets."

"I'll go for seventeen. My last offer."

"Mister," he said, "I could do it for twenty. But not for seventeen. You're an American. You understand. Don't you want me to have my commission?"

Not only colorful. Smart.

THE BIG BOOM

Life in Mexico is one fiesta after another. I cannot get my shoes from the shoe repairman this morning.

"He has gone to his village for the fiesta."

If there is not a national fiesta, there are local fiestas. Not a day passes in Mexico without one. The Indians do not care. They order up the fireworks and knock off work. If you cannot get your shoes, go barefoot.

I am having a Corona Extra with Bill Shanahan, editor of the *Mexico City News.* Prices are up in Mexico.

"You cannot determine costs by the cheap labor in Mexico," said Shanahan.

"Some years ago, I was working for American Mine and Smelting over in Taxco. The big boss came to my boss and said: 'I want to know something: Tell me why it is that in Taxco it costs us more to drive a shaft than anywhere else in the world. Write a report I can show to New York.'

"The boss said: 'Very well.' He said to me, 'Write this letter:

" 'Paragraph: You want to know why it costs more to drive a shaft in Taxco than anywhere else in the world?

" 'Paragraph: In most parts of the world, people want to improve their social and economic position. Not so in Taxco.

" 'Paragraph: In Taxco, people work as a pastime between fiestas of which there are seldom fewer than two every month. When they work, they work slowly.

" 'Paragraph: There is also the cost of dynamite. Each village competes to have the biggest, loudest fireworks with the biggest boom. There is nothing to equal dynamite for this purpose. More of our dynamite goes into fireworks than goes into the shaft.

" 'Paragraph: This increases the expense and makes it more expensive to drill a shaft in Taxco than anywhere else in the world.

" 'Paragraph: Very truly yours.' "

TOURIST HEAVEN

Acapulco, beloved of the American tourist; 40 beaches, 250 hotels. In the winter season, the town services 60,000 tourists at a clip. The town lies on a little landlocked Mexican bay. Bougainvillaea climbs every patio wall. And coco palms curve into the sky, exactly as prescribed by tropical travel writers.

It is six and a half hours from California or Chicago or New York. By Eastern, Western, CMA, Pan American, Air France, or Aeronaves de Mexico. About $270 per couple round trip, family plan. From snow to palm trees and back again.

It is raining to beat the band. This is considered very unseasonable weather and is blamed variously on the atom bomb; Veracruz on the opposite coast (for having hurricane weather); Tlaloc, the Aztec rain god, who probably hates tourists anyway.

"We came here 14, 15, 20 years ago," says the American colony. "It *never* rains at this time of the year. I don't know what's causing it." No? Well, I will tell you. I am causing it.

When I was the brass-polishing pride of the Merchant Marine, we used to put into Acapulco. (I regret to say I have counted this up on my fingers and find my last visit to Acapulco was 28 years ago.)

What I mean, it seems to me it was *always* raining in Acapulco. I spent most of my time in this port soaking-wet and securing canvas hatch covers. I was young and expendable. I drew all the wet work.

I do not think the town had one hotel at that time. When people wanted to visit Mexico City, they rode our ship way up to Mazatlán where they could catch a train.

My memory of Acapulco is a sandy plaza and a sandy bar on the corner. We carried an old sock ashore and filled it with sand—a matter of precaution.

It rained on me. It rained on the sailors of the Manila galleons in the old days. It rained on Drake when he beat up this port in the *Golden Hind* in 1575. Don't tell me about rain and atom bombs.

Scattered about the town and on the high cliffs that hide the bay are the homes of the Americans. The Americans discovered Acapulco 5, 10, 15 years ago. They constantly lament the good old days.

"Why, there were only a half dozen hotels. And the beaches! Nobody on them. And prices—you could live on $5 a day."

You cannot live on $5 a day today. But plenty of Mexican families are making it on less. My waiter handles house, wife and two children on $3.20. But the tourist rates come high at Acapulco. We tourists are a demanding bunch. It is only fair that we pay for such things as waking the cook from his siesta to get dinner on time.

Personally, I like the rain. It cools things off. Besides, this is the way I remember Acapulco. The tourists do not like the rain and have been departing, blaming such things on the Hotel Association and the Chamber of Commerce.

They are wrong. I believe the American colony that it has not rained for 5, 10, 15 years. I will bet it has not rained for 28 years.

Not since the good old days when I came here with a sock of sand in my hip pocket.

I think I bring the rain. I am hotter than Tlaloc as a rainmaker. For me, it *always* rains in Acapulco.

STORMY WEATHER

It has been raining for five days now in Acapulco. Great slashing, tropical rains. Booming on the rooftops and firing cascades of water from the rain gutters into the narrow Mexican streets. The sky is thick with cloud. The Pacific, far below our cliffs, is the color of lead. The sea is rough and there are hurricane winds to the north. This morning when I went down to the beach, they were bringing in the body of a drowned fisherman.

When I was the youthful pride of the Merchant Marine, my ship recruited its quartermasters from Acapulco. They were short, dark sailors and all of them seemed to be named Ramírez.

One of them called Manuel told me he had been wrecked in one of these storms. They call them "Tchuantepecs." He swam for eight hours. As he swam, he prayed to the Virgin of Guadalupe. He promised to burn a fortune in candles.

As things looked blacker, Manuel made harder promises.

"I promees to geev up the smokeen."

After a while he thought he saw a shark fin.

"I pray more ahnd I promees eef I get ashore, I no more dreenkeen."

Manuel swam on. Things were tough all over.

"Then I say, 'Eef I get on the shore, I no more chaseen the girls.' "

A short time later, his feet hit bottom and he climbed up on the beach.

"What did you do, Manuel?"

"Oh, I burn the candles and I no smokeen or dreenkeen or chaseen the girls for two weeks. Then I theenk, Ees better to be een the ocean than leev thees way. I get dronk, smoke, chase the girl. I make new promees. I promees nevair make such promees again."

Manuel and I had the gangway watch in Acapulco. Our job was to greet the townspeople who came aboard. There was no road to the fishing village of Acapulco in those days. When a ship came in every-body came aboard to touch the outside world.

They all wore big pistols and, in the excitement, were apt to pull them out and shoot a few holes in the overhead out of sheer exuberance. It was our job to take their pistols and check them. They let them go reluctantly. Every once in a while, they would come back to see if they were all right.

They do not carry pistols openly in Acapulco any more. But they carry them. There has been a recent roundup of pistols. The police sometimes get a thousand in one search.

"Here they love the pistol," a Mexican told me today. "They treat the pistol like a girl. They talk to it and clean it and look at it.

"One time I hired a man. He wanted to be a waiter. I put him in the kitchen, washing dishes. All day he washed dishes with the pistol in his belt.

"Then I moved him to waiter. He wore a short jacket and the pistol showed. I said to him, 'Man, you must not wear the pistol. It is bad for business. It frightens the tourists.'

"The tourists would look at this man with the pistol. He would say very politely, 'I suggest the shrimp cocktail.' They would tremble and say, 'Anything you say. Anything.' But they did not come back.

" 'Take off the pistol,' I told him. 'A waiter with a pistol spoils the digestion.'

" 'Ah, patrón,' he said, 'then put me back in the kitchen. For I cannot be content as a waiter if I must be separated from my love.' "

The telephone is still a mechanical marvel. The girl who handles the telephone is a genius. Too proud and haughty to engage in more than bare essentials.

For this reason, it is difficult to get a call through. My hotel operator flings the number to the local operator. She flings it like a duchess throwing a coin to a beggar.

The local operator will hand it on disdainfully to the Mexico operator. She will pass it with finger tips to the Mexico hotel opera-tor. If any one of them puts on too much airs, somebody along the line may become so proud she will cancel the whole thing. Then I must start all over.

"The Mexico City telephone does not answer, señor."

"That seems impossible. It is a large, luxury hotel. They have three telefonistas and an elegant switchboard."

"It is out of order. It does not function."

"When will it function?"

"Who knows? Possibly not until tomorrow."

"I will try again this afternoon."

"Very well, señor."

A half hour later my operator is on the phone. "Will you talk now, señor?"

"To whom?"

"On your call. We are ready with Ford Motors of Mexico."

"I am not calling Ford Motors of Mexico. I am calling the Hotel Hilton."

The phone then breaks off. The operator has washed her hands of me. She will not answer.

After another half-hour penance, the phone rings again. I am talking to Mexico City now. All in-between operators are going to let me do it myself. Let me see if I can do it if I'm so smart.

"Coca-Cola de Mexico," says a sharp new voice.

"I am calling the Hotel Hilton."

"On the part of whom?"

"Is this the Hotel Hilton?"

"No, señor. This is Coca-Cola de Mexico."

Oh.

This morning I rang for the maid. I should know better, I should indeed.

"There seems to be no hot water."

The maid looked in the shower. Water out of a shower is God's mystery to Mexico.

"It is not very cold," she said, testing it with her hand.

"Nevertheless, it is not hot. When will it get hot?"

This is like asking, "When will it stop raining?" But the maid is accustomed to us tourists.

"I will ask, señor. I return immediately."

That was several hours ago. I caught a glimpse of her in the hallway. But she saw me, too, and ducked around the corner. No smart tourist is going to corner that pigeon with foolish questions. The phone is ringing again.

"Your party does not answer."

"What party?"

"The Banco de Mexico."

SELDEN RODMAN

Cuernavaca, Taxco, Acapulco, 1960s

"ECCENTRICS COME HERE BECAUSE THERE IS ALWAYS A RECEPTIVE AUDIENCE."

Selden Rodman is no doubt best known today for his many books on Hai-tian painting, which his devoted work has done much to popularize. But in other decades Rodman was known as a respected poet and anthologist, and his books of interviews with writers and artists are now important sources of information. Rodman was also a constant traveler and one of the best-informed writers on Latin America. Among his many books are accounts of his own travels and guides to Peru, Colombia, Panama, and Mexico. In 1960 the Mexican government sponsored an exhibition of his art collection at the San Carlos Academy. The following selection is from The Road to Panama, *published in 1966.*

Rodman met William Spratling in 1956, when they both visited Mi-guel Covarrubias on his deathbed in a Mexico City hospital, and the art-ist suggested that Spratling fly Rodman down to Taxco in his private plane. The two men—writers, art critics, Mexicanists both—shared many interests and mutual friends, but where Rodman saw a compatriot,

201

Spratling sensed a rival. Spratling flew them to Taxco in his open-cockpit twin-seater, giving Rodman a few frights high above the mountains, and spent the rest of the day showing him around the craft workshops and Rancho Spratling at Taxco Viejo.

"I had expected to spend the night at Spratling's," Rodman wrote in a book of memoirs. "For some reason he announced that he was more than usually cantankerous, and I'd be more comfortable in Taxco. I drove into town . . . encountered a guide who found me a cheap hotel and a good restaurant, where we had enchiladas and tequila, and thank God for American Tourism, silver, and William Spratling, that quaint combination that has kept this beautiful hill town, outwardly at least, precisely as it was in Humboldt's time."

Perhaps Rodman wasn't asked to spend the night because Spratling, whose door was always open to an endless stream of celebrity guests through the years, was peeved at something unexpected that happened. The American television newsman Charles Collingwood, long with CBS, arrived with his wife to meet Spratling but was delighted to find Rodman there. Collingwood shared Rodman's intense interest in Haiti, had read his books, and praised them highly. Spratling's version of the story is that he didn't invite Rodman to stay because Rodman "talked too much." He probably did. To Collingwood.

In a later book, published in 1969, Rodman wasn't quite so generous. He called Taxco a "tourist trap" and Spratling a "dilettante" whose contributions to the town "have been a dubious blessing." Maybe the jukeboxes got to him.

THE ROAD SOUTH FROM TOLUCA, THROUGH Taxco, Iguala and Chilpancingo, leads directly to Acapulco. Taxco is another Guanajuato, a hill town with winding cobblestoned alleys and tiled roofs, so perfectly preserved that tourists would have overrun it by the thousands even if William Spratling hadn't revived the silver industry and lured them in with his hammered jewels and tableware. My first visit to Taxco was with Spratling, who flew me in with a cargo of silver sheets, landing his tiny open-cockpit two-seater in a cow pasture during a thunderstorm. That was in 1956, and Spratling had just completed a new wing to his home, to display his pre-Columbian "Remojadas" sculptures. This Totonac culture of the Veracruz region flourished, he told me, between A.D. 200 and 600. The figurines have a uniquely humorous air. One smiling face I liked especially had a small hand cupped over the sardonically half-open mouth, as if to say, "Don't believe a word you hear; they're all fakers!" An American dental surgeon, Milton Leof, has an equally distinguished collection of "Remojadas" in Taxco. For those who are not aficionados of sculpture and folk art, however, it will be enough to contemplate the gorgeous pink limestone façade of Santa Prisca. This jewel of the Mexican baroque was financed in the early 1700s by the silver king, José de la Borda, who is reputed to have said, "God gives to Borda, and Borda gives to God."

For those who *are* carried away by sculpture and folk art, there is a roadside stand on the highway just outside of Iguala where one can carry away (at prices ranging from five cents to two dollars) the most off-beat ladies of high fashion imaginable. Moulded from clay in a tiny village of Guerrero, six hours from here over the mountains by muleback, these attenuated female figures, with weirdly sorrowful faces, are painted from base to crown with birds, beasts and flowers in black and terra cotta.

Acapulco is for those who like great beaches, deep-sea fishing, hunting, yachting, fifty first-class hotels and fifty thousand American tourists. Some of the latter look as though they must have been imported from Southern California in flying boxcars. Complaining children. Distracted mothers. Philandering husbands. Fat-flanked teen-agers in skintight bikinis. Gray-haired schoolteachers in rhinestone-studded sunglasses—also in skintight bikinis. Retired businessmen with female companions of every age from nineteen to ninety. During my first visit, one of these paunchy tycoons and his girl friend had just been dredged from the bottom of the bay. They had had rocks attached to their feet. The guide, who took them out in a rowboat and stripped their jewels before killing them, had just been apprehended. Fortunately for Acapulco—because the tourists hadn't been concealing their intentions of going to a "safe" American resort next time—the guide had turned out to be an American.

Quebrada means "cliffside," and this is the word that doubles for the famed divers who now perform at the Hotel Mirador. The cliff on which the hotel stands is at the neck of a narrow inlet. One hundred and fifty feet below, the surf crashes into this pocket and then withdraws with a frustrated bellow, leaving the jagged rocks exposed like teeth. Sitting in the bar waiting for the show fills me with the same sense of guilt I feel at the bull ring: why am I here? is it the possibility of death that really draws me? A diver clambers up the virtually perpendicular cliff across the defile. We watch him kneel and cross himself at a tiny shrine to the Virgin of Guadalupe. Then, to a roll of drums, the diver seizes a flaming torch in each hand and soars out into the velvety night. The incoming wave must be caught exactly at its crest to prevent death on the rocks. He catches it. . . .

Puerto Vallarta, up the coast a long way, has received ample coverage as a hideaway for publicity-crazed lovers; but Zihuatanejo, much closer to Acapulco, is a fishing village with real fish. Bill Negron, who likes to live dangerously, made the round trip from Cuernavaca in 1964 with his eight-year-old son on one of those pensioned relics of the U.S. transportation system, a Flecha Roja bus. A letter from him described the coastal road as "a proving ground for tanks," and the driver who negotiated it at night as having worn sunglasses and scorning to use the bright-dim floor button. "Once, just for the hell of it, he jumped out on a blind turn at the edge of a four-thousand-foot drop to inspect the motor. Satisfied, he pulled a gun out of his belt, fired into the air once, climbed back, and continued driving."

They arrived at noon after the twelve-hour ride, "feeling like two sprung tuning forks," and were immediately spotted by the local welcoming committee and offered a thirty-peso trip across the bay. Dragging their "matrimonial hammocks" out of the bus, they explained that they were only looking for a couple of coconut palms on the beach—"though two dollars American for room and board here certainly beats the tariff at the Acapulco Hilton." In a few minutes they were being offered the same trip for twenty pesos. "Adapting fast to this hot village where no one is in a hurry," Negron wrote me, "I responded, 'See you after we eat, maybe,' whereupon we had a marvelous dinner of fish soup with thick chunks of *huachinango,* followed by deep-fried *ojotones,* a local fish of great delicacy, and the usual tortillas." By the following morning, the price of the fishing boat had come down to ten pesos, and a wonderful time was had by all, the catch including several gigantic sea turtles.

As Bill concluded his report: "The sun beats down heavily here. But in Shangri-La who cares?"

CUERNAVACA: PEOPLE OF LEISURE

I have lived in Cuernavaca longer than I have lived anywhere else in Mexico, but I find it hard to describe. Dozens, perhaps hundreds, of rich Americans, some of them socialites, some celebrities in the theatre, some dilettantes or hangers-on, live here. But Mexican millionaires, and celebrities from the political and art worlds, invariably have second homes in Cuernavaca too. Their worlds never mix, and seldom touch. Nor will they have anything to do with the young artists, Mexican and American, who come to Cuernavaca weekends. Then of course there are the natives, who live off all these intruders — some well, but most poorly; surely detesting their affluent guests, but rarely showing it. Before the 1950s, when the high-speed toll road from the capital knifed into Cuernavaca (and beyond, to Iguala), Cuernavaca was an end in itself. But by the time this highway is completed to Acapulco, Cuernavaca may become only a place where the Jet Set and the tourists stop for lunch, take a quick look at the Riveras in the Palace of Cortés, and pass on. Which will be too bad. For Cuernavaca, with its perfect climate, its leisurely pace, and its tropical garden homes sprawling up and down the *barrancas*, is one of the most attractive cities in the Americas.

There are hotels, pensions, and houses-to-rent for all incomes in Cuernavaca, but for reasons too involved to relate, my wife and I spent the winter of '64 in the largest and most bizarre of them, the Casino de la Selva. This complex of bungalows, bowling alleys, swimming pools, overhead kiddie-cars, and razzle-dazzle art works caters almost exclusively to weekending Mexicans. Its proprietor is an eccentric Spaniard named Manuel Suarez, who has made a fortune selling concrete water tanks to the Mexicans and would like to resell them Hernando Cortés. He goes about this difficult task by presenting an effigy of the Conqueror (the only one in Mexico) in bronze on a rampant charger. Then he makes his apologies to the Indians by filling a garden with little pre-Columbian replicas, and to the intellectuals by offering a cast of Dr. Atl, larger than life, and filling his recreation halls with nationalistic murals. According to latest reports, Siqueiros has just been hired to paint "the largest mural in the world" around a convoluted pyramid at the Casino. And it seems perfectly predictable that neither Suarez nor the Mexicans will see any irony whatsoever in the fact that Siqueiros' entire life—

when not engaged in threatening capitalists (like Suarez) for the Communist Party—has been devoted to making romantic heroes of Cortés' victims.

Angry men of genius like Charlie Chaplin and Erich Fromm come to Cuernavaca to simmer down; but milder eccentrics come here because there is always a receptive audience. Bill Negron and I encountered one of the oddest of the latter on the tennis courts east of the Casino, just before taking off for Guatemala. He was an American named Harry Bennett. His age: 68. His profession: promoter, retired. His avocation: tennis, which he still plays remarkably well. His trademark: a limp cigar butt in the corner of his mouth, which hasn't been lighted for thirty years. We asked him whether it was the *same* cigar butt, and that was his opening. Shifting the butt to the other corner of his mouth, he uncrossed his bow legs, gave us a squinting smile, and whipped a mimeographed document from his hip pocket. "This will answer all your questions," he said briskly, "but I'm running out of copies on this trip and would like it back."

Entitled *Stranger than Friction*, the first paragraph read: "Friction is a physical phenomenon the explanation of which is controversial even among physicists. Since it has nothing to do with this tale, it will be skipped." The six pages following proceeded to tell how a dentist thirty years ago said to him: "Harry, the roof of your mouth would be all right on the bottom of your shoe. . . . Cancer may develop unless you give up smoking." After much anguish, snarling and sneering at friends, etc., our hero went to Havana—of all places—and was urged to just hold a cigar in his mouth. When he got back to New York it was still there: "My friends were astounded at the change in me. . . ." He visited his dentist: "Egad, cancer had flown from my oral zodiac!" He offered ten dollars to anyone catching him lighting the butt, but once at Parícutin, following inadvertently his guide's suggestion that he light it on the hot lava, a friend demanded payment but got only ten pesos—"Mexican dollars!" The remainder of the article was devoted to technical explanations: "Since, by the process of attrition, lixiviation, and occasional amputation of the soggy stump, the length of the cigar decreases, the observer is puzzled; the logical reason, amputation, does not seem to occur to him." My own reaction, I'm afraid, was exactly that of a passenger on the Grace Line who had watched Harry for six days and finally slipped a note ("in a childish scrawl") under his door. The note said: "WHEN ARE YOU GOING TO LIGHT THAT DAMN CIGAR?"

Robert Brady is at the opposite pole from Harry Bennett. He is a painter – interior decorator who has spent a small fortune restoring a colonial palace on the street called Netzahualcoyotl. The palace is part of the cathedral compound that is believed to have housed Cortés during the building of the more formal palace on the Zócalo. From the exterior, all is Spanish reticence: massive, eyeless walls of tan-pink adobe. But once through the studded oaken portal, patio after patio opens up, disclosing pools, fountains, scarlet and yellow-flowering vines, giant trees, sculpture niches, and a tower in which hangs a giant chandelier that once graced the cathedral at Puebla. Among Mexicans whose homes I have visited, only Tamayo's is furnished with such impeccable taste. Brady paints the low arches and vaulting of the four-foot thick walls white, and then pierces them with deep niches for back-lighted sculpture. The unpierced walls are hung with handsome tapestries in primary colors, of his own design, or used as a setting for Pátzcuaro plates, Michoacán masks, Guerrero figurines or candlesticks from Metepec. Only in his choice of contemporary paintings —where he seems to prefer the chic Chouchu Reyes and Rafael Coronél to such uncompromising exponents of the great tradition as Sepúlveda, Muñoz, Arévalo, Cuevas, and Góngora—could I find anything to quarrel with in Brady's taste.

It was across the street in the home of Margaret Jessup, ten years earlier, that I had listened to a monologue that could serve as a threnody for Cuernavaca's fading splendor. Eduardo Bolio Rendán, a Mexican of pure Spanish ancestry, was then writing a book to be called *Unworldliness as a Fine Art*. He expounded his theory of the three "historical disasters" that have kept Mexico from realizing its potential. The first occurred at the time of the Conquest. "If Mexico had been conquered two hundred years earlier," he said, "its conquerors would have been Byzantines, men of the Middle Ages, whose viewpoint would have coincided with that of the great Indian cultures already here. But Cortés, though he came out of the medieval court of Isabella la Católica, was caught up in the belated Renaissance of the epoch of Charles V. Though he tried, at least half-heartedly, to build an independent empire, with free Indians intermarrying with Spaniards, he was recalled and disgraced. Similarly, the Franciscans and Dominicans, true medievalists who sympathized with the Indians' other-worldly culture—their inability to acquire property, measure accurately, think in commercial or scientific terms—lost out to the secular Church, in particular to the Jesuit order, which established the disastrous pattern by which Mexico was gradually 'middle-classed' and shorn of its individuality.

"The second disaster," he continued, "occurred when the 'liberal' Maximilian was ousted by the 'conservative' Juárez. Only Bulnes's interpretation of Juárez' character is to be relied on. Juárez was an Indian, to be sure, but an Indian who had become a petty lawyer, and hence dedicated to solid middle-class ideals such as 'progress' and 'social comfort.' Maximilian, a true aristocrat, at once espoused the Indian cause, thus alienating the secular Church, which had brought him to Mexico in the hope that he would reinstate its lost privileges. Juárez triumphed because he was wholly the tool of American interests. At one point, he even offered half of Mexico's territory to the United States—an offer that your Congress was too embarrassed to accept."

"But, Señor Rendán," I interrupted, "wasn't half of Mexico's territory already ceded to the United States?"

"That came later."

"But wasn't the Treaty of Guadalupe Hidalgo signed in 1848?"

"Perhaps. But dates are not important. I can never remember my own birth date. It is the spirit of history that matters, and if you are interested in the larger picture, I shall continue."

"By all means, do."

"Well, as I was saying, Juárez' acquiescence in American materialism was Mexico's second disastrous failure to realize his destiny. . . ."

"And the third?"

". . . was Ambassador Dwight Morrow, whose reign and diabolical influence I myself saw at first hand here in Cuernavaca."

"Morrow? I thought that Morrow only gave the Palace of Cortés to Diego Rivera, and his daughter to Charles Lindbergh."

"Morrow taught the petty middle-class lawyers, who had hitherto been content with a few hundred or a few thousand pesos, to think in terms of millions. He introduced the legalized larceny of the House of Morgan with his confounded 'liberalism'; and from that point on, the Mexican revolution became the rule (in the name of social benefits, security, industrialization) of Calles, Alemán, Avila Camacho and Company."

"You leave out Cárdenas?"

"Cárdenas is a rich man, too; but Cárdenas' aim has always been power—to work behind the scenes. Cárdenas is the real ruler of Mexico, even today. He has a home here in Cuernavaca, of course, like the rest of them, and when anything goes wrong he calls a meeting, *sub rosa*, and the orders go out to the puppets who occupy the nominal offices, from the president on down.

"The golden age of Mexico," Rendán continued, "was the age of Porfirio Díaz, but Díaz unfortunately made two mistakes. He failed to democratize the country when he might have, leaving the Indians out of his scheme of things entirely; and he lived too long, losing his grip and thus preparing the way for the decade of anarchy that followed his exile.

"Mexico today," he went on sadly, "has lost its chance to be a great nation. Individuality persists among the sixty or seventy per cent of the people not yet reduced to middle-class status. But the percentage—what with the success of industrialization, social security, and the infiltration of American tourism with its gadget-mindedness—is diminishing rapidly. In fifty years, every Mexican will be an undifferentiated consumer type, like you Americans. Already the country is flooded with cars, radio sets, and Pepsi-Cola—as you can see. Why, I can remember when every woman in this town could cook. And cook well. All they know how to do now is open cans and push the contents in front of you—and they don't *like* to do even *that*."

"The legacy of Zapata?" I said with a smile.

"Do you know John Steinbeck?" he asked.

I said I had known him.

"Well, he was here for some weeks writing the scenario for that absurd movie—*Viva Zapata!* I think they called it. One day at a cafe in the Zócalo, I came up to him at his table and said: 'Why in the name of God don't you hire a taxi just for one afternoon and go out into the countryside and see what your hero really did—how he destroyed all the wealth of this richest of Mexican states, totally destroyed it—instead of writing this absurd rot about his noble idealism?'

"But don't misconstrue my position," Rendán added. "While I'm not a professional radical like Steinbeck, neither am I a hopeless reactionary like Evelyn Waugh. Waugh was here, too, and I said the same thing to him. 'Instead of assuming that the secular clergy is doing good and is being persecuted unjustly, why don't *you* hire yourself a cab and go out and talk to the average Indian, who truly loves God and the saints and his own church, but hates the grasping priests with all his heart and all his soul? But you won't,' I said to him, 'because the truth would interfere with your dogma.'

"No," Rendán said, "the truth is always beautiful—because it is true. How many of us can face it? Mexico will lose, is already losing, its chance to face the truth."

As we were saying good-bye under the blue jacaranda in the garden, he pointed to the hills fading in the twilight. "Do you see that haze?" he said. "I can remember when the atmosphere here, forty or fifty years ago, was absolutely clear—every day, all day."

"You mean it's the smog of the capital, reaching even this far?" I asked.

"Not necessarily," he replied with a smile. "It's more than that. It's creeping all over Mexico. The haze of modernity."

SOUTH OF MEXICO CITY

CHARLES MACOMB FLANDREAU

Puebla and Misantla, ca. 1906

"ALTHOUGH FELIPE GETS FRIGHTFULLY DRUNK,
NEGLECTS HIS WIFE FOR OTHER WOMEN, AND
REGARDS A MACHETE AS THE MOST CONVINCING
FORM OF ARGUMENT, HE HAS EXCELLENT
QUALITIES."

Charles Macomb Flandreau was born in 1871 in St. Paul, Minnesota, where his father had been an agent for the Sioux Indians, a member of the Minnesota constitutional convention, a judge, and a successful law yer. Charles and his younger brother, Blair, grew up in a world in which authority and wealth went in hand with competence, generosity, and learning. In 1879 the family moved to Europe and traveled on an extended Grand Tour. In 1891 Flandreau entered Harvard University. Soon after graduation, he began writing amusing sketches of his experiences there, which led him to write The Diary of a Freshman. *First serialized in the* Saturday Evening Post *and later published as a book, it was called by Alexander Woollcott "the most engaging college story ever published."*

When his father died in 1903, Flandreau inherited enough money to let him live at ease for the rest of his life. He moved to Mexico, where his brother already owned a coffee plantation "sixty miles from

*anywhere in particular," near the town of Misantla in the state of Vera-
cruz. He settled in, thoroughly if not comfortably, as* hacendado. *Soon
his impressions of rural Mexican life began appearing in* The Bellman,
*a literary magazine published in Minneapolis. When he gathered the
pieces into a book a few years later, he had a hard time finding a publisher, but finally* Viva Mexico! *was published by Appleton in 1908.*

Over the next sixty years, Viva Mexico! *went through dozens of
reprintings and became one of the most widely read books ever written
about Mexico. For many Americans, certainly, it may have been the first
book to "introduce" them to Mexico and inspire an interest in travel
there. In the early decades of the century, it was nearly as important in
its own way as* Terry's Mexico, *the indispensable companion on the
journey, which first appeared in 1909.*

In the fifties, Sybille Bedford had looked in vain for a copy of Viva
Mexico! *before her trip there, but she was able to borrow a library copy
in Mexico City. She read it aloud to her companion as they traveled,
even copying several pages into her journal and later quoting them in*
A Visit to Don Otavio. *She declared Flandreau's work "the most enchanting, as well as extremely funny, book on Mexico."*

While Flandreau was surely the hacendado, *the boss of the* hacienda, *the* señor, *he had a great and rare capacity to view people of a
quite different sort with honesty, humor, and compassion. He had little
interest in tourist sights or even in the capital itself, although he visited
them. Instead, he wrote most often of local people, local scenes in the
countryside, and the daily life of the coffee plantation. Much of what he
wrote is very funny. All of it is written with extraordinary grace. "If one
is not inclined to exaggerate the importance of exactitude and is perpetu-
ally interested in the casual, the florid, and the problematic," he wrote,
"Mexico is one long, carelessly written but absorbing romance."*

While I was working on this Reader's Companion to Mexico, *I
told Octavio Paz about it. He was very enthusiastic and asked, almost at
once, if I was including a piece by Flandreau. He thought* Viva Mexico!
*was one of the best books ever written by a foreigner about his country.
His copy, he told me, had been a gift from Elizabeth Bishop.*

ONE DECEMBER MORNING, WHILE I WAS AIM-
lessly strolling in the white, dry sunlight of Puebla, I wandered

into the cathedral. The semireligious, semiculinary festival known as Christmas had come and gone for me in Jalapa, but as soon as I went into the church and walked beyond the choir, the awkward situation of which in Spanish cathedrals shows on the part of Catholics an unusual indifference to general impressiveness, it was apparent—gorgeously, overwhelmingly apparent—that here Christmas still lingered. This cathedral is always gorgeous and always somewhat overpowering, for, unlike any other I can recall, that which, perhaps, was the original scheme of decoration looks as if it had been completed a few moments before one's arrival. We have learned to expect in these places worn surfaces, tarnished gilt, a sense of invisible dust and tones instead of colors. So few of them look as they were intended to look that, just as we prefer Greek statues unpainted, we prefer the decorations of cathedrals to be in the nature of exquisite effacement. In the great church of Puebla, however, little is exquisite and certainly nothing is effaced. On entering, one is at first only surprised that an edifice so respectably old can be so jauntily new. But when, during mass, one passes slightly before the choir, and is confronted by the first possible view of any amplitude, it is something more than rhetoric to say that for a moment the cathedral of Puebla is overpowering.

The use of gold leaf in decoration is like money. A little is pleasant, merely too much is vulgar; but a positively staggering amount of it seems to justify itself. My own income is not vulgar; neither is Mr. Rockefeller's. The ordinary white and gold drawing-room done by the local upholsterer is atrociously vulgar, but the cathedral of Puebla is not. Gold—polished, glittering, shameless gold—blazes down and up and across at one; from the stone rosettes in the vaulting overhead, from the grilles in front of the chapels, from the railings between which the priests walk to altar and choir, from the onyx pulpit and the barricade of gigantic candlesticks in front of the altar, from the altar itself—one of those carefully insane eighteenth-century affairs, in which a frankly pagan tiempolito and great lumps of Christian symbolism have become gloriously muddled for all time. Gold flashes in the long straight sun shafts overhead, twinkles in the candle flames, glitters from the censers and the chains of the censers. The back of the priest at the altar is incrusted with gold, and to-day—for Christmas lingers—all the pillars from capital to base are swathed in the finest of crimson velvet, fringed with gold. It isn't vulgar, it isn't even gaudy. It has surpassed all that and has entered into the realm of the bewildering—the flabbergastric.

As I sank upon one of the sparsely occupied benches "para los señores," there was exhaled from the organ, somewhere behind and above me, a dozen or more bars of Chopin. During the many sartorial interims of the mass the organ coquetted frequently with Chopin as well as with Saint-Saëns, Massenet, and Gounod in some of his less popular but as successfully cloying moments—and never anywhere have I seen so much incense. As a rule, unless one sits well forward in churches, the incense only tantalizes. Swing and jerk as the little boys may, it persists in clinging to the altar and the priests, in being sucked into the draught of the candle flames and then floating up to the sunlight of the dome. It rarely reaches the populace until it has become cool and thin. At Puebla they may be more prodigal of it, or they may use a different kind. It at any rate belches out at one in fat, satiating clouds of pearl-gray and sea-blue, and what with Chopin and all the little gasping flames, the rich, deliberate, in-crusted group about the altar, the forest of crimson pillars and the surfeit of gold, I experienced one of those agreeable, harmless, ecclesiastical debauches that in Mexico, where the apparatus of worship does not often rise above the tawdry, and the music is almost always execrable, are perforce rare.

Toward the end of it, the central and most splendid figure among those at the altar turned to execute some symbolic gesture and I recognized his grace, the Bishop. More than half incrusted with gold and, for the rest, swathed in white lace over purple, he was far more splendid than when, two years before, he had confirmed my godchild Geronimo, son of Felipe, in the weatherworn church at Mizantla. But he was none the less the same poisonous-looking old body with whom on that occasion I had had "words." I recognized, among other things, his fat, overhanging underlip. By its own weight it fell outward from his lower teeth, turned half about and disclosed a rubbery inside that, with its blue veins against a background of congested red, had reminded me, I remember, of a piece of German fancy-work. Undoubtedly it was his grace on a visit to a neighboring see and officiating through the courtesy of a brother bishop in the great cathedral.

Strange, I thought, that such a looking old person should be associated in my mind with so pretty an incident and so springlike a day. For the sight of him took me back, as the saying is, to a hot, radiant February morning when the sun blazed down upon the ranch for the first time in two weeks and I had ridden into the village to have Geronimo, a charming child of six, confirmed. There was the inevitable Mexican delay in starting, while horses and mules fled around the pasture refusing to be caught, while the cook made out "la lista"—three cents worth of this and six cents worth of that—while mislaid tenates were found, provided with string handles and hung over pommels. But we staggered off at last—Felipe leading on foot with a sky-blue bundle under one arm (it was a clean pair of trousers) and his loose white drawers rolled up to his thighs. I wondered why, on this great occasion, he did not wear the neckerchief of mauve silk we had given him at Christmas until a moment later I discovered it in two pieces around the necks of his wife and Geronimo. His wife followed him on a horse, and Geronimo, astride at her back, clutched at her waist with one hand and with the other attempted most of the way in to prevent his cartwheel of a hat from bumping against his mother's shoulder blades in front and falling off behind. Then a San Juan Indian in fluttering white, bearing on his back Felipe's sick baby in a basket, pattered along over the mudholes with the aid of a staff. Trinidad, the mayordomo, followed next on his horse, and I came last on a mule, from where I could see the others vanishing one by one into the shady jungle, scrambling below me down wet, rocky hillsides and stringing through the hot pastures full of damp, sweet vapors and hidden birds that paused and listened to their own languid voices.

The river was high and swift after the rain, and for those who counted on another's legs to get them across, there was the interminable three or four minutes when one takes a reef in one's own, unconditionally surrenders to the steed, tries not to look down at the water, and with a pinched smile at the opposite shore reflects that: "If the beast keeps three or even two of his little hoofs on the stones at the same time until we reach the sand bar—how trivial! But if he doesn't he will go swirling downstream like an empty barrel, my head will smash against the first boulder, and it will all be very sad."

The bishop's advent had, if not quite the importance of a fiesta, at least the enlivening qualities of a fiestita. There was so much movement and talk and color in the drowsy town, and so many drunken Indians shook hands with me and patted me on the back, that if it had not been Thursday, I should have known it was Sunday. The bishop had not been to Mizantla for some said five and others eight years. But in either period it seems that unconfirmed children pile up amazingly. Grouped about the weed-grown open space on the church's shady side there were almost four hundred of them, not including parents and godparents, and this was the second of the three days' opportunity.

But there was the same vagueness as to when the ceremony would begin that there had been about the date of the previous visit. Some, remembering perhaps that most gringos have an inscrutable prejudice in favor of the definite, courteously named an hour—any hour; two, five, half past six. Others recalled that evening was the time, while a few assured me the bishop had come and gone the day before. Nobody, however, seemed to care, and I asked myself as Felipe and Geronimo and I sat on a crumbling parapet and watched the bright colored crowd: "Why should I care? What difference does it make whether I sit here in the shade or in the shade at the ranch?"

But at last there began to be a slow activity—a going in and a coming out at the door of the priest's house. I watched people go in empty-handed and come out with a slip of paper in one hand and a long yellow candle in the other. The slip of paper left me cold, but the tapering yellow candle mystically called. In Jalapa I had often stood for an hour staring at the moderate revolutions of the great hoop on which the pendent wicks grow fatter and fatter as the velero patiently bathes them in boiling tallow, and I had yearned to possess one. Yet, heretofore, I had denied myself; the desire, it seemed to me, was like that craving for heirlooms and ancestors on the part of persons to whom such innocent sensualities have been cruelly denied. To-day, however, long virtue was to have a short, vicarious reward, for Geronimo's little soul was at the moment entirely in my hands, and it was but proper that his way to heaven should be lighted by a blessed candle. So when I came out of the priest's house I, too, had one ("Bang!" went sixpence) as well as the "certificate of confirmation" ("Bang!" went another), on which was written my godchild's name, and the names of his parents and my name. It took hours for everyone to be supplied, but they were as nothing compared to the hours we waited in the church for the bishop. Except in front of the altar, the nave had been fenced off by a continuous line of benches facing inward, and on these the children stood with their sponsors behind them. Like most Mexican children, their behavior was admirable. They rarely cry, they rarely quarrel, and their capacity for amusing themselves with nothing is without limit. Had I the ordering of this strange, unhappy world, I think all children would be born Mexican and remain so until they were fifteen. That they in a measure outgrow their youthful serenity, however, seemed to be proved by exhausted relatives all about me who, after the first hour of waiting, began to roll their eyes when they met mine and dispatch a succession of Sister Annes to peer through the windows of the priest's sala. "Está dormiendo" (he is sleeping), in a hoarse whisper, was repeated so often that—my breakfast had been a cup of chocolate and a cigarette—the hinges in my knees began to work both ways, and just outside the church door I recklessly bought and ate something (it cauterized me as it went down) wrapped in a tortilla. When I returned, the bishop, with three priests behind him, was standing at the top of the altar steps. He was wearing his miter and the tips of his fingers lightly touched one another, as a bishop's fingers should, on the apex of his stomach. It was a thrilling moment.

Then, combining, in a quite wonderful fashion, extreme rapidity with an air of ecclesiastical calm, he made his confirmatory way down one side of the nave, across the end, and up the other, preceded by one priest and followed by two. The first gathered up the certificates (no laying on of hands unless one has paid one's twenty-five centavos) and read the name of the child next in line to the bishop, who murmured the appropriate formula, made a tiny sign of the cross on a tiny forehead with the end of a large, dirty thumb, and moved on. The second, with a bit of absorbent cotton dipped in oil, swabbed the spot on which the cross had been signed, while the third, taking advantage of the general rapture, gently relieved everyone of his blessed candle (it had never been lighted) and carried it away to be sold again.

But by the time the first priest reached my family party he had grown tired and careless. Instead of collecting the certificates singly, he began to take them in twos and threes with the result that they became mixed, and Geronimo was confirmed, not as Geronimo, but as "Saturnina," which happened to be the name of the little snub-nosed Totonac girl standing next to him. When I realized what had happened, I protested. Whereupon his grace and I proceeded to have "words." With exceeding bitterness he then reperformed the rite, and if the eyes of the first priest could have killed, I should have withered on my slender stalk. The priest with the cotton also sought to annihilate me with an undertoned remark to the effect that my conduct was a "barbaridad," but the third was not only simpático— he was farther away from the bishop. As, with much tenderness, he disengaged Geronimo's reluctant fingers from the candle, he severely looked at me and winked.

Then we wandered down to the shabby little plaza, where I bought Geronimo some toys and Felipe wanted to buy me a drink. But as Felipe was still looking prematurely old as the result of something suspiciously like delirium tremens a few weeks before, I sanctimoniously declined and bade them good-by.

There is no twilight in those tropics, and before the mayordomo and I reached home, darkness gathered in the deep valley, crept behind us up the mountainside, and all at once, as they say in Spanish, "it nighted." It was impossible to see the trail or even the sky, and we lurched on and on as through an interminable world of black velvet. Most of the way I kept my eyes shut—crouching down on the pommel to escape overhanging vines and the terrible outstretched fingers of mala mujer. Twice we lost our hats, and once my mule stuck deep and fast in the mud until we jumped into it ourselves and pulled him out. On this road after dark it is usually difficult to think of anything except that in a little while one's neck will be broken; but that evening, with my eyelids squeezed together and my feet prudently hanging free of the stirrups, I kept recalling Felipe's clumsy, charming devotion to his ethereal little son and the satisfaction he had unconsciously displayed when Geronimo toddled out of the church—confirmed.

Although Felipe gets frightfully drunk, neglects his wife for other women, and regards a machete as the most convincing form of argument, he has excellent qualities; but I shouldn't think of him as religious exactly. And yet—and yet—Felipe and his wife are really married (it seems rather snobbish of them, but it's a fact), and from the knowledge that his children have been baptized by the priest and confirmed by the bishop, he gets some sort of an agreeable sensation.

D. H. LAWRENCE

Market day in Oaxaca, 1924

"THAT IS WHY THEY LIKE YOU TO BARGAIN,
EVEN IF IT'S ONLY THE DIFFERENCE OF A
CENTAVO."

*On October 20, 1924, D. H. Lawrence and his wife, Frieda, arrived in
Mexico City. It was his third trip to Mexico, and Lawrence's reactions,
as usual, veered from one extreme to another. He spent some time in the
capital, seeing such people as Edward Weston, W. Somerset Maugham
(who got out of his trip only a single short story, "The Bum," about an
English artist in Veracruz), and Zelia Nuttall, an American archaeologist who lived in Coyoacán and whose books provided source material for*
The Plumed Serpent.

*In mid-November the Lawrences moved to Oaxaca and stayed at
the Hotel Francia, at 20 de Noviembre 10. Amazingly, Lawrence found
the hotel "very pleasant." By the end of the month they had rented a
house, and he set to work rewriting his novel. He finished it at the beginning of February 1925 and at once fell ill, blaming his sickness on
Oaxaca and all of Mexico.*

In Oaxaca, he also wrote the first four sketches contained in
Mornings in Mexico, *published in 1927. Although he held the view,*

221

expressed in a letter written shortly after his arrival in the town, that "70% of these people are real savages," the tone of the four sketches is much lighter and warmer. He writes with real affection about such things as parrots and the dog Corasmin, about Rosalino, his mozo or household servant, and even with humor about the difficulties in buying some oranges on a walk to a nearby town.

Oaxaca's famous market has often been described by visitors. Lawrence observed the Indians coming into town and the life of the market itself, then looked behind those images for the essential human truths that animated them.

Nearly thirty years later, Sybille Bedford would say, in A Visit to Don Otavio, that "the writer who first made people of my generation aware of Mexico as a contemporary reality was D. H. Lawrence in his letters, Mornings in Mexico and The Plumed Serpent. Mornings in Mexico had a lyrical quality, spontaneous, warmed, like a long stroll in the sun."

☀ THIS IS THE LAST SATURDAY BEFORE CHRIST-mas. The next year will be momentous, one feels. This year is nearly gone. Dawn was windy, shaking the leaves, and the rising sun shone under a gap of yellow cloud. But at once it touched the yellow flowers that rise above the patio wall, and the swaying, glowing magenta of the bougainvillaea, and the fierce red outbursts of the poinsettia. The poinsettia is very splendid, the flowers very big, and of a sure stainless red. They call them Noche Buenas, flowers of Christmas Eve. These tufts throw out their scarlet sharply, like red birds ruffling in the wind of dawn as if going to bathe, all their feathers alert. This for Christmas, instead of holly-berries. Christmas seems to need a red herald.

The yucca is tall, higher than the house. It is, too, in flower, hanging an arm's-length of soft creamy bells, like a yard-long grape-cluster of foam. And the waxy bells break on their stems in the wind, fall noiselessly from the long creamy bunch, that hardly sways.

The coffee-berries are turning red. The hibiscus flowers, rose-coloured, sway at the tips of the thin branches, in rosettes of soft red.

In the second patio, there is a tall tree of the flimsy acacia sort.

Above itself it puts up whitish fingers of flowers, naked on the blue sky. And in the wind these fingers of flowers in the bare blue sky, sway, sway with the reeling, roundward motion of tree-tips in a wind.

A restless morning, with clouds lower down, moving also with a larger roundward motion. Everything moving. Best to go out in motion too, the slow roundward motion like the hawks.

Everything seems slowly to circle and hover towards a central point, the clouds, the mountains round the valley, the dust that rises, the big, beautiful, white-barred hawks, *gabilanes*, and even the snow-white flakes of flowers upon the dim *palo-blanco* tree. Even the organ cactus, rising in stock-straight clumps, and the candelabrum cactus, seem to be slowly wheeling and pivoting upon a centre, close upon it.

Strange that we should think in straight lines, when there are none, and talk of straight courses, when every course, sooner or later, is seen to be making the sweep round, swooping upon the centre. When space is curved, and the cosmos is sphere within sphere, and the way from any point to any other point is round the bend of the inevitable, that turns as the tips of the broad wings of the hawk turn upwards, leaning upon the air like the invisible half of the ellipse. If I have a way to go, it will be round the swoop of a bend impinging centripetal towards the centre. The straight course is hacked out in wounds, against the will of the world.

Yet the dust advances like a ghost along the road, down the valley plain. The dry turf of the valley-bed gleams like soft skin, sunlit and pinkish ochre, spreading wide between the mountains that seem to emit their own darkness, a dark-blue vapour translucent, sombring them from the humped crests downwards. The many-pleated, noiseless mountains of Mexico.

And away on the footslope lie the white specks of Huayapa, among its lake of trees. It is Saturday, and the white dots of men are threading down the trail over the bare humps to the plain, following the dark twinkle-movement of asses, the dark nodding of the woman's head as she rides between the baskets. Saturday and market-day, and morning, so the white specks of men, like sea-gulls on plough-land, come ebbing like sparks from the *palo-blanco*, over the fawn undulating of the valley slope.

They are dressed in snow-white cotton, and they lift their knees in the Indian trot, following the ass where the woman sits perched between the huge baskets, her child tight in the *rebozo,* at the brown breast. And girls in long, full, soiled cotton skirts running, trotting, ebbing along after the twinkle-movement of the ass. Down they come in families, in clusters, in solitary ones, threading with ebbing, running, barefoot movement noiseless towards the town, that blows the bubbles of its church-domes above the stagnant green of trees, away under the opposite fawn-skin hills.

But down the valley middle comes the big road, almost straight. You will know it by the tall walking of the dust, that hastens also towards the town, overtaking, overpassing everybody. Overpassing all the dark little figures and the white specks that thread tinily, in a sort of underworld, to the town.

From the valley villages and from the mountains the peasants and the Indians are coming in with supplies, the road is like a pilgrimage, with the dust in greatest haste, dashing for town. Dark-eared asses and running men, running women, running girls, running lads, twinkling donkeys ambling on fine little feet, under twin baskets with tomatoes and gourds, twin great nets of bubble-shaped jars, twin bundles of neat-cut faggots of wood, neat as bunches of cigarettes, and twin net-sacks of charcoal. Donkeys, mules, on they come, great pannier baskets making a rhythm under the perched woman, great bundles bouncing against the sides of the slim-footed animals. A baby donkey trotting naked after its piled-up dam, a white, sandal-footed man following with the silent Indian haste, and a girl running again on light feet.

Onwards, on a strange current of haste. And slowly rowing among the foot-travel, the ox-wagons rolling solid wheels below the high net of the body. Slow oxen, with heads pressed down nosing to the earth, swaying, swaying their great horns as a snake sways itself, the shovel-shaped collar of solid wood pressing down on their necks like a scoop. On, on between the burnt-up turf and the solid, monumental green of the organ cactus. Past the rocks and the floating *palo-blanco* flowers, past the towsled dust of the *mesquite* bushes. While the dust once more, in a greater haste than anyone, comes tall and rapid down the road, overpowering and obscuring all the little people, as in a cataclysm.

They are mostly small people, of the Zapotec race: small men with lifted chests and quick, lifted knees, advancing with heavy energy in the midst of dust. And quiet, small, round-headed women running barefoot, tightening their blue *rebozos* round their shoulders, so often with a baby in the fold. The white cotton clothes of the men so white that their faces are invisible places of darkness under their big hats. Clothed darkness, faces of night, quickly, silently, with inexhaustible energy advancing to the town.

And many of the serranos, the Indians from the hills, wearing their little conical black felt hats, seem capped with night, above the straight white shoulders. Some have come far, walking all yesterday in their little black hats and black-sheathed sandals. To-morrow they will walk back. And their eyes will be just the same, black and bright and wild, in the dark faces. They have no goal, any more than the hawks in the air, and no course to run, any more than the clouds.

The market is a huge roofed-in place. Most extraordinary is the noise that comes out, as you pass along the adjacent street. It is a huge noise, yet you may never notice it. It sounds as if all the ghosts in the world were talking to one another, in ghost-voices, within the darkness of the market structure. It is a noise something like rain, or banana leaves in a wind. The market, full of Indians, dark-faced, silent-footed, hush-spoken, but pressing in in countless numbers. The queer hissing murmurs of the Zapotec *idioma*, among the sounds of Spanish, the quiet, aside-voices of the Mixtecas.

To buy and to sell, but above all, to commingle. In the old world, men make themselves two great excuses for coming together to a centre, and commingling freely in a mixed, unsuspicious host. Market and religion. These alone bring men, unarmed, together since time began. A little load of firewood, a woven blanket, a few eggs and tomatoes are excuse enough of men, women, and children to cross the foot-weary miles of valley and mountain. To buy, to sell, to barter, to exchange. To exchange, above all things, human contact.

That is why they like you to bargain, even if it's only the difference of a centavo. Round the centre of the covered market where there is a basin of water, are the flowers: red, white, pink roses in heaps, many-coloured little carnations, poppies, bits of larkspur, lemon and orange marigolds, buds of madonna lilies, pansies, a few forget-me-nots. They don't bring the tropical flowers. Only the lilies come wild from the hills, and the mauve red orchids.

"How much this bunch of cherry-pie heliotrope?"

"Fifteen centavos."

"Ten."

"Fifteen."

You put back the cherry-pie, and depart. But the woman is quite content. The contact, so short even, brisked her up.

"Pinks?"

"The red one, Señorita? Thirty centavos."

"No. I don't want red ones. The mixed."

"Ah!" The woman seizes a handful of little carnations of all colours, carefully puts them together. "Look, Señorita! No more?"

"No, no more. How much?"

"The same. Thirty centavos."

"It is much."

"No, Señorita, it is not much. Look at this little bunch. It is eight centavos."—Displays a scrappy little bunch. "Come then, twenty-five."

"No! Twenty-two."

"Look!" She gathers up three or four more flowers, and claps them to the bunch. "Two *reales*, Señorita."

It is a bargain. Off you go with multicoloured pinks, and the woman has had one more moment of contact, with a stranger, a perfect stranger. An intermingling of voices, a threading together of different wills. It is life. The centavos are an excuse.

The stalls go off in straight lines, to the right, brilliant vegetables, to the left, bread and sweet buns. Away at the one end, cheese, butter, eggs, chicken, turkeys, meat. At the other, the native-woven blankets and *rebozos*, skirts, shirts, handkerchiefs. Down the far-side, sandals and leather things.

The *sarape* men spy you, and whistle to you like ferocious birds, and call "Señor! Señor! Look!" Then with violence one flings open a dazzling blanket, while another whistles more ear-piercingly still, to make you look at *his* blanket. It is the veritable den of lions and tigers, that spot where the *sarape* men have their blankets piled on the ground. You shake your head, and flee.

To find yourself in the leather avenue.

"Señor! Señor! Look! Huaraches! Very fine, very finely made! Look, Señor!"

The fat leather man jumps up and holds a pair of sandals at one's breast. They are of narrow woven strips of leather, in the newest Paris style, but a style ancient to these natives. You take them in your hand, and look at them quizzically, while the fat wife of the huarache man reiterates, "Very fine work. Very fine. Much work!"

Leather men usually seem to have their wives with them.

"How much?"

"Twenty reales."

"Twenty!"—in a voice of surprise and pained indignation.

"How much do you give?"

You refuse to answer. Instead you put the huaraches to your nose. The huarache man looks at his wife, and they laugh aloud.

"They smell," you say.

"No, Señor, they don't smell!"—and the two go off into fits of laughter.

"Yes, they smell. It is not American leather."

"Yes, Señor, it is American leather. They don't smell, Señor. No, they don't smell." He coaxes you till you wouldn't believe your own nose.

"Yes, they smell."

"How much do you give?"

"Nothing, because they smell."

And you give another sniff, though it is painfully unnecessary. And in spite of your refusal to bid, the man and wife go into fits of laughter to see you painfully sniffing.

You lay down the sandals and shake your head.

"How much do you offer?" reiterates the man, gaily.

You shake your head mournfully, and move away. The leather man and his wife look at one another and go off into another fit of laughter, because you smelt the huaraches, and said they stank.

They did. The natives use human excrement for tanning leather. When Bernal Díaz came with Cortés to the great market-place of Mexico City, in Montezuma's day, he saw the little pots of human excrement in rows for sale, and the leather-makers going round sniffing to see which was the best, before they paid for it. It staggered even a fifteenth-century Spaniard. Yet my leather man and his wife think it screamingly funny that I smell the huaraches before buying them. Everything has its own smell, and the natural smell of huaraches is what it is. You might as well quarrel with an onion for smelling like an onion.

The great press of the quiet natives, some of them bright and clean, many in old rags, the brown flesh showing through the rents in the dirty cotton. Many wild hillmen, in their little hats of conical black felt, with their wild, staring eyes. And as they cluster round the hat-stall, in a long, long suspense of indecision before they can commit themselves, trying on a new hat, their black hair gleams blue-black, and falls thick and rich over their foreheads, like gleaming bluey-black feathers. And one is reminded again of the blue-haired Buddha, with the lotus at his navel.

But already the fleas are travelling under one's clothing.

Market lasts all day. The native inns are great dreary yards with little sheds, and little rooms around. Some men and families who have come from far, will sleep in one or other of the little stall-like rooms. Many will sleep on the stones, on the earth, round the market, anywhere. But the asses are there by the hundred, crowded in the inn-yards, drooping their ears with the eternal patience of the beast that knows better than any other beast that every road curves round to the same centre of rest, and hither and thither means nothing.

And towards nightfall the dusty road will be thronged with shadowy people and unladen asses and new-laden mules, urging silently into the country again, their backs to the town, glad to get away from the town, to see the cactus and the pleated hills, and the trees that mean a village. In some village they will lie under a tree, or under a wall, and sleep. Then the next day, home.

It is fulfilled, what they came to market for. They have sold and bought. But more than that, they have had their moment of contact and centripetal flow. They have been part of a great stream of men flowing to a centre, to the vortex of the market-place. And here they have felt life concentrate upon them, they have been jammed between the soft hot bodies of strange men come from afar, they have had the sound of strangers' voices in their ears, they have asked and been answered in unaccustomed ways.

There is no goal, and no abiding-place, and nothing is fixed, not even the cathedral towers. The cathedral towers are slowly leaning, seeking the curve of return. As the natives curved in a strong swirl, towards the vortex of the market. Then on a strong swerve of repulsion, curved out and away again, into space.

Nothing but the touch, the spark of contact. That, no more.

That, which is most elusive, still the only treasure. Come, and gone, and yet the clue itself.

True, folded up in the handkerchief inside the shirt, are the copper centavos, and maybe a few silver pesos. But these too will disappear as the stars disappear at daybreak, as they are meant to disappear. Everything is meant to disappear. Every curve plunges into the vortex and is lost, re-emerges with a certain relief and takes to the open, and there is lost again.

Only that which is utterly intangible, matters. The contact, the spark of exchange. That which can never be fastened upon, forever gone, forever coming, never to be detained: the spark of contact.

Like the evening star, when it is neither night nor day. Like the evening star, between the sun and the moon, and swayed by neither of them. The flashing intermediary, the evening star that is seen only at the dividing of the day and night, but then is more wonderful than either.

JOHN SKEAPING
Oaxaca, 1949

"IT IS A JOY TO SEE THE SKILL WITH WHICH THESE POTTERS TURN OUT GREAT BOWLS WITHOUT USING A WHEEL."

British artist and sculptor John Skeaping arrived in Mexico in September 1949. He had gone there to recover his health and bore a note from his doctor that recommended a diet of fish, mashed potatoes, and milk. His friends projected his life expectancy in Mexico at about a week. Skeaping survived, and The Big Tree of Mexico, *his wonderful record of that visit, was published in London in 1952.*

Skeaping's intention was to befriend the famed Indian potters of Oaxaca, not so much to learn their ancient techniques as to see if it might be possible to communicate with them beyond a superficial level. A craftsman himself, he hoped their shared art would be the basis for a bond. The Mexico City friends to whom he had introductions were not encouraging.

But six months later, when it came time to leave, he had to spend several days visiting all of his new Indian friends to say good-bye. One woman led him about her village. "She pointed to some person: 'Say good-bye to her, she will be dead when you come here again; and to him,'—pointing out some child—'he will be dead too.' " And when it came time for his actual departure, he was sent off in a flurry of fire-works, mezcal, gifts, and tears.

For most visitors to Mexico, achieving anything like Skeaping's experience would be out of the question. Only a man of his great heart and great humility could write, as plainly as he does at the end of his book, "I wanted to live with the Indians; I was told that it was quite impossible; I did it."

AFTER SEEING SOMETHING OF THE SUR-rounding country and meeting a few Indians untouched by modern civilisation I wanted to wander deeper into Mexico. There was such a vast difference between the simple country Indians and the city dwellers. I felt that I would be safe with the country people in spite of all that I had been told. So it wasn't very long before I packed my things and moved down to Oaxaca, where I had originally intended to go.

John Grepe went with me to Oaxaca one weekend to help me find a place where I could live. He had never been to this city before and was pleased to come along and see what it was like. The drive to Oaxaca from Mexico City is one of the loveliest in the country. Although I have made the journey many times, I never get tired of it. First there is a climb up a mountain over ten thousand feet high, where one goes right up into the clouds. Mexico City, which is itself over a mile and a half above sea level, can be seen far below deep down in the valley of Mexico. One can imagine what sort of view Cortés had when he first caught sight of Mexico as he and his men marched between the still higher mountains of Popocatépetl and Ix-taccihuatl which stand towering to the right and eternally covered with snow. What a sight these mountains are when one sees sunlit snow-covered fragments of them through the holes in the clouds! They are immense and dominate the whole landscape. On a clear day they can be seen from a hundred miles in almost any direction.

Then comes a long run down to Puebla, famous for its pottery and tiles, and the country opens out into a vast plain with fields of maize, herds of goats (there are about seven million in Mexico), teams of oxen ploughing the fields, and occasional small villages. Just before Puebla there is a small town called Cholula which, with a population of about four thousand, has over three hundred and fifty churches. According to the guide book, Cortés and his followers built a church on the site of every pyramid where human sacrifices were offered. Tourists love to be shown places where human sacrifices were supposed to have taken place. The churches are in various states of disrepair, though practically all of them have well-preserved domes covered in tiles of gold, green, and yellow. Shining in the sunlight the place looks like a giant flower-bed of great golden blossoms standing up amongst the greenery. It is a strange sight at night. Most of the churches have a neon cross of purple, red, green, or blue perched on top of the domes. Nothing else can be seen of the churches at night, and the crosses, which seem to be suspended in mid-air, are like a scene from a Walt Disney cartoon.

Beyond Puebla right into the heart of Mexico everything becomes still more lovely. In November, when I first made the journey, all the flowering trees are in full bloom. There are blue, red, yellow, and white flowers, blue morning glory climbing up the bushes and an infinite variety of flowers on the ground. As you drive along the road, vultures rise at the very last moment from the carcasses of dead dogs on which they have been gorging themselves. Some of them can hardly rise with the weight of their bellies. About the size of a turkey and brown in colour, these birds which look so lovely in flight are horrible-looking creatures when you see them on the ground tearing at the body of some dead animal, which they clean to the skeleton in a very short time.

The heat becomes terrific, and the road gets so hot that you have to keep watch on the pressure of your tyres for fear they will burst. You dare not stop for longer than it takes to let the air out of them, for the car soon gets as hot as an oven and if you touch the metal parts you burn your hands.

John and I kept saying, "Look at that! Look at this! Isn't it wonderful? Isn't it marvellous?" until we got sick of hearing each other. First red earth, then brown. Vast sugar plantations, great wastes where soil erosion has taken away all the earth, leaving only weird conical shapes on which nothing grows. In this district where there is very little agriculture the people, from the youngest children to the oldest men and women, do little else but make hats. No matter whether they are standing, talking, minding goats, riding donkeys, or just walking along the road, they are always weaving a straw hat and carrying one or two finished or unfinished products on their heads. If you stop and ask any of them how far it is to a certain place, they will always reply: "Pues, un sombrero a sombrero y medio" (Well, a hat to a hat and a half).

After ten hours' driving we reached Oaxaca and installed ourselves temporarily in a hotel on the main square. The Zócalo, as the square is called, is colonnaded on all four sides. Opposite the hotel is the municipal building; on both the other sides are cafés and shops. There is a bandstand in the centre surrounded by high Indian laurels with flower-beds underneath.

Oaxaca is a very attractive little town with a population of about forty-two thousand, predominantly Indian. Almost all the buildings are of one storey, due mainly to the severity of an earthquake which knocked the tops off most of them in 1931. Tales are still told of the extraordinary things which happened during the great quake of '31. An Indian woman walking along the high road carrying her baby suddenly disappeared in a great crack which opened up in the earth right under her feet. She instinctively held the child up over her head. The wretched mother was buried alive but the child was found unharmed lying on the broken surface of the road.

There are frequent mild earthquake shocks in Mexico which rattle one's bed at night, and lightning flashes are vivid and continuous almost the whole year round. They are especially violent during the rainy season, from June to October. I think that much of the Indian's character is a direct reaction to the power of the elements; his own ferocity, fatalism, and sense of insecurity are products of the violent meteorological contrasts of the country. When it rains it comes down in sheets, covering the ground in inches of water in a matter of a few minutes; visibility is reduced to nothing, and it is impossible to drive a car, which would be washed about all over the road.

The landscape surrounding Oaxaca is magnificent. The town lies in a valley enclosed by mountains covered with impenetrable forests. The name Oaxaca is a Spanish corruption of the Indian name Huaxyacac, which means "a place covered with trees." When the sun goes down everything turns a fierce indigo blue with the wildest of clouds creeping round the hill-tops. Then the lightning begins its wicked spitting and one expects almost anything to happen, but the next day all is sunny and an air of peace prevails. There is something vital about Oaxaca, something very real and living, something at the same time sinister yet kindly. Whatever it is, it grips everyone who comes there, with the exception perhaps of the two-day tourists who are rushed from the ruins of Monte Albán to those of Mitla with a vulgar guide spouting inaccurate information into their ears. All they do is to photograph everything and look at nothing. For the most part they sit in the sidewalk cafés, talking to phoney fat painters, or they photograph plume dancers.

The night of our arrival, when dinner was over, John and I strolled into the Zócalo, where the marimba was being played on the bandstand. This instrument is of Guatemalan origin. In appearance it is like a wooden version of the xylophone except that gourds are slung under the wooden keys to give greater resonance to the note when struck by the hammer. Players number from three to eight persons according to the size and length of the instrument. The music is wonderful and exhilarating, especially from this particular marimba, which is reputed to be the best in all Mexico.

The square was packed with Indians sitting, listening to the music, or walking about. They wear shirts of every colour, red, yellow, violet, and blue, white trousers, and gaily coloured zarapes. Boys were selling brightly coloured lollypops stuck all the way up sticks, or carrying glass "cages" full of green, red, and yellow jellies. Men wandered through the crowd with clusters of balloons floating drunkenly in the air like great bunches of bacchanalian grapes; others had cross-barred poles from which hung all kinds of little toys and charms. The whole square was lit by the many twinkling lights concealed in the trees.

It was pleasantly cool at this time of night, which was a great relief after the intense heat of the day. We were tired but incapable of dragging ourselves away from the scene. Like the vultures on the carcasses, we were afraid of missing one scrap.

We spent the day after our arrival roaming around the market, which spreads over a large area, partly in the streets and partly under cover. It is one of the best markets I have seen in Mexico. We pushed our way through the crowds of Indians, some sitting on the sidewalk with little heaps of fruits or vegetables, always in pyramids of five tomatoes, five potatoes, five lemons, and so on. They sit motionless all day, patiently waiting to sell a few things to earn a peso.

Hundreds of them with no traffic sense whatever wander in the middle of the road and don't get out of the way until they are practically pushed off by one of the rickety old buses which crawl through the market streets, leaking oil from the sump and spewing hot water out of the capless radiators, stopping for nothing except to discharge and pick up passengers at the street corners. When a bus stops it disgorges bundles of Indian women with their babies tied on their backs, large baskets of sweet buns on their heads, some of them carrying turkeys by their legs, the heads hanging down and dragging along the road. Then another jam of people will try to get on all at once, and no one objects to anyone who cares to go straight to the head of the queue without waiting his turn.

We had to walk with caution so as not to trip over the strings crossing the pavements in all directions. These are used to keep up the big white awnings supported on poles at the roadside. An old woman passed us with a baby tied on her back. The baby was eating a piece of water-melon and letting the seeds fall down the neck of the woman, who seemed to be completely unaware of what was happening. We hurried past the corner canteens holding our breath so as to avoid the pungent mixed aroma of mezcal and urine which emanates from these places, past the meat stalls in a row down the outside wall of the market with lumps of shapeless bloody meat, a long flabby-looking ox tongue or a set of horns hanging on bits of wire and string from an iron bar. As we passed the stalls hordes of flies would rise from the bowls of lard. We saw a man on the pavement chopping a skull in half with a very unpractical-looking axe which seemed to be set on the handle at too acute an angle. He looked as though he would chop his foot off at any moment.

Going into the market proper we passed the old-iron stall, smothered in bunches of keys, bits of scrap iron, and old tin cans which I could not imagine anyone wanting to buy. The next stall in violent contrast had shining daggers and swords with engraved blades and carved bone handles; all these are forged in Oaxaca, famed for its metal work. Inside the covered part of the market was a riot of colour: women in pink, yellow, blue, and green satin dresses and wearing the typical indigo blue reboso wound around the head like a turban with the ends hanging down at the side and back of the head; their hair braided and plaited with blue or red ribbons. Oranges, bananas, and less familiar fruits were piled alongside vegetables of every kind. Chickens tied in pairs by the legs squawked from under the stall tables. A shaft of sunshine came streaming through a hole in the roof and shone on the fountain where the people came with old gasoline tins for water. Wherever we looked was a woman feeding her child, her breast poking through a gap in a ragged blouse. The younger women seemed like Sienese paintings of the Madonna and Child.

We came to the part of the market where the Indians eat. Long tables with rickety chairs or benches were placed in rows so close together that the diners at the different tables were sitting back to back. At the end of each table a charcoal fire in a brazier belched out a sickly blue-yellow smoke as a woman fanned it, quite oblivious to the fat boiling over. The smell nearly made us sick. We ran for the open air, jumping from side to side to avoid puddles of dirty water, holes in the ground, and large dislodged paving-stones. There were dogs, dogs everywhere; the starving animals yelped as they were whacked on the back with sticks for trying to steal bits of garbage from under the tables. And nursing infants, always the nursing infants.

Trios of musicians, two men with guitars and a little boy beating a drum, entertained the diners with slightly out of tune versions of old American dance songs to which they imparted a Latin-American flavour. The song sellers in the streets were surrounded by small crowds clad in white in varying states of filth. We thrust ourselves forward to peer over the forest of sombreros to get a closer view of what was going on. The three musicians were singing a song and accompanying themselves on guitars, reading from a sheet of music held up by a little boy.

Hundreds of little dark-skinned Indians went shuffling barefoot in the streets carrying great loads strapped to their foreheads which would be too heavy for the average European to lift. In some parts of Mexico where the Indians always carry great loads they place a big stone on the back of the neck on their return journey, since they cannot walk properly without carrying a weight of some kind. When the weight is very great the carriers lean forward from the ankles. They can keep going at a jog-trot carrying a bed, or two armchairs, or a wardrobe. It is cheaper to move house this way than to hire a van. When they have to stop to let the traffic pass they keep up the jogging backwards and forwards until they can go on again.

In the pottery section of the market there were stacks of pots of all shapes and sizes strewn on the ground like pebbles on a beach. Women sat among piles of plates and jugs with scabby babies in wooden boxes beside them. Water was flowing down the open drain, into which a man was sweeping garbage with a flat straw broom.

Out in the street an old man carried water in two gasoline tins converted into a water-carrier. Latin-American music screeched from the juke-boxes in the cafés, and just to emphasize the fact that the Indian can stand an unlimited amount of musical noise, a loud-speaker van passed slowly down the street grating out some Mexican "corrido" (a special kind of song which has a great many yelps and pistol shots in it), interspersed with the raucous voice of the announcer offering two tablets of soap, a large comb, a small comb, a packet of pins, and a reel of cotton, all for fifty centavos. We ran past a stall of over-ripe fruit, as the owner gently and without concern fanned thousands of wasps into the air. They only returned again or went to the next stall, which sold crude sugar sweets and other native candies.

Finally we passed up the road leading to the Zócalo and sat down in wicker chairs at a sidewalk café to have a beer before resuming our explorations. A tired, distraught-looking Indian passed by carrying a dead girl across his shoulders.

The Zócalo is the hub of life in the town. Everyone congregates to sit in the cafés surrounding the square. In the middle there is a constant procession of young men and girls circling around in opposite directions. The men go one way and the women the other, so that they can get a look at each other. If they meet anyone that they know they pair off and go to the cafés for a drink.

Under each arch of the colonnaded square is a little tobacco kiosk about the size of a telephone booth, swarming with bees during the day. In the centre of the square is the bandstand of hammered iron and marble, the roof painted bright red. Here the band and the marimba play on alternate nights. There is always a big audience of Indians, and there they stand or sit until it is time to catch the last bus back to their villages.

The band of Oaxaca has been active for over a hundred years. It was started by French and Austrian musicians who were sent over to Mexico in the time of Maximilian. The famous French painter Douanier Rousseau was sent to Mexico as a flute player, and it was here that he got the vivid impressions for the jungle pictures he was to paint when he returned to France and became an artist. Since its inauguration the band has kept going with varying fortune. Sometimes it has been reduced to no more than fifteen players with salaries down to fifty centavos per performance, but it has never given up. Now it is such a good orchestra that when the famous American conductor Leopold Stokowsky was in Oaxaca he was so impressed by their performance that he asked to be allowed to conduct it, and in fact did so on an occasion that is still proudly talked about.

In the afternoon of that day John and I drove out on the Coyotepec road and lay sunning ourselves on the side of the hill just watching the Indians walking slowly behind the oxen in the fields. On the way back we stopped at the village of Coyotepec which is famous for its black pottery. We went into a hut and spoke with a man and his wife who were making jars for mezcal. We got very little information and they gave the impression that they were a bit nervous of our coming to visit them before we had seen the head man of the village. As we left we were stopped in the road by a woman who asked us if we had been to call on her brother. "He is the head man here," she said, "and you should go and see him first." We explained that we didn't know that but would see him next time we came to Coyotepec, as now we had to go back to Mexico City.

One thing I always do in a strange town, especially when I am in a foreign country and looking for a place to work or for information, is to search out a craftsman of some sort. They are always honest and intelligent people. When we got back to Oaxaca I talked to an old Indian stone-mason who was working on repairs to the cathedral. I told him that I had come to work at my sculpture for a time in Oaxaca and that I wanted a place where I could do as I liked undisturbed. He said that he thought he knew of a young man who was himself interested in art and might have a suitable place. "Come back here at six o'clock when I have finished my work and I will take you to him," he said. So that evening I went with the old man to the outskirts of the town to meet his friend. His name was Martin del Campo,* a young Mexican painter and architect, and a very intelligent fellow. He lived in a very nice little house with his American

* Martin del Campo was burned to death in a motor car accident in the summer of 1951.

wife. They agreed to let me have a room in the garden which was ideal for a studio and for which they would not allow me to pay any rent. I was delighted to have things fixed up so easily and felt it was a good omen. Next day we returned to Mexico City, where I started to make my preparations for living in Oaxaca.

Mexico is far too complex a place for first impressions to mean much. I realised this before I had been at Oaxaca a few weeks. I decided that I should need to spend at least a year in the State of Oaxaca alone. There are ninety-one thousand six hundred and forty-four square kilometres in the State, and that takes plenty of time to get to know. Much of it is virgin forest which has never been penetrated by civilised man, and a great many of the villages are only accessible on horseback. The forests are full of wild animals: jaguars, leopards, pumas, tapirs, wolves, foxes, and any number of smaller animals which sometimes venture into the gardens of houses that lie outside the towns. All this, together with the study of Indians, is enough to keep one busy for several lifetimes. I found it difficult at first to sleep at Oaxaca because of the incessant barking of dogs, the crowing of cocks, and the explosion of fireworks. Most of the dogs are semi-wild and roam the streets at night, where one often sees them huddled together in little groups for warmth. There are frequent fights amongst them when one of them has something to eat, or when a rabid dog comes out of his day-time hideout to attack the other dogs in the streets. Everywhere one sees dead dogs, either run over or killed in fights.

Oaxaca has a peculiar and rather sinister charm at night. In the less populated streets there are vultures roosting in the branches of the Indian laurel trees. Little groups of Indians covered with their multi-coloured zarapes are huddled in doorways. They have no homes to go to and sleep anywhere in the streets. There are glowing lights in nearly every street from the many charcoal fires; women are cooking something for the night meal, and there are always stray dogs in attendance. Then there is the sound of horses' hooves, and a group of police mounted on small wiry ponies come along in their rather ill-fitting cream uniforms on their way to the outlying parts of the town, or to the villages where they will pitch camp for the night. They tether their horses to a tree and sit under the branches, wrapped in their zarapes, heating coffee over charcoal fires.

There is always a sprinkling of unconscious drunks lying in the gutters. When the Indians get drunk they fall down in the streets and stay there maybe for the whole night and half the next day. No one minds, and the traffic makes a little detour to avoid running over them. Everyone is allowed to do as he likes, provided he is not interfering with the freedom of anyone else. The police interfere only at the point when interference with someone else's liberty begins. The Mexican is in this respect highly civilised and truly democratic.

I couldn't start work until I had got some clay, so I went down to the market to the pottery section. I stopped at a heap of little animals and birds in black clay. "What can we sell you, merchant?" asked the old woman. I bought one or two things from this woman by way of introduction. "Where does this clay come from?" I asked her. "The whistles" (for all the little animal objects were whistles) "come from Coyotepec and the casseroles come from Santa María Atzompa," she told me. I asked her if it was possible to get clay from either of these places, and she told me to go to Santa María Atzompa and see her brother, who might let me have some. She told me how to get there. "Is it a good road?" I asked. "Yes, very good. How do you propose to go?" "By car." "Yes, it is a good road for a car."

At that time I hadn't learned that all roads over which an ox cart can travel are good roads to the Indians, and oxen can pull a wagon up a mountain-side. I set out for Atzompa, expecting to cover the five miles in about ten minutes at most. As soon as I got off the paved highway on to the rough earth track I knew what I was in for. First of all I nearly scraped off the battery on a rock; then I became bogged in a sand hole. Two Indians stood by and watched me dig the car out with my hands. If it had been an ox cart and not a mechanical contrivance they might have offered to help me. As it was they just stood there like two terra-cotta figures watching me sweat my guts out in the blazing heat and dust. I got going again, always in second gear, which made the car as hot as a furnace, down a steep lop-sided bank and through a river, into bottom gear and up a dried mud hill on to some rough rocks, I sweating and the car boiling. Finally I got on to a dusty road that went through the middle of a village. I pulled to one side to let an ox wagon pass, laden with maize straw as big and as high as a hay-stack. Then I proceeded slowly to avoid the many semi-wild and half-starved mangy dogs that rushed out of every yard in a suicidal way, trying to bite the tyres of the car.

These dogs had no traffic sense at all. They rush in front of a car and try to stop it with their skinny bodies. That's why one sees so many disembowelled dogs lying on the roads. The Mexicans never try to avoid them. They just run them down and go on. The owners of the dogs never try to control them and don't seem to care much what happens to them. I can never understand why each house has at least two dogs when they are treated so indifferently. The only thing which an Indian does to his dog is to throw a great rock at it when he wants it to get out of the way, rocks that break their legs and ribs. Half the dogs in Mexico are lame or going about with one leg hanging on a bit of skin, a leg that was broken and never mended maybe a year or so before.

At the end of this village I asked how far it was to Atzompa, and a small group of men, all speaking at once, said, "The next village." "Can I get there with my car?" "Yes," they said. "Is it a good road?" "It is a beautiful road." "If it's no better than the one that I have just come on, it's a bad road, a very bad road." "The bus goes along it," they told me. The buses are all about twenty years old and all very high up off the ground, high enough to be able to drive over a small forest. They rush along these tracks in a cloud of dust with the passengers packed in and rattling about like dice in a box. How they don't get their bones broken is a mystery.

But a journey in one of these buses is an entertaining experience well worth the risk of a broken bone or two. They are designed to accommodate midgets only. Anyone over five feet four inches is in danger of being brained by banging his head on the roof. The driver sits at his ease in his shirt sleeves and wears a battered army-type cap. In front and just above his head is a miniature altar made out of a coloured postcard of the Virgin of Guadalupe, surrounded with paper flowers covered with tinsel illuminated by a small red electric light. Innumerable charms and toys dangle on strings from the roof. Miniature bottles, babies' shoes, and spiders on strings dance up and down with every movement of the bus. Stuck on the windscreen just below the Virgin is a paper cut-out of a vulgar pink nude with the inscription, "Don't distract the driver." All the same, his head is turned half the time towards the passengers, with whom he talks continuously. Then there are the usual notices about smoking and spitting, which are a mere formality; the Indian never ceases to spit no matter where he is.

Well, I got to Santa María Atzompa and after several enquiries I found my man sitting in his yard, making pots. All these yards are much the same: a square of dust fenced off with organ cactus, small heaps of maize straw, some rubbish mixed up with broken pottery, a pig, a donkey, two or three dogs, and some long-legged hens without a feather on their necks.

I walked up to the man who was squatting in front of the adobe hut made of large sun-dried unfired bricks and thatched over with maize straw. "Buenos días," he said; "Buenos días," I replied. "Sit down," said the man as he dragged a log towards me. There I sat for a while, watching the man working, neither of us saying anything. It is a joy to see the skill with which these potters turn out great bowls without using a wheel. They just have one saucer face downwards and another face upwards, placed on top of the inverted one, and this they use as a wheel. They turn things out very rapidly and just a fraction out of the symmetrical, which makes the pots really alive. No two are ever exactly the same. Inside the hut was a woman making casseroles. With her seemingly boneless fingers she was creating three patterns at once, one with her thumb and the other two with her first and second fingers of the same hand. What made the thing look like magic was that she wasn't looking at her work but at the huddled figure of another woman who was squatting in a dark corner, talking to her. Once round, and the pattern met up perfectly.

Presently, and without raising his head from his work, the man said, "You are American." Everyone who is not Mexican is a "gringo" or American to the Indians. "No, I'm English," I said. "Where do you come from?" he then asked. "From England." Then there was a silence as the man fixed the leg on to a little horse that he was now making. "What's England near to?" was his next question. "It's near to France." "What's France near to?" "Spain," I said. Then he wanted to know if it was anywhere near Egypt. Why Egypt? I suppose he had heard that there was such a place. "No, it isn't. It's a long way from Egypt," I told him. Then there followed a conversation between the man and his wife in the hut, all in Zapotec, none of which I could understand, and when this had finished there was another silence before the man came back to the question of where England was.

"How far away is England?" was his next question. "About eight thousand kilometres." Anything which consists of more than single units means absolutely nothing to these people, so the potter tried another line of interrogation after a short pause. "How long would it take you to get there?" "About two weeks." "Ah! that would be walking, of course."

I began to wonder how I was going to convey to this man where and what England was. "No," said I, "five days in a train from here to New York and then nine days in a boat." "Is it your own boat?" "No, it belongs to a company." "Would it hold six people?" "No, it holds hundreds of people," I said. The old man got on with his work in silence. This last incredible statement had been too much for him. Then he started humming to himself and once again opened the conversation. "Do you live in the town or in the country?" "In the town," I said. "Is it a big town?" "The biggest in the world." "Is it as big as Oaxaca?" Well, I knew that mentioning square miles, eight and a half million inhabitants, or anything like that was just wasting time, so I racked my brains to find a way of conveying the size of the place to him. Finally I struck on what I thought was a watertight answer, an explanation that he could understand. "Look," I said, "if you got into a car or a bus and drove in a straight line for two hours, starting at one end of the town, at the end of the two hours you would still be in the town." "Ah!" said the man, "when you did that you must have been driving round and round in a circle without being aware of it." I gave up, and we spent the next quarter of an hour on all fours whilst I drew maps of the world in the dust.

I must have been there at least an hour before I came to the point of my visit to him. It never does to rush these people; if you ask them a direct question, the answer will always be a negative one. You have to sniff around cautiously like a dog going from tree to tree and then to the side of the wall before you make your intentions clear. I got my clay all right in the end and a bottle of beer into the bargain.

The Indian knows that he is at a disadvantage with any white face and he is always on the defensive, even when approached by a prospective client for his wares. The only way to get on with him is to take endless trouble to understand him and respect all his peculiarities without expecting him to return the compliment.

This man was once approached by an American who asked him if he would make two truck loads of his little animal figures to send to the States. "I will pay you twice as much for them as you can get in the market," he said. "I could make them but I don't want to," the Indian answered. "I work only when the inspiration comes upon me and I leave off when I am tired. Maybe to-morrow I shan't want to make animals; what then? No, I won't do it. You go and buy them in the market like everyone else does; you'll get them cheaper there."

I was much encouraged by this first contact with one of the Indian potters, and it seemed to me that we were going to get along together quite well. There was no hostility either to my visit or to my request, and I began to have high hopes that I wouldn't have to abandon my original plan after all. I wanted to cross the "fence" into the Indian world, which seemed to be quite a life apart from that of the rest of Mexico and the Mexicans. The only contact that the Indians have with the whites is as servants.

Roughly, the population is divided into three sections, Indians, Mestizos or cross-breeds, and people of direct Spanish descent. There are many different tribes of Indians throughout Mexico, who between them speak seventy distinct languages and some fifty sub-dialects of these. Practically all the Indians speak Spanish, otherwise intercommunication in the markets would be impossible. The unfortunate people are the Mestizos, who have a great inferiority complex, as they are not wholly acceptable to either side.

One thing is certain: all classes of inhabitants of the United States of Mexico adhere very strongly to the belief that "those who are not for us are against us," and that is why one gets such positive reactions from them all. There is nothing negative about Mexico. I started out with the determination that I would get to know and understand the Indians, and realised that the quickest way this could be accomplished was through the medium of my work.

I soon got going with my clay and turned out a great many things. I was trying to work as the Indians do, making the simplest things free from any artistic taboos. The Indians do not think of themselves as artists; I doubt very much if they know what the word art means as they only apply the term "artist" to persons who perform in the theatres. A potter will also be a good ploughman behind a pair of oxen. He will know when it is going to rain or the wind change its direction. He will know a good ox from a bad one. He can build a house, a kiln, or a cart, and beat a wife as well as any other Indian. He is just a man who through centuries of tradition and practice has skill and knowledge in the use of clay. He likes working it, and that is all there is to it. The result is that his work has love and sincerity combined with the simplicity and skill which, to me, make the perfect work of art. Whilst this simple life and approach are most desirable, it is terribly difficult, perhaps impossible, for a person to adopt it after years of sophistication. Can it be done at all? Can one remove one's self, or anything else, for that matter, out of its context? If it can be done, are the results always going to be disastrous? Will both the thing removed and the new context into which it is introduced suffer in consequence? I strongly suspect that they will, though much depends upon how it is done. If one is going to revert to the simple life it cannot be done as an experiment but must be done of necessity and for some definite reason.

I came to Mexico to work with the Indian potters and to see their point of view. Now, having recovered from the first shock of being told that it was going to be impossible, I was determined at all cost, even at the cost of my life, to carry out my wishes. I felt that, after all, my life was a paltry thing if it had to be watered down to be preserved.

GRAHAM GREENE

Palenque, 1938

"I DIDN'T REALLY CARE A DAMN ABOUT PALENQUE."

For six weeks, in April and May of 1938, Graham Greene traveled in Mexico. He hated virtually every second of it.

Greene was already a veteran of extensive travels in West Africa, but Mexico—"this hating and hateful country," he learned to call it— didn't appeal to him at all. His British publisher had commissioned him to write a book about the situation of the Catholic church, which had been under attack by the Mexican government since 1924. Churches had been closed, priests were forbidden to wear clerical garb in public, foreign religious were expelled from the country. Some priests had been tortured or executed. Conditions were especially unpleasant in the southern states of Tabasco and Chiapas, and Greene, a convert to Catholicism, was often horrified by the sight of churches reduced to rubble.

Greene's book, The Lawless Roads *(more diplomatically titled An-other Mexico by his American publisher), appeared in 1939. Although he wrote with passion about the piety of the average rural Mexican, and*

246

although he met with a number of bishops in his travels, Greene didn't look closely enough to see any priests of the sort Charles Macomb Flandreau had described so vividly in Viva Mexico! *thirty years earlier. On the other hand, it was this tropical southern landscape that provided the story and setting for Greene's great novel* The Power and the Glory.

Green didn't confine his dislike to the government. He couldn't bear Mexico City, for example: "the shops full of tourist junk, silver filigree and gourds and rugs and dead fleas dressed up as little people inside walnuts, all the fake smartness and gaiety, El Retiro and the Cucaracha Bar and the Palace of Art, the Avenida Juárez smelling of sweets, and all the hidden hate." Surely his attitude wasn't improved any by the fact that Mexico was then in the process of expropriating foreign oil interests, of which Britain's share was second only to that of the United States. Greene's jumble of ill-assorted impressions tells us clearly where the hate was. And it wasn't hidden at all.

He sneers at everything. After describing the fashionable shopping streets, 5 de Mayo and Madero, he notes that nearby, on Tacuba, "you can buy your clothes cheap if you don't care much for appearances." And he sneers at the Hotel Regis, "where the American Rotarians go," and at the Independence Monument, "all vague aspiration and expensive golden wings," and at the Alameda and its "bourgeois families under the great trees." And then he heads south, where he knows things are worse.

At that time, there was no land route from central Mexico to Yucatán. Going by way of Veracruz, he sails on a questionable craft to Frontera in Tabasco. From Frontera it takes eleven hours by boat up the Río Grijalva to reach Villahermosa. From there he wants to go to San Cristóbal de las Casas but, failing to find reliable guides, he yields to the inevitable and decides to fly from Villahermosa to Salto de Agua. To make his misery complete, he has only two books with him. He has finished Cobbett's Rural Rides and has been rationing Trollope's Dr. Thorne at the rate of twenty pages a day. On his last night in Villahermosa, he comes to the end of the Trollope, only to discover that his copy is misbound and lacks four pages near the conclusion.

Selden Rodman visited Palenque in 1956, when it was accessible only by narrow-gauge railway. After his train was derailed, he had to complete the journey on horseback. In sharp contrast to Greene, Rodman felt this was "the perfect way of entering a Maya ruin in the jungle. . . . It was good to see Palenque, as . . . I saw it that late *afternoon, in the eerie, ruined light. The jungle setting, the compactness of the temples, the devastating power and purity of the stucco reliefs led one to feel that everything at Palenque reached perfection."*

Today, the route from Frontera to Villahermosa is on Mexican highways 180, 186, and 199 to Palenque. South of Palenque, at Ocosingo, MEX 199 joins a road that goes to San Cristóbal de las Casas. This is the road taken by Ronald Wright in 1985.

SALTO DE AGUA

WHEN I GOT UP, I THREW AWAY EVERYTHING inessential—like used socks—and put on riding-boots and breeches; I wasn't to take them off very often in the next ten days. I was still uncertain whether I was bound for Palenque or not. I had set myself two jobs—to get to Villahermosa and to cross Chiapas; Palenque was only a side issue, a blind for officials, and now suddenly I found it taking possession of my route—I was being driven there like a sheep through a gate. The manager of the aviation company had given me a letter of introduction to the storekeeper at Salto, asking him to supply me with a reliable guide—to Palenque. I was not an archaeologist. I felt only the faintest curiosity about these ruins which the few people who had visited them claimed to be finer than Chichén Itzá. I was on my way home now by way of Las Casas—I didn't want to delay any longer, and my flying friends, with whom I had dined in mess the night before, had told me Palenque was two full days' ride from Salto. That meant five days in all. Well, one could only leave it to fate.

The airport was up on top of the hill beyond the cemetery. The great gateway, the black letters "SILENCIO," and the wall where the prisoners had been shot rolled by, and a few vultures lifted heavily.

A friend of mine, José Ortega, was flying the plane, a little cramped red six-seater. I sat up in front beside him and we took off ten minutes early. Far below Tabasco spread out, the Godless state, the landscape of a hunted man's terror and captivity—wood and water, without roads, and on the horizon the mountains of Chiapas like a prison wall. After a quarter of an hour we came down—no sign of a village—to a tiny clearing in a forest. A man sat on a horse and watched us taxi in, then trotted away down a narrow path and disappeared. Three people left the plane, a peasant woman with a basket and two men carrying leather satchels and umbrellas; they walked off—like season-ticket holders—into deep forest. We rose again and the same landscape unrolled like a Chinese picture: an endless decorative repetition. This was the dry season: you could see the hollows—like thumb-marks—waiting for the rains. The mountains came nearer—heavy black bars one behind the other—and a silver horizontal gleam upon the ground was a waterfall. "You thought Villahermosa was hot," Ortega said. "You wait. And the mosquitoes . . ." Words failed him.

Salto lay right under the mountains on a bluff above a rapid green river which one must cross by dug-out canoe from the little rough landing field. The wooded mountains rose steeply at the back, shutting out ventilation. It was nine-thirty in the morning, and Chiapas, and no one spoke a word of English. A man carried my suitcase and my hammock ahead of me along the river bank, past the tin-roofed shacks where men lay in hammocks drearily swinging in the great heat, trying to construct a private current of air. Ortega's little red plane moved back across the merciless sky, like an insect on a mirror, towards Villahermosa. I had a sense of being marooned . . . even the dentist would have been welcome. The man carried my suitcase into a dark store with its back to a tiny dry plaza and laid it down; he said something I couldn't catch and disappeared. There were casks of— something, and Indians with curious pointed straw hats looked in and out again. I was overcome by an immense unreality: I couldn't even recognise my own legs in riding-boots. Why the hell was I here?

For the first time I was hopelessly at a loss because of my poverty of Spanish; always before there had been *someone* who spoke English—except on the *Ruiz Cano,* and my needs there had been few and my destination self-evident. Now I felt a mistake might land me anywhere. And, of course, that letter of introduction seemed doomed to land me in Palenque. It took a long time in my bad Spanish to make the storekeeper understand that I didn't really care a damn about Palenque: I was much more eager to get to Las Casas— that "very Catholic" city—by the beginning of Holy Week. Could he find me a guide to Yajalon instead of to Palenque? He said he'd try, and every few hours during the day I visited him—to learn that he hadn't yet found a guide for anywhere at all. He *had* found me a lodging—a bed made out of packing-cases with a straw mat laid on the top in a room partitioned off with plywood from the rest of a one-room house. I was to pay two pesos fifty for room and food, and the food at lunch-time proved unexpectedly good. I don't really mean good, of course: one's standard in Mexico falls with brutal rapidity.

There was nothing to do all day but drink warm expensive beer in the only cantina. The beer was expensive because it had to come on muleback across the mountains. In the plaza there was no life at all: two wooden seats, a mineral-water stall, some dogs and flies— no church, of course. A horse tethered outside the schoolroom stamped and stamped, sometimes a mule team rattled across a little wooden bridge going towards the mountains, but long before midday the Indians had all cleared off and life went dead. There wasn't so much as a lottery seller here. At sunset I called desperately in at the store; no, he hadn't been able to find a guide for Yajalon; maybe in two or three days . . . but I hadn't even *Dr. Thorne* to occupy me now. With a sense of doom I fell back on Palenque. . . . Well, yes, he could find me a guide *there,* and by the time I got back again he would without doubt have found the Yajalon guide. And at Palenque, he said to encourage me, there was a German-American with a fine *finca* and a beautiful daughter—*muy simpática.*

This German with his beautiful daughter had been a legend, a mirage which had been flashing on and off ever since Mexico City. I had heard rumours of them first in the lounge of the bright chromium Reforma, but in Villahermosa the flyers had told me that the girl didn't exist—nor her father. And as the storekeeper had never been to Palenque, I took the information with reserve. Perhaps once—years ago—there had been a German with a beautiful daughter. . . . Anyway, the mules and the guide were to call for me at five in the morning. How many days' journey? Only one day to the village, the storekeeper said, perhaps ten hours' riding, and rashly I left it at that—I was so eager to get on—although the flyers had told me it was a good two days' journey.

The dark came down punctually at six, and I sat outside my room on a hard chair, smoking to keep the flies away. My landlord sat on another chair, dumb with misery—he had toothache—and again inevitably with night the place took on the lineaments of home. This was what I knew well—a few hours were enough in so tiny and barren a place: the row of huts by the river, two parallel tracks running into the little plaza, the palms and the cantina at the corner, and the wooden bridge over a small ravine and a track running off into the hills. One might have been here for years without knowing the appearance of the place any better. The fireflies moved like brilliant pocket torches, and a small boy stood by the track with a flaming brand making mysterious animal noises into the dark.

At eight o'clock I climbed under my mosquito-net and put my mackintosh cape under my head as a pillow. Oddly enough, sleep came at once—luxuriously. A hard bed has its compensations: I remember once in a third-class compartment between Toulouse and Paris dreaming with a rich sentiment and gentle sensuality of Miss Merle Oberon and waking on the hard narrow vibrating seat to find the grey sky over the grey stone, the Paris suburbs already going by. So now, on the packing-cases, I dreamed of a Mr. Wang, also known as Mr. Moon, who was to guide me—somewhere. He was dressed in the most extravagant robes—all silk and gold embroidery and dragons—and when I said I much preferred walking to riding, he immediately assumed that I was offering him my horse. He was complacent and difficult—another more seedy guide complained that Mr. Wang had "put one over him"—but nevertheless Mr. Wang left across the hard night an impression of enormous luxury, well-being, and romance. "It is long since I saw the Prince of Chang in my dreams."

Then somebody rattled on my door, and something animal muttered and stamped and blew windily in the dark street. Mr. Wang evaporated with his silken robe into Chiapas air. I looked at my watch: it was only four o'clock and I cried out a protest and turned over and sought Mr. Wang again in sleep. Somebody on the other side of the wooden partition groaned and muttered, and the animal stamped.

THE LONG RIDE

I left my suitcase behind, and because it seemed absurd to think of rain I foolishly abandoned my cape and took only the net, a hammock, and a ruck-sack.

At a quarter past four I got up and dressed by the light of my electric torch, folded up the huge tent-like mosquito-net. Everybody in Salto was asleep but my guide—a dark, dapper young man of some education who had come from Las Casas by way of Yajalon—and his father, who had prepared us coffee and biscuits in his home. It was the cool and quiet beginning of one of the worst days I have ever spent. Only the first few hours of that ride were to provide any pleasure—riding out of Salto in the dark with one sleepy mongrel raising its muzzle at the clip-clop of the mules, the ferry across the river in the earliest light, the two mules swimming beside the canoe, with just their muzzles and their eyes above the water like a pair of alligator heads, and then the long banana plantations on the other bank, the fruit plucked as we rode tasting tart and delicious in the open air at dawn.

The trouble was, the way to Palenque lay across a bare exposed plateau, broken only occasionally by patches of forest and shade, and by nine in the morning the sun was blindingly up. By ten my cheap helmet bought in Veracruz for a few pesos was just the damp hot cardboard it had pretended not to be. I had not ridden a horse for ten years; I had never ridden a mule before. Its trot, I imagine, is something like a camel's: its whole back heaves and strains. There is no rhythm you can catch by rising in the stirrups; you must just surrender yourself to the merciless uneven bump. The strain on the spine to the novice is appalling: the neck stiffens with it, the head aches as if it had been struck by sun. And all the time the nerves are worn by the stubbornness of the brute; the trot degenerates into a walk, the walk into an amble, unless you beat the mule continually. "Mula. Mula. Mula. Echa, mula," the dreary lament goes on.

And all the time Palenque shifted like a mirage; my guide had never been there himself: all he could do on the wide plain was to keep a rough direction. Ten hours away the storekeeper had said, and after four hours I thought I could manage that quite easily, but when we stopped at an Indian's hut about eleven in the morning (six hours from Salto) and heard them talk as if it were now not quite half-way, my heart sank. A couple of wattle huts like those of West African natives, chickens and turkeys tumbling across the dusty floor, a pack of mongrels and a few cows listless in the heat under some thorny trees—it was better than nothing on that baked plateau, and I wished later we had stayed the night. They swung a string hammock up and I dismounted with immense difficulty. Six hours had stiffened me. They gave us tortillas—the fat, dry pancake with which you eat all food in the Mexican country—and an egg each in a tin mug, and coffee, delicious coffee. We rested half an hour and then went on. Six hours more, I said, with what I hoped was cheerfulness to my guide, but he scouted the notion. Six hours—oh, no, perhaps eight. Those people didn't know a thing.

I can remember practically nothing of that ride now until its close; I remember being afraid of sun-stroke my head ached so—I would raise my hat for coolness, and then lower it from fear; I remember talking to my guide of the cantinas there would be in Palenque and how much beer and tequila we would drink. I remember the guide getting smaller and smaller in the distance and flogging at my mule (*"Mula. Mula. Echa, mula"*) until I overtook him at a trot that wrenched the backbone. I remember that we passed a man with the mails travelling on a pony at a smart canter and he said he'd left Palenque in the night. And then somewhere on that immense rolling plain, in a spot where the grass grew long, the mule suddenly lay down under me. The guide was a long way off; I felt I could never get up on that mule again; I sat on the grass and tried to be sick and wanted to cry. The guide rode back and waited patiently for me to remount, but I didn't think it was possible—my body was too stiff. There was a small coppice of trees, some monkeys moved inquisitively, and the mule got on its feet again and began to eat.

Can't we stay the night somewhere, I said, in some hut, and go on to-morrow? But the guide said there wasn't a single hut between here and Palenque. It was two o'clock in the afternoon; we had been riding for nine hours, with half an hour's break; Palenque was, he said, about five hours away. Couldn't we string our hammocks up to the trees and sleep here? But he had no hammock and besides, there was no food, no drink, and lots of mosquitoes, perhaps a leopard. I think he meant a leopard—they call them tigers in Chiapas—and I remember how Victorian Dr. Fitzpatrick had met one on his ride across these mountains, standing across his path. It is rather terrifying to believe you cannot go on, and yet to have no choice. . . .

I got back into the saddle, thanking God for the big Mexican pommel which you can cling to with both hands when all else fails, and again the ride faded into obscurity—I didn't talk so much now about the cantina, I grumbled to myself in undertones that I *couldn't* make it, and I began to hate the dapperness of my guide, his rather caddish white riding-breeches—it was nothing to him, the ride; he rode just as he would sit in a chair. And then the mule lay down again; it lay down in the end four times before we saw, somewhere about five o'clock when the sun was low, a little smoke drifting over the ridge of the down. "Palenque," my guide said. I didn't believe him, and that was lucky, because it wasn't Palenque: only a prairie fire we had to ride around, the mules uneasy in the smoke. And then we came into a patch of forest and the ways divided; one way, the guide said—on I don't know whose authority, for he had never been here before—led to the German *finca*, the other to Palenque. Which were we to take? I chose Palenque: it was nearer and the lodging more certain, above all the drink. I didn't really believe in the German and his lovely daughter, and when after we'd been going a quarter of an hour we just came out on the same path, I believed less than ever in them. As the sun sank, the flies emerged more numerous than ever; they didn't bother to attack me; great fat droning creatures, they sailed by and sank like dirigibles on to the mule's neck, grappled fast, and sucked until a little stream of blood flowed down. I tried to dislodge them with my stick, but they simply shifted their ground. The smell of blood and mule was sickening. One became at last a kind of automaton, a bundle of flesh and bone without a brain.

And then a little party of riders came out of a belt of forest in the last light and bore news—Palenque was only half an hour distant. The rest of the way was in darkness, the darkness of the forest and then the darkness of night as well. That was how we began and ended. The stars were up when we came out of the forest, and there at the head of a long park-like slope of grass was a poor abandoned cemetery, crosses rotting at an angle and lying in the long grass behind a broken wall, and at the foot of the slope lights moved obscurely up towards a collection of round mud-huts thatched with banana leaves as poor as anything I ever saw in West Africa. We rode through the huts and came into a long wide street of bigger huts—square ones these, raised a foot from the ground to avoid ants, some of them roofed with tin—and at the head of the street on a little hill a big plain ruined church.

My guide apparently had learned where we could get food, if not lodging—a woman's hut where the school teacher lived, and while food was prepared we staggered out on legs as stiff as stilts to find the drink we had promised ourselves all the hot day. But Palenque wasn't Salto; the Salto cantina loomed in memory with the luxury of an American bar. In the store near the church they had three bottles of beer only—warm, gassy, unsatisfying stuff. And afterwards we drank a glass each of very new and raw tequila; it hardly touched our thirst. At the other end of the village was the only other store. We made our way there by the light of electric torches, to find they sold no beer at all: all we could get was mineral water coloured pink and flavoured with some sweet chemical. We had a bottle each and I took a bottle away with me to wash down my quinine. Otherwise we had to try and satisfy our thirst with coffee—endlessly; a good drink, but bad for the nerves. The school teacher was a plump complacent young half-caste with a patronising and clerical manner and a soft boneless hand: that was what the village had gained in place of a priest. His assistant was of a different type: alert, interested in his job for its own sake and not for the prestige it gave him, good with children, I feel sure. After we had eaten, he led us up the street to his own room, where we were to sleep. It was a small room in a tin-roofed hut beside the ruined church, which they used now as a school. He insisted that I should take his bed, my guide took my hammock, and our host tied up another for himself from the heavy beams.

I think the hut had once been a stable; now it seemed to be divided by thin partitions into three. In one division we slept, in another small children cried all night, and behind my head, in the third, I could hear the slow movements and the regular coughing of cows. I slept very badly in my clothes—I had cramp in my feet and a little fever from the sun. Somewhere around midnight there was the sound of a horse outside and a fist beat on the big bolted barn door. Nobody moved until a voice called, *"Con amistad"* (with friendship), and then the stranger was let in. I put on my electric torch and he moved heavily round the little room tying up a hammock; then he took off his revolver holster and lay down, and again I tried to sleep. It seemed to me that a woman's voice was constantly urging me to turn my face to the wall because that way I lay closer to Tabasco, the Atlantic, and home. I felt sick, but I was too tired to go outside and vomit. The hammocks creaked and something fluttered in the roof and a child wailed. There was no ventilation at all.

VISITING THE RUINS

Fate had got me somehow to Palenque, and so I thought I had better see the ruins, but it was stupid, after the long ride and the feverish night, to go next morning. And it was stupid, too, to start as late as seven, for it was nearly half-past nine before we reached them and the tropical sun was already high. It wasn't so much stiffness that bothered me now: it was the feel of fever, an overpowering nausea without the energy to vomit, a desire to lie down and never get up again, a continuous thirst. I had tried to get some mineral water to take with me, but our purchases had cleared the store right out, and all the time, if only I had known it, I was in one of the few places in Mexico where it was safe to drink the water. Springs rose everywhere; as we climbed through the thick hot forest they sparkled between the trees, fell in tiny torrents, spread out, like a Devonshire stream, over the pebbles in a little clearing. But I didn't drink, merely watched with sick envy the mules take their fill, afraid that the streams might be polluted farther up by cattle, as if any cattle could live in this deep forest: we passed the bleached skeleton of something by the path. So one always starts a journey in a strange land—taking too many precautions, until one tires of the exertion and abandons care in the worst spot of all. How I hated my mule, drinking where I wanted to drink myself and, like the American dentist, chewing all the time, pausing every few feet up the mountainside to snatch grasses.

Nobody had properly opened up the way to Palenque; sometimes the guide had to cut the way with his machete, and at the end the path rose at a crazy angle—it couldn't have been less than sixty degrees. I hung on to the pommel and left it all to the mule and anyway didn't care. And then at last, two hours and a half from the village, the ruins appeared.

I haven't been to Chichén Itzá, but judging from photographs of the Yucatán remains they are immeasurably more impressive than those of Palenque, though, I suppose, if you like wild nature, the setting of Palenque is a finer one—on a great circular plateau halfway up the mountainside, with the jungle falling precipitously below into the plain and rising straight up behind; in the clearing itself there is nothing but a few Indian huts, scrub and stone and great mounds of rubble crowned with low one-storey ruins of grey rock, so age-worn they have a lichenous shape and look more vegetable than mineral. And no shade anywhere until you've climbed the steep loose slopes and bent inside the dark cool little rooms like lavatories where a few stalactites have formed and on some of the stones are a few faint scratches which they call hieroglyphics. At first you notice only one of these temples or palaces where it stands in mid-clearing on its mound with no more importance than a ruined stone farm in the Oxford countryside, but then all round you, as you gaze, they open up, emerging obscurely from the jungle—three, four, five, six, I don't know how many gnarled relics. No work is in progress, and you can see them on the point of being swallowed again by the forest; they have looked out for a minute, old wrinkled faces, and will soon withdraw.

Well, I had told people I was here in Chiapas to visit the ruins and I had visited them; but there was no compulsion to see them, and I hadn't the strength to climb more than two of those slopes and peer into more than two of the cold snaky chambers. I thought I was going to faint; I sat down on a stone and looked down—at trees, and nothing but trees, going on and on out of sight. It seemed to me that this wasn't a country to live in at all with the heat and the desolation; it was a country to die in and leave only ruins behind. Last year Mexico City was shaken more than two hundred times by earthquake. . . . One was looking at the future as well as at the past.

I slid somehow down on to the ground and saw my guide set off with the Indian who guards the site towards another palace; I couldn't follow. With what seemed awful labour I moved my legs back towards the Indian huts; a kind of stubbornness surged up through the fever—I wouldn't see the ruins, I wouldn't go back to Palenque, I'd simply lie down here and wait—for a miracle. The Indian hut had no walls; it was simply a twig shelter with a chicken or two scratching in the dust, and a hammock and a packing-case. I lay down on my back in the hammock and stared at the roof; outside, according to authorities, were the Templo de las Leyes, the Templo del Sol, the Templo de la Cruz de Palenque. I knew what they could do with their temples. . . . And farther off still England. It had no reality. You get accustomed in a few weeks to the idea of living or dying in the most bizarre surroundings. Man has a dreadful adaptability.

I suppose I dozed, for there were the Indian and the guide looking down at me. I could see the guide was troubled. He had a feeling
of responsibility, and no Mexican cares for that. It's like a disused
limb they have learned to do without. They said if I'd move into the
other hut they would get me coffee. I felt that it was a trap: if they
could make me move, they could make me get on that mule again
and then would begin the two-and-a-half hour ride back to Palenque.
An hour had lost meaning; it was like a cipher for some number too
big to comprehend. Very unwillingly, very slowly, I shifted a dozen
feet to another open hut and another hammock. A young Indian girl
with big silver ear-rings and a happy sensual face began to make corn
coffee—thin grey stuff like a temperance drink which does no harm.
I said to the guide, without much hope, "Why shouldn't we sleep
here?" I knew his answer—mosquitoes; he was a man who liked his
comforts. He brought up again that dream of a German with a beautiful daughter; I lay on my back, disbelieving. The *finca*, he said, was
only a little way from Palenque. We'd go there to-night in the cool.
I went on drinking corn coffee, bowl after bowl of it. I suppose it
had some tonic effect, for I have a dim memory of suddenly thinking,
"Oh, hell, if I'm going to collapse, I may as well collapse in the
village where the damned guide won't worry me. . . ." I got on the
mule and when once I was up it was as easy—almost—to sit there
as in a hammock; I just held on to the pommel and let the mule do
the rest. We slid down slowly over the tree-roots towards the plain.
I was too exhausted to be frightened.

And when time did somehow come to an end, I fell off the mule
and made straight for the schoolmaster's hammock and lay down.
I wanted nothing except just not to move. The plump complacent
schoolmaster sat on the steps and had a philosophical talk with a
passing peasant—"The sun is the origin of life," a finger pointed
upwards. I was too sick to think then of Rivera's school teachers in
snowy-white blessing with raised episcopal fingers the little children
with knowledge, knowledge like this. "That is true. Without the sun
we should cease to exist." I lay and drank cup after cup of coffee;
the school teachers had lunch, but I couldn't eat, just went on drinking coffee, and sweating it out again. Liquid had no time to be di-
gested; it came through the pores long before it reached the stomach.
I lay wet through with sweat for four hours—it was very nearly like
happiness. In the street outside nobody passed: it was too hot for life

to go on. Only a vulture or two flopping by, and the whinny of a horse in a field.

SIGHT OF PARADISE

The *finca* did exist. When the sun was low I allowed myself to be persuaded back on to the mule, and there beyond a belt of trees it lay, only a quarter of an hour out of Palenque—over a rolling down and a stream with a broken bridge, among grazing cows, and as we waded through the river we could see the orange trees at the gate, a tulipan in blossom, and a man and woman sitting side by side in rocking-chairs on the veranda—as it might be the States, the woman knitting and the man reading his paper. It was like heaven.

There was no beautiful daughter, though I think there must once have been one, from a photograph I saw in the *sala* (she had married, I imagine, and gone away), but there was this middle-aged brother and sister with an unhurried and unsurprised kindliness, a big earthenware jar of fresh water with a dipper beside it, a soft bed with sheets, and, most astonishing luxury of all, a little clear sandy stream to wash in with tiny fish like sardines pulling at the nipples. And there were six-weeks-old copies of the New York papers and of *Time,* and after supper we sat on the veranda in the dark and the tulipan dropped its blossoms and prepared to bloom again with the day. Only the bullet-hole in the porch showed the flaw in Paradise— that this was Mexico. That and the cattle-ticks I found wedged firmly into my arms and thighs when I went to bed.

Next day I lay up at Herr R.'s—a bathe at six in the stream and another in the afternoon at five, and I should have felt fine if it hadn't been for the heat. My shirt was being washed and I had only a leather jacket lined with chamois to wear; the sweat poured down all day and made the leather smell, and the chamois came off on my skin. Like most Mexican things it was a bit fake. At the evening meal the lamp on the table made the heat almost unbearable; the sweat dripped into the food. And afterwards the beetles came scrambling up on to the porch. No, it wasn't after all quite Paradise, but it contained this invaluable lesson for a novice—not to take things too seriously, not to attend too carefully to other people's warnings. You couldn't *live* in a country in a state of preparedness for the worst—you drank the water and you went down to bathe in the little stream barefooted across the grass in spite of snakes. Happy the people who can learn the lesson: I could follow it for a couple of days and then it went, and caution returned—the expecting the worst of human nature as well as of snakes, the dreary hopeless failure of love.

Herr R. had left Germany as a boy. His father wanted to send him to a military college, and he had told his father, "If you do, I will run away." He had run away and with the help of a friendly burgomaster had got papers and reached America. After that he'd never gone back. He had come down to Mexico as agent for various firms, and now he was settled on his own *finca*. There had been revolutions of course—he had lost crops and cattle to the soldiers and he had been fired on as he stood on his porch. But he took things with a dry cynical Lutheran humour; he had a standard of morality which nobody here paid even lip service to, and he fought them with their own weapons. When the agraristos demanded land he gave them it—a barren fifty acres he had not had the means to develop— and saved himself taxes. There had been, I suppose, that beautiful daughter (his wife was dead) and there were two sons at school now in Las Casas. He said of Las Casas, "It's a very moral town." I promised to take them out when I arrived: I should be in time for the great spring fair.

Walking in to the village to send his mail, we talked of the Church and Garrido. Though R. was a Lutheran, he had no ill to say of any priest he had known here in the old days. Palenque had not been able to support a permanent priest, and the priests who came to serve Mass on feast days stayed usually with R. at the *finca*. He had an honest Lutheran distaste for their dogmas which took him to queer lengths. There was one priest who was so sick and underfed that R. insisted he should not go to Mass before he had breakfasted. To ensure this, when his guest was asleep, he locked him in, but when he went to call him he found the priest had escaped to church through the window. One felt that the Mexican priesthood in that politely unobtrusive act had shown up rather well. Another priest, one who sometimes came to Palenque, was an old friend of Garrido. He had great skill in brickwork, and Garrido invited him under safe conduct to come into Tabasco and undertake a building job. But friendship and safe conduct didn't save him—when the work was finished he was murdered, though possibly Garrido's followers had gone too far and the dictator may have had no hand in his friend's death.

Garrido's activities did not stop at the border. He sent his men over into Chiapas, and though in this state the churches still stand, great white shells like the skulls you find bleached beside the forest paths, he has left his mark in sacked interiors and ruined roofs. He organised an *auto-da-fé* in Palenque village, and R. was there to see. The evil work was not done by the villagers themselves. Garrido ordered every man with a horse in Tabascan Montecristo to ride over the fifty-six kilometres and superintend—on pain of a fine of twenty-five pesos. And a relative of Garrido came with his wife by private plane to see that people were doing as they were told. The statues were carried out of the church while the inhabitants watched, sheepishly, and saw their own children encouraged to chop up the images in return for little presents of candy.

NIGHT ON THE PLAIN

It was six-thirty next day before we got properly started; the stiffness had been washed away in the shallow stream and my fever was gone, so we made far better time than when we rode from Salto. In less than five hours we reached the Indian huts where we had eaten on our way. After stopping for coffee, we pushed on three leagues more—distances in Chiapas are measured always in leagues, a league being about three miles. This time we intended to make the journey in two stages. Just short of our destination a sudden blast of wind caught my helmet and the noise of crackling cardboard as I saved it scared the mule. It took fright and in the short furious gallop which followed I lost my only glasses. I mention this because strained eyes may have been one cause of my growing depression, the almost pathological hatred I began to feel for Mexico. Indeed, when I try to think back to those days, they lie under the entrancing light of chance encounters, small endurances, unfamiliarity, and I cannot remember why at the time they seemed so grim and hopeless.

The old Indian woman (you cannot measure the age of the poor in years; she may not have passed forty) had a burnt pinched face and dry hair like the shrivelled human head in the booth at San Antonio. She gave us bad corn coffee to drink and a plate of stringy chicken to eat with our fingers. I lay all afternoon and evening in my hammock slung under the palm-fibre veranda, swinging up and down to get a draught of air, staring at a yellow blossoming tree and the edge of the forest and the dull dry plain towards Salto, striking with a stick at the pigs and turkeys which came rooting in the dust under my legs. I dreaded the night. For one thing, I feared the mosquitoes here in the open, and though I had my net with me, I hadn't the moral courage to go against the opinion of the inhabitants, who said there were no mosquitoes at all. And for another, I feared, unreasonably, but with a deep superstitious dread, the movements of the animals in the dark: the lean pigs with pointed tapir snouts, like the primeval ancestors of the English pig, the chickens, above all the turkeys—those hideous Dali heads, with the mauve surrealist flaps of skin they had to toss aside to uncover the beak or eyes. Suppose when night fell they chose to perch on the hammock? Where birds are concerned I lose my reason, I feel panic. The turkey cock blew out its tail, a dingy Victorian fan with the whalebone broken, and hissed with balked pride and hate, like an evil impotent old pasha. One wondered what parasites swarmed under the dusty layers of black feathers. Domestic animals seem to reflect the prosperity of their owners—only the gentleman farmer possesses the plump complacent good-to-live-with fowls and pigs; these burrowing ravenous tapirs and down-at-heel turkey cocks belonged to people living on the edge of subsistence.

And then a storm came cracking along the horizon through the heavy afternoon. It wandered in a circle, making the animals restless. They came in darts and rushes round the corner of the hut; the turkeys couldn't keep still; they scurried and hissed and raised their hideous and uneasy voices. I lay in the hammock and thought with longing of New York—Rockefeller Plaza rose in icicles of steel towards a cold sky; the ice-skaters moved in the small square under the stars; I thought of tea at the Waldorf, the little saucers of cinnamon sticks and cherries. This didn't seem to be the same world. I hit furiously at a pointed snout.

Punctually just before sunset the hens went to roost in the branches of a mimosa. The turkeys remained up later till dusk fell and then scrambled with difficulty into the overcrowded tree. Two children lit a fire at the end of a path going off towards the forest and then beat the path with brands from the fire. Why? Perhaps to ward off the spirits of the dead, perhaps to close the way out of the jungle to prowling animals. The sparks illuminated the mimosa tree with its strange dark feathered fruit. Somewhere on the plain too a great fire was burning, clearing the land for crops, and the lightning came edging up across the sky—the night was all flame and darkness. A few big drops began to fall.

At two o'clock everyone was asleep but the pigs and me; they still moved restlessly round the hut. Then the sound of horses came beating up across the plain—this is the romantic attraction of the Mexican countryside, the armed stranger travelling at night who may be a friend or an enemy. The door of the hut was barred shut. A horse whistled, stirrup irons jangled; when the lightning flared I could see four horses, and a man dismounting. He felt his way across the veranda and knocked at the door—"Con amistad." His belt drooped with the weight of his gun. He seemed to be the leader; the three others dismounted and unsaddled, and for a moment time reversed and on the lawn under the forbidding wall I dreamed of Stevensonian adventure.

The night became alive again; the turkeys lumbered down from the tree and hissed and squawked; candles were lit and coffee served. There was political and incomprehensible talk around the table – hammocks were slung. The owner of the hut seemed to have some objection to the stranger's gun. He rolled up a trouser to show bullet scars in his leg. The stranger laughed, took off his belt, and tossed it into his hammock; the bearded arrogant faces shone in the candlelight. My guide slept on, and presently they too went to sleep. The leader had the table made up as a bed and—more sensible than I—draped a mosquito-net; the others wrapped themselves in serapes on the ground.

And then the storm broke overhead terrifyingly. The lightning struck the ground within a hundred yards; one tethered calf was thrown up by the light every thirty seconds or so, till I wearied of the sight of it. The night was bitterly cold and the rain poured in under the veranda, wetting my hammock. I put on my leather jacket, but I had no mackintosh; I retreated farther under the veranda, trying to avoid the men on the ground; the hens slept on in the mimosa. I was wet and frightened. I said "Hail Mary's" to myself and shivered with the cold. Why was I scared of this storm and not of the one in

San Luis? I suppose the love of life which periodically deserts most men was returning: like sexual desire, it moves in cycles. At last the rain stopped and the lightning moved a little farther away. I got back into the wet hammock and dozed till four. I dreamed that I had returned from Mexico to Brighton for one day, and then had to sail again immediately for Veracruz. It was as if Mexico was something I couldn't shake off, like a state of mind.

RONALD WRIGHT

Palenque, 1985

"I KNOW OF NOWHERE IN THE WORLD
THAT HAS A SETTING LIKE PALENQUE'S.
DELPHI COMES CLOSE."

I first came to admire Ronald Wright's work when I reviewed his second book, On Fiji Islands, *for* Smithsonian *magazine. That sent me to his first book,* Cut Stones and Crossroads: A Journey in the Two Worlds of Peru, *one of the best books ever written about that country. Wright was born in England, lives in Canada, and is a Fellow of the Royal Geographical Society. He has contributed to many publications and has worked on both radio and television documentaries. His writing combines the best elements of archaeological and historical research with personal investigation and vivid journalism. His third book,* Time Among the Maya: Travels in Belize, Guatemala, and Mexico, *was published in 1989.*

That book, from which the following excerpt is taken, and two other recent volumes, all based on new studies of Maya art and the decoding of Maya hieroglyphs, bring the field up to date. The other books are The Blood of Kings: Dynasty and Ritual in Maya Art *(1986) by Linda Schele and Mary Ellen Miller and* A Forest of Kings: The

Untold Story of the Ancient Maya (1990) by Linda Schele and David Freidel.

Wright first saw Palenque in 1968 as a student. He visited the lands of the Maya several more times, and when a magazine sent him on assignment to a Maya site in Belize in 1985, he decided to examine the ancient Maya civilization in a book that would also deal with the Maya peoples who live in those lands today. He started out in Belize, in October 1985, circled south through Guatemala, then turned northward into the Mexican state of Chiapas. By December 12, the Feast of the Virgin of Guadalupe, he was leaving San Cristóbal de las Casas, headed northeast toward Palenque. This was the opposite direction from which Graham Greene, whom Wright quotes, had come to Palenque almost forty-eight years earlier. Both Wright's trip to the site and the site itself were very different from what Greene experienced.

The Hotel de las Ruinas, where Wright stayed, appears still to be standing, despite his description, and still accepting guests sin vergüenza.

☀ THE ROAD BETWEEN SAN CRISTÓBAL AND Palenque is a living thing that shakes its coils and sheds its skin according to the seasons. The pavement is fragile and discontinuous, buried under landslides, cracked by subsidence, held together with strips of gravel and clay. The forest thickens and fills with startling juxtapositions of tropical and temperate species as we wind down into the lowlands: a pine next to a palm; a liana chandelier hanging from an oak; an orchid beside a cactus, one prospering in the wet season, the other in the dry. It has been raining almost every day, and the clifftops dangle waterfalls like horses' tails.

There was a disturbance at the hotel last night. Two youths were fighting, stripped to the waist, evidently drunk. The loser was frog-marched out by the manager, who throws a good half nelson. I sat in the bar and watched the Guatemalan election results on TV. The campaign had sunk pretty low: Cerezo's supporters called Carpio and his colleagues a bunch of filthy *mariconcs* (queers); Carpio defended himself on television, offering to prove his virility with his opponents' wives and daughters; Cerezo's people said Carpio had insulted Guatemalan womanhood; and so on. Cerezo won, as predicted—the best hope for a country that has little else.

Guatemala: it seems now, after a week away, a microcosm of all the ugliness and beauty in the world; of stupidity and wisdom; evil and good—endless Manichaean opposites, and darkness with the upper hand. Things may not be wonderful in Mexico, especially for Indians, but almost all the people I've met here—the weavers and writers, the Chamulas who cleared us off their land, the Maya officials and policemen, the liberal bishop—if this were Guatemala these people would be dead.

Susanna came round with two friends for a drink—Monique, a French linguist, and Philippe, her brother. We smoked Gitanes and drank tequila, and watched an homage to John Lennon on this the fifth anniversary of his death. The next program, about famine in Africa, was broken by commercials for cat food.

I always seem to be setting off on a Death day; this time to see Palenque and what is left of the Chiapas rain forest before heading north and east to Yucatán. In eight days Janice will arrive at Cozumel. Monique and Philippe want to see Palenque, too, so we're sharing a taxi for the five-hour trip.

Philippe has no Spanish, and his English is as bad as my French, which makes conversation laborious. He's a civil servant from Toulouse, with a cartoonist's gift and sense of humor beneath the resignation in his eyes and shoulders. Monique is the dominant sibling: it's *Philippe!* this and *Philippe!* that, but he doesn't seem to mind. At eighteen she took a teaching job in Mali. The war had just ended, there were no jobs in France, and she had always wanted to go to Africa. The colonial service recruiters showed her a picture of waves crashing on a beach. Not until she got to Dakar did she discover that Mali is a landlocked country. It took a week of arduous travel to reach her posting in the interior. There was so little water she couldn't take a shower; her charges were insolent adolescent boys, who, being Muslims, despised a female teacher.

"They went on strike the day I arrived because they thought they should have been sent a man. They were full of anti-French ideas that they hadn't thought out properly. And the food! The food was the worst I have ever eaten in my life. Worse than anything we had during the war. When I left that place after two years I was on the point of a nervous breakdown!"

Her interest turned to the New World and she came to Mexico to study sixteenth-century Nahuatl and Spanish. Here was the fascination she had been looking for; she stayed.

The *taxista* is a jolly fellow named José Ticayehuatl. He's huge and has wisps of hair swept thinly over a head as smooth and brown as a football. A row of stitches adds to the likeness. "This," he says, tapping the scar. "Some bastard with a beer bottle gave me this."

He and Monique have hit it off. She, delighted with his surname, keeps trying to converse with him in Nahuatl. Unfortunately he doesn't speak *mexicano,* as he calls it. "My grandmother did, but I lost what words I had when we moved away from Puebla."

When it becomes clear that the *señora francesa* is not offended by a good joke, the conversation gets less academic. "This morning I had a very cowardly breakfast!" José announces, grinning gold to see if we can guess the punch line. "*¡Porque desayuné sin huevos!*" He breakfasted without "eggs," i.e., balls.

"Do you know what we call the governor of Chiapas?" José asks. "We call him the Tailor! Do you know why?" We have no idea.

"It's because every time the president asks him about trouble in Chiapas—what's the matter with the students? What's the problem with the Indians?—the governor replies, 'I am taking measures.' "

After a couple of hours, small plantations of coffee, fruit, and cacao appear beside the road, the coffee beans spread out in the sun to dry before being hulled. Round a bend comes a pickup truck, its windshield half obscured by an icon of the Virgin Mary. In the back of the truck young people are waving and singing, and behind them comes a procession of runners bearing torches. José crosses himself. It is, he says, the pilgrimage in honor of the Guadalupe Virgin.

Soon after the conquest of Mexico a baptized Indian named Juan Diego saw the Virgin Mary hovering above the abandoned temple of Tonantzin, Aztec mother of the gods. As a memento of the encounter, a miraculous painting of the Virgin appeared on the Indian's cloak. In Catholicism the line between heresy and sanctity has always been fine. (Saint Francis of Assisi, for one, very nearly ended on the wrong side of it.) The difference between beatification and the bonfire was usually a political decision. If Juan Diego had happened to see the Virgin, say, at Chamula in the eighteenth or nineteenth century, he and his followers would have been crushed. But in this case the church authorities saw an opportunity for mass "conversion" of skeptical Aztecs. The miracle was given papal approval; the two mother goddesses became one. Her name was changed to the Virgin of Guadalupe, but a few Nahuatl-speakers still call her Tonantzin.

At Agua Azul we stop to see the cataracts: broad cascades of turquoise water pouring from one natural basin to another. In the campground stands a solitary Winnebago (Idaho plates) surrounded by grazing cows; a large Brahma bull is lying in the restaurant doorway, vacantly chewing a banana skin.

PALENQUE

The eight-year-old Hotel Ruinas is almost a ruin itself: the concrete ceiling of the lobby is webbed with cracks and shored up by wooden poles. Despite this it's brightly lit, *"sin vergüenza,"* as Monique puts it—without shame.

I take a shortcut through the forest to see the ancient city at dusk. The woods are so dark I have to wear my glasses. There's a constant insect hum—an electrical sound—among huge trees and crumbling walls half buried by twelve centuries of decay. This part of Mexico is karst country, and water deposits limestone wherever it flows over rock. Here, in a small ravine below the city center, is a series of natural pools that might have been designed for an Edwardian production of *Swan Lake*. Each basin looks like a giant scallop shell, with stalactites dripping from the level rims like beards of candlewax. For the Maya this was a sacred spot—there are ancient walls and shrines wherever you explore. Several years ago a friend of mine ate magic mushrooms here and claims he saw a procession of Maya gods. His hippie days and mine are gone, but Palenque still has its hairy pilgrims. Two men and a slender dark-haired girl are bathing naked. "Want to smoke a number, man?"

I press on up the slope, reminded of the first time I saw this place. It was 1968 and I was nineteen. I'd been awarded a hundred pounds by Cambridge University as a travel bursary, enough for a cheap flight to New York and a bus to Mexico. I remember the interview with the committee that made the awards: "Mr. Wright, your records show that you passed the first-year Tripos with only a third-class degree; we don't usually give out funds to people with results like that. Can you tell us why we should make an exception?" I said lamely that I thought they would see a substantial improvement in the second-year results (not yet announced) and that a visit to Mexico would provide the stimulus I needed to follow a career in New World archaeology. They believed me.

The ruins are deserted by the time I emerge behind the site museum. Surrounding hills still have dabs of sunlight on their tips, but twilight is flooding the plazas, brimming over the terraces and steps. I know of nowhere in the world that has a setting like Palenque's. Delphi comes close, if you can imagine its hills and its view amplified and clothed in rain forest. The city straddles the geographical boundary between the Maya highlands and the lowlands of the Mexican Gulf. The buildings are cupped by steep hills as if resting in an open palm. To the north they look out over an immense plain, stretching without interruption to the sea some sixty miles away. The ceremonial plazas lie about two hundred feet above the plain, and the buildings rise another hundred feet from that. But there is none of the grandiosity of Tikal. Palenque's structures are buoyant, elegant, harmoniously proportioned to the magnificent hills with which many of them are engaged. In this—their articulation with nature's architecture—they replicate the setting of the city as a whole: its toes on the plain, its back in the mountains, the five doorways of its principal temple gazing out over the flatlands.

At the core of the city are two eminences: a labyrinthine palace with an extraordinary tower; and the Temple of Inscriptions. The palace stands on an artificial platform roughly one hundred yards on a side and thirty feet high; the temple crowns a nine-tier pyramid built against a hill. These buildings have been restored, and now, with the sun gone, their limestone walls glow ivory against the deepening jade of the forest.

In 1968 the road to the ruins had only recently been upgraded from a muddy track; not many visitors came. I'd been told it was possible to camp in the parking lot and had brought a tent and sleeping bag. It was late afternoon when I arrived, after hitchhiking from Villahermosa. An old Chol Maya was in charge. He lived in a wooden hut surrounded by turkeys and chickens in an uncleared corner of the main plaza. My Spanish was very bad then and so was his. But he kept saying, *"Hoy piesta, perigloso,"* until I caught on that there was to be some heavy drinking in a nearby village that night, and that he thought I would be safer if I slept up in the Temple of Inscriptions, out of sight.

It was lucky for me that I did, although not so much because of wandering drunks. I slept very lightly, with my penknife close at hand. I had never traveled outside Europe before and woke at every noise. The temple was far from deserted: there were bats in the roof and bees in the walls; a large rodent kept trying to steal food from my pack. Then there were less rational fears. I began to think of all the people who might have been sacrificed on the very spot where I lay, and about the long vaulted passage that led down from the chamber next to mine to a crypt deep in the bowels of the pyramid. There the Mexican archaeologist Alberto Ruz had made a sensational discovery some years before: a sarcophagus containing an ancient king guarded by the skeletons of several retainers who had accompanied their lord to the afterlife. If I was ever going to see a ghost, this seemed a likely place.

At about two in the morning a tropical storm blew up. First there was an outpouring of the sky, as if a layer of water had suddenly collapsed upon the earth. (It would surely have flattened my cheap tent.) Then came lightning of a brilliance I have never seen before or since. Besides individual bolts arcing down into the jungle, the whole turbulent sky would be illuminated for seconds, like a false ceiling of fluorescent lights. I sat in the doorway of the temple, a curtain of water falling before me, and watched the pale ruins and dark hills appear and vanish as the storm raged over Palenque. The thunder was felt as much as heard, a deafening blast in the heavens followed by a detonation deep within the pyramid, as if the old king and his retinue were trying to blast their way out of the underworld. Directly opposite me was the tower, a slender structure seventy feet high, pierced by large windows where Maya astronomers had once observed the planets. It rose above the mysterious galleries and jagged roof combs of the palace like a campanile, sometimes in black silhouette, sometimes drenched with magnesium light.

Tonight there is merely a chorus of frogs and cicadas, darkness rising to engulf my perch in that same temple doorway, a dying salmon glow over the western hills, and the stars lighting up one by one in the east above the tower.

I returned early to the ruins, entering through the proper gate this time. Monique and Philippe were still having breakfast. They take things slowly. Neither is very fit and both smoke far too much.

The sun is strong this morning; everywhere the skiffle of crickets follows your tread. Now, in broad daylight, I can see the changes that have taken place since my first visit, in 1968, and my last, in 1977. The plazas have been cleared of scrub and converted into smooth lawns dotted with fruit trees. The mosses and epiphytes that were colonizing even the restored buildings have been removed; everything has a white, scrubbed look. Workmen are carrying garbage bags by tumpline to a waiting truck. I hear them speaking Chol, thought by most experts to have been the version of Maya spoken here in the city's heyday. A cheering sound.

Those who doubt that Maya "palaces" were really residences should be convinced by Palenque's palace. It was built late in the Classic period by daring architects who experimented with new variations on the corbeled vault and kept the masonry bulk of the walls, roofs, and roof combs to a minimum. The galleries are lofty and broad, with airy porticoes and small windows in the T shape of Ik, the glyph for wind. The outer galleries look over the city from the palace perimeter; the inner ones enclose private courtyards decorated with sculptured panels and steps. Near the tower are remains of steam baths and lavatories.

If the cramped, ponderous architecture of Tikal's Central Acropolis may be compared in spirit to a Norman castle, then Palenque's palace is an Elizabethan country house. Traces of stucco molding still cling to the doorways—rococo compositions of vegetation and mythological beasts; a band of planetary signs (possibly a Maya zodiac) circles the rooms at the spring of the vault. Perhaps most surprising are the trefoil arches, formally, though not structurally, similar to Arab design. These have intrigued and misled visitors from Caddy's day until our own. I hear a "guide" trying to impress two blond gringas resting in the eastern courtyard:

"Hello, I'm Rafael. Wair jou from? United Stays?"

"Iowa, where the tall corn grows." (Giggles.)

"Look this one here, please. See this arc? This is Arabic arc!" The girls stare at the "arc," evidently baffled; Rafael stares at their breasts.

"Thank you," they say, and start to walk away.

"Hey! Jou now they have been found Arabic and even Hebrew writing in Palenque! I chow you. . . ."

Thanks to the work of Peter Mathews, Linda Schele, and others, the city has yielded its history over the last fifteen years. Their studies were coordinated in a series of conferences organized by Merle Greene Robertson, an artist who made Palenque her home and devoted herself to recording and publishing all the carved reliefs and modeled stucco. They found that the city was a minor center until shortly after the middle Classic hiatus. Then, during the long and illustrious reign of Pacal (Shield), the king buried beneath the Temple of Inscriptions, Palenque quickly rose to the first rank of Maya states. Women were important here: two queens ruled Palenque in their own right, and Pacal's mother, Lady Zac Kuk, was a power behind the throne.

She gave birth to Pacal on March 6, 603, and he was "crowned" when only twelve years old. An oval tablet, carved in bas relief and set into a palace wall, shows his installation, attended by his mother. The city rapidly extended its control over the western part of the Maya area and diffused its emblem glyph. Pacal died in 683, after ruling for sixty-eight years. At death he left a record of Palenque's dynastic history in the Temple of Inscriptions, which he built to be his mausoleum. It is architecturally more sophisticated than the pyramid-tomb of Ah Cacau, who came to power at Tikal during Pacal's last years. The burial chamber has a cross-vaulted ceiling more than twenty feet high, so well designed that it has survived thirteen centuries without a crack. In it stands a huge sarcophagus carved from a single block of stone, with a stone lid measuring twelve by seven feet.

The scene carved on the lid has been made famous by Erich von

Däniken's assertion that it reveals a spaceman taking off in a rocket. Actually, every element in the design is consistent with Maya iconography. Far from ascending to the sky, Pacal is falling back into the fleshless jaws of the earth-monster. Von Däniken's "exhaust flames" are the earth's ophidian teeth, and his "control panel" is a cruciform world-tree rising above the underworld's maw. The same world-tree appears on reliefs in the temples of the Sun, Cross, and Foliated Cross built by Pacal's heir and dedicated to the Palenque Triad, a holy trinity ancestral to the city's royal line. If one wants to entertain chimeras, the evidence for wandering Christians is much more compelling than the presence of astronauts. But must we always defame the inventiveness of human beings?

At the top of the four-story tower I find Philippe, coughing and struggling with a crumpled pack of Delicados—his Gitanes have run out and this local brand, popular with Mexican truck drivers, is the nearest thing he's found. He wipes his brow theatrically. "I sink ze Mayá must 'ave been very little people! I find her very difficult, ze stairs." He presses his palms together to emphasize the narrowness of the ascent. "I know now what ze Mayá look like." He hands me a sketch he's done on the back of an envelope. It's a clever pastiche of Maya art—a haughty patrician head with flattened brow and trailing plumes, and below that, instead of a torso, a pair of stocky legs and feet. "Voilà, ze Mayá!" He chuckles like a concrete mixer.

The top of the tower is almost at the level of Pacal's mortuary temple, and on the winter solstice the sun, viewed from here, sets directly above his crypt.

Philippe goes his own way. I climb the Temple of Inscriptions, descend by the vaulted passage to Pacal's dripping tomb, and return to look at the three great tablets that give the temple its name. They contain the longest text of any Maya monument—620 glyph blocks in all, recording the reigns of Pacal's ancestors, astronomical events, and a staggering projection into the future: on the west panel Pacal noted that the eightieth Calendar Round anniversary of his accession (80 × 52 years) would fall eight days after the completion of the current *pictun*, the cycle of twenty baktuns, or 8,000 years. So there they are: the Maya equivalents of October 13 and 21, A.D. 4772.

That's hubris. And as if the gods were tickled by his numerology, he died when eighty years old.

Pacal's son and successor, Chan Bahlum, looked to the past. His buildings, the three graceful temples in a hilly cul-de-sac east of the Temple of Inscriptions, are monuments to the symmetry of human and mythic time. In every one we see the new king, then forty-eight, receiving the regalia from ghostly Pacal (why this obsession; was there something smelly about his claim?). Not content with this, Chan Bahlum's inscriptions fix precisely the genealogy of the ancestral Palenque Triad, whose members were the Hero Twins (remembered much later in the *Popol Vuh*) and "God K," patron of royalty, who survived in Aztec times and was aptly named for a politician: Smoking Mirror. Like most gods, they were long-lived. The parents of these three were born in 3122 and 3121 B.C. The children came into the world on October 19, October 23, and November 6, 2360 B.C.

Even these dates are recent compared to others in the temple group. When Chan Bahlum died in 702, after ruling eighteen years, his younger brother and heir erected a fourth shrine to record the apotheosis of the departed king. On these reliefs Chan Bahlum is shown emerging victorious from the underworld exactly three solar years and one tzolkin after his death. He then dances across sacred waters toward his mother, the Lady Ahpo-Hel. The old queen rises and presents Chan Bahlum with the pixielike God K. The text then links Lady Ahpo-Hel to the moon goddess and reminds the reader of God K's first epiphany by the moon, nearly *one million* years before!

Chan Bahlum's younger brother, Kan Xul, was fifty-seven when he became king. He devoted himself to enlarging the palace, and apparently built the four-story tower in honor of his father, Pacal. After a reign of about eighteen years he was unlucky enough to be captured—and probably sacrificed—by the upstart city of Toniná, which lies about halfway between Palenque and San Cristóbal de las Casas. This ominous event revealed the political instability that was beginning to shatter the Classic Maya world. Palenque had a number of fleeting rulers during the rest of the eighth century; the city's last Long Count monument went up in 783. A dated pot suggests that a ruler with the Mexican name of Six Death took over the city in 799. This may have been part of a general movement of aggressive

Mexicans up the Usumacinta River. Ironically, Toniná outlived Palenque, and has the distinction of erecting the last Long Count stela known—in 10.4.0.0.0, or A.D. 909.

Palenque's great legacy is artistic. Stone suitable for stelae was rare in the area, so the city's sculptors developed bas relief on limestone tablets to a perfection that rivals or surpasses the best Egyptian work. The modeled stucco was equally fine. Outside walls of the palace and temples were covered in life-size reliefs of rulers and deities performing ritual acts. These are now badly damaged, but photographs taken in the last century give an idea of how they once looked. The figures are so graceful, and their attitudes so fluid, that many early travelers assumed they showed women and children dancing. The portrait heads of individual kings modeled in the full round are even more astonishing. Several have been dug up in perfect condition. Medallions on a palace wall show where eight or nine of them were mounted in a row. As with the best Greek marbles and Ife bronzes, one looks at these and feels instantly in the presence of an individual.

But not every visitor is impressed. Graham Greene, who came here in 1938 by mule, had this to say of the temples and their sculpture: "little rooms like lavatories where a few stalactites have formed and on some of the stones are a few faint scratches which they call hieroglyphics."

When I leave the ruins I notice a young man in a long white smock standing by the ticket office. With his mane of wavy black hair he resembles an amiable hippie hospital patient. He's selling spears, bows, and arrows tipped with flint blades. He is evidently a Lacandón, a group who live deep in the Chiapas forest and are thought to be descended from wandering Mayas never conquered or "reduced" by Spain. David left me a copy of *The Last Lords of Palenque,* a fine book about them by Victor Perera and Robert Bruce; I think I recognize the souvenir seller from a photograph.

"Yes, I'm in the book," he says in Spanish. "My name is K'in García, but my gringo friends call me Louis the Fourteenth."

"Louis the Fourteenth?"

"He was a king of France, across the sea," K'in García laughs, showing a row of fine white teeth with gold caps. "He looked like me."

"Which gringo friends?"

"The Na Bolom people."

Na Bolom, "Jaguar House," is the old mansion of Frans and Trudi Blom in San Cristóbal. Frans Blom was a Danish archaeologist; Trudi, now over eighty, is a Swiss pastor's daughter who came to Mexico in the 1940s and made herself champion of the Lacandón. Their home became a shrine and safe house. Ethnographic collections and a large library on the Maya are kept there; and any Lacandón who visits highland Chiapas may stay as long as he likes. Artists, photographers, and scholars are also welcomed.

I went to Na Bolom a few days ago. There were no Lacandón; Trudi Blom, now ailing, was not at home. The place seemed to have been colonized by a tribe of young Mexican artists, one of whom showed me around. He hurried through the few rooms that still have Lacandón artifacts and old photographs behind dusty glass, laughing scornfully at the Indians' rude appearance. He dwelt lovingly on wall after wall of paintings (most of them bad) done by himself and other members of the group.

K'in García is a son of Old Chan K'in, patriarch of Nahá and the last Maya priest openly to have resisted Christianity.

"I've read about your father. Is he well and still living at Nahá?"

Louis XIV beams a royal smile. "Yes, he is well. Do you know Nahá?"

"No, but I'd like to go there. Would it be all right if I just turn up?"

"Of course. People can visit Nahá—when the road is good. Do you want to buy a bow?"

"I'm afraid not. Couldn't carry it."

"Would you like to take my photograph?"

K'in García poses with his weapons, a figure from an ancient relief.

"I charge four hundred pesos a picture," he adds, after I've snapped three or four.

EARL H. MORRIS

The Temple of the Warriors, Chichén Itzá, 1925

"THE HEAVY AIR MUTED THE SWASH AND
CLINK OF MACHETES AS LITHE BLADES SLICED
THROUGH VINES AND UNDERBRUSH, OR
GLANCED OFF FROM HIDDEN STONES."

The Maya city of Chichén Itzá, in Yucatán, had been abandoned less than half a century when the Spaniards arrived in the New World, and Spanish soldiers even fought a battle with local Indians on the steps of one of its pyramids. But it wasn't until the nineteenth century that the world really became aware of American antiquity. Incidents of Travel in Central America, Chiapas and Yucatán *was published in 1841 and was followed two years later by* Incidents of Travel in Yucatán. *Written in a lively style by a young New York lawyer, John Lloyd Stephens, these books introduced readers everywhere to the romance of New World archaeology.*

Stephens's books, along with the rediscovered work of a sixteenth-century Spanish bishop of Yucatán, Diego de Landa, led a New Englander named Edward Herbert Thompson to an interest in the Maya when he was still a teenager. And Thompson was lucky. In 1885, at the age of twenty-five, he was sent to Mérida as American consul. Later he bought a small cattle ranch, about three square miles in size, seventy miles from Mérida. The ranch included the ruined city of Chichén Itzá. Thompson spent years exploring the ruins, then still covered by centuries of vegetation, and made many important discoveries of graves and temples.

In the early years of the Mexican Revolution, the Carranza government accused Thompson of illegally exporting antiquities. Sought by the government and fearing his life was in danger, he made a hasty and hazardous escape by boat to Cuba. His hacienda, still containing much of his collection, was burned and only some walls were left standing. Later the whole estate was confiscated. In 1914, at the urging of the great Maya scholar Sylvanus G. Morley, negotiations began between the Mexican government and the Carnegie Institution in Washington, which proposed to undertake a major study of the site. Political turmoil prevented the agreement from going into effect until 1924. In that year, when the Carnegie Institution took over the exploration and restoration of Chichén Itzá, the team had time only to make a quick survey of the site. In 1925 they returned, headed by Earl H. Morris, and began work on what is known today as the Temple of the Warriors.

Morris had grown up in New Mexico and from an early age took part in excavations of Indian sites in the American Southwest and in Central America. By the time he went to Chichén Itzá, at the age of thirty-five, he had already won a reputation for his innovative methods, which combined solid archaeological knowledge with modern engineering techniques.

Today, the Temple of the Warriors, standing on flat ground and surrounded by the Court of the Thousand Columns, is a terraced pyramid with a handsome temple on the flat surface at its top. But that is not what Morris saw in 1924, nor what Stephens and Thompson had seen before him. Morris saw only an irregular mound about fifty feet in height, thickly covered by vegetation and with tall trees growing at its crest. Broken pieces of stonework lay scattered around, half buried in the undergrowth, and what might have been a section of wall protruded near the top.

In 1925 and in subsequent seasons, Morris also unearthed an even older temple, buried beneath this one, which contained the additional bonus of painted walls and columns that, hidden away for centuries, still preserved their brilliantly colored murals of ancient Maya village life.

As new evidence continually comes to light, interpretations of Maya civilization and the dating of both buildings and events in Maya history

*are frequently being revised, and all older accounts, including those of pi-
oneers like Morris and others, should be read in relation to the latest discoveries. Still, although Morris may not have had the whole picture, he
did have the unparalleled pleasure of discovery and the satisfaction of
bringing sunlight once again to an ancient civilization.*

*And he was luckier than one archaeologist who visited the Temple
of the Warriors in the 1980s and couldn't wait to reach the top, where
the Chac-Mool lies. Writing of the Chac-Mool in* Time Among the
Maya, *Ronald Wright declares, "All he has to do is wait. And sometimes, after aeons of waiting, fate sends an offering his way. Not long
ago a well-known archaeologist was unwary enough to climb the Chac-
Mool's pyramid when the sky had turned black with an impending storm;
he was killed by lightning on the spot."*

THE FIRST SEASON OF EXTENSIVE EXPLO-
ration by Carnegie Institution of Washington among the ruins
of the old Maya metropolis of Chichén Itzá was about to begin. Although we had come to Yucatán in May, 1924, at the close of the
Mexican revolution, we had found opportunity for little more than to
get the feel of the place before the advent of the rains made excavation among the fallen temples impracticable. Now [in early 1925] we
were on the ground early in the dry season, and had in readiness
foodstuffs, tools, and equipment for a long and, we hoped, a fruitful
campaign.

As our first undertaking, we wished to open a building of a type
not hitherto excavated, one which would not only yield important
historical data, but which, when repaired, would stand as a monument to the architectural genius of the Maya. Moreover, Doctor John
C. Merriam, President of Carnegie Institution, was to visit us only
three weeks hence, and we greatly desired to have something of special interest laid bare by the time of his arrival. Whether or not we
would succeed in this depended entirely upon our choice of a site.
Certain it was that among the wreckage of a city once magnificent,
nature had entombed many an object or structure which it would
quicken the pulse to behold, but it was equally certain that between
the spots where such lay buried there were stretches where our
workmen might delve for weeks among nothing but barren debris.

Thus far we had been unable to settle upon the spot where the spade should pry at the lock of time.

At dusk Pablo had halted before the *portal* of the Hacienda which served as field headquarters with the last load of our fifty tons of freight. Missing from it, lost upon the way, was the only rod of tool steel which in New Orleans, our distant base of supplies, I had included among the necessities for the season's work. I could see that rod made up into mason's chisels, bars for moving heavy stones, and put to half a dozen other uses for which only good tough steel would serve. As soon as the evening meal was over, Doctor Morley and I set out into the misty rain in search of it. As we bumped over the stony road it seemed as if a giant swell had molded the contour of its troughs and broken crests upon the floor of the shallow sea before Yucatán had been pushed above the waves. We moved as upon the back of a great measuring worm, now up, now down across the alternate sequence of swales and hummocks. Legend ran that once upon a time the rented Ford had been kicked blind by a mule. Wedged between a fender and the hood sat Isauro, from his hand a gasoline lantern pendant before the radiator in lieu of headlamps. From the roadway the eyes of a night bird gleamed ruby red as it turned to face the glare, while just beyond twin orbs of green became a streak of phosphorescence as a wood cat abandoned quest of food to vanish into the sheltering haven of the bush. Gravel rattled against the hood, flung by the heels of a buck that crossed in front of us, racing in startled terror from this one-eyed monster of the night. Above, misshapen trees leaned inward to intertwine their branches, thus to hide the white scar that scored the jungle from the ruins to the railway at Dzitas.

While I held the rickety car to the road, scanning with peripheral vision the weeds that fringed the wheel tracks for a coveted gleam of metal, we reviewed once more the arguments for and against the several localities, one of which we soon must choose as a point of beginning. Under our contract with the Mexican Government, we had agreed to centre our activities upon the Court of the Thousand Columns, a huge cluster of ruined buildings flanking a five-acre open court in the northeastern quarter of the city. Towering above the northwest corner of the ranges of lower mounds stood a large and rugged pyramid, bush-clad and difficult to climb. We had worked our way upward through the tangle of vines upon the nearly vertical eastern slope to the stump of a fallen tree, clasped among the roots of which were wall stones bearing bits of a fresco done in vivid red and green. And on the western edge of the summit we had seen the huge capitals, each graven from a single block, that once had capped the serpent columns in the portal of a splendid temple. We knew that to free the temple and the pyramid upon which it stood of the debris of centuries, and properly to repair them, would constitute a task by no means easy. Nevertheless I recommended, since it appeared to me to offer the most striking possibilities of any ruin that lay within the limits defined by our concession, that we begin upon it at once.

"But, Earl," Doctor Morley asked, "have we had enough experience to tackle such a job?"

"I believe we can swing it," I replied.

"Well, old man, if you think so, go ahead," was the response.

And so, during our search for the lost rod of steel, was born, that rainy February night in 1925, the decision to explore the great architectural complex which was to be called the Temple of the Warriors.

The following Monday, as the white fog dissolved before the warmth of the rising sun, the heavy air muted the swash and clink of machetes as lithe blades sliced through vines and underbrush, or glanced off from hidden stones. A swarm of workmen, like white-coated ants, were slowly eating their way up the slope of the pyramid, while from the summit Old Juan, the Mayor Domo, perching like a battered eagle upon the stump of a wind-riven tree, watched and directed the brood below.

By sundown the hill was swept clear of all herbage except the larger trees, and the resultant rubbish had been dragged a safe distance away and piled in windrows, there to be burned some afternoon when the sap had dried and a wind was running. Now that it had been well barbered, one could form some notion of the actual size and contour of the knobby head that had grown so rank a thatch. Full fifty feet high it stood, and one hundred fifty feet broad in either direction at the base. The north and east faces rose in a steep unbroken slope from base to summit. The talus at the south side spread out upon the surface of the mound covering the north range of the

Court of the Thousand Columns. Near the southwest corner of the pyramid this north range reached a junction with the long, ruined hall forming the western boundary of the same court. Thence the latter structure continued northward as a mound twelve feet in height and fifty broad, entirely across and somewhat beyond the north end of the western skirt of the pyramid. Up the centre of the western side was a ramp of lesser gradient than the slope on either hand. Cluttered about the foot of it were scores of finely hewn blocks tumbled down from the stair steps with which the ramp had once been faced. When the last workman had answered the call of the bell that clanged from the ruined church atop the knoll beside the Hacienda, I climbed that ramp. At three-fourths the height of the pyramid it gave upon a nearly flat terrace which I knew marked the level of the platform which had flanked the front of the temple. Upon it, half buried, lay the tail pieces of the serpent columns, and midway between them rested a more than life-size sculpture of a semireclining human figure, headless, battered, and pitted by the rains of centuries. Farther up the slope were strewn great blocks from the shafts of the columns, and near the summit protruded a single stone from each of the jambs, thus indicating the breadth of the tripartite doorway.

A turn or two back and forth across the irregular crest of the elevation gave me the form and approximate size of the temple. Here and there a stone with its smooth face in vertical position, depending upon the direction in which the tooled surface pointed, revealed the inner or outer line of a wall. Between such stones I stepped the distance from north to south and from east to west. The building was somewhat more than sixty feet square, and faced the west. A partition in the north and south axis divided it into two long chambers of practically the same size. In each of these a few top blocks of square columns stood just above the mould, and I could see that all four sides of these were carved. Apparently there were two rows of columns running from north to south in each chamber. Quick-falling darkness finally drove me from the temple top, but the stars had described a wide arc of their circle before sleep obscured the images that my mind cast upon the curtain of closed lids as I viewed that tumbled hill from every angle that imagination could devise, and sought to project my vision beneath the shroud of humus and fallen masonry. Ere dawn I had to know where each of the fifty workmen, who would emerge from the mist when again the church bell clanged, was to ply his spade.

If we were to have made appreciable headway on the tangled heap within the three weeks' limit which was our immediate objective, speed was necessary, but to speed caution could not be sacrificed. Moreover, the attack was not unlike that of an army upon a fortress, and the first blow of the vanguard had to be struck in its proper relation to the whole campaign.

Across the northern two-thirds of the eastern slope, some six feet from the summit, a line of faced stones sloping outward showed that even the inner course of the rear wall had fallen to that height. Along this expanse I placed a row of workmen as close together as they could conveniently use their tools. They were to dig toward the west, thus slicing off the upper half of the debris that filled the eastern chamber. The stone and crumbled mortar removed was to be cast down the slope behind them. This was crude, rough work, for there was little chance of finding even a sculptured stone in the roof debris. The more intelligent appearing of the men I had separated from the rest. These were divided into two groups. One was placed at the southwest, the other at the northwest corner of the platform in front of the temple. The surface earth was the black humus of decayed vegetation. At a depth of about one foot it gave way to undisturbed masonry. This level was traced across the entire front and then inward toward the temple wall. As the depth of debris increased, root action had been less pronounced. Soon a film of white mortar began to appear as a coating over the surface of the rough masonry, and not long after a pick blade scraped upon a beautifully polished red-tinted floor. We had established our first definite point—the exact level of the platform which led toward the temple door. Inward the drift was run toward the ragged line where, at a higher level, the material from the fallen roof, with its intermingled network of stumps and roots, was being broken down and cast behind, thus bringing the vertical banks ever so slowly toward an eventual meeting.

Ere long a shout echoed from the lips of one of the diggers at the front of the temple. His pick had loosened a sculptured stone from the wreckage. Most of those about him dropped their tools and crowded close to view and to speculate what might be this bit of carving. Carefully I watched them to judge the relative keenness and interest of each of them as they gazed at the fanged jaw, which the finder was wiping clean of earth, for from that group I must gradually select the few to whom would be entrusted the difficult and meticulous bits of excavation that I knew would, sooner or later, be encountered. Pick and shovel are the tools of a lowly and misunderstood profession. Casually it would seem that any lump of animate matter with sufficient intelligence to guide food and drink to his lips could wield them with all the effectiveness lying within the possibilities of such gross implements. Never was a notion more erroneous. There are almost as many different kinds of picks and shovels as there are of artists' brushes, and each one is shaped for a definite and specific use to which it may be put with blundering stupidity or consummate skill. Sufficient mental alertness quickly to recognize the object which his pick point or shovel blade has laid bare, an ability to evaluate the mechanical relationship between the components of the mass to be moved, and good co-ordination between eye and hand, are, far more than size or strength, the essentials to the making of a master craftsman in the art of digging ditch or driving tunnel. And if ever the touch of the master is needed, it is in archaeological excavation. There even an additional qualification is almost prerequisite—that of interest in the work. A single careless blow can reduce an exquisite pottery vessel to a hundred frayed and tattered sherds; mar a plaque of jade beyond hope of restoration, or destroy utterly some feature of a priceless sculpture.

Before noon of the first day carved stones were coming from the debris all across the front of the temple. For the most part they were thin flat blocks graven in low relief, component elements of large mosaic panels which had adorned the upper reaches of the outer wall. Each one was carried directly forward from the spot at which it was found and added to a heap of its fellows. Karl Ruppert stood with paint pot in hand, ready to brand each stone in a way that would facilitate the task of fitting the mosaics together again when the time came for reassemblage.

The tail pieces of the serpent columns we left as they lay. As the breast of the excavation moved inward, the debris was taken out from beneath each of the heavy rectangular blocks of the toppled shafts, and the stone was let down upon the pavement of the platform, the same side up, and in exactly the same position relative to the others in which it had been found. Corners and flakes had been riven from some of the blocks by the heat of bush fires. Old Juan watched for these among the stones and crumbled mortar which caved down under the picks of the workmen. Much of his thirty years' residence at Chichén had been spent among the ruins, and in consequence he had developed what amounted almost to instinct for recognizing fragments of worked stone. Very often he stooped to recover some ragged spall that might help to fill out a splintered block, for as keenly as we did, he looked forward to the day when this pair of serpent columns would be re-erected in its entirety.

The serpent column, upon which the architects at Chichén specialized, is perhaps one of the most bizarre architectural concepts the world has ever seen. The head, with wide-flung jaws and protruding tongue, lies flat upon the floor plane of the building, jutting forward from the line of the front wall. From behind it the body rises vertically, functioning as the shaft of the column. At the height of the capital, it turns forward at a right angle and continues for a distance sufficient to reach beyond the jutting molding which occurs just above it, then bends vertically upward. This terminal portion is graven to represent the rattles of the rattlesnake, surmounted by a tuft of flowing plumes. No ordinary serpent this, but the Plumed Serpent, the patron deity of Chichén Itzá, combining the qualities, both mystic and mysterious, of the most subtly powerful of the creatures of the earth, and of the bird, master of the element wherein man had no power or domain.

In front of several of the ruins scattered throughout the city lay fallen serpent columns, battered and splintered by the vicissitudes of time. In no known instance was the head of one of them complete. So deep was the debris where we were digging that the heads which we knew should there be present were completely buried, and being thus protected, we hoped that they might be in nearly perfect condition. But there was no predicting what fate they might have suffered before detritus from the walls above had entombed them.

When, near the northwest corner, the temple wall was finally uncovered, findings there injected a new element into our calculations. Because of the height of the mound above the level we had been following, we fully expected to find a series of steps leading up from that level to the entrance of the temple. The highest columns known to exist elsewhere in the city had an altitude of little more than nine feet, hence it was to be expected that the ones in the building we had chosen to explore would be of no greater height. The tops of those which showed above the earth upon the summit were more than twelve feet above the frontal platform, hence our conclusion that the floor of the temple would be at a higher level. Since there were no steps the columns would have a height of between twelve and thirteen feet, and moreover, owing to its greater depth, the debris to be moved from the interior of the building would have a bulk one-fourth greater than that upon which we had calculated, which of course would lengthen the time of excavation.

The portion of the front wall which had been buried was in excellent condition. It rose to a height of more than four feet with a decided inward slant, at the top of which ran a bevelled molding course. Resting directly upon the molding at the northwest corner was the finely carved tooth-studded lower jaw of a grotesque mask, and southward from it spread other features of the mask. Midway between the corner and the north jamb of the door, above one tall course of plain-faced stones, were the basal stones of a mosaic panel, graven to represent the huge clawed feet of a bird. And adjacent to the jamb there remained in place a considerable part of a mask like that found at the corner, except that it was conformed to a flat surface, whereas the median line of the other formed the apex of the corner so that one-half of the mask faced west and the other half north. The half of the wall south of the doorway duplicated these conditions. As a result, we had the key for the rebuilding of these walls to a considerable height. It remained only to fit together the blocks of the mosaics which had been recovered from the debris, and to see that the masons put them back in their proper places in the walls. This sounds easy in the telling, but days, even weeks, of tedious labor had elapsed ere the task was done.

As the diggers drew in upon the area where the serpents' heads should be, Ruppert and I were as restless as dogs which watch at the mouth of a hole for a rabbit to be poked out. Manuel pried down a rough stone, and beyond it I saw a glint of red. "Wait," I ordered before another blow could be struck, and took the pick in my own hands. In an interval that seems devoid of duration as I look back upon it, I had loosened earth and stone from one entire side of the great head, and willing hands had scraped it away behind me. The masterly piece of carving, waist-high, and four feet long, stood before us unmoved and scarcely marred, in almost perfect condition. The upper jaw was flung far upward to reveal a wide-open mouth, painted a dark and brilliant red, and studded, contrary to anatomical veracity, with a huge pair of fangs in the lower as well as in the upper jaw. The eye was a deep-sunken cavity filled in with a black paste which outlined a yellow-white pupil, and above the socket was carved an inverted crescent painted a deep and pleasing blue. From the angle of the jaw a spiral whorl reached backward toward a collar of bright green feathers, beyond which long graceful plumes, also green, were carved to turn upward on the first vertical block of the shaft of the column. From the flat top of the head two short curving horns struck upward. One of them was broken off and missing, and one tooth or fang was gone from the lower jaw.

Sweat molded the flimsy white shirts of the workmen to every contour of their supple torsos as they clawed away the mass that impeded access to the other side of this sculpture, and to the second one that lay beyond. By quitting time both heads stood free, one as nearly perfect as the other. There was no difficulty now in visualizing exactly what had taken place. Slowly at first the topmost portion of the temple wall had crumbled. Plaster and mortar washed down by the rains, then later stones from face and hearting of the wall, had built up an accumulation around the heads, to a height sufficient slightly more than to cover them. Then the whole upper half of the front of the building had fallen outward *en masse*. The two columns swung forward as a severed tree might fall. The lower blocks, wedged by the massive heads, stood firm, but those above lay as we had found them, like sections sawed from a prostrate trunk. Not four inches of earth separated the upflung jaws from the blocks that rested directly above them, but that small layer had been enough to cushion the shock and to preserve these heads in the condition in which we dreamed of finding them.

To the inner line of the door jambs the drift was dug, and then the workmen were transferred elsewhere. The face of the cut was now twelve feet high. The surface beyond would serve as a platform from which to work during the replacement of the serpent columns, stronger and more effective than any that we could build. Also the trees that had been left standing on top of the mound would come in handy as anchor posts for brace ropes and tackle lines. We set up an

A made of two stout timbers, strongly lashed together a short distance below their tops, between one column and the bank of debris behind it. From somewhere in the bush Isauro, son of Juan, and his squad, brought a straight slender trunk of hard wood forty feet long. This we laid horizontally so that it rested in the crotch at the top of the A, the butt protruding beyond the forward face of the column some four feet above it, the tip reaching far back onto the mound. To the butt was lashed a powerful chain block. With this improvised hoist once erected, all was in readiness to begin the rebuilding of the column.

Those elements of the two shafts which had fallen farthest forward had been moved at some time since their collapse, to the extent that from position alone it was impossible to tell to which column a particular one belonged. So we aligned them upon the ground, matching the carving on each with the lines that crossed onto the block above, and the block below. Half of the top stone of the shaft of the south column was missing. Finally Old Juan found it at the foot of the pyramid. Certainly it had been pushed over the brink of the temple platform by human hands.

One by one the rectangles of stone were hoisted, swung into place, the corners plumbed, and the crack beneath wedged so that the block could not sag out of line when the tackle was loosened. Then the crack was sealed with mud, except for a short distance at its highest point. Here a metal pipe was inserted, and through it liquid cement was poured until the crack was completely full. Thus each unit that was added was firmly knit to the one beneath, so that when finished, the column was, in effect, monolithic. The individual blocks of the shaft varied in weight from four hundred to seven hundred pounds, hence were not difficult to raise. With the capital or tail piece the situation was not so simple. It weighed well over a ton, but that was not the chief obstacle. The block, when viewed from the side, was shaped much like a builder's square. When in position it stood as if with the short arm pointing vertically upward, and the free end of the blade resting upon the shaft of the column. As a result the centre of gravity lay forward of the face of the column, and the stone would not remain in position unless supported. Originally the lintels which spanned the door rested upon these tail pieces so that they were bound in place by the tremendous weight of the superstructure. But, as we had no idea of replacing the upper reaches of the building, some other plan of anchorage must be devised.

Upon a bed of wooden rollers the great tail piece was dragged into position beside the column. Ropes, soft but strong, were passed about it, and through these was slipped the hook of the chain block. To the rhythm of Old Juan's "Yo heave," the heavy stone rose till it swung clear of the shaft. The tip of the long horizontal pole, to the butt of which the tackle was attached, served as a sweep, free to move through an arc of more than forty-five degrees. By means of it the tail piece was swung over the capital, and the chains were slackened until it came to rest upon the stone beneath, just where it had originally been placed some centuries before. The tip of the sweep was tied to a stump, and weighted down with logs as an extra precaution, for the capital was poised, ready, if a rope gave, or any feature of the hoist weakened, to crash down upon and shatter the gorgeous head which lay directly beneath it.

Now there came a use for that rod of tool steel that no one had foreseen. We did not find it the night that we searched so long, but two days later it came to the Hacienda on the back of a native who had picked it up and hidden it, to bring it in when convenience dictated, with the hope of a piece of silver for reward. In the forge that we had set up beneath a huge laurel tree I gave one end of it the shape and temper of a miner's drill. All the following day the clang of steel on stone pulsed through the bush as four workmen, led by Ruppert, who knew the handling of a churn drill, stood on a scaffolding above the poised capital and drove the rod deeper and deeper into the shaft beneath. At length the column was pierced from top to bottom and the bore extended well beyond into the foundation. Then a rod of soft iron three-fourths inch in diameter and of the proper length was threaded at one end and split at the other so that the tip of an iron wedge would fit into the slot. The rod was let down into the bore in the column and driven until the wedge had spread the lower end as wide apart as the diameter of the hole would permit. Then the space around the rod was poured full of liquid cement. When this had set, a recess was cut into the top of the capital surrounding the tip of the rod, a plate was fitted over the latter and drawn down tight with a heavy nut. When the countersunk area had been filled with cement not one trace remained visible of the fourteen-foot bolt which united column, capital, and even the foundation beneath into one unit of solid substance which could not fall, barring an earthquake or the actual breaking of stone.

The night after the tackle was removed from the second completed column I sat upon the brink of the terrace and gazed long at the weird and beautifully graven emblems that stood clear limned against the pale white sky, quite lost in the wilderness of my own imaginings. Ere the end I wondered if I were the only one who watched the portal of this ancient shrine. Perhaps in that limbo to which all old discarded gods are at length consigned, one among the host felt a glow of warmth in his long-cold breast as he beheld these symbols of his cult, that for ages had lain among the dust, erect once more, bright beneath the tropic moon, battered, time-scarred, but eloquent of the power and magnificence of the deity to whose glory they had been wrought from the living stone.

ILKA CHASE

Mérida and Chichén Itzá, 1971

"I CHICKENED OUT AT CHICHÉN ITZÁ."

When I was a child, Ilka Chase was a popular television personality, often appearing on the celebrity panels of game shows. I thought her, like Arlene Francis and Kitty Carlisle Hart, an extremely elegant lady. She starred on Broadway in the thirties and wrote a best-selling autobiography in 1942. In the best years of radio she was a major star, later moving easily into television. Over those years, she wrote many books, including a series of lively and amusing accounts of her travels. They reveal a woman both gracious and intelligent, open to adventure, appreciative of quality, and quick to spot anything silly or false.

In February 1971 she set out to tour Yucatán and Guatemala on her own, before joining a tour of South America that would start from Mexico City. She was a celebrity, and the appropriate people rushed forward everywhere to show her around, even in Yucatán. Nothing ruffled her. She could go to see an overweight dancer perform, as she did in Mérida, and keep a straight face. She could visit Cuernavaca, as she did later, and lunch with Helen Hayes, who had a house there. And she could also produce a better, if rather obvious, reason than most archaeologists as to why more virgins weren't sacrificed at the Sacred Well. Her style is breezy and occasionally tart—typical is the way she describes where the ruins are "conveniently situated"—and she must have been great fun to travel with.

The Mayaland Hotel, where Chase and so many other visitors have stayed at Chichén Itzá, is still popular. The main building of the nearby Hotel Hacienda Chichén was built on the burned-out ruins of Edward Thompson's old hacienda, and the hotel's eighteen guest cottages originally housed the teams of Carnegie Institution archaeologists who excavated and restored the ruins. Modern visitors, scholars and tourists alike, might be tempted by the posh, dignified, and comfortable Villa Arqueológica operated here by Club Med. On his 1985 visit, Ronald Wright treated himself to a stay here.

In Mérida, the Hotel Mérida (now the Hotel Mérida Misión), at number 491 Calle 60, a couple of blocks from the Plaza Mayor, remains one of the city's major hotels. (A 1965 guidebook noted with satisfaction that "the hot water is always hot.") The restaurant Los Tulipanes on Calle 43 remains popular too. Local people were still using the cave of the cenote beneath the restaurant as a swimming pool in 1967, so the show that Ilka Chase describes seeing there in 1971 was then a fairly new attraction in Mérida. It caught on with tourists. The restaurant is still presenting it today just as Chase saw it then.

Mérida, with its port city of Progreso, was for centuries the gateway to Yucatán. In the nineteenth century it won renewed fame for its wealth, beauty, and sophistication, all produced by the enormous value of the hemp exports it sent around the world. Today the same highway, MEX 180, that connects Mérida with Chichén Itzá continues on to the city's modern rival, Cancún, 200 miles (320 kilometers) away on the other side of the peninsula.

While Mérida has been described by travelers for centuries, Cancún appears nowhere in the literature. In 1967 a government computer study picked the spot as an ideal place for a resort. Construction began in 1970, the airport was completed in 1973, and the first hotels began greeting guests in 1974. Until then, the spot didn't even appear on maps.

The 1965 edition of Terry's Guide to Mexico, revised by James Norman, briefly mentions the "utter isolation" of nearby Isla Mujeres, noting that "there are no night clubs, swank hotels, and promenades" and "there is little to do." Struggling to find something to offer, Norman then *adds, "An hour or more boat ride across the channel, just S of Puerto Juárez, is the Island and Lagoon Cancuen. The first provides good fishing waters, the latter has an unexplored Maya ruin. The island has undoubtedly the whitest sands in the world." And that's it.*

☀ I HAD BEEN A LITTLE APPREHENSIVE ABOUT the first leg of the journey since I would be alone, but an old and dear friend, Romney Brent, who lives in Mexico City and who would be our peerless leader in South America, had assured me he would alert Willie Calderone, a young English-speaking chauffeur-guide whom he knew, who would meet me at the Mérida airport. On him I could depend as a little child upon a strong wise father.

Had he been there, maybe I could have. As it turned out he was otherwise engaged, but I was not alone. I was met with ruffles and flourishes. His sister was there and his mother was there. Also a travel agent, a newspaper reporter, a photographer and a TV cameraman.

The few passengers with whom I had struck up an acquaintance on the flight were no more astonished than I by the surging entourage. My bafflement was due to the fact that I had reckoned without an influential friend, one Mr. Jack Howard of the Scripps-Howard newspaper and television chain. Having journalistic contacts south of the border, and learning I was going to those parts, Mr. Howard had alerted them and they had rallied.

It was lucky the travel agent was along since he was the only one who could speak both Spanish and English. He interpreted the interview between me and the reporter while the lights flashed, the portable TV camera ground and feeling like a visiting head of state— Mrs. Golda Meir or Prime Minister Indira Gandhi perhaps—I clutched the flowers that had been sent by Romney.

Like all reporters, my man wanted to know how I liked his native city. My knowledge of it being limited to the walk from the plane to the airport lobby where they had descended on me, I was able to say that I admired the handsome brown and white marble paving of the corridor. A few more such pungent comments and I was released.

We drove to the hotel where Willie eventually appeared and it was agreed that he would pick me up at nine the next morning.

The Mérida is a quite nice second-class hotel, the main floor especially so. There are two pretty patios, one with a fountain and swimming pool. During the occasional quiet spells it is extremely pleasant but for the most part, rasping piped-in music assaults the ears destroying all tranquillity and privacy and the clientele is shoddy.

The rooms, if a bit threadbare, are clean and the cashier a bit lighthearted. Scrutinize your bill and—when cashing a traveler's check count your pesos—they were agreeable and prompt about making readjustments but they were understaffed and the hotel was crowded.

The next morning Willie showed up on schedule and we drove around Mérida. The city itself is not enthralling but the climate of Mexico is seductive. The day was hot and dry, the sky a marvelous clear blue and great beautiful trees cast inviting shadows. Mérida was founded by Don Francisco de Montejo the Younger in 1542 and the so-called palace, a large town residence, was built in 1549.

The house is owned and still inhabited by an eccentric old customer named Solariega who is, Willie assured me, a direct descendant of the original Don Francisco. The difference in names, he explained, was because "sometimes no men in a heneration, only wims." Men usually are outnumbered by wims and certainly outlived by them.

One is allowed to visit the house and the proprietor himself, a fairly laborious comedian, acts as guide.

A large hammock is strung between two pillars of an arcade and there, Señor Solariega told us, he sleeps every night. He spread it out to show how wide it was. "I have seven children." I did not know whether they had all been conceived there—doing such work in a hammock would, I should imagine, be quite tricky—or whether possibly they all shared it with him.

Foreigners, the sophisticated and the rich sleep in beds but, at least in that part of Mexico, the great majority of people do sleep in hammocks. In a hot climate they are a good deal more airy than a solid mattress.

The most colorful and interesting sight of the city is the market.

It is an enormous two-storied building, not as picturesque as an open market, but probably more hygienic, and the fruits and flowers and vegetables are arranged with skill and artistry. A little farther along in an arcade with many open stall shops, I bought a guayabera for Norton. They are stitched and pleated shirts that have pockets, are designed to be worn without a tie and hang outside the trousers. They are good looking and cool and would be perfect for the clammy sweltering months of summer in many parts of the U.S.A.

In the course of the day Señor Lavin, publisher of the paper whose reporter had interviewed me the night before, had phoned to say his wife was coming to fetch me for dinner.

Unfortunately he was unable to accompany her but the señora, a small woman, was a more than able lieutenant, even on that hot evening very dashing in a see-through blouse, suede skirt and boots, supplementary lashes and a rich auburn wig. What would I like to do, she asked. Since it was now seven-thirty I began to think of food, but I was in a somewhat Spanish land. *Dine* at *seven-thirty?*

She was vague about food although murmuring that of course we would eat, but would I not like to do a little shopping first? Then there was an underground river she thought I would enjoy and after that we were to go to a concert which would begin about half-past nine. I was confused about the underground river, it sounded *very* strange, and if the concert continued until eleven o'clock or longer I doubted that I would be alive to eat, but she was graciously giving up her evening to me and who was I to upset the customs of the country?

She piloted me to a shop, Canul, Calle 59—as in New York the streets are numbered rather than named—496 where, because I was embarrassed not to, I bought a second guayabera for my dear husband which he did not need. Finally we took off for the subterranean waters. To my delight I found they were below a restaurant, a large open air affair called Tulipanes, and my hostess said we had time to eat before the performance started. The food was very good. Fresh shrimp and chicken baked in banana leaves. The performance itself was a curious affair.

We descended a steep flight of stone steps into a dark, shadowy grotto, where a concrete platform bordered a large pool of gray water, a *cenote* or reservoir. Banquets were placed against the curving stone walls and there were small tables for the customers and their drinks.

The ancient Mayan, Toltec, and Aztec civilizations believed that the god Yum Chac, a distinctly unpleasant character, inhabited the *cenotes,* and to appease him they frequently tossed in young virgins. Most of them drowned but occasional sturdy survivors were hauled out by ropes. They were then supposed to relay tales of the gods and people of the murky depths. If they had any sense one imagines they must have said, "Great god, he say throw no more virgins. Him much displeased by idea." One would also assume that the brighter members of the female sex would have dispensed with their virginity as quickly as possible.

Be that as it may, the evening's entertainment was a kind of facsimile of the gruesome rite.

The already dim lights were lowered still further and down the stairs to the rhythm of tom-toms pounded by two semi-naked youths, floated two girls in white, the victims. They were escorted by a chap I took to be the high priest with flames sprouting from his high head dress and a kingly figure with plumed crown.

Despite oneself, the dim grotto, the flaring flames, the beating of the tom-toms evoked a kind of awe and tension which unfortunately, from the dramatic point of view, was rudely dissipated by waiters hurrying down the stone staircase and threading their way through the cast to serve whisky and Margaritas to the customers.

Still, one got one's money worth. One of the half-naked lads did a dance which included placing his bare feet in the live flames of a small brazier set on the ground, the king's feathered headdress caught fire and was snuffed out by the bare hands of a quick-thinking waiter, there was the flash of a knife blade, an anguished scream from the victim and from the gray water emerged a weird figure, the god Yum Chac. The lights went out, the show was over.

This pastiche was followed by a more worldly spectacle at the Teatro Colonial where we were joined by a pretty girl, Alys, one of Señora Lavin's six children. Usually a movie house, tonight the theatre had been turned into a concert hall where a Mexican artist, Pilar Rioja, was giving a performance of Spanish dances.

The first thing to strike me was the lady's girth. She was a buxom one, that Pilar, almost impossibly so for a Spanish dancer. However, she danced with vigor and skill and under circumstances that would have daunted a lesser spirit. The movie screen, though veiled by a gray curtain, was set very near the footlights with the result that the unfortunate woman had to cavort on a stage only about ten feet deep. This doesn't allow much leeway for sweeping choreography. She was accompanied by a pianist who starred on his own while the señorita was changing costumes, of which she had a large selection. When he was resting she did her own accompaniment which demanded considerable agility. Backstage she would set up a record and burst through the curtain right on the button of the correct beat, skirts swinging, castanets chattering. The lady had spunk.

In the course of the evening I remarked to Señora Lavin that I was about to take off for Guatemala. She evinced considerable surprise coupled with alarm.

"All by yourself?"

"That's right. My husband couldn't come on this trip."

"But do you feel safe?"

"Why yes, why not?"

Something stirred dimly in my memory. Had I not read that there *had* been some anti-American feeling? However, that is universal and frequently passive and if I recalled correctly, the newspaper accounts were already several months old.

"But you are a woman," continued my hostess, "and you don't speak Spanish and those mountain roads . . . you have no *idea*. Ooh, I wouldn't do it," and she gave a little shiver.

I don't pretend that she didn't give me food for thought but although she could not have been more friendly or hospitable, I felt that perhaps political assessments should be left to her journalist husband. Still I would seek further advice.

The next morning I called the American consulate. A man answered and since it was Saturday I asked if the consul was in that morning, and if he could tell me his name.

"You're speaking to him," said the voice.

"Oh."

I told him who I was and explained my problem. "Is it all right for Americans to go to Guatemala?"

"We haven't heard anything from the State Department indicating that it isn't all right," he said, adding helpfully, "Of course that doesn't necessarily mean that it *is* all right."

"I see. Well, forget the State Department. What do you hear from Henry Kissinger?"

There was a kind of gargle at the other end of the wire. "I realize I'm not being very helpful," he said, "but you know as much as I do."

On the record there seemed no reason not to pursue my original plan, but first I would visit Chichén Itzá, the site of the great Mayan ruins and the reason a traveler goes to Mérida in the first place.

The drive takes nearly two hours and is reasonably tedious but once one arrives there all is forgiven.

The Mayaland Hotel at Chichén is charming: spacious and airy with a big swimming pool, tropical gardens and pretty private cottages. Price: $26 a day. It is a delightful place for either an overnight stay or, if one has the time, a more protracted one. Too bad the food is poor.

The ruins are conveniently situated, the equivalent of a couple of blocks, down the road from the hotel. There are two sites, and the afternoon of my arrival I chose the one known as New Chichén.

It is strange to think that when European culture was in abeyance an extraordinary civilization existed on the other side of the world. Chichén Itzá flourished between 461 and 623 although in the tenth century the man-god Kulkulcan occupied it as his capital.

Today almost all that remains of its past glory are huge heavy pyramids, public buildings, and intricate carvings of warriors, feathered serpents, and Kulkulcan.

In the dining room of the Mayaland I was both startled and interested to see that one or two of the native waitresses precisely resembled the carvings of the god and assorted dignitaries of antiquity. The same backward-sloping foreheads, the same high abrupt bridge of a long nose. Mayans really did look like that!

Although by no means as bloodthirsty as the Toltecs, whose religious rites involving human sacrifice and cannibalism were of a revolting cruelty, the Mayans were not averse to a *little* human sacrifice. Just now and then. To keep their hand in.

If one has the stamina to climb the steep interior staircase of the great pyramid, El Castillo, he will see a stone jaguar with jade eyes, the altar upon which men and young women met their gory deaths.

As I hesitated at the foot of the staircase thinking I *might* steel myself for the climb, an American came down. "How was it?" I asked. "It's clammy up there," he said. "There *is* a jaguar with little teeny jade eyes. I don't know as you'd find it worth the effort." I chickened out at Chichén Itzá.

In 1904 an American, Edward Thompson, began dredging Chen Ku, the deep sacred well or *cenote* of New Chichén, whose perpendicular limestone walls drop seventy-five feet to the water which is about forty feet deep. They found jewelry, coins, knives and human skulls, and in 1961, when the National Geographic Society financed an expedition, they brought up not only human bones, but those of thousands of animals who had also been sacrificed.

Of course, even the bloodthirsty couldn't spend *all* their time sacrificing. As Mr. Lincoln so shrewdly observed, "you can't fool all of the people all of the time." Nor could the Toltecs and the Mayans—to some extent Chichén Itzá was a mixture of both cultures—murder all of the people all of the time.

Indeed, there is evidence that they did have other diversions. There are the ruins of a ball court where the great, great grandfather of what is today's soccer was played. It is an enormous and massive affair that could easily hold several thousand people.

The solid rubber balls used in play were a foot in diameter and might not be touched with the hands, but were propelled by knees, hips, and buttocks. The object was to knock them through great stone rings twenty feet above the level of the court.

So difficult was this feat to accomplish that the winner was allowed to take what clothes and possessions he could snaffle from any spectator. One may imagine the wild scramble of the audience to get away from the pastime it had come so eagerly to watch. Sometimes, if he was in the mood, the victor was permitted to behead the captain of the losing team.

One of the most impressive buildings stands in Old Chichén. It is the observatory, resting on a tremendous base of two huge terraces, the lower one 225 feet long and 150 feet wide. One may fairly say that the Mayans were prolific builders and it is very nearly impossible—one would be too exhausted physically and culturally—to take in all of Chichén Itzá in a day even in the most superficial fashion, so that in a sense the hotel's check-out time has something to do with the visitor's schedule. It is 2 P.M. Most people arrive after lunch, do one side of the road in the afternoon, the other the next morning, have luncheon and depart. It is a good plan. You should husband your energies, for it is very hot in Yucatán. A dry heat and tolerable, but it does take something out of you.

I had arranged with Willie Calderone that he would be at the Mayaland Hotel to pick me up at one-thirty the day after my arrival. However, since he had asked if I could not give him some money in advance I made a bet with myself he would not show up. I won it too, although he did send a replacement, Luis, with a cock and bull story about Willie's car having broken down. Had he failed to get the advance money I suspected that his car would have been working like a dream. Even so I was in luck for Luis's car was air conditioned and much more comfortable.

It was a Sunday and on the return trip to Mérida we passed through a village where a bullfight was in progress. Having seen my first and only bullfight in northern Spain at the age of sixteen where the shock was such that I vomited all over the stands I know that they were not for me. However, Luis was eager and assured me they did not kill the bull.

"Please, please, can we not stop off to see it?"

From the way he spoke I gathered it might be a rather cruel game but that in the end they would release the animal and probably considerable local color would be involved.

I let myself be persuaded to get out of the car and to climb a primitive ladder to reach chairs on a sort of makeshift platform in what had to be the most rickety bull ring of modern times. It appeared to be constructed of wattles and banana leaves and on it, teetering precariously upon broken-down chairs, were masses of Mexicans, chiefly women, with masses of children; bawling, nursing, laughing, and hanging over flimsy railings like washing over a clothesline. It was a death trap par excellence and I was grateful it was out of doors. In case of fire one *might* have a fighting chance.

Down in the ring were three or four men on horseback and in the hot sun, tethered to a post, was a cadaverous steer, a big red X painted on his sunken flanks.

"Oh," said Luis cheerfully, "on Sunday they always have three. The other two they let go but this one is marked. They'll kill him."

That did it. As though he had pressed a button, tears of rage, pity, and shame for the human race poured down my cheeks.

"Not in front of me they won't. Come on," and I groped my way as hurriedly as I could back through the rows of rickety chairs and along the platform till we reached the ladder. Half the time missing my footing I slid and tumbled down it, bruising my arms and legs, tearing my dress, while Luis lowered himself after me imploring me to be careful. *"Señora, señora, despacio, despacio por el amor de dios!"*

My reaction was beyond his comprehension and he kept asking in a bewildered way, "But why? What? What upsets you?"

"It's monstrous," I stammered, "monstrous to slaughter a help-less animal in that brutal way. For sport. For glee! Let's get out of here." I jumped into the car and slammed the door. With a shrug he got into the driver's seat and with a reluctant glance behind him at the bull ring and the missed delights of the kill, he headed for Mérida.

Back at my hotel as I was waiting in the lobby for the elevator the doors opened and out stepped a most elegant young toreador. He was wearing a skin-tight suit of green and gold and with his dark curls and flashing dark eyes was quite beautiful. He smiled at me as he passed. I wished him all the worst.

The next morning Willie picked me up again and when I confronted him with the improbable tale of his car breaking down he shrugged and laughed good humoredly. He had been out with his girl.

Our destination was Uxmal, another pyramid site well worth a visit. It is a later period and not as large as Chichén Itzá, but in some respects it is more rewarding. There is greater variety and finer carving. Uxmal was once a great city, and there is still much to be unearthed, but what there is today is impressive, especially the enor-mous courtyard of which the governor's palace forms one entire side. It is rich with friezes and chiseled decorations and a truncated col-umn which was originally a ten-foot-high stone phallus stands before it. Today it is of more modest proportions, a mere five feet. Even so . . .

NORTH OF MEXICO CITY

DANE CHANDOS

Uruapan and Paricutín, 1948

"FROM MINUTE TO MINUTE THE COUGHING
OF THE VOLCANO CAME LOUDER, LIKE THE
SNARLING OF A LION."

Early in the 1940s, about twenty years after D. H. Lawrence spent time there working on The Plumed Serpent, *an American named Peter Lilley began building a house in the town of Ajijic on the shore of Lake Chapala. Writing under the pseudonym Dane Chandos, he recounted the checkered story of its construction in his 1945* Village in the Sun, *which* The New Yorker *called "a pleasant, sunlit book."*

The house was large and located directly at the water's edge, and when it was finally finished—or almost finished—friends suggested Chandos take in a few paying guests. In House in the Sun, *published in 1949, he reported his adventures and misadventures as an amateur hotel keeper. He was clearly a genial host to friends and paying customers alike, as well as a careful and affectionate observer of Mexican customs, and his books were both praised and popular at the time they were published.*

In the following excerpt he takes a pair of guests, Professor and

Mrs. Fountanney, and a servant named Silvanito to the town of Urua-pan and the volcano Paricutín.

The birth of Paricutín came after a decade of ominous seismic activity in the region. At about five o'clock in the afternoon on Sunday, February 20, 1943, an Indian farmer named Dionisio Pulido saw smoke rising from the middle of his cornfield. As he hurried to the spot, the earth literally opened at his feet. Pulido ran for his life to the nearest village and reported what he'd seen. By the time he returned with neighbors, his cornfield was disappearing beneath a rapidly growing volcanic cone. A column of flame, ash, glowing rock, and red-hot lava was shooting into the sky, and the eruption had jiggled the needles on a seismograph 2,200 miles away in New York City.

Where Dionisio Pulido had been sowing corn there was now a roaring volcano, its cone growing visibly wider and taller by the minute. The villagers raced back to town, telephoned Mexico City for help, and then gathered in the village church of Parangaricutiro to pray for what they hoped would be more reliable assistance. None came and, before long, they had to abandon church and village to an inexorable river of lava. Only the church's tower was left standing.

The following weeks, with the volcano shooting rocks nearly a mile into the air, brought devastation to the region. Five thousand people were displaced, several villages were buried entirely, and Uruapan was knee-deep in ash. Within two years the base of the volcano's cone had spread to a mile or so in diameter and about 1,400 feet in height, forever changing the landscape of the valley.

Paul Bowles saw the volcano late in 1944. "The fire shot out all night every ten seconds with a magnificent roar," he wrote. Nearly thirty years later, he described that roar as "a sound deeper and viscerally more exciting than any sound I have ever heard."

Dane Chandos describes the volcano as it was in 1948. Today, the tower and white marble apse of San Juan de Parangaricutiro can still be seen rising above the black lava that covers the village. Since 1952, Paricutín has been silent, content to cast a long shadow. Buried deep within it is the point in space, hard to imagine now but harder to forget, where Dionisio Pulido was sowing corn in his field that quiet Sunday afternoon.

☀ WE TURNED OFF THE MAIN HIGHWAY A LITTLE
before sunset and entered on the last seventy kilometers of the
steep and sinuous road to Uruapan. As we began to climb, the air
freshened, and soon we were driving among pine forests beneath lofty
crags. Here and there were meadows full of cattle, and once we
passed a little sparkling stream. The villages too contributed to the
Alpine atmosphere; their little houses were of adobe no longer but
sturdily built of wood with widely overhanging eaves. By now the
lamps were lit, and in their soft glow was a mellow feeling of comfort
and cheerfulness. In the dusk you could imagine yourself back in the
old Austria, scenting the sharp tang of resin and listening to the
friendly buzz of talk by the Weinstube. Perhaps Maximilian too,
when he paid his first state visit to Michoacán, which he described
as the most troublesome province of his empire, took fresh heart in
this mountain air and was carried back in memory to the great post
highway from Vienna to Trieste.

The road wound in and out with unbelievable intricacy, past
woods, over bridges, around a series of hills that all seemed, in the
gathering gloom, to be of the same curiously familiar shape--squat
flattened cones, smooth and regular, their outlines blurred with a
haze of pine trees. The sun had already set, but a faint glow remained ahead of us in the west.

"It looks as if we're catching up the sun, señor," said Silvanito,
spitting tangerine seeds out of the car.

And indeed the light ahead was growing rosier, pulsating every
quarter minute or so and giving the impression that behind the hills
some titanic firework master was touching off, at fixed intervals, a
chain of Bengal lights. Suddenly, however, one of them decided to
act like a Roman candle. A burst of crimson light gushed over the
summit of one of the flat-topped hills, setting on fire the clouds behind it.

It was our first view of the volcano, but the flames were still
many miles away and only coincidence had placed the little peak directly between them and ourselves. One thing, however, was suddenly clear to me. Of course these hills were familiar. They were
textbook volcanoes, familiar to every child who has had an illustrated
geography primer. There they were, uniform in shape, diverse in
size, hundreds upon hundreds of them swarming over the mountain
country, an army of inverted cooking pans, cool now, but, no doubt,

each in its day another Paricutín, carrying ruin and destruction over the whole state. For all Michoacán is of volcanic origin, and there is still a large waste area southeast of Uruapan, known as the Bad Lands, which, once a rich agricultural district, was turned into a desert by the sudden appearance two hundred years ago of the volcano Jorullo, in circumstances curiously similar to those attending the birth of Paricutín in 1943. Perhaps these violent and temporary volcanoes arise at fairly frequent intervals, safety valves for the whole region.

We left the red glare of the mountain behind us to the right, and as we ran downhill into Uruapan, twinkling lights began to appear through the pine trees below. The town lies in a fertile basin, famous for its flowers and orchards, but in the cold and feeble light of the street lamps its personality was austere, and the houses, whitewashed and tiled, seemed to crouch secret and watchful beneath their wide eaves. Although it was not late, there were few people about.

I had not stayed in Uruapan when I visited Paricutín some years before, but I knew of a hotel. Its appearance didn't promise anything luxurious, but we were all ready for bed and prepared to make the best of whatever accommodation it offered. I knocked on the modest wooden door, and then we waited. After about five minutes it was opened by a very small boy. He blinked at us for a moment, and then said solemnly and in English, "Tourist mansion! Come in! You will like to know it!"

The hotel had been in darkness when we went to bed and I hadn't noticed my surroundings. In the morning I opened my door onto a huge patio, a shining cloister filled with flowers—azaleas, begonias, geraniums, stars of Bethlehem, in row upon row of neat white classical vases, draped with foliage and crowned with color. Among the flowers were many bird cages filled with parrots, mocking birds, cockatoos, and budgereegahs. A flaming bougainvillea rioted along one wall, and among its crimson blossoms a family of white canaries sang and chattered—little white stars gleaming in the morning sun. After the severity of the hotel front this brilliance was startling enough, and the unexpected effect of space was heightened by the view through an archway of another patio overlooking a rose garden.

This element of surprise persists wherever the patio is the focal point of the house. Guadalajara has many mean-looking streets, but often enough the dingy, plastered façades and barred and shuttered windows conceal elegant and flowery courts. Where an American or North European house displays a bold front to the world, the charms of the Spanish home are turned inward as if jealous or scornful of the world's admiration. Withdrawn and reserved as the Spanish character itself, the patio has, all the same, older and more distant origins. Perhaps the courts of the Alhambra at Granada are the most renowned and elegant of Spanish patios, with their myrtles and fountains, their slender clustered colonnades and pavilions brilliant with mosaic and stalactite and multicolored stucco. But all these glories are concealed behind severe and frowning battlements, and all were the work of Islam. In the twisted lanes of Cairo or Damascus, or in any city of the Moslem world from Fez to the Indies, are innumerable homes, humbler Alhambras, reserved and exquisite, hiding from a world of violence and maintaining sacrosanct the privacy of the family. This was the way of life and the chosen type of abode that Spanish colonists took to their new lands, from Seville to Havana, from Havana to Mexico, from Acapulco to Manila, a way of life on which, long before the days of anthems and flags and all the other trappings of an imperialistic age, the sun never set.

The Fountainneys joined me for breakfast in the patio, among the flowers and the birds. The Professor had already been up and about for an hour. He was in great form and ordered three fried eggs with his ham.

The day was blue and brilliant. High above the rose garden Paricutín's white and lilac plume of smoke towered into the sky. After breakfast we explored the town. By day it was colorful and animated, displaying none of the mystery of the night before; hills rose on all sides and fir trees screened the view at the ends of all its cobbled lanes; everywhere there were flowers; down the main street one little plaza succeeded another, and in the gardens palms and pines, rose's and plumbago and oranges and limes grew side by side; everywhere there were arcades, borne on slim pillars fashioned from pine trunks on square brick bases.

The market in Uruapan sprawls cheerfully through four or five steep and narrow streets, and so closely are the booths crowded together that they attain the effect of an oriental bazaar. The air is full of the scent of fruit, piled in mounds of every imaginable variety and color. There are nuts of all kinds arranged in neat little heaps, casseroles and cookpots of every size, laid out on rows and grouped in sets, little round white cheeses, and mats, fans and other types of plaited work. Where the last street merges into the plaza, we found the lacquer stores.

Lacquer is a specialty of Uruapan, which exports this ware to every part of the republic and to the United States. A great variety of objects are made, from matchboxes to large trays, including many different patterns of gourd, bowl, and calabash, most of the forms being useful rather than purely ornamental. Lacquerware as made in China and Japan has many country cousins, from the delicate work on Srinagar papier-mâché to the gay, and sometimes crude, Pontypridd trays of early Victorian times. Uruapan ware is, in composition, more like the lac of Burma than true oriental lacquer, being made from the juices exuded by a plant bug related to the cochineal insect.

The best examples of lacquerware in Uruapan are treated with a kind of gesso or clay, and the designs are incised, picked out in colored pigment, lacquered, and polished by hand. The work is gay and brilliant and is characterized by a profusion of many-petaled surface flowers, but the designs, though often crude and barbaric, are robust and forceful, and occasional pieces are attractive.

Even before the days of the volcano, Uruapan had a tourist trade on account of its climate and its beautiful surroundings, including the famous waterfall of Tzaráracua, and the national park, which I particularly wanted to see. It is a large natural garden clinging to the sides of a gorge, through which, in foaming cataracts, rushes a clear, cold river. It lies a little way out of town, so we went there in the car, which we parked outside the gate, leaving Silvanito in charge of it, free to gossip with anybody who might pass.

The fact that there was no entrance fee may have had something to do with the air of neglect that hung over the garden, but perhaps this added to its charm. The paths were weed grown and heavily shaded by tall evergreen trees, and the undergrowth pressed thickly on either side. Save for the shafts of sunlight that thrust powerfully through the leaves every few feet, polka-dotting the path with slate and silver, the effect would have been most somber. However, in spite of the heavy scent of coffee blossom, the air was fresh, and there was none of the insect-peppered opacity that you find in tropical forests, where the sun's rays struggle with a haze of motes, like torchlight in a dark and dusty attic. The garden was wholesome and alive with the ripple of innumerable springs; its pellucid conduits, tinkling and artificial, ran merrily down the slopes of the gorge through a maze of fern-encrusted channels, their waters bubbling musically over pebble beds and swirling round mossy boulders. And above the myriad rustles and gurglings of the tiny streams, like the roll of drums behind an orchestra, the roar of the torrent was everywhere. Across the gorge was slung a sturdy wooden bridge, steeply roofed as if against Alpine rocks and snow, and here we sat down and looked about us. The setting was intimate, the details lavish. Beneath our feet the river churned and raced, massive boulders rumbling in its narrow bed. In and out, between the stony masses, darted a little flashing kingfisher, pursued, and evidently worried, by a pair of lilac-polled hummingbirds. All along the steeply sloping banks, in the shade of giant Indian laurels, were ranged huge banana plants, their tattered leaves anything up to a dozen feet in length, the largest I had ever seen.

And there was tropical color as well as tropical size. In the interstices of many trees there were orchids in bloom, clumps of delicate odontoglossum, and here and there a vivid queen cattleya. I like orchids and think myself fortunate in being able to see so many, for Mexico has a great variety and indeed is said to be the world's largest producer of the only species in general commerce—the vanilla. In some private gardens there are fabulous collections of orchids; here, in Uruapan, they were distinguished neither for their rarity nor their profusion, but the occasional exotic touches of color—rose pink, violet, cinnamon, and speckled chestnut—lent extra brilliance to the scene. Down below, zigzagging and hovering over the broken surface of the water, whirled dragonflies, blue and scarlet, green and puce, like vivid slivers of the lavish masses of bougainvillea and morning glory that festooned the treetops on either bank. High among the blossoms, their murmurs submerged in the thunder of the cataract, the bees moved drowsily.

Beside us on the bridge a student leaned against the coping, deeply absorbed in a mathematical textbook; a little way up the stream, in a natural rock basin, three naked Indio boys were frisking in the water, somersaulting and slapping each other with lily pads. Apart from these, there was no one in all Uruapan who cared to share this loveliness with us.

I had to give in about the volcano. The Professor was very keen to go, and since our way home went right past the dirt road leading to the mountain, it seemed rather mean not to start a few hours earlier and take him.

I had visited Paricutín in its younger days, and it had certainly been an alarming and brilliant spectacle. It had astonished the world by its sudden appearance, though, as is usual in such cases, there had been warning signs for some time before. There seems to be sympathy between volcanoes. The Neapolitans will tell you that when Vesuvius is quiet the mud volcano, the Solfatara, will be at its most active and that when the mud ceases to bubble they may expect the lava. Numerous portents heralded Paricutín's birth—earthquake shocks, subterranean rumblings, the sudden appearance and equally sudden disappearance of hot springs in the nearby mountains, and a minor eruption of the great peak of Colima. Then one day a Tarasco farmer, plowing his corn patch, was startled to see a jet of smoke gush up from a dip in the field a few yards away. The earth trembled, and as he watched, the cracks in the soil widened, the ground heaved up, and flames poured out with the smoke. A new volcano had been born. In a few weeks it had piled itself a cone hundreds of feet high, from which it spewed lava and hot boulders, and far away in Ajijic we could hear the dull rumble of the explosions. Soon after that I had gone there with Mexican friends. We reached the neighborhood late; darkness had fallen, and we should have missed the narrow track that led to the volcano but for the stream of cars creeping along it. The way was terrible, and with every bump we lurched from side to side, but, once started, it was impossible to turn back against the flow of cars. There seemed no reason why we should ever arrive anywhere. We could hear the explosions, but they sounded no nearer than they had done a couple of hours before. We could see a glow high in the sky, but round each corner we met only blackness again. For more than three hours we went on like this. Then, suddenly, we turned one more corner, the road opened out into a field, and there was the volcano, a dark regular cone with a firework show on top of it.

It was a fantastic sight. As though it were breathing, the volcano gave off deep resonant explosions, and with every breath there arose a shower of incandescent rocks. The larger ones were hurled out of the crater. The smaller, thrown straight up into the air, fell straight down again, but the volcano's agitated breath came so short that almost always, before they dropped again into those boiling depths, a new breath caught them, so that they bounced up and down like celluloid balls on a fountain in a shooting gallery. They were not all the same color, these flaming rocks and stones. Some were electric white, some were tinged with rose, and here and there one was red or sprouted fiery hair. The reverberations were continuous and the ground shook. From time to time there came a greater shock, and the larger boulders were hurled higher. Sometimes there came a little lull, and then the small bouncing stones, glowing duller and duller, would fall back into the crater. We stood directly beside a small lava stream, but it was still molten and had hardly formed a crust. The shaking body of the earth, the explosions coming like hurried breath, the tongue of lava, and the fiery spittings made it very easy to understand how man had invented his dragons. It was like being on the dragon's back, rather too near the head.

Later Paricutín changed character. First he poured out rivers of lava. Upon Parangaricutiro, the nearest large village, the lava advanced, and most of the inhabitants fled, taking with them the image from the church. The village was engulfed. Then he gave out dust, nothing but dust and more dust. More than a hundred miles away in Ajijic we were showered for several weeks with black grit, and all round the volcano there was desolation. In Uruapan, fields and orchards were blighted and the dust settled on the houses, on the roofs, on the sills, everywhere. It drifted through every crevice. It filled and fouled the ponds and pools, and the parched cattle died, choked to death. It killed the poultry. It even killed some children who had gone to glean in the stricken fields, a storming flurry of it catching and suffocating them. Then it rained, and a fine mud came through the air; then more dust, forming a treacherous cake over the mud. In the towns the roofs collapsed, and for days on end only a murky half light came from the hidden sun. Priests rode round the dark, choking streets in cars, standing on the running boards and calling the people to penance, to avert this retribution for their sins. From Uruapan, whither the first refugees had fled, people were now fleeing down the dim and muffled roads. This went on for weeks. High officials visited the region and relief was organized. Then the dust abated. No longer did it quench the sky. The lava still flowed but slowly. Experts prophesied that Paricutín would last only a few years, a nova among volcanoes. But all around it the country was a desert. This was what the Professor wanted to see.

Since my first visit the local authorities had done much to turn what was once the roughest of tracks into a practicable dirt road, and no doubt, if the tourist traffic had increased, further improvements would have been made. But what had been a torrent of cars had now, with the decreasing activity of the mountain, dwindled to a trickle. It only requires the appearance of a new volcano, an event reported mistakenly at least once a year, for Paricutín's tourist value to fall still further, and the road will crumble and eventually disappear back into the earth as adobes do. As it was, the going was rough. After a mile or more we came to an arroyo over which was a wooden bridge, some of whose planking for no apparent reason had been removed. Two small boys smirkingly directed us to a hamlet that lay off the road to our right, loudly demanding centavos and, to my surprise, matches. These small blackmailers were firmly repulsed by a flood of invective from Silvanito, and we lumbered down into the village, where I asked a man the way to the volcano.

"Who knows," he answered. No note of interrogation in his voice, no smile, nothing. A woman in a nearby doorway, ragged and emaciated, said coldly, "To the left." And suddenly, for the first time in Mexico, I was aware of what D. H. Lawrence called the "obsidian stare," impenetrable, defiant, and hostile. I am not in sympathy with Lawrence's attitude toward the Indios in their relations with the whites; I am more at home with earlier and less emphatic writers— with. Mme. Calderón de la Barca, who notices everything and pontificates about nothing, or with Charles Macomb Flandreau, whose wit and penetration is always tempered with kindness and geniality. But here, in this remote Tarasco village, I could see eye to eye with Lawrence. There was hatred and mockery in the atmosphere. I suppose it was hardly surprising. To the Tarasco countryman the volcano has brought ruin, misery, and starvation. He has had no part in the profits of the hotelkeepers and taximen of the town, and it is only natural that he has little sympathy for the wealthy travelers who come in cars with lavish picnic baskets to chatter and gloat over the cause of all his troubles.

We were all glad to leave the village. At the corner the Professor asked an elderly man the distance to the mountain.

"I do not know the road to Paricutín," he said gravely, as though he were a stranger in a big city. "They say it is ten kilometers."

By the time we had gone nearly twice that distance, we had risen several hundred feet, crossed numerous rickety plank bridges, and changed a wheel. The sun had disappeared, and the sky wore an unearthly, sulphurous tint. Dust was in the air, in the car; dust grated between our teeth; the road, which had been steep and stony, was now muffled with gray volcanic dust, save where the deep ruts had a filling of red pumice. Through the ranks of sickly pines, tattered and moth eaten like half-fledged birds, wound sleek ribbons of gray silt brought down by the rains. It was some time since we had seen any animals, and the only sign of life was provided by a raven enjoying some nameless repast on a withered thorn tree. At our approach he heaved himself into the air and flapped clumsily ahead round a bend in the road, the scarlet flesh in his beak glowing against his plumage like the last live ember in a half-consumed coal fire. As we followed him round the curve, the landscape opened up into a slate-gray expanse fringed by ragged firs, and away beyond, squat and drab, crouched the volcano, a huge inverted flowerpot from which a mournful plume of gritty, dusty smoke poured into the still air.

The road ends a few kilometers short of the volcano, and if you want to get closer, you must go on foot or hire mules in the settlement of tumble-down shacks where those who have refused to leave the remnant of their fields now live. It was soon evident that Silvanito wanted nothing further to do with the mountain.

"The car will be quite safe, señor," he said in a tragic voice, "for I shall guard it."

"Don't you want to come with us?"

"Certainly that, yes. But who knows if somebody might not put sugar in the gasoline, like that time in Guadalajara."

I looked around at the congeries of miserable huts with their two or three patches of gray and stunted corn. It was clear there was no sugar here to waste, but I made sure the gas tank was locked.

"But, señor," said Silvanito, rather pink, "it would be bad if we lost one of the little valves of the tires. For the doubts one must stay and watch the car."

Several small boys had appeared from nowhere to look at us, so I suggested giving one of them a few centavos to look after the car.

"I do not have confidence," said Silvanito, grandly, "in these of up here."

So we left him and started up the rough track, guided by a child who said he'd show us where to hire the mules. At a bend in the road I looked back; six small boys were clustered round the hood of the car gaping, while Silvanito expounded.

The mules were expensive, but our guide, a cheerful young native of the village of Paricutín, who introduced himself as Gerónimo López-to-serve-you, explained this by the fact that their food had come from many miles down the valley. As we rode along he talked.

"It came very slowly," he said, pointing to the tangled sea of gray-brown lava surrounding the half-submerged tower of Parangaricutiro's parish church. "Six months it took to flow, and now there are fifteen kilometers of it, or so they say."

In what is left of the village a few inhabitants still live. The Professor busied himself speculating about the effect of volcanic grit on the egg production of some scraggy hens we saw. I asked the guide if no one had been trapped in the village by the eruption.

"We all had good warning," he said, "though when that Dionisio, who first saw the smoke, came running to his neighbors, we didn't think much about it. You see, there was always a hole in that field from which the air blew very hot, and the boys would throw each other's sombreros into it so that they were cast back many meters into the air. It was a favorite game, so I for one didn't take Dionisio too seriously. But in the next hours there was much noise and smoke and fire, and the Señor Cura himself went up to look at it. When he came down the hill he called a meeting, and those of Paricutín came down to Parangaricutiro here, and we all put ourselves and our homes at the mercy of God. But later, when the dust and stones fell heavily and the ground shook, we were afraid to go into the church for Mass, for we thought it might fall down on us when we were inside. Of course, many people said it was a punishment for our sins, so naturally we were afraid, and we built a little chapel of wood outside. But now, as you may imagine, they say that if we had trusted in God more the lava would have stayed away from the village, but I do not think so."

He talked on, and the mules picked their way across the jagged surface of the lava. Mrs. Fountanney rode easily, looking straight ahead, never speaking; every now and then she leaned forward and patted her mule's neck. The Professor sat rigidly on his mount, cross-questioning the guide and stopping every few yards to focus his binoculars.

From minute to minute the coughing of the volcano came louder, like the snarling of a lion, full of menace but without the terror of his full-blooded roar. Our guide said he thought it wiser not to go any closer, and at the summit of a little hillock we halted. The air was heavy and still, and across the valley the huge bulk of the volcano now appeared in its true impressive proportions. The Professor dismounted and set up the tripod of his camera. Thin white smoke, like incense before an altar, arose round the base of the mountain, from the narrow streams of hot lava that still crept from the fissures in its flanks. From the crater itself mushrooms of black smoke burst forth every few seconds, and, as they began to break up, the noise of the discharge reached us across the intervening space, like the muffled roar of cannon.

"We say in these parts," said Gerónimo, "that it's a poor fire that won't warm somebody's pot. But who knows."

Optimism is inherent in the Mexican character, and the Indio is the master of making the best of things. This had been rich land inhabited by a prosperous community. Now it was a lunar desolation. What the lava had spared was a desert of gray volcanic silt, flat and smooth as satin, save where the rain had worn small pinnacles beneath the pumice stones that speckled its surface, giving the appearance of a rash of tiny mushrooms. On all the hillsides around us the trees still stood in their serried thousands, but it was as if they had been blasted bare by many lightnings; stripped and sere, their stark trunks looked brittle as old bones, giving the hills the grizzled, spiny appearance of hedgehogs. This was not a mere pocking of destruction leaving untouched places; this was not a leveling of tree and building, leaving the old earth ready to receive seed and spore, and in a season to put forth new greens; here not a square inch was spared; this land was totally dead.

The Professor ran here and there, enjoying himself, sifting ash through his fingers, examining volcanic rock, poking at lava. Mrs. Fountanney and I stared in silence across the waste—grassless, birdless, insectless.

"Look at that low bough," she said, pointing to a ruined tree near the path. "You would have said, wouldn't you, that it was meant for children to swing on?"

And suddenly we both wanted to go home, back to the fertile Chapala lakeside. We called to the Professor, and, as we turned our mules to go, a little speck of white caught my eye—a poppy, barely rooted in the gray ash, was bravely struggling to put forth its one stunted flower. Perhaps Gerónimo's optimism was not so preposterous after all. Flowers don't give way to despair. Why should he?

On the way back to the highway in the car, we passed a tumbledown shack, ash colored amid the poisoned fields. A family was sitting beside it, a chocolate-dark Tarasco and his wife, a little girl, a boy of ten or so. They had a burro and some bundles, cookpots and two chickens crowded into a wicker cage. I stopped and greeted them. Only the man could speak Spanish, and the others muttered together in the harsh, guttural Tarasco tongue. I asked if any of them wanted a lift.

"Thank you, señor," replied the man, "but we have come home."

They would not change their minds. Hopeful and unreasoning as the little poppy itself, they were prepared for the struggle to strike new roots into their ruined homeland. We left them there, squatting amid the cinders, gray brown and desolate as the blasted earth, patient and dignified as the hills themselves, waiting for goodness knows what, goodness knows when.

ELIZABETH BORTON DE TREVIÑO

An American bride in Monterrey, 1930s

"EVENTUALLY I LEARNED ALL THE WEAPONS OF
BARGAINING, THE LOOK OF SCORN, THE FALSE
STARTS AWAY, THE EYEBROW LIFTING, THE EYES
ROLLED HEAVENWARD."

*Elizabeth Borton was born in Bakersfield, California. After graduating
from Stanford, she went to Boston to study the violin and there began
a long newspaper career with the* Boston Herald, *writing about music,
dance, and, from Hollywood, film. In the 1930s her editor assigned her
a series of articles on Mexico, and within a week her life had changed
forever. Almost before she knew what was happening, she had been
courted and wed by the son of a fine old Mexican family (somewhat reduced in circumstances by years of revolution) and set up as mistress of
a household in provincial Monterrey.*

*Though little more than a hundred miles from the U.S. border, she
had to struggle, in those early years, to adapt to life in an alien culture.
Day by day, and with many frustrations, she learned to cope with the
complexities of Spanish names, the traditions of household management
and family relationships, and the language, remembering especially not to
provoke general hilarity by using the Castilian version of Spanish she had
learned in school.*

Her memoir of those first years, My Heart Lies South (1953), is an invaluable record of traditional Mexican social life, besides being funny, heartwarming, free of sentimentality but rich with sentiment. And it's filled with wonderful stories, both hair-raising and hilarious, about everything from parrots to the impenetrable ways of the Mexican post office. In 1962 she added another volume to her memoirs, Where the Heart Lies.

Señora Treviño began writing books for children in the mid-thirties, and in the fifties and sixties she wrote several novels for adults. El Guero, an adventure tale for young readers, is based on the boyhood of her father-in-law, and I, Juan de Pareja won the 1965 Newbery Medal. Here Is Mexico, published in 1970, is an introduction to that country for young people.

In later years, living in Cuernavaca, she became a great señora, often sought out as an important source of information about the country. At one point in her memoir, for example, she refers to the old family recipes she was given by Mamacita, her mother-in-law. Those recipes had first been written down by Mamacita's own great-grandmother. When Diana Kennedy, the leading American authority on Mexican food, was preparing her now classic cookbook, The Cuisines of Mexico (published in 1972 and in a revised edition in 1986), Señora Treviño was one of those she consulted for advice. And some of those same recipes learned by the young bride in Monterrey are no doubt still in use today.

The house where Señora Treviño first lived in Monterrey, at Morelos 829, was half a block and just around the corner from the cathedral. Mamacita, who helped her learn Mexican ways, lived at Bolívar 492. Modern Monterrey, Mexico's third largest and most industrialized city, is much changed from the small provincial town Señora Treviño knew in the thirties. Still, in her 1970 Here Is Mexico, she wrote that "the social life of the city remains profoundly Mexican. The old patterns of city life brought from Spain—surveillance of daughters, an elaborate ceremony of courtship, rigid ideas about fidelity, honor, and respect for elders—are adhered to by all classes."

Señora Treviño still lives in Cuernavaca.

☀ THERE ARE A NUMBER OF CHARMING "COLO-nias" or residence sections in Monterrey, many of them modern and very much in the American style, but I had fallen in love with Mamacita's old-fashioned Mexican house, and I wanted a patio, and barred windows, and a fountain. She was against this idea, for she loved everything bright and new, herself. But at last I found a little house which had everything I had been looking for except the fountain. The barred windows curved outward in a very pregnant manner, the floors were all tiled in a pattern of rust and gray, and there were *two* patios. My address: Morelos 829. Here I lived the early years of my marriage.

The rooms closed with great wooden shutters against the dangerous night air, and the *dispensa* or food-storage room, and the kitchen and dining room were divided from each other by long windy corridors. But though these arrangements had certain disadvantages, there is no tranquility quite equal to that of a garden within high walls, where you can wander barefoot in your nightgown on a heavenly summer morning.

I had to achieve my garden with the help of many potted ferns and plants, since my patio was entirely paved, but before long I had a kind of thick flowering jungle there. Climbing vines twisted everywhere and hung down over the recessed doorways.

In Monterrey homes the *dispensa* is supposed to be locked, to prevent pilfering of rice and sugar by the servants, and the ice box (almost always kept in the dining room) is also padlocked against possible lowering of the level in the milk bottles, and other depredations. Keys to all these things, plus keys to the silver drawer and dish closets, to the linen press, to the clothes closets and trunks and desks are supposed to hang from the belt of the lady of the house. Not for nothing is she known in Spanish as *ama de llaves,* or keeper of the keys. As I lost all my keys frequently, we soon gave up and left ourselves to chance, and the servants took good care of my treasures because the *señora* was so evidently less than capable.

It took us months to save up enough money to buy curtain material for the eleven fifteen-foot high windows, and I slowly collected the indispensable implements of housekeeping . . . the mops and buckets, the wash board, feather dusters on very long poles, and the sundry gourds, clay cooking vessels, scraps of rope which were used as dish scourers and many strange vegetables which served as soap, scouring pads, and hot-dish protectors. A root called *amole* is soaked in water to generate rich suds that wash floors without leaving any scum, the dried membranes of certain squashes make wonderful dish cloths, and little pats of earth molded into cakes serve to clean brass and copper.

My *sala* or living room was furnished for some time exclusively with a small Rosencranz piano which I had found for sale in a poor section of the city. It had been made in 1840 before Mr. Edison, and had two small candle-holders flanking the portrait of Mozart just above the music rack. Several thousand generations of cockroaches and crickets rioted in its insides, but I fumigated it and bought it new felts, and it has gladdened my home ever since.

I had been given presents of money with which to buy linens and dishes, and Mamacita offered to help me shop for them. I wanted bright Mexican woven cottons and the brilliant glazed ware of Oaxaca and Guadalajara. Mamacita was horrified; only Indians and poor people used that stuff. She marched me straight to Monterrey's best home-furnishings store, and made sure I bought correct Czecho-Slovakian and English china and glass. She herself gave me fine white damask tablecloths.

Many years later she visited an old friend in Mexico City, a lady famous for her chic and elegance, and was seated at luncheon at a table set with Mexican pottery and blue glass. Overcome with remorse as she remembered my tastes, she rushed out and bought me the country-style things I admired, to atone. But of course her resistance to the cheap hand-made native crafts was typical of provincial Mexican elegance at the time. Even today, it is mostly folk-lore conscious foreigners and "arty" people who use the native goods in their homes. Mexicans like fine French and Spanish furniture, the most delicate of Limoges china, and Persian rugs. But the strong hand of the United States is to be seen in the bathrooms and the kitchens.

Of tremendous importance in setting up housekeeping in Mexico are the servants. Life is geared to them and since every home employs at least two, and since their families and relatives are regularly succored, hospitalized, dosed, fed and loaned money, one performs a sort of private social service in hiring them.

Instead of the vacuum cleaner, the washing machine, and the mangle, you have Lupe and Torquata and Tencha. Instead of packaged mixes and frozen foods and things in cellophane, you have a Chonita who goes out every day with her basket and the *gasto* which is the daily allowance for food. With this she travels to the market and buys everything, haggling and pinching and tasting and enjoying a good chat with her friends. Then she comes home and contrives three meals for her *patrona* and the family, herself and the other servants, and all their relatives and friends who may drop in.

Even baby sitters are unknown, for as soon as a new baby arrives in any family a new *nana* (nurse) or *pilmama* (an Indian word for wet nurse) is hired, whose duties are to tend the baby, wash and feed him, change him, entertain him, love him, take care of all his clothes, and if necessary, feed him at the breast. In Mexico a good clean fat *pilmama* is infinitely preferred to a formula, by parents in general, and always by the baby. So tremendously important is the *pilmama* or *nana* that she, as much as the ubiquitous mother-in-law, is often the cause of domestic struggles between husband and wife. I have known wives to flounce home to mother until their husbands got rid of the *nana* who had brought them up and was still a power.

Mamacita gave me sage advice about hiring servants, but wisely did not hire for me herself, for servants obey and respect the person who engages them and pays them. Therefore I had to do the hiring in order to be in a position to fire as well, if this seemed to be indicated. Mexican servants wisely recognize only one boss.

"For cook," Mamacita told me, "choose a woman who is fat, for this means that she is probably healthy and likes to eat. If she likes to eat she will taste the food as it cooks and season it properly. Beware these thin women who cook with disdain, for they don't make anything taste good.

"But for your housemaid, choose a *solterona* (old maid), if you can find one. They are slightly embittered at life for having passed them by and they take out their frustrations in cleaning and scrubbing. Also, they keep a sharp and envious eye on the other servants and have them all terrified of their tongues, so they keep a house in order. Never hire a young and pretty girl for housemaid, for they spend their time at the window looking for their sweetheart, and playing the radio when you are out, and they steal your powder and perfume."

My first servants all drifted away from me after a few months, despite my tearful pleadings, giving me one vague excuse or another or none, until it became apparent, even to the most myopic, that there was going to be an heir in the house of the fifth Treviño. Then all the servants came back to me, smiling, patted my protuberance affectionately, and were eager to work for me again, since they were now assured that I wasn't one of those crazy foreign women who didn't want children. No one cared to endure the bad luck of working in a house unblessed by the patter of little feet and the lusty squalling that makes the whole world kin. "It was too quiet, too sad," they all told me. "But now that there will be a *niño!* Maybe even twins. . . ." And their eyes shone with anticipation.

In my earliest days as a *señora* I was troubled because I didn't know how to arrange the meals. I had to learn that one always began with a *sopa,* which is a dish made of rice, macaroni, or some paste; then went on to meat and vegetables and salad, and finally to dessert. And always, after the meat, the beans. No butter was to be served, but instead, always, there must be a *salsa,* . . . a sharp sauce of tomatoes and chile, and various spices. At first I had to throw myself on the mercy of the servants, in planning dinners that my husband would eat, and one servant left me in disgust, complaining to Mamacita that the little *señora* didn't know how "to command."

Another maid was almost too religious for me, though Mamacita had told me to be sure to hire a pious girl and let her go daily to mass and Rosary, for such were less likely to "dawn" pregnant after their day off, having on their side all the righteousness of the church in the constant and unremitting battle of the sexes.

This girl was Tomasa.

I asked her, "Can you make bread, muffins, cookies?"

"God willing," she answered.

I hired her, and she spent the first day arranging her room, nailing up pictures of all her favorite saints, her little basin of Holy Water, and a small altar where she installed the Holy Family with candles and flowers.

Whenever I asked her to make a dish she didn't know she would crash right down on her knees and ask God to send her the recipe. Usually He did and very good recipes too, though He is fonder of lard than I am. Whenever she served the table she would pause in the doorway of the dining room, roll her eyes heavenward and say aloud, "Dios Mio, please don't let the *señora* criticize this dish, for You know how I burnt my finger and what a chore it is to grind up all those chiles anyhow."

This always effectively silenced me, especially as it was also her practice, when setting a dish before me, to make the sign of the cross above it, but one day my husband dared to protest against one of the holy recipes, and Tomasa left us, never to return, declaring she couldn't outrage her immortal soul by working for heathens.

Some servants are very sensitive and take umbrage at the most innocent of actions or gestures. Luis and I often conversed in English, with the result that one little maid left me and ran home to her mother, reporting that the *señores* were always saying things about her in Arabic. I was startled until Luis explained that among the country people *Arabe* means any heathen tongue, and when they say to anyone, "Say it in Christian!" it means "Speak Spanish!"

Pregnancy is the occupational disease of the servant girls, and an astute *señora* can tell within a few weeks when any girl has gone the way of all flesh. I was never clever at this, which made my servants embarrassed for me, so generally they gave notice, and said they were going away to fulfill a vow, or to visit an aunt in a distant part of the country, or to work in a factory. Later I would learn that they were "expecting" and were working in another house. The psychology behind their leaving me was that they "had pain" to tell me they had become pregnant while working in my house, for fear I might think they had smuggled in a man at night, or while I was out. However, *fait accompli*, they could go to work in the house of a stranger, complete with mythical husband, or not, as they pleased, but certainly without pain.

However, once the baby arrived, pride would burgeon, and not one could resist bringing the treasure to show me, and indeed there isn't anything more adorable than a new Mexican baby, round, brown and pink as an apricot, with black silken hair and eyes like black marbles. Often I invited these new mothers to return to work for me, for they are fanatically devoted to their children, and when they are allowed to have their children with them, they are happy and diligent.

I had one maid who didn't leave when she became pregnant. As time went by and she waxed rounder and more mysterious daily, I at last ventured to ask a few questions.

"Josefina, can it be that you are expecting a child?"

Downcast lashes, but the firm answer.

"*Sí, señora.*"

"But good heavens," I thundered, for Mamacita would have been disapproving if I hadn't got in a stroke for morality and God's law, "I thought you were a widow!"

"I am. The baby's father is just a friend of mine, nothing more."

"But Josefina," sadly, "I thought you were so *seria!*" (*Seria* means serious, or roughly "no nonsense.")

"Oh *señora,*" she sighed, as if speaking of an acquaintance, "you have no idea how sneaky I am!"

In those early days when I had so much to learn, the servants were very patient with me. Not one but served me tenderly as nurse whenever I was ill, no matter what her other duties; not one but brought me presents of flowers, vegetables, or handwork on my saint's day, even long after they had left my employ; and never did anyone leave me because of extra work caused by my children and my varied and maddening animals.

One of them, Maria, hired as cook, took on the care of the plants as well, and cooked abstractedly, one eye on the traffic in the street. Whenever an *arriero* (muleteer) went by with his train of burros, she was out like a flash with broom and dustpan, sweeping up hot potent fresh manure for the finest flowers. She stole cuttings for me, and wheedled roots and slips from the gardeners in houses that had lawns, and from friends of hers who worked for other *señoras* who kept fine plants.

Servants are part of the fabric of my life in Mexico and I cannot think of life without them, and yet they are not an unmixed blessing. Hilaria, for instance.

Hilaria had an innocent interest in *muertitos* (the dead), and would leave work any time to attend a funeral, especially if it were the funeral of a child. Then she would weep luxuriously for days.

There was Nieves. Nieves was a maiden lady of a certain age, in my employ as housemaid. The passing years had not embittered her at all, but had caused her to grow only more coy and flirtatious. Every afternoon she would pose in a window, with a rose in her graying hair, inviting passing workmen and startled gentlemen bound for home and supper, to "fly to the bosom of their dove" and she would indicate her own ample bosom.

There was Maura, who wasted away for love before my horrified eyes. She was a fine sturdy blooming two hundred pounds when Cupid felled her with a dart. She went down to one hundred and twenty, resisting the proposals of her lover that they indulge in a little reasonable dalliance while saving up enough money to get married on. But she held out, though she told me it was breaking her spirit, and all the while she was afraid some other less rigidly moral girl would catch him. She married him triumphantly in church, with bell, book, and candle, her virginity intact, and she secured such an absolute domination over the unfortunate young man who is her husband that she beats him, they tell me, and he will not lift a finger to protect himself, so intense is his respect for her.

There was Teresa who nearly committed suicide with my husband's pistol because her sweetheart (a policeman) hadn't phoned when he said he would. That is, she grabbed the gun, which Luis kept on the top shelf in his closet, roared that she was going to blow her brains out, and almost did, had it not been for my washwoman who threw herself into the fray and fought with her. The gun went off, and the bullet went through the door of my children's bedroom.

I have learned a lot from my maids, especially humility, one of the Christian virtues to which I never gave much thought in my heedless youth. Once I would have felt superior to an illiterate; our education teaches us many such vain assumptions. But I learned that all my illiterate servants have, in general, excellent memories that would put to shame the writers (and readers!) of "Improve Your Memory" books. They could give me long complicated messages without an error, and could do sums in their heads faster than I can with pencil, paper, and eraser.

They have an intellectual integrity formed by their own experiences at first hand, unadulterated by watered-down and half-understood ideas at second hand, or from reading ideologies and printed manifestos foreign to their life and setting. They are capable of very sensible judgments because they have never learned to mix their thoughts with "escape literature."

One maid, Severia, asked permission to go to a meeting which had been organized by a *lider* (leader) in order to form the servant girls into a union. What this meeting was, and who the *lider* was I do not know, but Severia came home with the report that it had been proposed in the meeting that one day all the servants would expropriate their patron's house, just as the government had expropriated the oil of the foreign companies in Mexico.

"And what do you think of this plan, Severia?" I asked.

"Well, *señora,* it doesn't sound practical to me. It is all very well for me to expropriate your house, with the *dispensa* full of rice and beans and lard. But when they are gone, who will buy me more? Not you, for I can scarcely expect you to give me your kitchen and also a salary. So where would I be, then? No, *señora,* and not even the government would give me the rice and beans, for I have heard government promises before. So, if you are willing, let us continue as we were, I cook for you, and you pay me my salary. Agreed?"

I agreed.

I was wringing my hands and worrying about world troubles one day when Severia asked me why I was afflicting myself. I explained to her about what bad things were being done all over the globe.

"*Señora,* you go to mass, you are a Catholic, are you not? Do not think about those bad people, *señora,* God will attend to them in his own good time. I am certain of this, for there must have been many bad times before, and yet here we are, you and I, are we not?"

I am inclined to think Severia's solution of the world's ills may, in the eye of Time, have as much sense to it, and more, as the drastic remedies we have often recommended, and sometimes take.

In my first weeks and months in Monterrey, I was so busy learning the Mexican way of running a household and getting acquainted with Papacito and Mamacita and Luis's eight brothers and sister Adela, that I didn't realize that I was being snubbed. I was. No one came to call on me except the wife of the American vice-consul (dear Penny!) and I made no Mexican friends. This was because, in the tight social organization of a Mexican provincial town, where courtship is a long process, a dance with intricate steps, in which everything must be done according to tradition, I had blithely spoiled the pattern.

I, an interloper, a foreigner, had deprived some Monterrey *señorita* of a perfectly good husband. And a Monterrey man, who should have had to court and pass inspection and submit to the rules for at least two years, had got himself married with practically no trouble and in a matter of a few months, too! It was setting a terrible precedent, and we were let strictly alone, to teach us a lesson and to teach other Monterrey young men that such goings-on were not looked on kindly.

But when some months had gone by and it was observed that

Luis was going to be a papa, hearts softened and we were forgiven. Besides, by that time Luis's youngest brother Roberto was involved in his unbelievable, fantastic, and very correct courtship of Beatriz. We were let off the hook.

One by one shy *señoritas* and *señoras* came to visit me, and when my first son Guicho, "The Little General," was born, I was "in."

But meanwhile I was occupied learning to shop and conducting my first quarrels with my husband. Matrimonial squabbles are always about 1, Love and/or 2, Money. In the love department we had no trouble. But we did a good deal of noisy adjusting to the problem of money. Right away we came up against the whole matter of the *gasto*.

Gasto means "expense" and is generally used to indicate exactly the sum set aside for the daily purchase of food and household necessities.

There may be a few Monterrey husbands, naturally careless fellows or contaminated by the United States, who turn over to their wives a fixed sum with which to run the house every month, or who even pass over to her their earnings so that she may control expenses, savings, and what-not. These are, in the cautious north of Mexico, a race as rare as hen's teeth. Most Monterrey men provide only the daily *gasto* and this is calculated with great cunning. As a matter of fact the custom has certain advantages even I can see.

Firstly, the little woman, who has always had a small daily amount of money to spend on fripperies from her papa, continues a habit she is used to. She is also made to watch where the money goes (easier taught with small sums) and is not tempted to make expensive down payments on floor-waxing machines and imported cake beaters.

One bride, who had never managed more than ten pesos in her life, was given three hundred pesos as a monthly *gasto* by her American husband and she so fell a prey to the first sales talk she had ever heard that she bought ten hams. In general, since Mexican women are reared under a heavy mantle of protection and are kept from harsh contacts with the voracious world of commerce, it is considered rash to give a woman as much as fifty pesos at a time. She is likely to plunge right out and buy a couple of hats or do something else equally foolish.

My *gasto* at first was three pesos a day, and was far beyond my station, as Luis' total monthly salary at that time amounted to three hundred pesos (at that time worth about eighty-five dollars). With my *gasto* I was supposed to buy meat, milk, vegetables and fruit, bread and such staples as sugar, rice, beans, and coffee. Luis had fixed the *gasto* after long worried discussions with Adela's husband, and they had calculated in a certain amount of slack because of my inexperience with Mexican ways. But I barely made ends meet and was constantly in a tearful turmoil because the cook would come and report that there was no lard or no rice or no eggs, after the shops had closed.

Luis was very patient with me, . . . at first. I so often had to borrow a *tostón* (fifty centavos) against the next day's *gasto,* that he would frequently invite me out to supper in order to let me catch up with my debts. What upset him was that I would not bargain. But I couldn't. It embarrassed me to try. It gave me the feeling that I was supposed to do somebody out of a rightful profit, or let them do me out of some of Luis' money. Both ideas paralyzed me.

While I bought some groceries from a Spanish grocery shop, I was supposed to go to the big market, or *"parian"* as they call it in Monterrey, where, under one enormous roof, countless vendors had set up their stalls in a wild confusion of boxes and counters and noise and milling-about of people.

The market men soon sized me up. The Mexicans simply pretended not to understand my Spanish, or if they saw that I was determined to haggle, they began at a price about five hundred per cent higher than they were willing to settle for, and allowed me to beat them down a little.

The Chinese fruit and vegetable men confused me by saying my dialogue as well as their own.

"How much are string beans?" I would ask.

"Fifty centavos. Very expensive. The man must be crazy," they would reply.

There was nothing to do but pay the fifty cents or slink away.

My husband struggled to teach me proper procedure. The strongest lesson was administered when I bought the pineapple.

I had bought the blasted pineapple (after gritting my teeth and bargaining for the better part of half an hour) for a peso. When Luis saw the peso pineapple he struck his brow with the flat of his hand (a gesture which means "God help us all!") and said, "They take advantage of your blond hair. They think you are a *tourist!* Come. Watch me, and see how to do it."

He strode into the market with me some three or four abashed yards behind him. He went to the fruit stall and looked around scornfully, and then pushed a few fruits with a disdainful forefinger.

The vendor hurried over, snarling, "Don't touch, if you don't intend to buy!"

"Dirty place you have here," remarked Luis. "Look at that pile of peelings over in the corner. I must remember to tell the inspector."

"What inspector?"

"Treviño. My brother." (No brother was an inspector, but as there are thousands of Treviños in northern Mexico, there may well have been one who was an inspector.)

"I pay my license right on the dot!" defensively.

"But you've got some fruit there that ought to be condemned. Those pineapples, for instance."

"What? Those beautiful pineapples! They're worth a peso and twenty centavos apiece!"

Luis took a paper from his pocket and seemed to consult it.

"What's that?" Suspiciously, from the vendor.

"Government prices on fruit. Just a moment. I'm checking up on pineapples . . ."

"Look, I could let you have one for seventy centavos. As a favor."

"Apples, fifty centavos a kilo. Bananas . . . let's see now. . . ."

"Fifty centavos for a pineapple! I'm losing money, too."

Luis pretended to be momentarily interested.

"You mean one of those small pineapples over there? The ones that look bruised?" Incredulous.

"Well, take them for forty centavos each. I haven't got all day."

Luis bought two pineapples for forty centavos each. He and the vendor parted full of mutual admiration.

I went over and held out my hand to Luis.

"How do you do?" I inquired. "Let me present myself. My name is Mrs. Mud."

That's how I lost the *gasto.* Luis turned it over to the cook. At the time, it seemed fair enough. But it hurt, all the same, to be demoted.

However, marriage is a game of give and take. I had taken a wallop. It was soon my turn to give one.

It happened this way.

The *gasto* was to cover purchases for food. But as time went by we began to need other things. Flea powder for Policarpo, the cat. Hairpins. Electric light bulbs. Dish towels. Tooth paste. Tacks. Shoe polish.

Luis said I had only to tell him what was needed and he would bring it from town. But I wanted to look in shop windows and wander in and out of stores. In short, I wanted to shop.

It went hard with me to ask for the money for each little item. So my list was rather extensive when I brought myself to present it. Luis went over it with some trepidation. It came to more than fifty pesos. An appalling sum.

"But I only earn three hundred pesos," he wailed. "And extra, with some commission I make. But I have to save the commissions for the baby. You can only buy one thing at a time." He gave me the exact amount indicated for the purchase of the first item on the list, Poli's flea powder.

I soon found that I was expected to wheedle the money for each purchase when the moment seemed propitious, beginning, "Lindo . . ." (which means "Pretty boy"). I refused to call Luis "Lindo." I refused to coax and plead and kiss for what I thought I should have proffered me as a right. Mexican women go through the little form, Mexican men adore the game. But I was a hard-headed foreigner.

I stamped my foot. I demanded a charge account.

Luis almost fell dead. Only very rich people had charge accounts. Nobody would let us open one; we weren't important enough.

Finally we worked out a compromise. Luis said I could go to the shops and choose what was needed and sign a *"vale"* for it. (A *vale* is a sort of IOU, a chit.) This sounded to me rather like an honorable charge account, so I agreed. Next day after siesta, I went to a shop and bought face powder and soap and signed a *vale,* and to another shop where I bought two *metres* of unbleached muslin and some thread and signed a *vale.* I window-shopped luxuriously and arrived home about an hour later. Two young men were guarding my door. They were holders of the *vales* I had signed. They demanded immediate payment. I had no money and Luis wasn't home. We had a dramatic scene in broken English and broken Spanish and several varieties of dirty looks were exchanged. This occurred at about five in the afternoon.

At five-thirty the shop owners phoned to ask me when I intended to pay. At six both young men were back. But I had to report that my husband had not yet arrived. They acted as if they knew very well he was that moment hiding behind the door, but they left. At six-thirty they were back. I wouldn't answer the door. At eight the next morning, they both appeared again, and presented the *vales*. Luis paid them both.

But I had had enough. I would sign no more chits, I said. I asked Luis for an allowance. He explained that this was not sensible; I might buy more than I needed.

"You treat me as if I had been locked up all my life like a Mexican girl!" I accused.

"I am not a rich American!" he countered.

"You are domineering and bossy!" I wept.

Then he shouted at me the worst epithet . . . the thing most horrible!

"You want to be *independent!*" he roared, and stormed out of the house.

What could I do? We had had a terrible, an awful quarrel. Luis had left the house in a temper. I was in tears. I did what any bewildered bride would do. I went home to Mama. But as my own mother was thousands of miles away, it was to Mamacita that I went with my tale of woe.

She listened to me. Then she laughed heartily. Then she suddenly got mad and said many things to herself in loud annoyed Spanish. Then she calmed down, and was very thoughtful for a while. Suddenly she patted me, and said, "*Yo voy arreglarlo. I feex.*"

She went to her desk and wrote out a list of about fifty ten-centavo and twenty-centavo purchases. She also wrote out Luis's business address. Then she briefed me. I followed her instructions to the letter.

I made all the small purchases, one by one, and signed a *vale* for each, and directed the collector to Luis's office. All afternoon a parade of boys with chits passed through his office. All were so small that he couldn't refuse to pay. He couldn't do any work. He was interrupted every ten minutes. He was busy all afternoon paying for two quinine tablets, half a dozen hooks and eyes, twenty centavos of bicarbonate, one yard of white tape, four sheets of writing paper and two envelopes, etc., etc.

I waited for his return home in the evening with some uneasiness. It was just possible that he might be annoyed. But he walked in calmly and announced that he was going to give me an allowance. It would grow larger with his salary, when that grew.

"Santo Remedio" or Holy Remedy, as they say. I suspected that he had discerned the fine hand of Mamacita in the parade of boys with *vales*. But the dove of peace flew in the door of Morelos 829 once more and there were no more quarrels.

Eventually I learned all the weapons of bargaining, the look of scorn, the false starts away, the eyebrow lifting, the eyes rolled heavenward. I got the *gasto* back.

But I had learned a lesson too.

One has no rights with a Mexican husband. Mexican women flatter and tease and love them into generosity. Or they simply outwit them.

JOHN W. HILTON

Guaymas, 1940s

"I LIKE THE FISHING, AND I LIKE TO JUST RIDE
OUT IN THE BLUE BAY AND LOOK BACK AT THE
WHITE TOWN AGAINST GREAT, RED-LAVA HILLS."

John Hilton was raised in China by his missionary parents, and by the time he was twelve he had traveled widely. He went to school in California, where he hunted for gems in the desert and became a gem cutter. When the company he worked for failed in 1929, Hilton moved to Thermal, California, and went into business for himself as a gem dealer. He also took up painting and writing and contributed many pieces about the southwestern deserts to magazines and newspapers.

During the 1940s Hilton and his wife, often accompanied by another couple, traveled frequently throughout the desert country of Sonora, south of Arizona. They hunted birds and collected reptiles, visited abandoned mining towns, explored the wild Yaqui country, and listened avidly to the tales of local people.

His Sonora Sketch Book, published in 1947, was based on his memories, sketches, notes, and letters from those explorations. It is a charming and unpretentious book, not, as he says in the preface, an "attempt to produce timely or 'significant' literature," but rather an "experiment in sharing these memories."

When Mexico and the United States were negotiating the 1848 Treaty of Guadalupe Hidalgo, the U.S. government tried to acquire as much Mexican territory as possible. But a government aide carrying confidential instructions from President Polk got only as far as Veracruz before he fell ill and died there of fever. His dispatch case went astray, and when it reappeared it was in Mexican hands. The Mexicans learned that, while the United States insisted on getting most of what we now call the American Southwest and the entire state of California, the negotiators would try to get Baja California only if the Mexicans did not hold out too firmly. The Mexicans, forewarned, held out very firmly and managed to retain Sonora, Sinaloa, and Baja California, thus preserving for themselves a Pacific coastline that stretches, in all, about three thousand miles.

For more than a century nothing much changed on that coastline. Fishing continued in the scattered coastal villages, and shipping from the East continued to arrive through the little port of Acapulco. Then, in the middle of the twentieth century, Mexico began to develop the coast as a resort area, Club Med moved in with an extensive building program, and half a dozen sleepy and nearly inaccessible villages became fashionable international playgrounds.

Guaymas, in Sonora, is a port on the Gulf of California, the Sea of Cortés, 266 miles due south of the border crossing at Nogales. It is nearly as quiet and remote today, except for Club Med's regular air service, as it was when John Hilton and his friends visited there in the forties. The Hotel Playa de Cortés that he mentions was opened by the Southern Pacific Railway in 1936 and is still in business in the resort area at Playa Miramar on Bocochibampo Bay. And the fishing he enjoyed so much then is still good, especially for marlin and sailfish. The major changes are the village's growth to a population of over 150,000 and the music drifting out of the Club Med.

THE FIRST TIME THAT I SAW GUAYMAS WAS on the fourth of May. We had battled bad roads and dust across the thornbrush-and-cactus studded desert from Hermosillo south, and, much as I like deserts, the water was a welcome sight. The sun was low. Just as we were shown to our rooms, facing the bay in the old Gran Hotel Almada, it was reflected in purple counterpoints on the iridescent water. There was nothing between our second-story room and the water but a wide sidewalk, edged by a concrete sea wall, and as we looked down we could see myriads of small fish swimming busily about; our first taste of the teeming life that characterizes the Gulf of California.

Any town has some building or person, or perhaps a combination of both, to serve as a typical reminder of that locality. To me, such a spot is the Gran Hotel Almada. Perhaps there are other hotels in town equally interesting; and I am sure that the Playa del Cortez out on Miramar Bay is considerably more modern and palatial; but we got started with the Almada, and that seems to be the spot to which we always return when coming to Guaymas. There, in its spacious patio, where one can drive his car for safety, and sign the register without getting out, I have had many pleasant experiences and conversations. In the old bar, where the sea captains used to congregate, one can always find entertaining persons and cool drinks to share with them.

The church bells bothered me that first night. They seemed to be right in the room and struck the hour, "más o menos," with a persistence that was appalling. I would just get soundly to sleep when the sudden clanging would almost raise me out of bed, and it seemed that it was only a few minutes until the whole process was repeated again. Noises are funny. After several nights in Guaymas, if someone had asked me whether I heard the same church bells in the night, I would probably have answered, "What church bells?"

The first thing we heard in the morning was the laughter of children, right under our window. They seemed to be having a hilarious time for themselves, and I finally got up and looked out on the sidewalk below. The sea wall was draped with clothing of all sorts and in every state of deterioration. Right out in front were dozens of newsboys and bootblacks, taking their morning dip in the bay, without benefit of bathing suits. They were amusing to watch. The joy of living seemed to radiate from every pore of their brown skins. Soon they put on their clothes and gathered up their shine boxes, or bundles of papers, and went off to their daily grinds.

Passers-by of both sexes seemed to think nothing of the boys' nudity, and called to them from the sidewalk banteringly, as they went about their early morning walks or shopping tours.

One other time we had a room facing the land instead of the sea, and every morning we watched a strangely beautiful spectacle. Just as the rising sun turned the naturally red cliffs to an incandescent rose, the goatherds started up the mountain; apparently the goats were retained in corrals of some sort at the base of the hills, but grazed on the mesas above. The trail was composed of dozens of switchbacks up the side of the almost vertical volcanic upthrust. Goats of many hues, and small boys shouting to one another and to their flocks, made a sinuous parade as they zigzagged up the cliff through the sunrise.

For breakfast we had papayas, toast, and black coffee, and it broke the cook's heart. She had prepared steak, chicken and beans. We assured her that we would be back for such a meal at noon, but she looked cheated though the price was the same (one peso each) regardless of what we ate. The waitress told us that a cook likes to see people eat, and when they turn something down the cooks feel that they have been personally insulted. We were about to go out in the kitchen and try to explain why the first course had been entirely sufficient, when a band took our minds off the whole matter.

Then we realized that today was "Cinco de mayo," and that this day was to the Mexican people what Fourth of July is to us. It was a parade; the first of the day—and only the beginning. Later, all the shops closed while they had parades of every school, police force, military unit, representatives of the navy, and fraternal and labor organizations—all bearing the Mexican flag with its tri-colors of red, white, and green, and the ancient symbol of the eagle perched on a cactus with a snake in its mouth. Each group had music of some sort, and the streets were gay, though dusty.

The dry season was at its height. Everything was like tinder. The air even felt dry for a spot so near the sea, and the very palms in the plaza drooped. The city water supply ran low at this time of the year, and none could be spared. Caged birds could be seen through patio doorways, spreading their brightly colored wings for added ventilation; flowers drooped, and there was dust on the gardenias.

In spite of all this we liked Guaymas. We liked it well enough to come back again and again. The town and the old hotel hold a lot of pleasant memories—stories I heard at the bar: of the fabulous Vermilion Sea (the Spaniards' first name for the gulf); tales of pearl divers from the Lower California ports, and their adventures in the deep; of the great manta rays that smothered and killed men; of giant octopi, capable of overturning a boat; of "burrow shells" that caught the feet of divers. The old-timers could sit by the hour and recite tales of everything from sea serpents to mermaids, and I am sure that they had told the stories so often that they believed them themselves.

They told me of Don Juan Ocio, who was a common soldier and a guard at the mission Loreto; how a great "chubasco"—which, as near as I could discover, is a sort of waterspout that sweeps in from the gulf and deposits marine life over the desert—came to Loreto. It seems that this particular storm was unusually violent, and it dropped tons of pearl oysters out on the dry land, where the Indians gathered them and had great feasts. They had no use for the pearls, and the story goes that Juan Ocio traded some old clothes and other trinkets for about ten gallons of the finest. He then quietly marketed a few, bought his way out of the army, settled at La Paz, and became one of the wealthiest and most influential men of that period.

Then there was the tale of the king of the pearlers at La Paz; a little naked boy, who was found by the first Spaniards, playing on the beach with pearls as large as marbles. He was soon traded out of this treasure and, in the celebration that followed in the camp of the Spaniards, they decided to crown him king of the pearlers. They did, with much pomp and bogus ceremony. The little boy became a sort of mascot for the colony, and whenever a diver found an exceedingly fine gem, he was forced to pay tribute. They asked him what he wanted and he said, "Bring me some worms." These were a soft white grub, to be found by turning over rotten logs. Soon a regular measurement was agreed upon. Fellow divers would examine the pearl and pronounce it a "three-worm gem," or a ten, or a twenty; whereupon the lucky finder was forced to crawl about on his hands and knees and find the required tribute for the little black monarch. Of course, he was accompanied by his fellow divers, who did everything in their power to make him seem, if possible, even more ridiculous. The King grew up as all kings do, and finally died leaving an equally dark-skinned heir; but the new monarch had changed his tastes. Although the diver still had to go about on all fours in a mock worm-hunt, he presented the despot with a gift of coins, beads, or sweetmeats; more to his liking.

Another tale that is retold with many variations is the tale of the Pearl without Shame. It starts with a woman who, though beautiful, was as shameless as the pearl that finally caused her downfall. When a lover asked for her favors she would say simply, "Bring me a pearl"; and if the pearl was large and fine enough, that man was very happy for a while; but the woman had no shame. She had one consuming desire: to own more and finer pearls, which she wore at all times. She amassed a great fortune in these lovely gems, all paid for in the same manner. Then a strange man came by. He was of noble descent, but poor. He too was smitten by the beauty of this lovely siren, and she said, "Bring me a pearl." He had no money, so he learned to dive, and eventually he found two very fine pearls. One was a lovely pink, but the other was a strange, changeable color, passing from gray to purple. It was a fascinating gem, but the other divers refused even to touch it. They told the finder that he had better throw it into the sea, for it was "la perla sin vergüenza" (the pearl without shame), and it would spoil any pearls that touched it. The young man returned with the two pearls, which he had kept separated. He decided that, if the woman had remained true, he would give her the pink pearl of fabulous worth; but if she had been unfaithful, he would have her at the price of the beautiful, but shameless, pearl.

When he got back to Guaymas he found that she had married a Spaniard of great wealth, but was still willing to pay her usual price for a fine pearl. The young man hid his fine pink pearl, and called at the house when the wealthy husband was well away on a voyage. His revenge was complete. In a few days all the fine lady's pearls began to fade, and finally only the great gray-and-purple one shone with its sinister luster. The young man then circulated the story that the pearls had died of grief for the shamelessness of the wearer, and the lady, unable to bear the disgrace, finally threw herself into the bay. Her ghost, I am assured, can be heard wailing on stormy nights along the sea wall.

Yes, the old Hotel Almada has many a tale and memory about it; and, although the room service is unpredictable, and the plumbing dates back to nineteen hundred, I hope they never modernize it.

I stopped there the last time with some American friends, and we had the largest room in the place. The ceiling was so high, and the single electric light so dim, that we actually were disappointed when we looked up and didn't see stars. Our room was equipped with a bath that would have been big enough for a whole hotel suite in an American hostelry, and it too had a ceiling about twenty feet high, from which protruded a gadget that looked like a railroad whistle (which it may have been), but we were assured it was a shower head. A string was attached to a handle on this contraption and hung down to within a few inches of the zinc-covered floor. On the end of this string was a ring in which the bather was supposed to hook one toe and hold the throttle open, while the water came tumbling down from the heights and nearly knocked him flat.

We had made the rounds of the more interesting spots of Guaymas, in what had not been an entirely uneventful evening, and a shower of any sort sounded like a good idea. The hilarious time we all had, operating the plumbing, raised a racket that must have awakened every guest in the hotel, and in this country would have ended in a prompt ejection. But there, no one seemed to mind. When we finally had all had our baths, and settled down to sleep, the shower kept right on dripping. The spring, or whatever held the valve closed, had weakened, it seems. At any rate, the regular drip every twelve and a half seconds, hitting that zinc floor with a TAP— TAP—TAP, became very annoying. My friend Harlow Jones rolled over in his bed and propped himself up on one elbow. "We have to do something about that damned thing," he said, "it sounds like a W.P.A. worker pounding tacks." We tried everything—including stacking all the furniture in the room under it, so we could tie the lever back firmly—but it still dripped. Finally Max Felker, who is an inventor, turned over in bed. "If you guys will shut up," he promised, "I'll fix that so-and-so thing." Whereupon, he rose deliberately and took a towel from the rack, bundled it into a ball, and placed it directly under the drip. The noise stopped—and the rest of the hotel guests probably sighed a deep sigh of relief, for it was two A.M.

Yes, I like Guaymas. I like the fishing, and I like to just ride out in the blue bay and look back at the white town against great, red-lava hills, and see the little red islands, studded with giant cacti that grow right down to the shoreline. I like to watch the rookeries of great sea birds of all sorts that inhabit these little islands, and hear their strange cries as they rise and wheel overhead. One day I thought I had found an island covered with a new species of Cephalocereus. Cacti of this group are usually crowned by masses of white wool in the top where the flowers appear. Here, right in front of me, was a whole island covered with giant cereus plants, each topped with a white crown. The size alone would indicate a new species, as there are no described members of the genus so large, and nothing of the sort reported from this locality.

I am a cactus collector, and it looked as if I were about to make botanic history. I ordered the boatman to swing in close to the little island and, as we came nearer, it was apparent that I had made a terrible mistake. The tip of each plant was simply the roost of some guano-depositing bird, and the white crowns would probably wash off with the summer rains, along with the dust of Guaymas. We returned another way, and I spotted a huge and architecturally beautiful building, all alone on a distant shore. I asked the boatman to go closer, but he refused. It was the slaughterhouse, and he assured me that only the fact that no wind blew in our direction had prompted him to get even that close. It stood there so grand and lonely, mirrored in the shining bay like something from a fairy tale. It was the prettiest slaughterhouse I ever saw.

PAUL THEROUX

Nuevo Laredo, 1978

"THE SMELL OF NUEVO LAREDO RISES. IT IS
THE SMELL OF LAWLESSNESS; IT IS SMOKIER,
SCENTED WITH CHILIS AND CHEAP PERFUME."

*Mexico's border towns pose a special problem for any observer. And so do
the U.S. towns along that same border. It's hard to imagine sending the
folks back home a picture postcard of Nogales, Arizona, or San Ysidro,
California. Are border towns really representative of either country?*

*In Tijuana, the pavements are shattered, the buildings are crum-
bling, and most of the wares offered in the market and arcades are generally tasteless and mass-produced. On my last visit, while Sanborn's
department store and a few other places offered genuine crafts, the vendors in Avenida Revolución seemed convinced that gringos were visiting
their city for the sole purpose of buying lurid plastic figures of Bart Simpson, which were displayed everywhere in blue and yellow abundance.*

*In Nogales one time, a slick huckster whose stand was within sight
of the international gate insisted, in English, on selling me, and for
thirty dollars each, some perfectly ordinary Mexican shirts. I declined.
In fact, I had only been passing by and had not even stopped to look at
his wares. The price quickly dropped to eighteen dollars. I still declined.*

"Amigo," *the vendor said, his arm sliding around my shoulder, "these other merchants, they wrap your shirts in a paper package. Me? I treat you right." He glanced over his shoulder to make certain no other customers, less favored than I, could hear and grow jealous. "I treat you right," he breathed. "I give you a plastic shopping bag."*

A few hours later, at the opposite edge of town, where the road led off into a dusty landscape and where few tourists ventured, I bought identical shirts, in Spanish and for five dollars each, from an elderly señora *who was memorably gracious.*

And the Indian women sitting on the broken pavement, with babies slung in rebozos *on their backs, still look just like the triangular figures in a painting by Zuñiga or a drawing by Rivera, as solid and permanent as their country's mountains and pyramids.*

The United States and Mexico share a border 1,950 miles long, from the Pacific Ocean to the Gulf of Mexico. Although the barrier doesn't quite stretch into the water at either end, most of that distance is fenced. On one side of it is apparent poverty; on the other side is apparent wealth. In El Paso, people can look out the windows of their air-conditioned office towers into the humble interiors of shacks in Ciudad Juárez, just as residents of Ipanema and Copacabana can look out at Rio de Janeiro's hillside favelas. *The difference is that El Paso and Juárez are in different countries.*

That fence may draw a clear line in the sand, but the line grows blurred when the winds of history blow across it. In 1848, at the end of a painful war, Mexico gave up more than half its territory to the United States. Looked at from the other side, about one-fourth of what is today the United States was once Mexican land. And the holes torn at regular intervals in that frontier fence attest to the continuing exchange of money, goods, services, people, and culture. At crossing points in Tijuana, Mexicali, Nogales, Ciudad Juárez, Nuevo Laredo, and Matamoros, at half a dozen other major checkpoints, and at unmarked spots in the desert and on the banks of the Río Grande, the traffic never stops.

While I was working on this book I heard comedian Rich Hall tell a joke that neatly sums up the interdependence so obvious along the border. "The President says he can solve the border question by digging a ditch. He wants to dig a ditch along the whole Mexico-California border. But I don't think it'll work. After all, who does he think is going to dig that ditch?"

After the success of The Great Railway Bazaar, *which chronicled his journeys by train through Asia, Paul Theroux set out by train from Boston and headed toward the southernmost tip of South America. The* Old Patagonian Express, *published in 1979, tells the story of that trip.*

Because railroad lines do not cross this border, Theroux entered Mexico on foot, walking across the International Bridge from Laredo, Texas, to its sister city in Mexico, Nuevo Laredo. Laredo's wicked sister, some might say.

☀ IT WAS A RAINY NIGHT IN LAREDO — NOT late, and yet the place seemed deserted. A respectable frontier town sprawling at the very end of the Amtrak line, it lay on a geometric grid of bright black streets on a dirt bluff that had the clawed and bulldozed look of a recent quarry. Below was the Rio Grande, a silent torrent slipping past Laredo in a cut as deep as a sewer; the south bank was Mexico.

The city lights were on, making the city's emptiness emphatic. In that glare I could see its character as more Mexican than Texan. The lights flashed, suggesting life, as lights do. But where were the people? There were stoplights on every corner, WALK and WAIT signs winked on and off; the two-story shop fronts were floodlit, lamps burned in the windows of one-story houses; the street lights made the puddles bright holes in slabs of wet roads. The effect of this illumination was eerie, that of a plague city brightened against looters. The stores were heavily padlocked; the churches lit up in cannonades of arc-lamps; there were no bars. All that light, instead of giving an impression of warmth and activity, merely exposed its emptiness in a deadening blaze.

No traffic waited at the red lights, no pedestrians at the crosswalks. And though the city was silent, in the drizzly air was an unmistakable heart murmur, the *threep threep* of music being played far away. I walked and walked, from my hotel to the river, from the river to a plaza, and into the maze of streets, until I was almost certain I was lost. I saw nothing. And it could be frightening, seeing — four blocks away — a blinking sign I took to be a watering hole, a restaurant, an event, a sign of life, and walking to it and arriving soaked and gasping to discover that it was a shoe store or a funeral parlor, shut for the night. So, walking the streets of Laredo,

I heard only my own footsteps, the false courage of their click, their faltering at alleyways, their splashes as I briskly returned to the only landmark I knew—the river.

The river itself made no sound, though it moved powerfully, eddying like a swarm of greasy snakes in the ravine from which every bush and tree had been removed in order to allow the police to patrol it. Three bridges linked the United States to Mexico here. Standing on the bluff I heard the *threep threep* louder: it was coming from the Mexican side of the river, a just discernible annoyance, like a neighbor's radio. Now I could see plainly the twisting river, and it struck me that a river is an appropriate frontier. Water is neutral, and in its impartial winding makes the national boundary look like an act of God.

Looking south, across the river, I realized that I was looking toward another continent, another country, another world. There were sounds there—music, and not only music but the pip and honk of voices and cars. The frontier was actual: people did things differently there, and looking hard I could see trees outlined by the neon beer signs, a traffic jam, the source of the music. No people, but cars and trucks were evidence of them. Beyond that, past the Mexican city of Nuevo Laredo, was a black slope—the featureless, night-haunted republics of Latin America.

A car drew up behind me. I was alarmed, then reassured when I saw it was a taxi. I gave the driver the name of my hotel and got in, but when I tried to make conversation he responded by grunting. He understood only his own language.

In Spanish I said, "It is quiet here."

That was the first time on my trip that I spoke Spanish. After this, nearly every conversation I had was in Spanish. But in the course of this narrative I shall try to avoid affecting Spanish words and will translate all conversations into English. I have no patience with macaronic sentences that go, " '*Carramba!*' said the *campesino,* eating his *empanada* at the *estancia* . . ."

"Laredo," said the taxi driver. He shrugged.

"Where are all the people?"

"The other side."

"Nuevo Laredo?"

"Boys' Town," he said. The English took me by surprise, the

phrase tickled me. He said, now in Spanish again, "There are one thousand prostitutes in the Zone."

It was a round number, but I was convinced. And that of course explained what had happened to this city. After dark, Laredo slipped into Nuevo Laredo, leaving the lights on. It was why Laredo looked respectable, even genteel, in a rainswept and mildewed way: the clubs, the bars, the brothels, were across the river. The red-light district was ten minutes away, in another country.

But there was more to this moral spelled out in transpontine geography than met the eye. If the Texans had the best of both worlds in decreeing that the fleshpots should remain on the Mexican side of the International Bridge—the river flowing, like the erratic progress of a tricky argument, between vice and virtue—the Mexicans had the sense of tact to keep Boys' Town camouflaged by decrepitude, on the other side of the tracks; another example of the geography of morality. Divisions everywhere: no one likes to live next door to a whorehouse. And yet both cities existed because of Boys' Town. Without the whoring and racketeering, Nuevo Laredo would not have had enough municipal funds to plant geraniums around the statue of its madly gesturing patriot in the plaza, much less to advertise itself as a bazaar of wickerwork and guitar-twanging folklore— not that anyone ever went to Nuevo Laredo to be sold baskets. And Laredo required the viciousness of its sister city to keep its own churches full. Laredo had the airport and the churches; Nuevo Laredo, the brothels and basket factories. Each nationality had seemed to gravitate to its own special area of competence. This was economically sound thinking; it followed to the letter the theory of comparative advantage outlined by the distinguished economist David Ricardo.

At first glance, this looked like the typical sort of mushroom-and-dunghill relationship that exists at the frontiers of many unequal countries. But the longer I thought about it, the more Laredo seemed like all of the United States, and Nuevo Laredo all of Latin America. This frontier was more than an example of cozy hypocrisy; it demonstrated all one needed to know about the morality of the Americas, the relationship between the puritanical efficiency north of the border and the bumbling and passionate disorder—the anarchy of sex and hunger—south of it. It was not as simple as that, since there were obviously villainy and charity in both, and yet crossing the river (the Mexicans don't call it the Rio Grande; they call it the Río Bravo del Norte), no more than an idle traveler making his way south with a suitcase of dirty laundry, a sheaf of railway timetables, a map, and a pair of leak-proof shoes, I felt as if I were acting out a significant image. Crossing a national boundary and seeing such a difference on the other side had something to do with it: truly, every human feature there had the resonance of metaphor.

It is only two hundred yards, but the smell of Nuevo Laredo rises. It is the smell of lawlessness; it is smokier, scented with chilis and cheap perfume. I had come from the tidy Texas town and could see, almost as soon as I left it, the crowd of people at the far end of the bridge, the traffic jam, the catcalling and horn blowing, some people waiting to enter the United States, but most of them merely gaping across the frontier which is—and they know it—the poverty line.

Mexicans enter the United States because there is work for them there. They do it illegally—it is virtually impossible for a poor Mexican to enter legally if his intention is to seek work. When they are caught, they are thrown into jail, serve a short sentence, and then are deported. Within days, they head back to the United States and the farms where they can always find work as low-paid day laborers. The solution is simple: if we passed a law requiring United States farmers to hire only men with entry visas and work permits, there would be no problem. There is no such law. The farm lobby has made sure of that, for if there were no Mexicans to exploit, how would these barrel-assed slavers be able to harvest their crops?

Closer, I could see the chaos particularized. The lounging soldiers and policemen only made it look more lawless, the noise was terrifying, and, at once the national characteristics were evident— the men had no necks, the policemen wore platform shoes, and no prostitute was without her natural ally, an old woman or a cripple. It was cold and rainy; there was an atmosphere of impatience in the town. Still February, the tourists were not due for months.

Halfway across the bridge, I had passed a rusty mailbox bearing the sign CONTRABAND. This was for drugs. The penalties were posted in two languages: five years for soft drugs, fifteen for hard. I tried to peek inside, but unable to see anything I gave it a whack with my fist. It boomed: it must have been empty. I continued to the barrier, five cents in the turnstile slot, and as simply as boarding a bus I was in Mexico. Although I had been growing a mustache to make myself visibly Latin, it was clearly not working. I was waved through the customs gate with four other gringos: we looked innocent.

There was no question that I had arrived, for while the neckless men and the swaggering cops and maimed animals had a certain sullen statelessness, the garlic seller was the personification of Latin America. He was weedy and wore a torn shirt and a greasy hat; he was very dirty; he screamed the same words over and over. These attributes alone were unremarkable—he too had a counterpart in Cleveland. What distinguished him was the way he carried his merchandise. He had a garland of garlic cloves around his neck and another around his waist and ropes of them on his arms, and he shook them in his fists. He fought his way in and out of the crowd, the clusters of garlic bouncing on his body. Was there any better example of cultural difference than this man? At the Texas end of the bridge he would have been arrested for contravening some law of sanitation; here, he was ignored. What was so strange about wearing bunches of garlic around your neck? Perhaps nothing, except that he would not have done it if he were not a Mexican, and I would not have noticed it if I hadn't been an American.

Boy's Town—the Zone—is aptly named, since so much of it wickedly reflects the sexual nightmare-paradise of forbidden boyhood fantasy. It is fear and desire, a whole suburb of libido in which one can see the dire consequences in every greedy wish. It is the child who numbly craves the thrill of a lover's hug, but no child enjoys this fantasy without knowing the equal and opposite anxiety of being pursued by the same creature. Months of wintry weather and rain and off-season idleness had turned the prostitutes of the Zone into rather woeful examples of demon lovers. They were the howling, sleeve-tugging, arm-grabbing, jostling embodiment of the punitive part of sexual fantasy. I felt like Leopold Bloom steering his timid way through the limitless brothel of night town, for here one could not express an interest without risking humiliation. What made it worse for me was that I was merely curious. Intending neither to condemn nor encourage, I was mistaken for that most pathetic of emotionally damaged souls, the nearsighted voyeur, a kind of sexual barnacle fastening my attention upon the meat market. *Just looking,* I'd say; but prostitutes have no patience with this attitude.

"Mister!"

"Sorry, I have to catch a train."

"What time is it leaving?"

"About an hour."

"That's plenty of time. Mister!"

The urchins, the old ladies, the cripples, the sellers of lottery tickets, the frantic dirty youths, the men selling trays of switchblades, the tequila bars and incessant racketing music, the hotels reeking of bedbugs—the frenzy threatened to overwhelm me. I had to admit a certain fascination, and yet I feared that I would have to pay for my curiosity. *If you're not interested in this,* said a pretty girl hiking up her skirt with a casually lazy gesture, *why are you here?*

It was a good question but, as I had no answer, I left. I went to the office of Mexican Railways to buy my train ticket. The town was in great disrepair—no building was without a broken window, no street without a wrecked car, no gutter not choked with garbage; and in this clammy season, without any heat to justify its squalor or give it romance, it was cruelly ugly. But it is our bazaar, not Mexico's. It requires visitors.

Some citizens remain pure. Paying for my sleeper on the Aztec Eagle, I mentioned to the friendly manager that I had just come from the Zone.

She rolled her eyes and then said, "Shall I tell you something? I do not know where that place is."

"It's not far. You just . . ."

"Don't tell me. I have been here two years. I know my home, I know my office, I know my church. That's all I need."

She said that my time would be better spent looking at the curios than idling in the Zone. On my way to the station, I took her advice. Inevitably there were baskets and postcards and switchblade knives; but there were also plaster dogs and plaster Christs, carvings of women squatting and religious junk of every description: rosaries the size of a ship's hawser with beads like baseballs, rained-on ironwork rusting on sidewalk stands, and gloomy plaster saints—martyred rather savagely by the people who had painted them, and each bearing the inscription *Souvenir of Nuevo Laredo.* A curio (the word, practically self-explanatory, is short for "curiosity") is something that has no purpose other than to prove that you arrived: the coconut carved with an ape's face, the combustible ashtray, the sombrero— they are useless without the Nuevo Laredo inscription, but a good deal more vulgar than anything I saw in the Zone.

Not far from the station there was a man melting tubes of glass and drawing them thin and making model cars. His skill amounted almost to artistry, but the result—always the same car—lacked any imagination. The delicate work, this glass filigree, took hours; he labored to make what could have been something beautiful into a ridiculous souvenir. Had he ever made anything else?

"No," he said. "Only this car. I saw a picture of it in a magazine."

I asked him when he had seen the picture.

"No one ever asked me that question before! It was ten years ago. Or more."

"Where did you learn to do this?"

"In Puebla—not here." He looked up from his blowtorch. "Do you think a person could learn anything here in Nuevo Laredo? This is one of the traditional arts of Puebla. I have taught my wife and children to do it. My wife makes little pianos, my son makes animals."

Over and over, the same car, piano, animal. It would not have been so disturbing if it was a simple case of mass-producing the objects. But enormous skill and patience went into the making of what was in the end no more than junk. It seemed a great waste, but not very different from the Zone, which turned lovely little girls into bad-tempered and rapacious hags.

Earlier that afternoon I had left my suitcase at the station restaurant. I had asked for the baggage department. A Mexican girl sitting at a table on which someone had spewed pushed her tin plate of beans aside and said, "This is it." She had given me a scrap of paper and written PAUL in lipstick on the suitcase. I had no lively hope of ever seeing it again.

Now, trying to reclaim it, I gave the scrap of paper to a different girl. This one laughed at the paper and called a cross-eyed man over to examine it. He laughed, too.

I said, "What's so funny?"

"We can't read her writing," said the cross-eyed man.

"She writes in Chinese," said the girl. She scratched her stomach and smiled at the paper. "What does that say—fifty or five?"

"Let's call it five," I said. "Or we can ask the girl. Where is she?"

"Chee"—now the cross-eyed man was speaking in English—"chee go to the veech!"

They thought this was hysterically funny.

"My suitcase," I said. "Where is it?"

The girl said, "Gone," but before I could react, she giggled and dragged it out of the kitchen.

The sleeping car of the Aztec Eagle was a hundred yards down the track, and I was out of breath when I reached it. My English leak-proof shoes, specially bought for this trip, had sprung a leak; my clothes were wet. I had carried the suitcase on my head, coolie-style, but all that served to do was provoke a migraine and funnel rainwater into my collar.

A man in a black uniform stood in the doorway, barring my way. "You can't get on," he said. "You haven't been through customs."

This was true, although I wondered how he could possibly have known it.

I said, "Where is customs?"

He pointed to the far end of the flooded track and said disgustedly, "Over there."

I heaved the suitcase onto my head again and, certain that I could get no wetter, splashed back to the station platform. "Customs?" I asked. A lady peddling bubble gum and cookies laughed at me. I asked a little boy. He covered his face. I asked a man with a clipboard. He said, "Wait."

Rain dribbled through holes in the platform roof, and Mexicans carted bales of their belongings and shoved them through the windows of second class. And yet, for an express train with a high reputation, there were not many passengers in evidence. The station was dingy and nearly deserted. The bubble gum seller talked to the fried chicken seller; barefoot children played tag; it continued to rain—and the rain was not a brisk purifying downpour, but a dark tedious drizzle, like flecks of falling soot, which seemed to taint everything it touched.

Then I saw the man in the black uniform who had barred my entry to the sleeping car. He was wet now and looked furious.

"I don't see the customs," I said.

He showed me a tube of lipstick and said, "This is customs."

Without inquiring further, he franked my suitcase with a slash of lipstick, then straightened and groaned and said, "Hurry up, the train is about to leave."

"Sorry, have I been keeping you waiting?"

JOHN STEINBECK

Cabo San Lucas, Baja California, 1940

"WE LOVE CARTA BLANCA BEER."

John Steinbeck first won attention in 1935 for his novel Tortilla Flat.
By 1962 his novels and other writings had earned him a Nobel Prize.

Sea of Cortez *was published in 1941. Steinbeck had studied marine biology at Stanford University before making up his mind to try writing, and the subject continued to interest him. In March and April of
1940 he and a friend, marine biologist Edward F. Ricketts, chartered a
boat and crew and spent six weeks in the Gulf of California, formerly
known as the Sea of Cortez. They collected innumerable samples of marine life and visited some of the Mexican coastal villages.* Sea of Cortez
combines Steinbeck's narrative of the trip with photos by Ricketts.

*After nearly four days and nights of running from San Diego, they
reached the tip of the Baja peninsula on March 17. They first went
ashore at Cabo San Lucas, where a tuna cannery and a few houses along
the beach were "the only habitations visible." Even a writer destined to
win the Nobel Prize would have had difficulty imagining San Lucas as*

an expensive resort town, but while many other things on the peninsula have changed very little in the last fifty years, Cabo San Lucas has enjoyed—if that's the word—considerable prosperity.

San Lucas lies on the gulf side of the point at the end of a highway that runs 1,050 miles (1,700 kilometers) south from the border crossing at Tijuana. Until the road was completed in 1973, most points on the peninsula were accessible only by boat or private plane. The road made possible the development of a number of areas to serve the interests of whale watchers, naturalists, auto racers, sport fishermen, and vacationers who prefer to concentrate on doing nothing whatsoever, a pastime for which Baja is eminently suited.

Cabo San Lucas has profited most of all. Its natural endowments include excellent game fishing for marlin and sailfish, a beautiful coastline for boating, good beaches, and plenty of sun. Today, the little village that Steinbeck saw has pretty much disappeared beneath a modern resort town, complete with expensive boutiques and restaurants, condos on the hillsides, and the kinds of hotels that have their own landing strips.

A popular bar in town, the Cabo Wabo Cantina, is owned by members of the Van Halen rock band. It seems fair to say that, except for its generic name, it has little in common with the cantina where Steinbeck and Ricketts had a couple of Carta Blancas in 1940. Certainly it has to count as a plus that there's now electricity and the beer is cold.

Today, Cabo San Lucas is connected by regular air service to Los Angeles, as well as to Tijuana and other Mexican cities, and by ferry service across the gulf to Puerto Vallarta.

One of Steinbeck's more memorable passages about his visit concerns the eager little boys who helped collect marine specimens on the beach in hope of a few centavos. Many of those same boys, now grown men, have probably spent the last dozen years or so carrying drinks to hotel guests or trying to sell them souvenirs in hope of a few (devalued) pesos.

AT TWO A.M. WE PASSED POINT LAZARO, ONE of the reputedly dangerous places of the world, like Cedros Passage, or like Cape Horn, where the weather is always bad even when it is good elsewhere. There is a sense of relief when one is safely past these half-mythical places, for they are not only stormy but treacherous, and again the atavistic fear arises—the Scylla-Charybdis fear that made our ancestors people such places with monsters and enter them only after prayer and propitiation. It was only reasonably rough when we passed, and immediately south the water was very calm. About five in the morning we came upon an even denser concentration of the little red *Pleuroncodes,* and we stopped again and took a great many of them. While we netted the *langustina,* a skipjack struck the line and we brought him in and had him for breakfast. During the meal we said the fish was *Katsuwonus pelamis,* and Sparky said it was a skipjack because he was eating it and he was quite sure he would not eat *Katsuwonus pelamis* ever. A few hours later we caught two small dolphins, startingly beautiful fish of pure gold, pulsing and fading and changing colors. These fish are very widely distributed.

We were coming now toward the end of our day-and-night running; the engine had never paused since we left San Diego except for idling the little time while we took the *langustina.* The coastline of the Peninsula slid along, brown and desolate and dry with strange flat mountains and rocks torn by dryness, and the heat shimmer hung over the land even in March. Tony had kept us well offshore, and only now we approached closer to land, for we would arrive at Cape San Lucas in the night, and from then on we planned to run only in the daytime. Some collecting stations we had projected, like Pulmo Reef and La Paz and Angeles Bay, but except for those, we planned to stop wherever the shore looked interesting. Even this little trip of ninety hours, though, had grown long, and we were glad to be getting to the end of it. The dry hills were red gold that afternoon and in the night no one left the top of the deckhouse. The Southern Cross was well above the horizon, and the air was warm and pleasant. Tony spent a long time in the galley going over the charts. He had been to Cape San Lucas once before. Around ten o'clock we saw the lighthouse on the false cape. The night was extremely dark when we rounded the end; the great tall rocks called "The Friars" were blackly visible. The *Coast Pilot* spoke of a light on the end of the San Lucas pier, but we could see no light. Tony edged the boat slowly into the dark harbor. Once a flashlight showed for a moment on the shore and then went out. It was after midnight, and of course there would be no light in a Mexican house at such a time.

The searchlight on our deckhouse seemed to be sucked up by the darkness. Sparky on the bow with the leadline found deep water, and we moved slowly in, stopping and drifting and sounding. And then suddenly there was the beach, thirty feet away, and with little waves breaking on it, and still we had eight fathoms on the lead. We backed away a little and dropped the anchor and waited until it took a firm grip. Then the engine stopped, and we sat for a long time on the deckhouse. The sweet smell of the land blew out to us on a warm wind, a smell of sand verbena and grass and mangrove. It is so quickly forgotten, this land smell. We know it so well on shore that the nose forgets it, but after a few days at sea the odor memory pattern is lost so that the first land smell strikes a powerful emotional nostalgia, very sharp and strangely dear.

In the morning the black mystery of the night was gone and the little harbor was shining and warm. The tuna cannery against the gathering rocks of the point and a few houses along the edge of the beach were the only habitations visible. And with the day came the answer to the lightlessness of the night before. The *Coast Pilot* had not been wrong. There is indeed a light on the end of the cannery pier, but since the electricity is generated by the cannery engine, and since the cannery engine runs only in the daytime, so the light burns only in the daytime. With the arrived day, this light came on and burned bravely until dusk, when it went off again. But the *Coast Pilot* was absolved, it had not lied. Even Tony, who had been a little bitter the night before, was forced to revise his first fierceness. And perhaps it was a lesson to Tony in exact thinking, like those carefully worded puzzles in joke books; the *Pilot* said a light burned—it only neglected to say when, and we ourselves supplied the fallacy.

The great rocks on the end of the Peninsula are almost literary. They are a fitting Land's End, standing against the sea, the end of a thousand miles of peninsula and mountain. Good Hope is this way too, and perhaps we take some of our deep feelings of termination from these things, and they make our symbols. The Friars stood high and protective against an interminable sea.

The tip of the Cape at San Lucas, with the huge gray Friars standing up on the end, has behind the rocks a little beach which is a small boy's dream of pirates. It seems the perfect place to hide and from which to dart out in a pinnace on the shipping of the world; a place to which to bring the gold bars and jewels and beautiful ladies, all of which are invariably carried by the shipping of the world. And this little beach must so have appealed to earlier men, for the names of pirates are still in the rock, and the pirate ships did dart out of here and did come back. But now in back of the Friars on the beach there is a great pile of decaying hammer-head sharks, the livers torn out and the fish left to rot. Some day, and that soon, the more mature piracy which has abandoned the pinnace for the coast gun will stud this point with gray monsters and will send against the shipping of the Gulf, not little bands of ragged men, but projectiles filled with TNT. And from that piracy no jewels or beautiful ladies will come back to the beach behind the rocks.

On that first morning we cleaned ourselves well and shaved while we waited for the Mexican officials to come out and give us the right to land. They were late in coming, for they had to find their official uniforms, and they too had to shave. Few boats put in here. It would not be well to waste the occasion of the visit of even a fishing boat like ours. It was noon before the well-dressed men in their sun helmets came down to the beach and were rowed out to us. They were armed with the .45-caliber automatics which everywhere in Mexico designate officials. And they were armed also with the courtesy which is unique in official Mexico. No matter what they do to you, they are nice about it. We soon learned the routine in other ports as well as here. Everyone who has or can borrow a uniform comes aboard—the collector of customs in a washed and shiny uniform; the business agent in a business suit having about him what Tiny calls "a double-breasted look"; then soldiers if there are any; and finally the Indians, who row the boat and rarely have uniforms. They come over the side like ambassadors. We shake hands all around. The galley has been prepared: coffee is ready and perhaps a drop of rum. Cigarettes are presented and then comes the ceremonial of the match. In Mexico cigarettes are cheap, but matches are not. If a man wishes to honor you, he lights your cigarette, and if you have given him a cigarette, he must so honor you. But having lighted your cigarette and his, the match is still burning and not being used. Anyone may now make use of this match. On a street, strangers who have been wishing for a light come up quickly and light from your match, bow, and pass on.

We were impatient for the officials, and this time we did not have to wait long. It developed that the Governor of the southern district had very recently been to Cape San Lucas and just before that a yacht had put in. This simplified matters, for, having recently used them, the officials knew exactly where to find their uniforms, and, having found them, they did not, as sometimes happens, have to send them to be laundered before they could come aboard. About noon they trooped to the beach, scattering the pigs and Mexican vultures which browsed happily there. They filled the rowboat until the gunwales just missed dipping, and majestically they came alongside. We conducted the ceremony of clearing with some dignity, for if we spoke to them in very bad Spanish, they in turn honored us with very bad English. They cleared us, drank coffee, smoked, and finally left, promising to come back. Much as we had enjoyed them, we were impatient, for the tide was dropping and the exposed rocks looked very rich with animal life.

All the time we were indulging in courtliness there had been light gunfire on the cliffs, where several men were shooting at black cormorants; and it developed that everyone in Cape San Lucas hates cormorants. They are the flies in a perfect ecological ointment. The cannery cans tuna; the entrails and cuttings of the tuna are thrown into the water from the end of the pier. This refuse brings in schools of small fish which are netted and used for bait to catch tuna. This closed and tight circle is interfered with by the cormorants, who try to get at the bait-fish. They dive and catch fish, but also they drive the schools away from the pier out of easy reach of the baitmen. Thus they are considered interlopers, radicals, subversive forces against the perfect and God-set balance on Cape San Lucas. And they are rightly slaughtered, as all radicals should be. As one of our number remarked, "Why, pretty soon they'll want to vote."

Finally we could go. We unpacked the Hansen Sea-Cow and fastened it on the back of the skiff. This was our first use of the Sea-Cow. The shore was very close and we were able just by pulling on the starter rope to spin the propeller enough to get us to shore. The Sea-Cow did not run that day but it seemed to enjoy having its flywheel spun.

The shore-collecting equipment usually consisted of a number of small wrecking bars; wooden fish-kits with handles; quart jars with screw caps; and many glass tubes. These tubes are invaluable for small and delicate animals: the chance of bringing them back uninjured is greatly increased if each individual, or at least only a few of like species, are kept in separate containers. We filled our pockets with these tubes. The soft animals must never be put in the same container with any of the livelier crabs, for these, when restrained or inhibited in any way, go into paroxysms of rage and pinch everything at random, even each other; sometimes even themselves.

The exposed rocks had looked rich with life under the lowering tide, but they were more than that: they were ferocious with life. There was an exuberant fierceness in the littoral here, a vital competition for existence. Everything seemed speeded-up; starfish and urchins were more strongly attached than in other places, and many of the univalves were so tightly fixed that the shells broke before the animals would let go their hold. Perhaps the force of the great surf which beats on this shore has much to do with the tenacity of the animals here. It is noteworthy that the animals, rather than deserting such beaten shores for the safe cove and protected pools, simply increase their toughness and fight back at the sea with a kind of joyful survival. This ferocious survival quotient excites us and makes us feel good, and from the crawling, fighting, resisting qualities of the animals, it almost seems that they are excited too.

We collected down the littoral as the water went down. We didn't seem to have time enough. We took samples of everything that came to hand. The uppermost rocks swarmed with Sally Lightfoots, those beautiful and fast and sensitive crabs. With them were white periwinkle snails. Below that, barnacles and Purpura snails; more crabs and many limpets. Below that many serpulids—attached worms in calcareous tubes with beautiful purple floriate heads. Below that, the multi-rayed starfish, *Heliaster kubiniji* of Xanthus. With *Heliaster* were a few urchins, but not many, and they were so placed in crevices as to be hard to dislodge. Several resisted the steel bar to the extent of breaking—the mouth remaining tight to the rock while the shell fell away. Lower still there were to be seen swaying in the water under the reefs the dark gorgonians, or sea-fans. In the lowest surf-levels there was a brilliant gathering of the moss animals known as bryozoa; flatworms; flat crabs; the large sea-cucumber; some anemones; many sponges of two types, a smooth, encrusting purple one, the other erect, white, and calcareous. There were great colonies of tunicates, clusters of tiny individuals joined by a common tunic and looking so like the sponges that even a trained worker must await the specialist's determination to know whether his find is sponge or tunicate. This is annoying, for the sponge being one step above the protozoa, at the bottom of the evolutionary ladder, and the tunicate near the top, bordering the vertebrates, your trained worker is likely to feel that a dirty trick has been played upon him by an entirely too democratic Providence.

We took many snails, including cones and murexes; a small red tectibranch (of a group to which the sea-hares belong); hydroids; many annelid worms; and a red pentagonal starfish. There were the usual hordes of hermit crabs, but oddly enough we saw no chitons (sea-cradles), although the region seemed ideally suited to them.

We collected in haste. As the tide went down we kept a little ahead of it, wading in rubber boots, and as it came up again it drove us back. The time seemed very short. The incredible beauty of the tide pools, the brilliant colors, the swarming species ate up the time. And when at last the afternoon surf began to beat on the littoral and covered it over again, we seemed barely to have started. But the buckets and jars and tubes were full, and when we stopped we discovered that we were very tired.

Our collecting ends were different from those ordinarily entertained. In most cases at the present time, collecting is done by men who specialize in one or more groups. Thus, one man interested in hydroids will move out on a reef, and if his interest is sharp enough, he will not even see other life forms about him. For him, the sponge is something in the way of his hydroids. Collecting large numbers of animals presents an entirely different aspect and makes one see an entirely different picture. Being more interested in distribution than in individuals, we saw dominant species and changing sizes, groups which thrive and those which recede under varying conditions. In a way, ours is the older method, somewhat like that of Darwin on the *Beagle*. He was called a "naturalist." He wanted to see everything, rocks and flora and fauna; marine and terrestrial. We came to envy this Darwin on his sailing ship. He had so much room and so much time. He could capture his animals and keep them alive and watch them. He had years instead of weeks, and he saw so many things. Often we envied the inadequate transportation of his time—the *Beagle* couldn't get about rapidly. She moved slowly along under sail. And we can imagine that young Darwin, probably in a bos'n's chair hung over the side, with a dip-net in his hands, scooping up jellyfish.

When he went inland, he rode a horse or walked. This is the proper pace for a naturalist. Faced with all things he cannot hurry. We must have time to think and to look and to consider. And the modern process—that of looking quickly at the whole field and then diving down to a particular—was reversed by Darwin. Out of long long consideration of the parts he emerged with a sense of the whole. Where we wished for a month at a collecting station and took two days, Darwin stayed three months. Of course he could see and tabulate. It was the pace that made the difference. And in the writing of Darwin, as in his thinking, there is the slow heave of a sailing ship, and the patience of waiting for a tide. The results are bound up with the pace. We *could* not do this even if we could. We have thought in this connection that the speed and tempo and tone of modern writing might be built on the nervous clacking of a typewriter; that the brittle jerky thinking of the present might rest on the brittle jerky curricula of our schools with their urge to "turn them out." To turn them out. They use the phrase in speeches; turn them out to what? And the young biologists tearing off pieces of their subject, tatters of the life forms, like sharks tearing out hunks of a dead horse, looking at them, tossing them away. This is neither a good nor a bad method; it is simply the one of our time. We can look with longing back to Charles Darwin, staring into the water over the side of the sailing ship, but for us to attempt to imitate that procedure would be romantic and silly. To take a sailing boat, to fight tide and wind, to move four hundred miles on a horse when we could take a plane, would be not only ridiculous but ineffective. For we first, before our work, are products of our time. We might produce a philosophical costume piece, but it would be completely artificial. However, we can and do look on the measured, slow-paced accumulation of sight and thought of the Darwins with a nostalgic longing.

Even our boat hurried us, and while the Sea-Cow would not run, it had nevertheless infected us with the idea of its running. Six weeks we had, and no more. Was it a wonder that we collected furiously; spent every low-tide moment on the rocks, even at night? And in the times between low tides we kept the bottom nets down and the lines and dip-nets working. When the charter was up, we would be through. How different it had been when John Xantus was stationed in this very place, Cape San Lucas, in the sixties. Sent down by the United States Government as a tidal observer, but having lots of time, he collected animals for our National Museum. The first fine collections of Gulf forms came from Xantus. And we do not feel that we are injuring his reputation, but rather broadening it, by repeating a story about him. Speaking to the manager of the cannery at the Cape, we remarked on what a great man Xantus had been. Where another would have kept his tide charts and brooded and wished for the Willard Hotel, Xantus had collected animals widely and carefully. The manager said, "Oh, he was even better than that." Pointing to three little Indian children he said, "Those are Xantus's great-grandchildren," and he continued, "In the town there is a large family of Xantuses, and a few miles back in the hills you'll find a whole tribe of them." There were giants in the earth in those days.

We wonder what modern biologist, worried about titles and preferment and the gossip of the Faculty Club, would have the warmth and breadth, or even the fecundity for that matter, to leave a "whole tribe of Xantuses." We honor this man for all his activities. He at least was one who literally did proliferate in all directions.

Many people have spoken at length of the Sally Lightfoots. In fact, everyone who has seen them has been delighted with them. The very name they are called by reflects the delight of the name. These little crabs, with brilliant cloisonné carapaces, walk on their tiptoes. They have remarkable eyes and an extremely fast reaction time. In spite of the fact that they swarm on the rocks at the Cape, and to a less degree inside the Gulf, they are exceedingly hard to catch. They seem to be able to run in any one of four directions; but more than this, perhaps because of their rapid reaction time, they appear to read the mind of their hunter. They escape the long-handled net, anticipating from what direction it is coming. If you walk slowly, they move slowly ahead of you in droves. If you hurry, they hurry. When you plunge at them, they seem to disappear in little puffs of blue smoke—at any rate, they disappear. It is impossible to creep up on them. They are very beautiful, with clear brilliant colors, reds and blues and warm browns. We tried for a long time to catch them. Finally, seeing fifty or sixty in a big canyon of rock, we thought to outwit them. Surely we were more intelligent, if slower, than they. Accordingly, we pitted our obviously superior intelligence against the equally obvious physical superiority of Sally Lightfoot. Near the top of the crevice a boulder protruded. One of our party, taking a secret and circuitous route, hid himself behind this boulder, net in hand. He was completely concealed even from the stalk eyes of the crabs. Certainly they had not seen him go there. The herd of Sallys drowsed on the rocks in the lower end of the crevice. Two more of us strolled in from the seaward side, nonchalance in our postures and ingenuousness on our faces. One might have thought that we merely strolled along in a contemplation which severely excluded Sally Lightfoots. In time the herd moved ahead of us, matching our nonchalance. We did not hurry, they did not hurry. When they passed the boulder, helpless and unsuspecting, a large net was to fall over them and imprison them. But they did not know that. They moved along until they were four feet from the boulder, and then as one crab they turned to the right, climbed up over the crevice and down to the sea again.

Man reacts peculiarly but consistently in his relationship with Sally Lightfoot. His tendency eventually is to scream curses, to hurl himself at them, and to come up foaming with rage and bruised all over his chest. Thus, Tiny, leaping forward, slipped and fell and hurt his arm. He never forgot or forgave his enemy. From then on he attacked Lightfoots by every foul means he could contrive (and a training in Monterey street fighting had equipped him well for this kind of battle). He hurled rocks at them; he smashed at them with boards; and he even considered poisoning them. Eventually we did catch a few Sallys, but we think they were the halt and the blind, the simpletons of their species. With reasonably well-balanced and non-neurotic Lightfoots we stood no chance.

We came back to boat loaded with specimens, and immediately prepared to preserve them. The square, enameled pans were laid out on the hatch, the trays and bowls and watchglasses (so called because at one time actual watch-crystals were used). The pans and glasses were filled with fresh sea water, and into them we distributed the animals by families—all the crabs in one, anemones in another, snails in another, and delicate things like flatworms and hydroids in others. From this distribution it was easier to separate them finally by species.

When the catch was sorted and labeled, we went ashore to the cannery and later drove with Chris, the manager, and Señor Luis, the port captain, to the little town of San Lucas. It was a sad little town, for a winter storm and a great surf had wrecked it in a single night. Water had driven past the houses, and the streets of the village had been a raging river. "Then there were no roofs over the heads of the people," Señor Luis said excitedly. "Then the babies cried and there was no food. Then the people suffered."

The road to the little town, two wheel-ruts in the dust, tossed us about in the cannery truck. The cactus and thorny shrubs ripped at the car as we went by. At last we stopped in front of a mournful *cantina* where morose young men hung about waiting for something to happen. They had waited a long time—several generations—for something to happen, these good-looking young men. In their eyes there was a hopelessness. The storm of the winter had been discussed so often that it was sucked dry. And besides, they all knew the same things about it. Then we happened to them. The truck pulled up to the *cantina* door and we—strangers, foreigners—stepped out, as disorderly-looking a group as had ever come to their *cantina*. Tiny wore a Navy cap of white he had traded for, he said, in a washroom in San Diego. Tony still had his snap-brim felt. There were yachting caps and sweaters, and jeans stiff with fish blood. The young men stirred to life for a little while, but we were not enough. The flood had been much better. They relapsed again into their gloom.

There is nothing more doleful than a little *cantina*. In the first place it is inhabited by people who haven't any money to buy a drink. They stand about waiting for a miracle that never happens: the angel with golden wings who settles on the bar and orders drinks for everyone. This never happens, but how are the sad handsome young men to know it never will happen? And suppose it did happen and they were somewhere else? And so they lean against the wall; and when the sun is high they sit down against the wall. Now and then they go away into the brush for a while, and they go to their little homes for meals. But that is an impatient time, for the golden angel might arrive. Their faith is not strong, but it is permanent.

We could see that we did not greatly arouse them. The *cantina* owner promptly put his loudest records on the phonograph to force a gaiety into this sad place. But he had Carta Blanca beer and (at the risk of a charge that we have sold our souls to this brewery) we love Carta Blanca beer. There was no ice, no electric lights, and the gasoline lanterns hissed and drew the bugs from miles away. The cockroaches in their hordes rushed in to see what was up. Big, handsome cockroaches, with almost human faces. The loud music only made us sadder, and the young men watched us. When we lifted a split of beer to our lips the eyes of the young men rose with our hands, and even the cockroaches lifted their heads. We couldn't stand it. We ordered beer all around, but it was too late. The young men were too far gone in sorrow. They drank their warm beer sadly. Then we bought straw hats, for the sun is deadly here. There should be a kind of ridiculous joy in buying a floppy hat, but those young men, so near to tears, drained even that joy. Their golden angel had come, and they did not find him good. We felt rather as God would feel when, after all the preparation of Paradise, all the plannings for eternities of joy, all the making and tuning of harps, the street-paving with gold, and the writing of hosannas, at last He let in the bleacher customers and they looked at the heavenly city and wished to be again in Brooklyn. We told funny stories, knowing they wouldn't be enjoyed, tiring of them ourselves before the point was reached. Nothing was fun in that little *cantina*. We started back for the boat. I think those young men were glad to see us go; because once we were gone, they could begin to build us up, but present, we inhibited their imaginations.

At the bar Chris told us of a native liquor called *damiana,* made from an infusion of a native herb, and not much known outside of Baja California. Chris said it was an aphrodisiac, and told some interesting stories to prove it. We felt a scientific interest in his stories, and bought a bottle of *damiana,* intending to subject it to certain tests under laboratory conditions. But the customs officials of San Diego took it away from us, not because of its romantic aspect, but because it had alcohol in it. Thus we were never able to give it a truly scientific testing. We think we were going to use it on a white rat. Tiny said he didn't want any such stuff getting in his way when he felt lustful.

There doesn't seem to be a true aphrodisiac; there are excitants like cantharides, and physical aids to the difficulties of psychic traumas, like yohimbine sulphate; there are strong protein foods like *bêche-de-mer* and the gonads of sea-urchins, and the much over-rated oyster; even chiles, with their irritating qualities, have some effect, but there seems to be no true aphrodisiac, no sweet essence of that goddess to be taken in a capsule. A certain young person said once that she found sexual intercourse an aphrodisiac; certainly it is the only good one.

So many people are interested in this subject but most of them are forced to pretend they are not. A man, for his own ego's sake, must, publicly at least, be over-supplied with libido. But every doctor knows so well the "friend of the client" who needs help. He is the same "friend" who has gonorrhea, the same "friend" who needs the address of an abortionist. This elusive friend—what will we not do to help him out of his difficulties; the nights we spend sleepless, worrying about him! He is interested in an aphrodisiac; we must try to find him one. But the *damiana* we brought back for our "friend" possibly just now is in the hands of the customs officials in San Diego. Perhaps they too have a friend. Since we suggested the qualities of *damiana* to them, it is barely possible that this fascinating liquor has already been either devoted to a friend or even perhaps subjected to a stern course of investigation under laboratory conditions.

We left the truck and walked through the sandy hills in the night, and in this latitude the sky seemed very black and the stars very white. Already the smell of the land was gone from our noses, for we were used to the smell of vegetation again. The beer was warm in us and pleasant, and the air had a liquid warmth that was really there without the beer, for we tested it later. In the brush beside the track there was a little heap of light, and as we came closer to it we saw a rough wooden cross lighted indirectly. The cross-arm was bound to the staff with a thong, and the whole cross seemed to glow, alone in the darkness. When we came close we saw that a kerosene can stood on the ground and that in it was a candle which threw its feeble light upward on the cross. And our companion told us how a man had come from a fishing boat, sick and weak and tired. He tried to get home, but at this spot he fell down and died. And his family put the little cross and the candle there to mark the place. And eventually they would put up a stronger cross. It seems good to mark and to remember for a little while the place where a man died. This is his one whole lonely act in all his life. In every other thing, even in his birth, he is bound close to others, but the moment of his dying is his own. And in nearly all of Mexico such places are marked. A grave is quite a different thing. Here one's family boasts, or lies, or excuses, in material of elegance and extravagance. But that is a family or a social matter, not the dead man's own at all. The unmarked cross and the secret light are his; almost a reflection of the last piercing loneliness that comes into a dying man's eyes.

From a few feet away the cross seemed to flicker unsubstantially with a small yellow light, seemed to be almost a memory while we saw it. And the man who tried to get home and crawled this far— we never knew his name but he stays in our memory too, for some reason—a supra-personal being, a slow, painful symbol and a pattern of his whole species which tries always from generation to generation, man and woman, which struggles always to get home but never quite makes it.

We came back to the pier and got into our little boat. The Sea-Cow of course would not start, it being night time, so we rowed out to the *Western Flyer*. Before we started, by some magic, there on the end of the pier stood the sad beautiful young men watching us. They had not moved; some jinni had picked them up and transported them and set them down. They watched us put out into the darkness toward our riding lights, and then we suppose they were whisked back again to the *cantina*, where the proprietor was putting the record away and feeling with delicate thumbs the dollar bills we had left. On the pier no light burned, for the engine had stopped at sundown. We went to bed; there was a tide to be got to in the morning.

PERMISSIONS
ACKNOWLEDGMENTS

SYBILLE BEDFORD   From A Visit to Don Otavio by Sybille Bedford. Copyright © 1989 by Sybille Bedford. Reprinted by permission of the publisher Eland, Ltd.

ELIZABETH BORTON DE TREVIÑO   From My Heart Lies South. Thomas Y. Crowell, New York, 1953. Copyright © 1953 and 1972 by Elizabeth Borton de Treviño. Reprinted by permission of Ray Pierre Corsini, agent for the author.

PAUL BOWLES   From Without Stopping by Paul Bowles. Copyright © 1972 by Paul Bowles. First published by The Ecco Press in 1985. Reprinted by permission of Ecco Press.

WITTER BYNNER   From Journey with Genius by Witter Bynner. Copyright 1951 by Witter Bynner. Reprinted by permission of HarperCollins Publishers Inc.